Shojo Beat

ORESAMA TEACHER

1

Art by

...tsubaki

ORESAMA TEACHER

Volume 1
CONTENTS

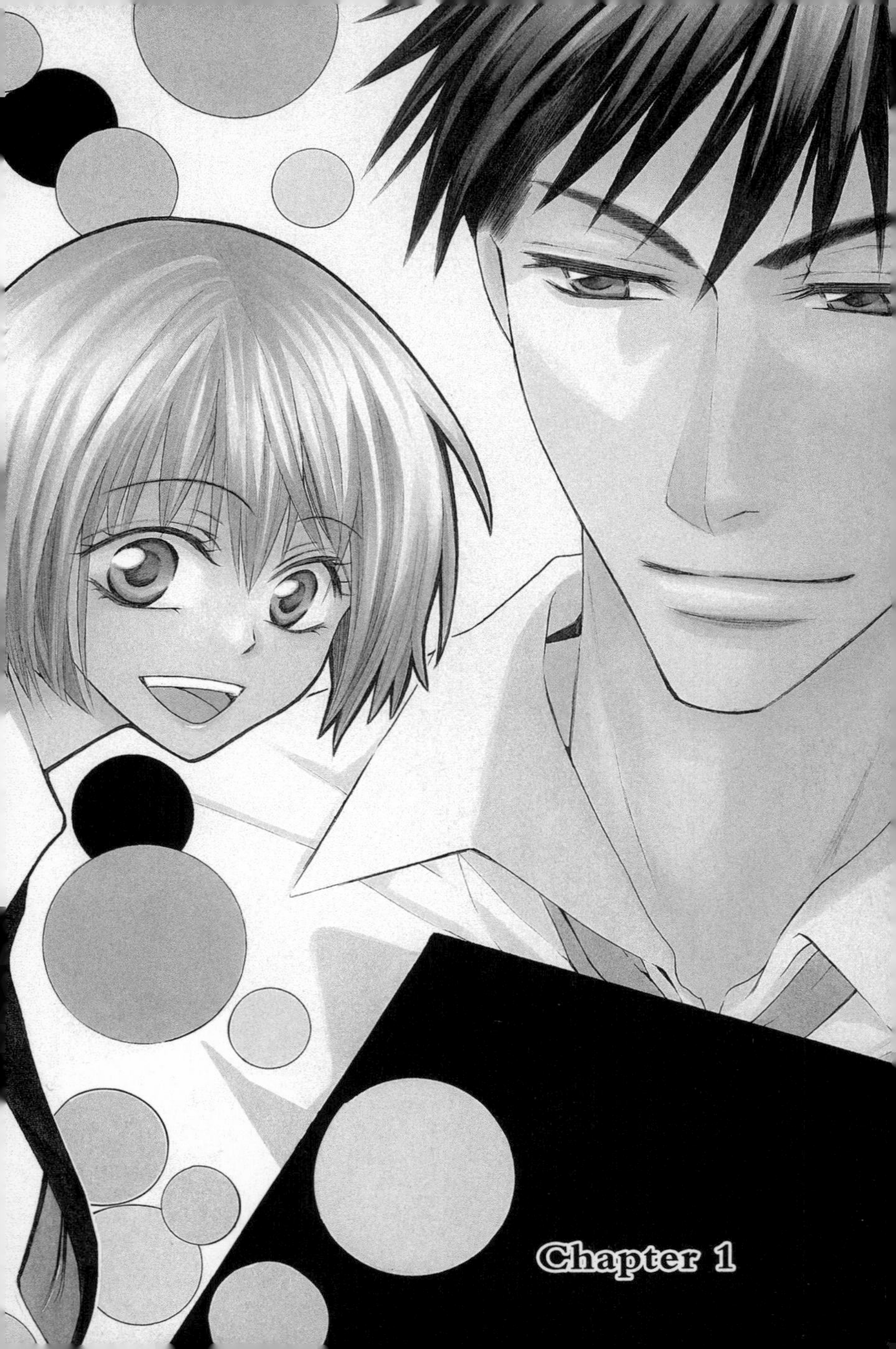
Chapter 1

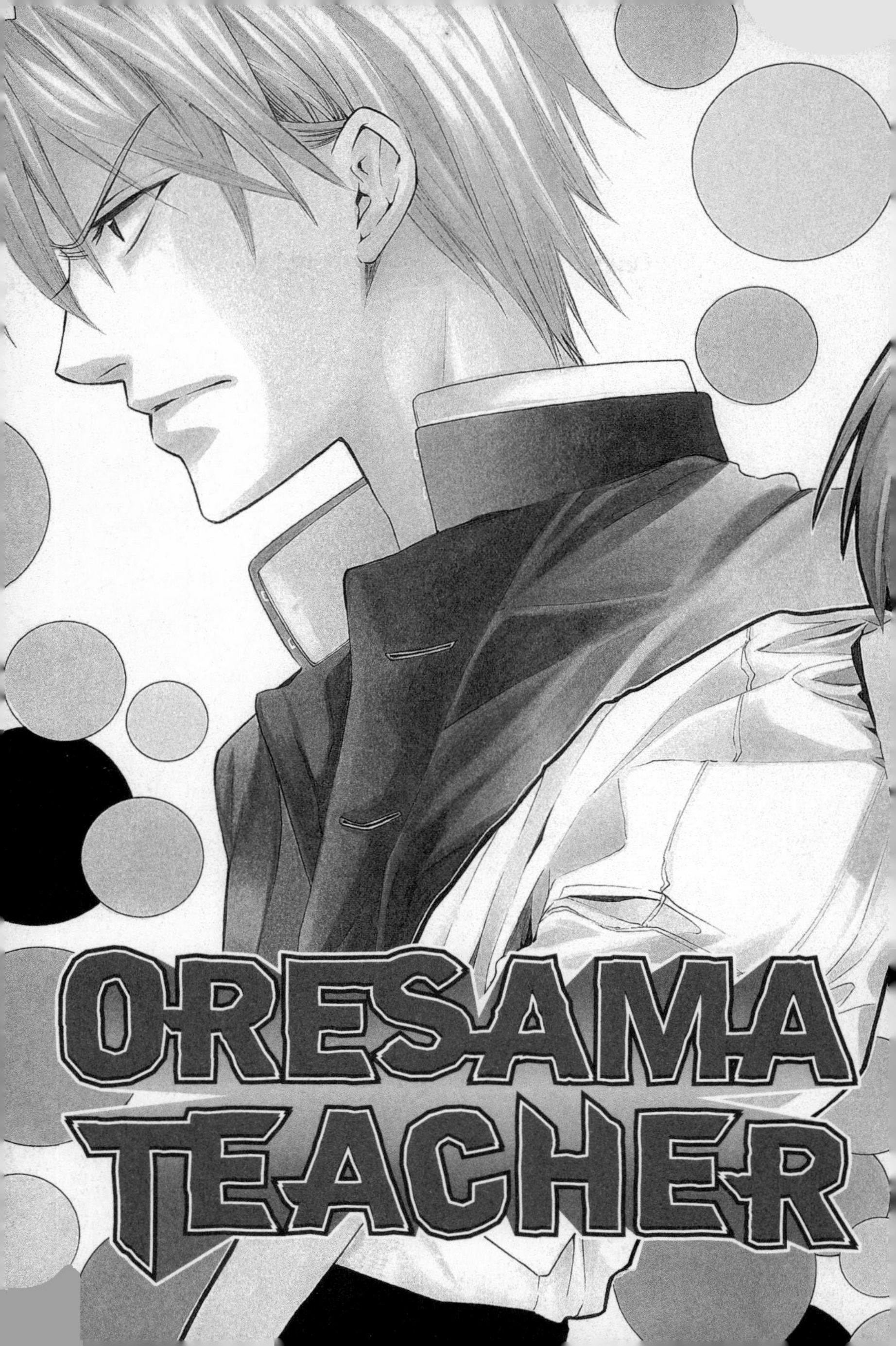
ORESAMA
TEACHER

Midorigaoka Academy

High atop a mountain in the countryside, this private school caters to wealthy students. However, low academic requirements have allowed delinquent students who have been expelled from their schools to gain admission.

Town is a 15-minute bus ride from the campus, and since most students live in the dorms, they only get into town on the weekend.

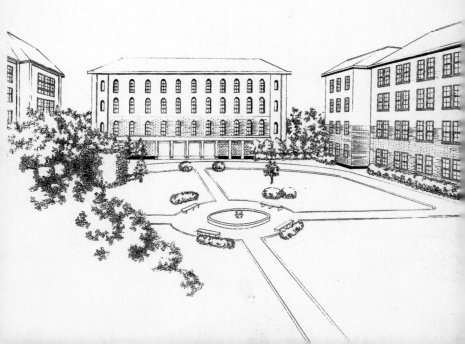

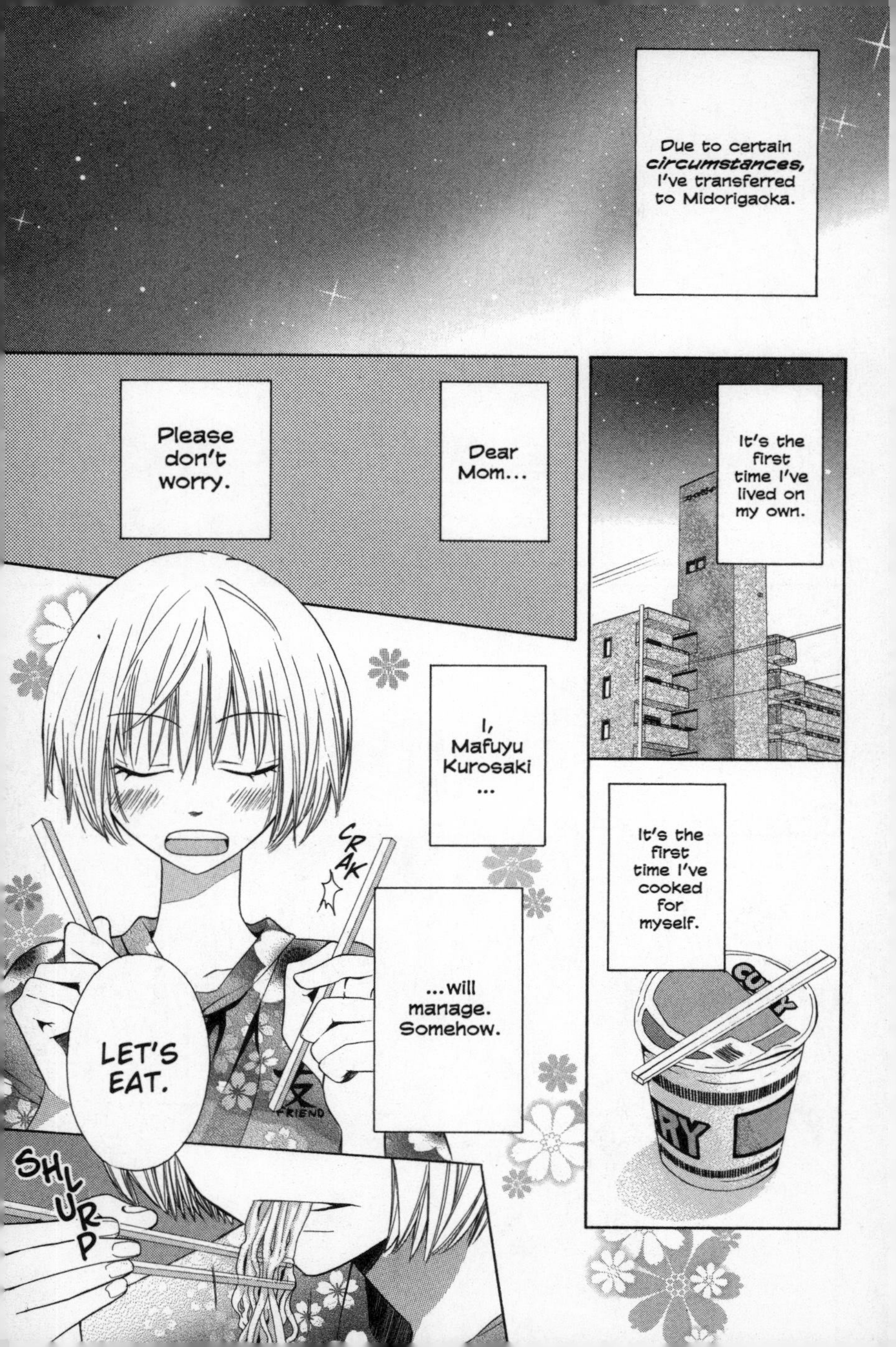
Due to certain *circumstances,* I've transferred to Midorigaoka.
It's the first time I've lived on my own.
It's the first time I've cooked for myself.
Dear Mom...
Please don't worry.
I, Mafuyu Kurosaki ...
CRAK
...will manage. Somehow.
FRIEND
LET'S EAT.
SHLURP

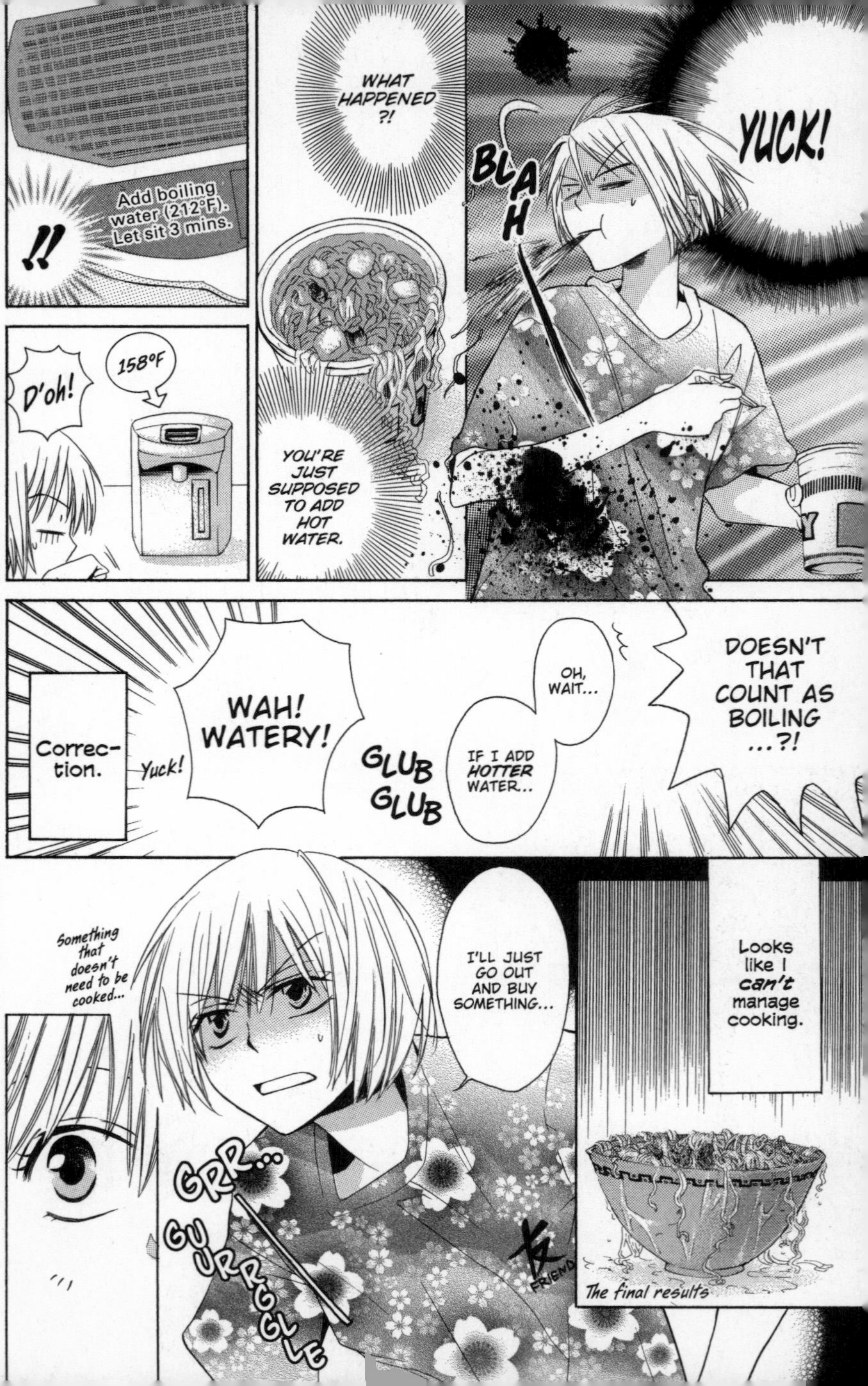

YUCK!
BLAH
WHAT HAPPENED ?!
YOU'RE JUST SUPPOSED TO ADD HOT WATER.
!!
Add boiling water (212°F). Let sit 3 mins.
158°F
D'oh!
DOESN'T THAT COUNT AS BOILING ...?!
OH, WAIT...
IF I ADD HOTTER WATER...
GLUB GLUB
WAH! WATERY!
Yuck!
Correction.
Looks like I can't manage cooking.
The final results
I'LL JUST GO OUT AND BUY SOMETHING...
Something that doesn't need to be cooked...
GRR...
GUURRGGLLE

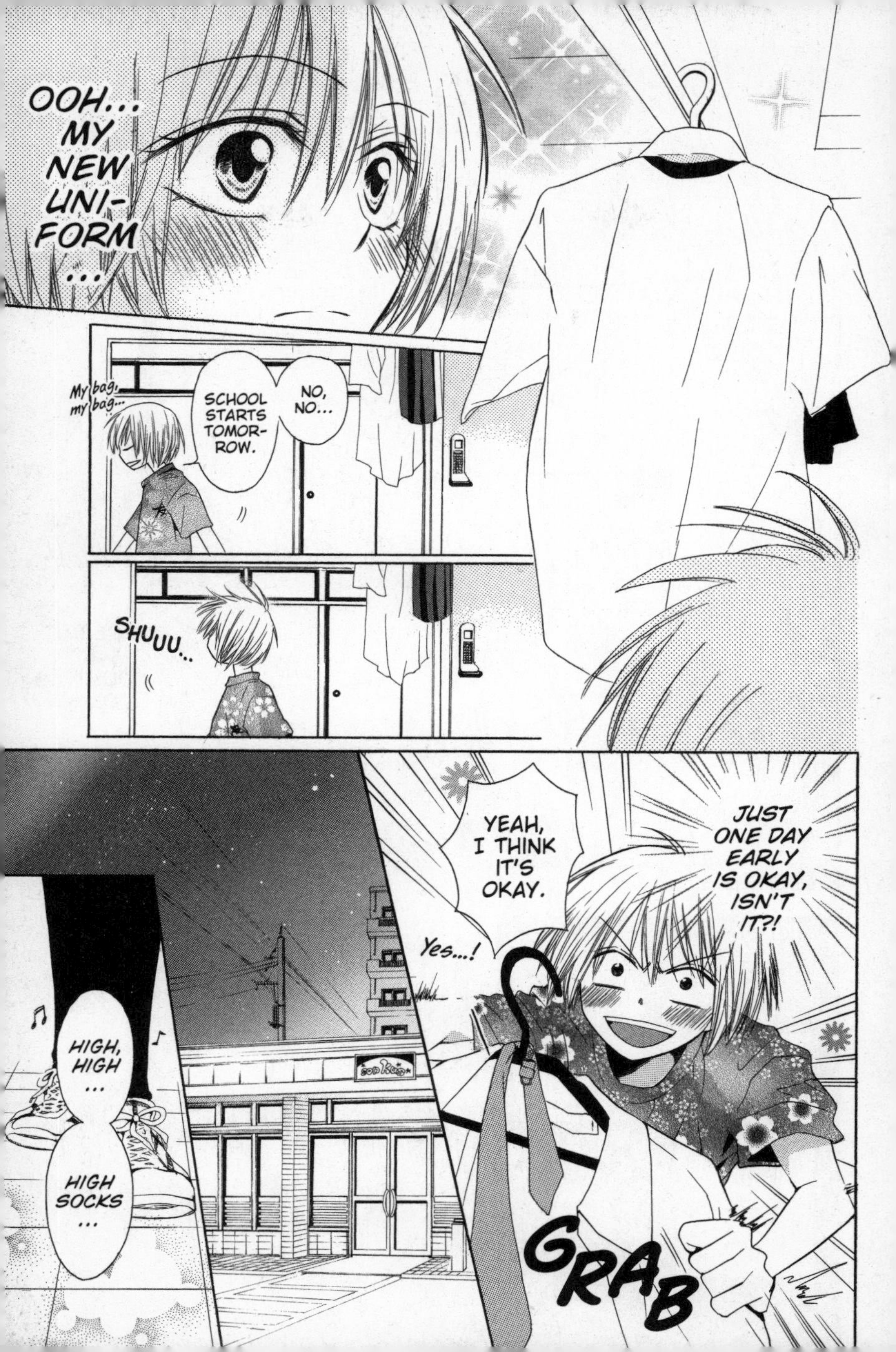
OOH... MY NEW UNI-FORM...
NO, NO...
SCHOOL STARTS TOMOR-ROW.
My bag, my bag...
SHUUU...
JUST ONE DAY EARLY IS OKAY, ISN'T IT?!
YEAH, I THINK IT'S OKAY.
Yes...!
GRAB
HIGH, HIGH...
HIGH SOCKS...

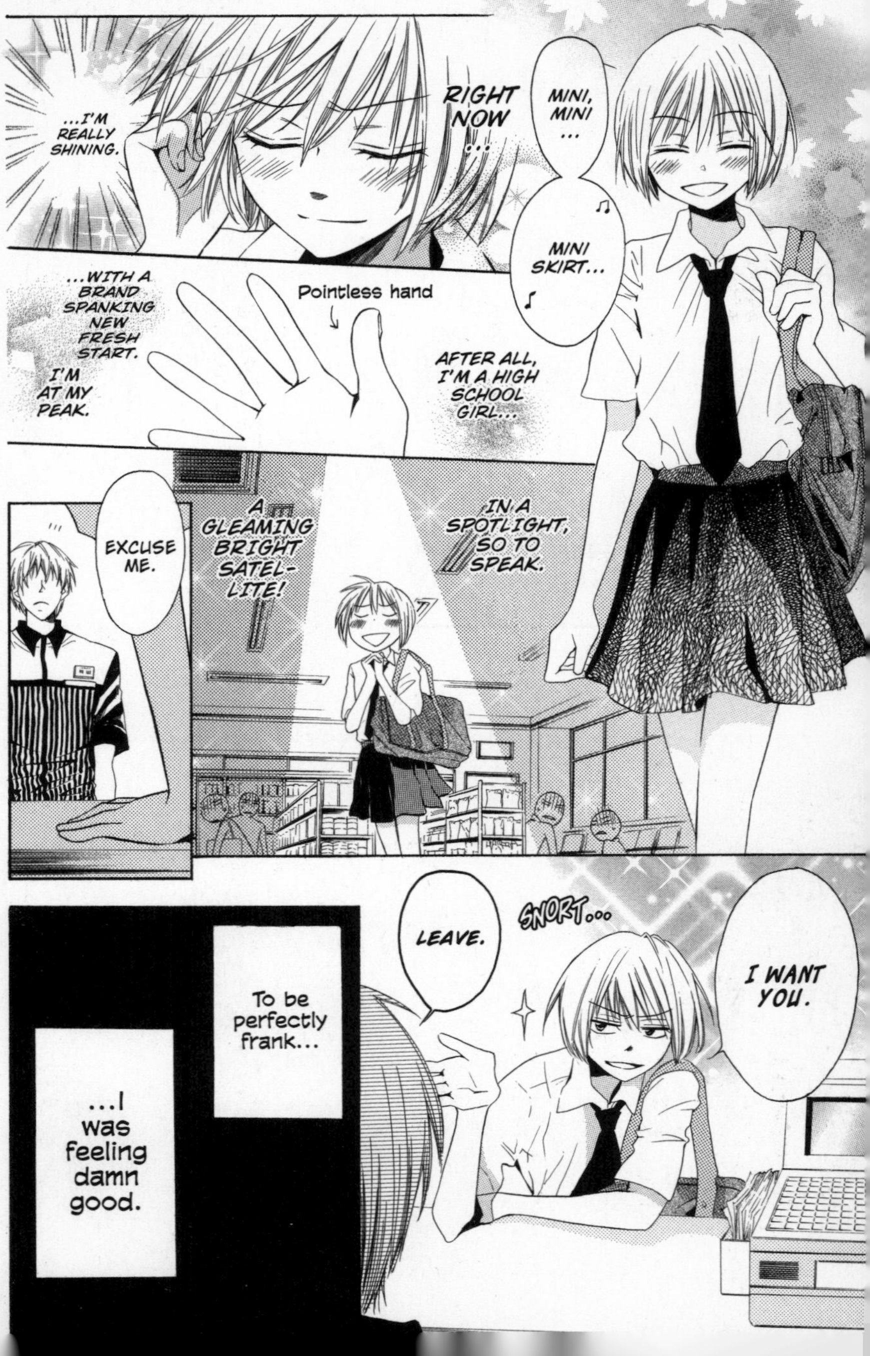
MINI, MINI ...
MINI SKIRT...
RIGHT NOW ...
...I'M REALLY SHINING.
AFTER ALL, I'M A HIGH SCHOOL GIRL...
Pointless hand
...WITH A BRAND SPANKING NEW FRESH START.
I'M AT MY PEAK.
IN A SPOTLIGHT, SO TO SPEAK.
A GLEAMING BRIGHT SATEL-LITE!
EXCUSE ME.
I WANT YOU.
SNORT...
LEAVE.
To be perfectly frank...
...I was feeling damn good.

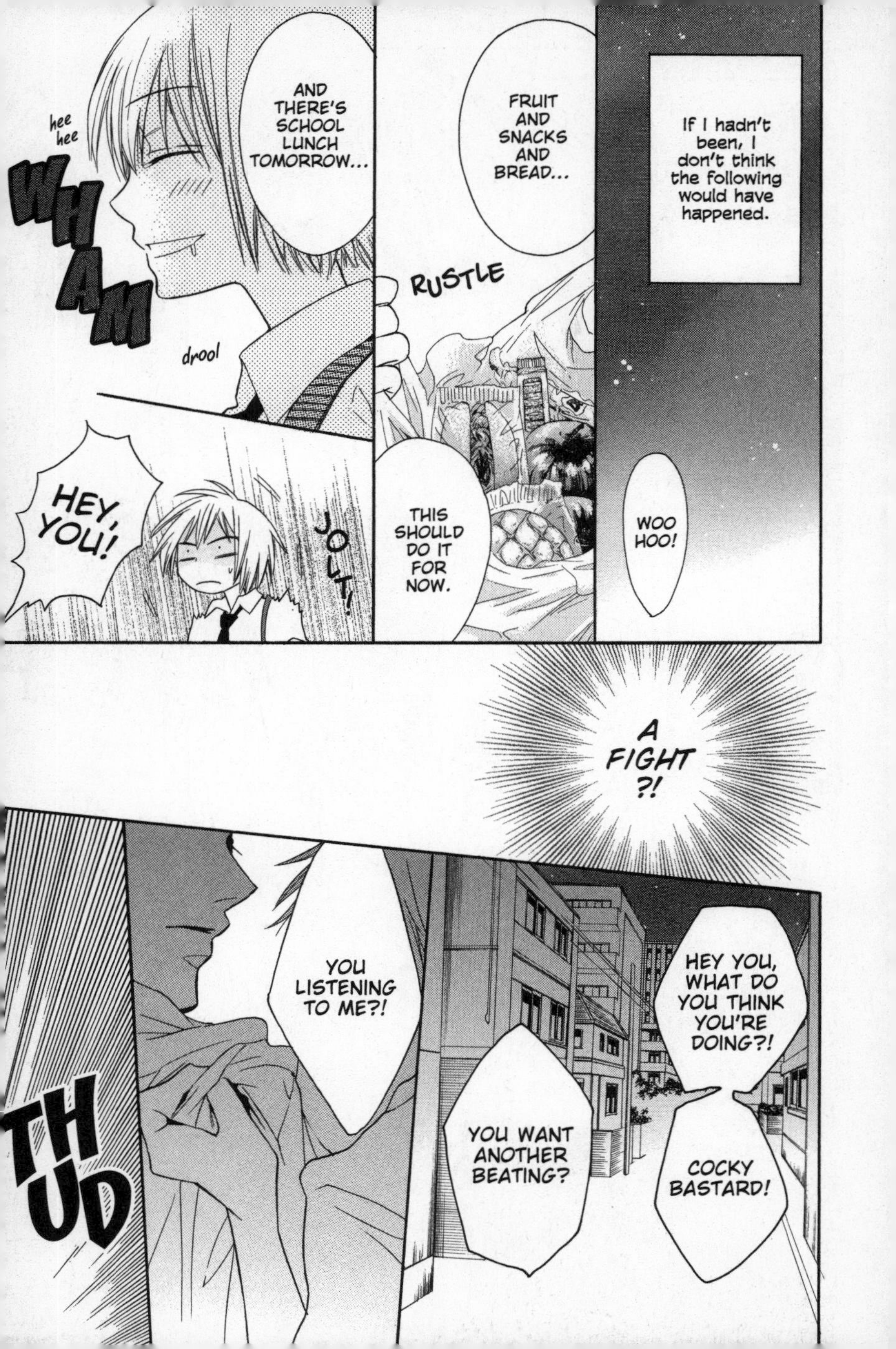
If I hadn't been, I don't think the following would have happened.
WOO HOO!
FRUIT AND SNACKS AND BREAD...
RUSTLE
THIS SHOULD DO IT FOR NOW.
AND THERE'S SCHOOL LUNCH TOMORROW...
hee hee
WHAM
drool
HEY, YOU!
JOLT!
A FIGHT ?!
HEY YOU, WHAT DO YOU THINK YOU'RE DOING?!
COCKY BASTARD!
YOU WANT ANOTHER BEATING?
YOU LISTENING TO ME?!
THUD

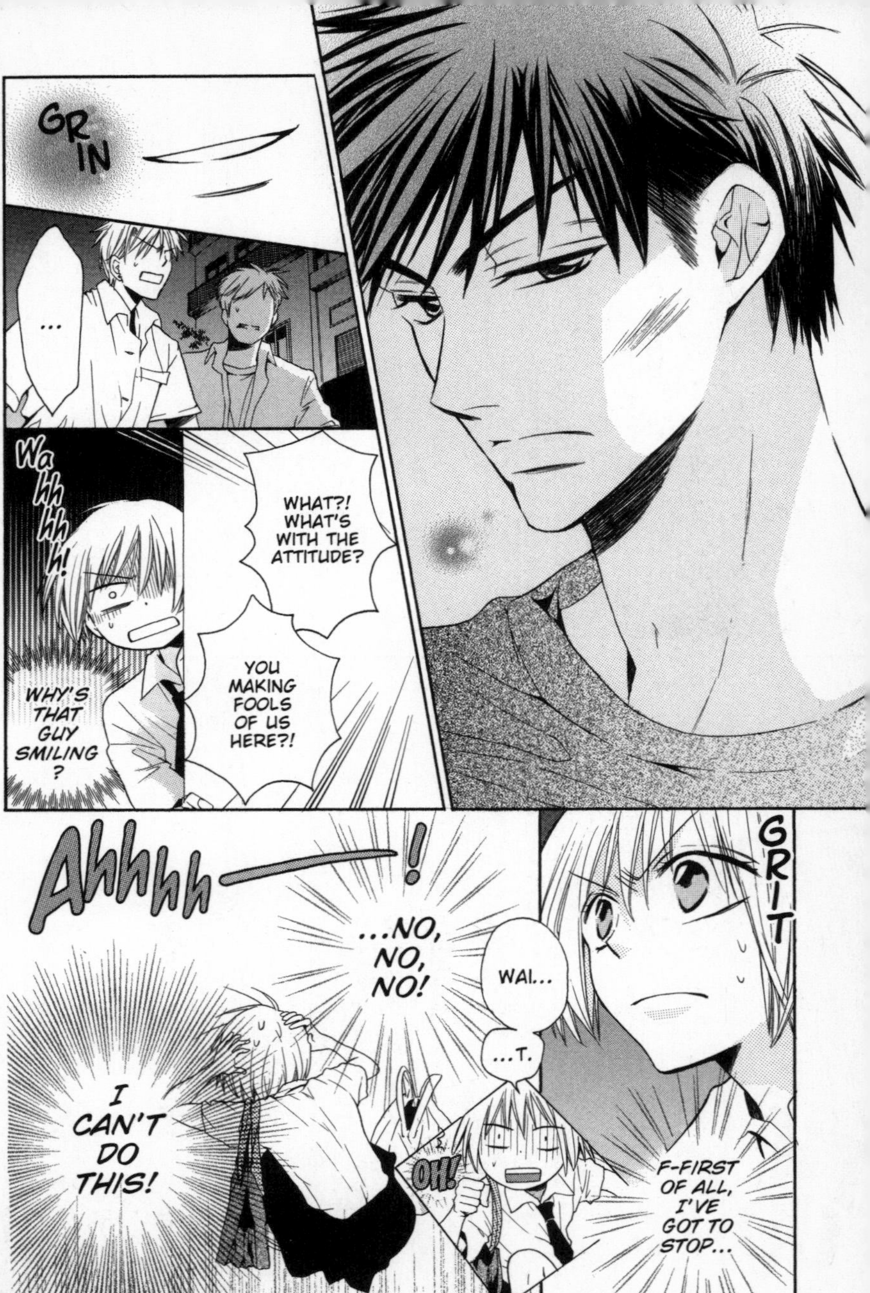
GRIN
...
WHAT?! WHAT'S WITH THE ATTITUDE?
YOU MAKING FOOLS OF US HERE?!
Wahhhhh!
WHY'S THAT GUY SMILING?
GRIT
F-FIRST OF ALL, I'VE GOT TO STOP...
WAI...
...T.
OH!
Ahhhhh——!
...NO, NO, NO!
I CAN'T DO THIS!

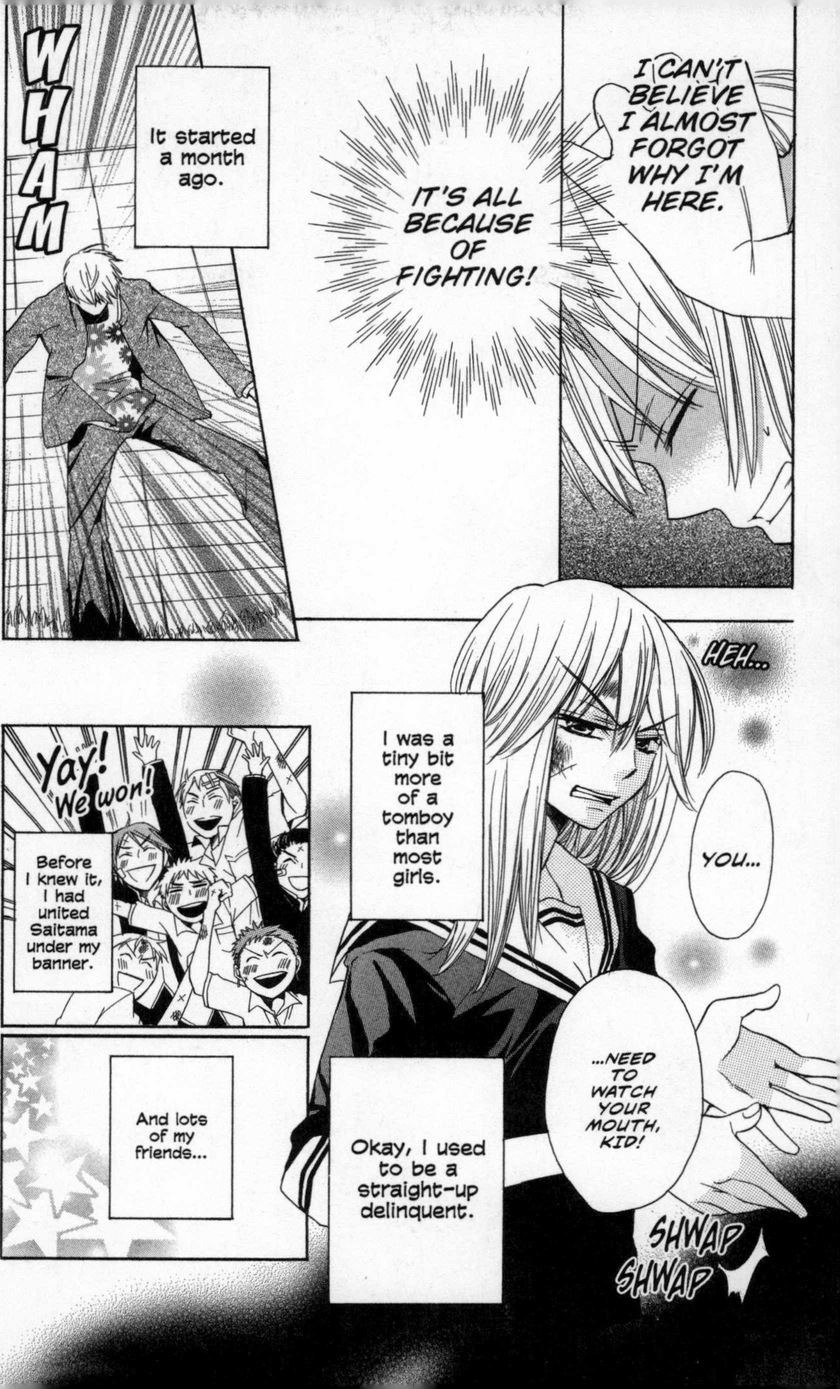

I CAN'T BELIEVE I ALMOST FORGOT WHY I'M HERE.
IT'S ALL BECAUSE OF FIGHTING!
It started a month ago.
WHAM
HEH...
I was a tiny bit more of a tomboy than most girls.
YOU...
...NEED TO WATCH YOUR MOUTH, KID!
Okay, I used to be a straight-up delinquent.
SHWAP SHWAP
Yay! We won!
Before I knew it, I had united Saitama under my banner.
And lots of my friends...

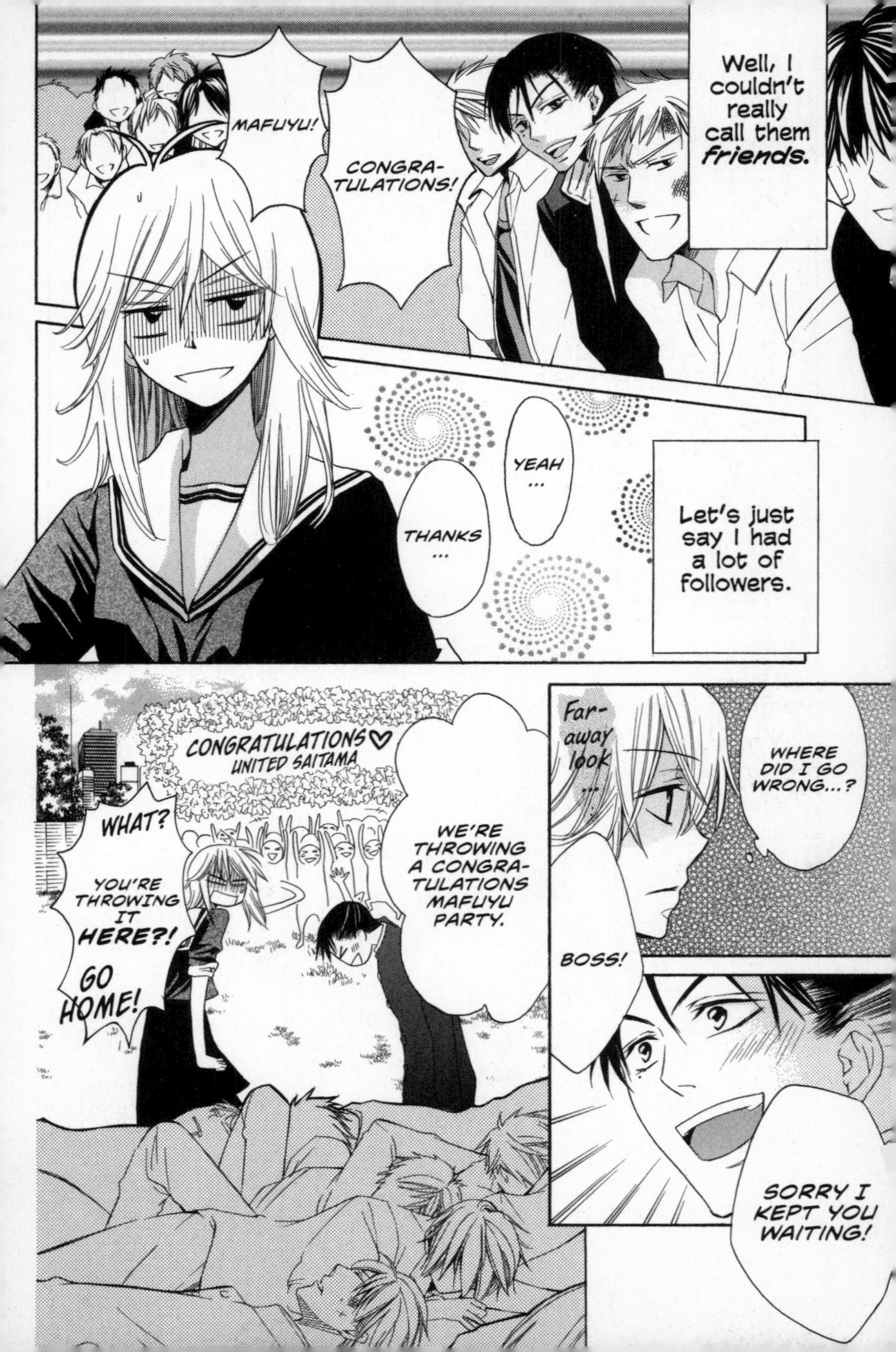
Well, I couldn't really call them *friends.*
MAFUYU!
CONGRA-TULATIONS!
Let's just say I had a lot of followers.
YEAH ...
THANKS ...
WHERE DID I GO WRONG...?
Far-away look ...
BOSS!
SORRY I KEPT YOU WAITING!
CONGRATULATIONS ♡ UNITED SAITAMA
WE'RE THROWING A CONGRATULATIONS MAFUYU PARTY.
WHAT?
YOU'RE THROWING IT HERE?!
GO HOME!

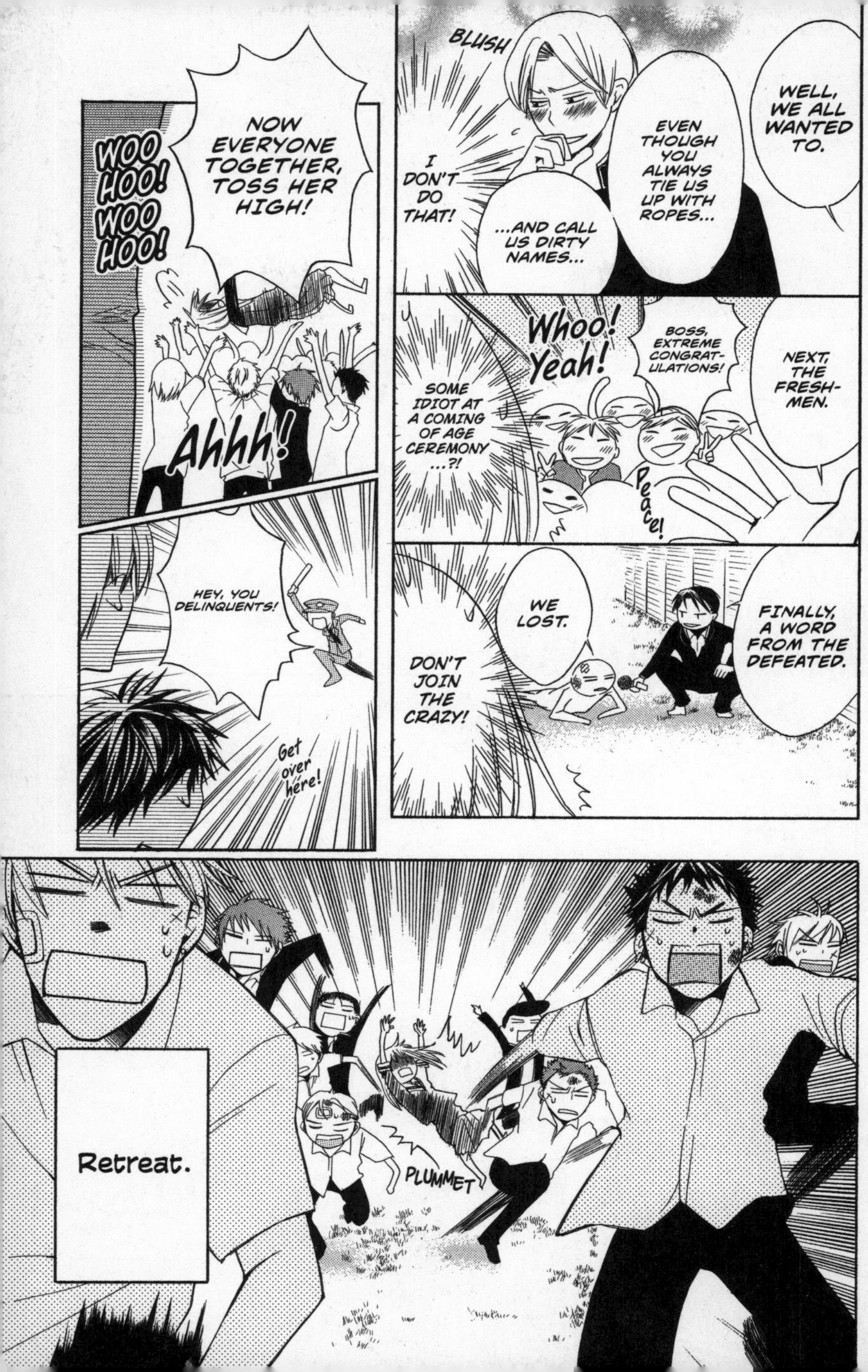

WELL, WE ALL WANTED TO.
EVEN THOUGH YOU ALWAYS TIE US UP WITH ROPES...
BLUSH
...AND CALL US DIRTY NAMES...
I DON'T DO THAT!
NOW EVERYONE TOGETHER, TOSS HER HIGH!
WOO HOO! WOO HOO!
Ahhh!
NEXT, THE FRESHMEN.
BOSS, EXTREME CONGRATULATIONS!
Whoo! Yeah!
Peace!
SOME IDIOT AT A COMING OF AGE CEREMONY ...?!
FINALLY, A WORD FROM THE DEFEATED.
WE LOST.
DON'T JOIN THE CRAZY!
HEY, YOU DELINQUENTS!
Get over here!
Retreat.
PLUMMET

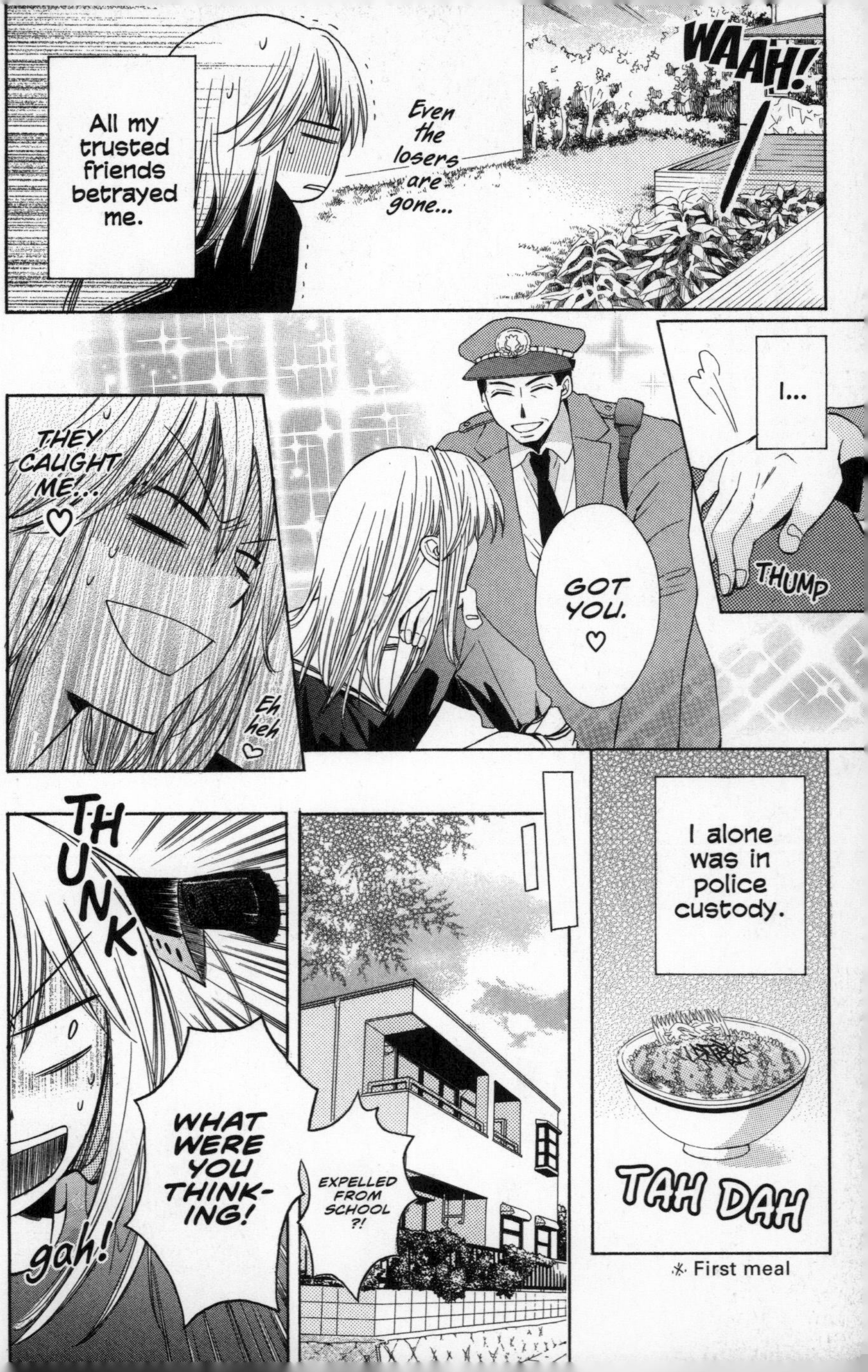
WAAH!
Even the losers are gone...
All my trusted friends betrayed me.
I...
THUMP
GOT YOU. ♡
THEY CAUGHT ME... ♡
Eh heh ♡
I alone was in police custody.
TAH DAH
※ First meal
EXPELLED FROM SCHOOL?!
WHAT WERE YOU THINKING!
THUNK
gah!

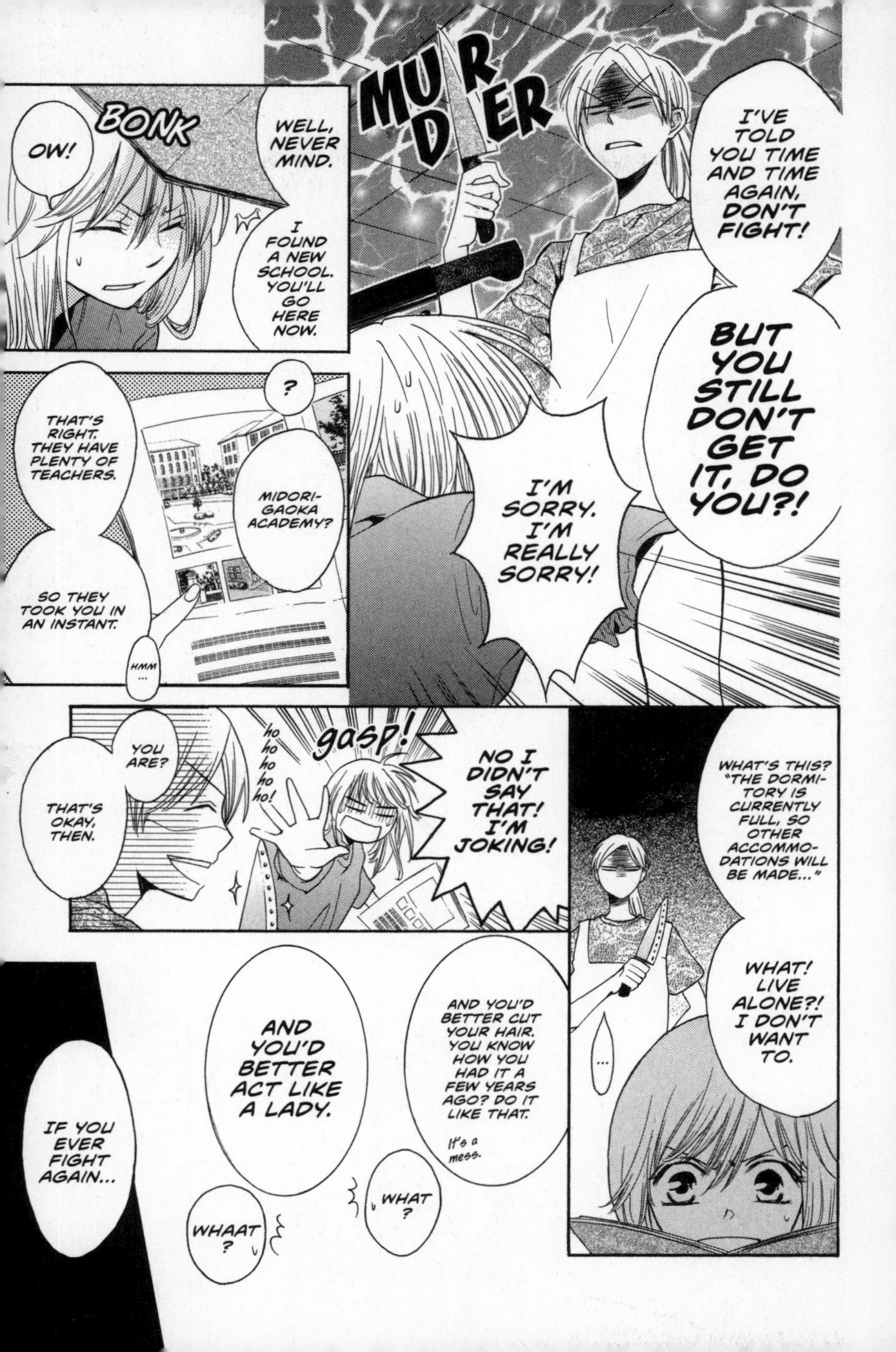
MURDER
I'VE TOLD YOU TIME AND TIME AGAIN, DON'T FIGHT!
BUT YOU STILL DON'T GET IT, DO YOU?!
I'M SORRY. I'M REALLY SORRY!
WELL, NEVER MIND.
BONK
OW!
I FOUND A NEW SCHOOL. YOU'LL GO HERE NOW.
?
MIDORI-GAOKA ACADEMY?
THAT'S RIGHT. THEY HAVE PLENTY OF TEACHERS.
SO THEY TOOK YOU IN AN INSTANT.
HMM...
WHAT'S THIS? "THE DORMITORY IS CURRENTLY FULL, SO OTHER ACCOMMODATIONS WILL BE MADE..."
WHAT! LIVE ALONE?! I DON'T WANT TO.
...
NO I DIDN'T SAY THAT! I'M JOKING!
gasp!
ho ho ho ho ho!
YOU ARE?
THAT'S OKAY, THEN.
AND YOU'D BETTER CUT YOUR HAIR. YOU KNOW HOW YOU HAD IT A FEW YEARS AGO? DO IT LIKE THAT.
It's a mess.
AND YOU'D BETTER ACT LIKE A LADY.
WHAT?
WHAAT?
IF YOU EVER FIGHT AGAIN...

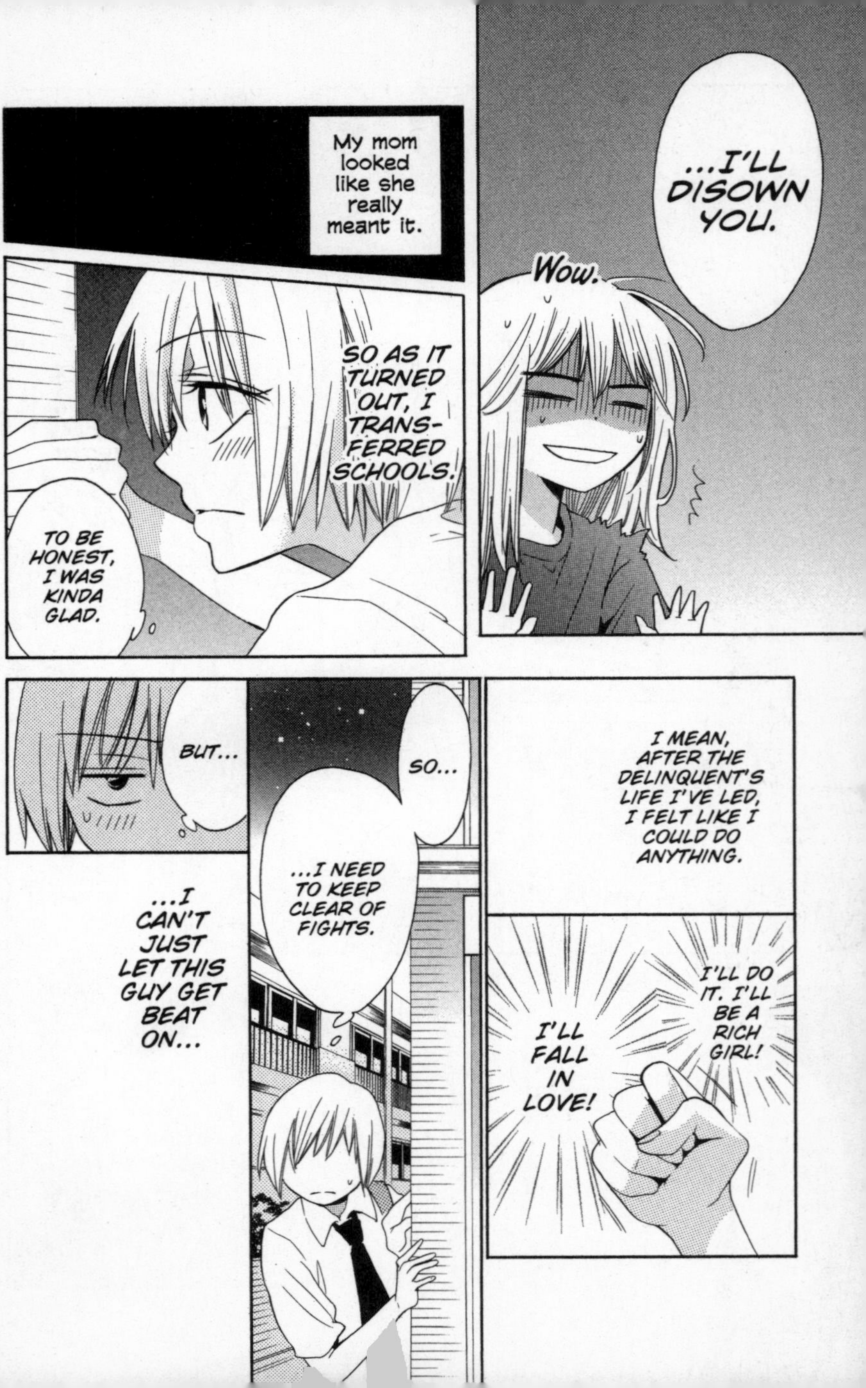

...I'LL DISOWN YOU.
Wow.
My mom looked like she really meant it.
SO AS IT TURNED OUT, I TRANSFERRED SCHOOLS.
TO BE HONEST, I WAS KINDA GLAD.
I MEAN, AFTER THE DELINQUENT'S LIFE I'VE LED, I FELT LIKE I COULD DO ANYTHING.
I'LL DO IT. I'LL BE A RICH GIRL!
I'LL FALL IN LOVE!
SO...
...I NEED TO KEEP CLEAR OF FIGHTS.
BUT...
...I CAN'T JUST LET THIS GUY GET BEAT ON...

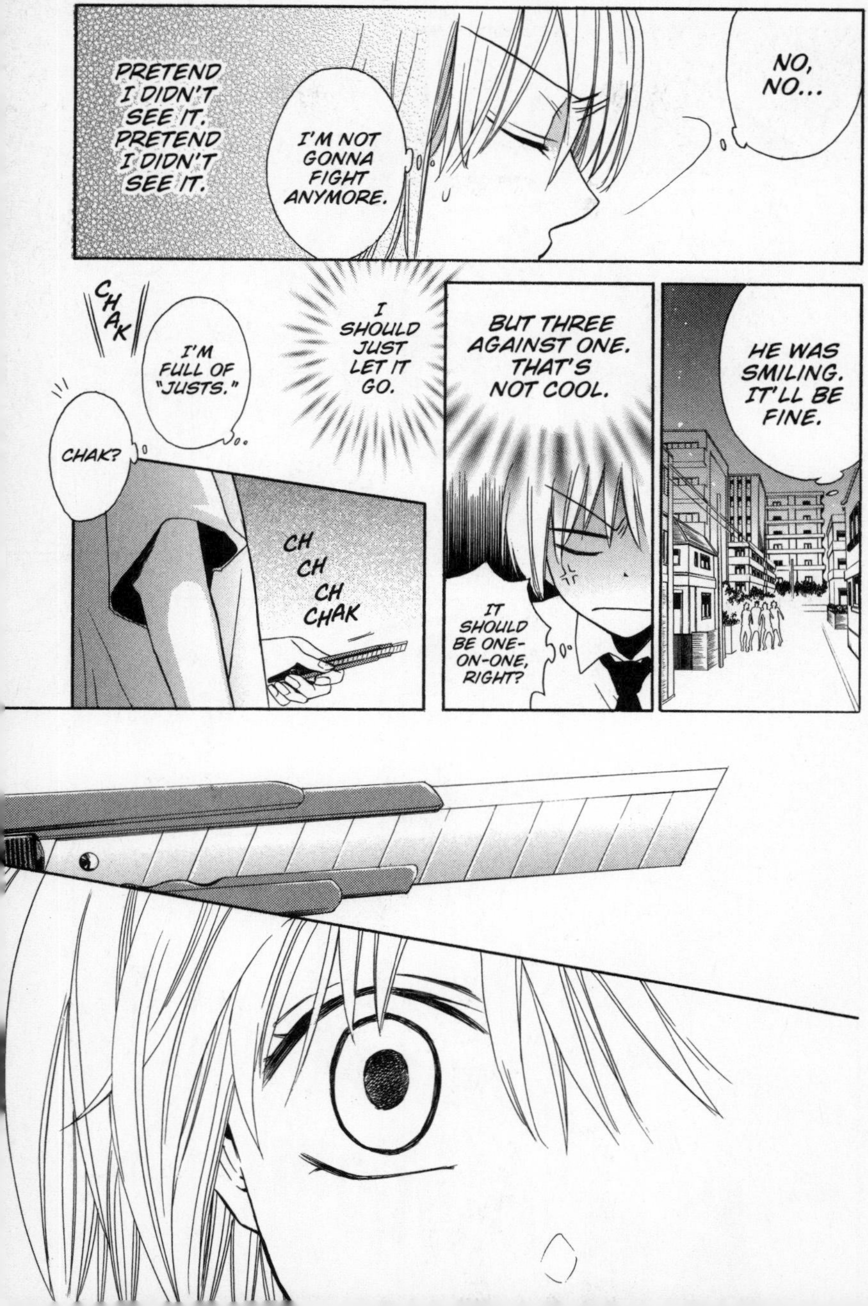
NO, NO...
I'M NOT GONNA FIGHT ANYMORE.
PRETEND I DIDN'T SEE IT. PRETEND I DIDN'T SEE IT.
HE WAS SMILING. IT'LL BE FINE.
BUT THREE AGAINST ONE. THAT'S NOT COOL.
IT SHOULD BE ONE-ON-ONE, RIGHT?
I SHOULD JUST LET IT GO.
I'M FULL OF "JUSTS."
CHAK
CHAK?
CH CH CH CHAK

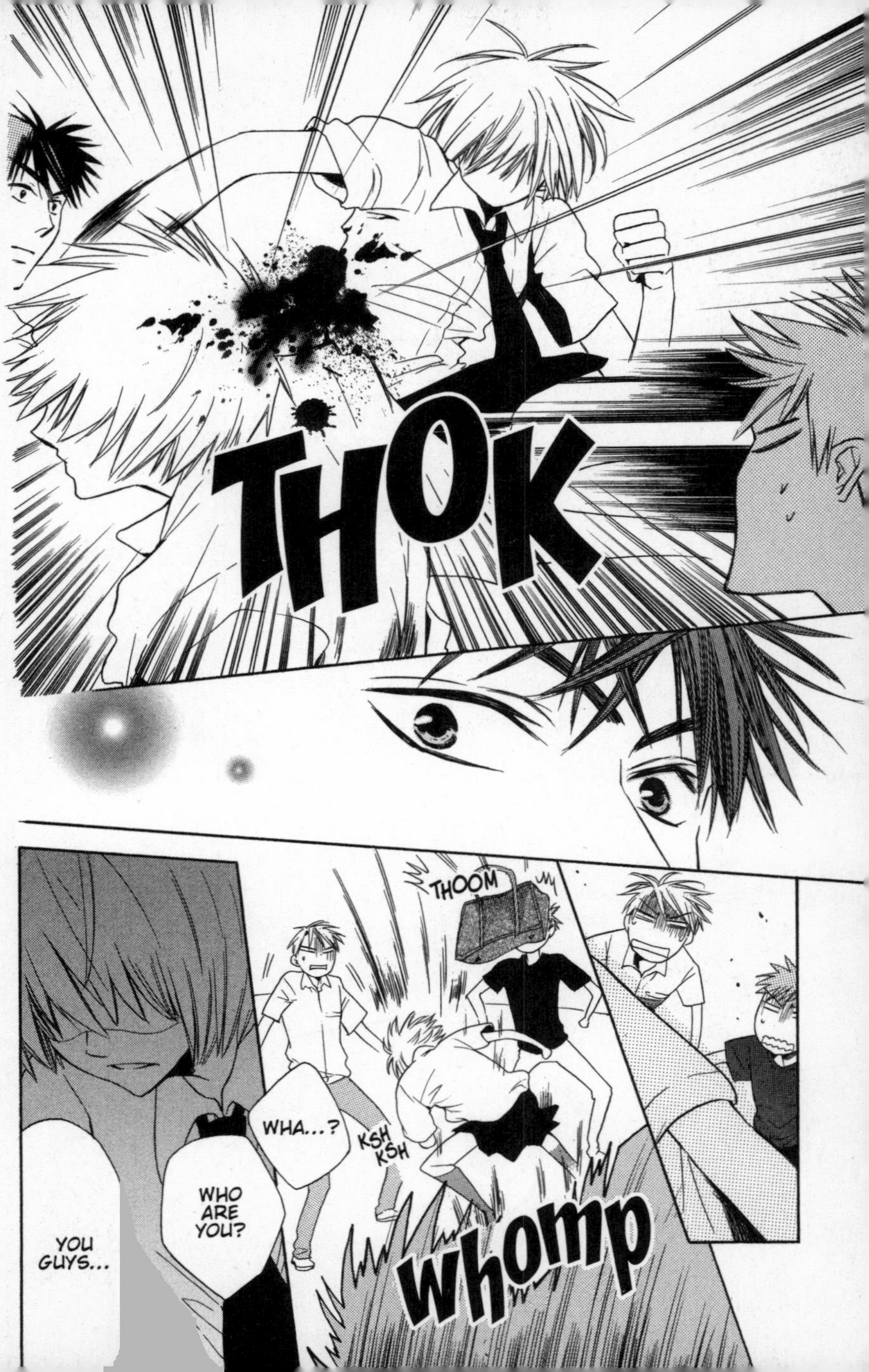
THOK
THOOM
WHA...?
KSH KSH
whomp
WHO ARE YOU?
YOU GUYS...

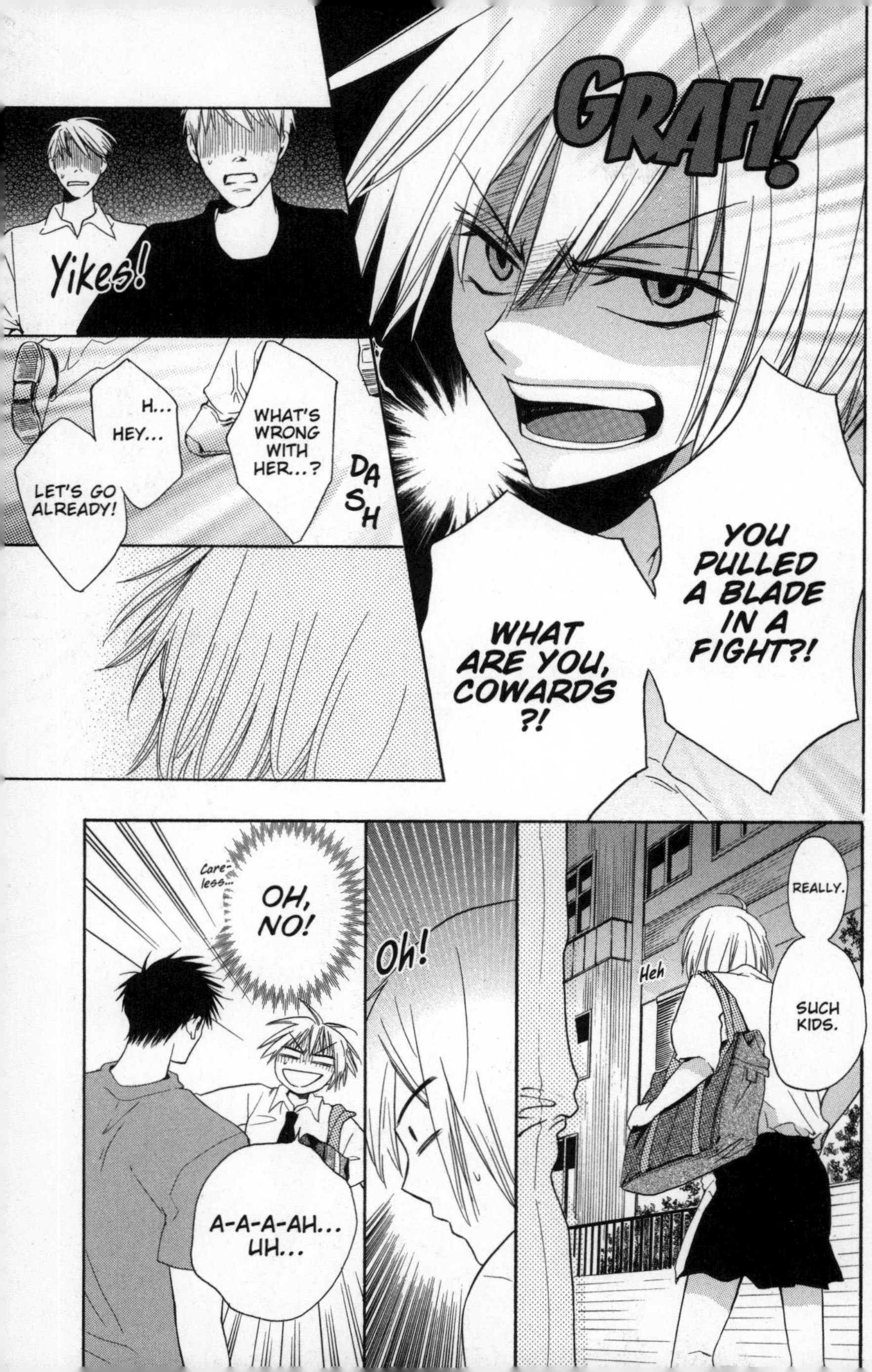
GRAH!
YOU PULLED A BLADE IN A FIGHT?!
WHAT ARE YOU, COWARDS?!
Yikes!
DASH
WHAT'S WRONG WITH HER...?
H... HEY...
LET'S GO ALREADY!
REALLY.
SUCH KIDS.
Heh
Oh!
OH, NO!
Care-less...
A-A-A-A-AH... UH...

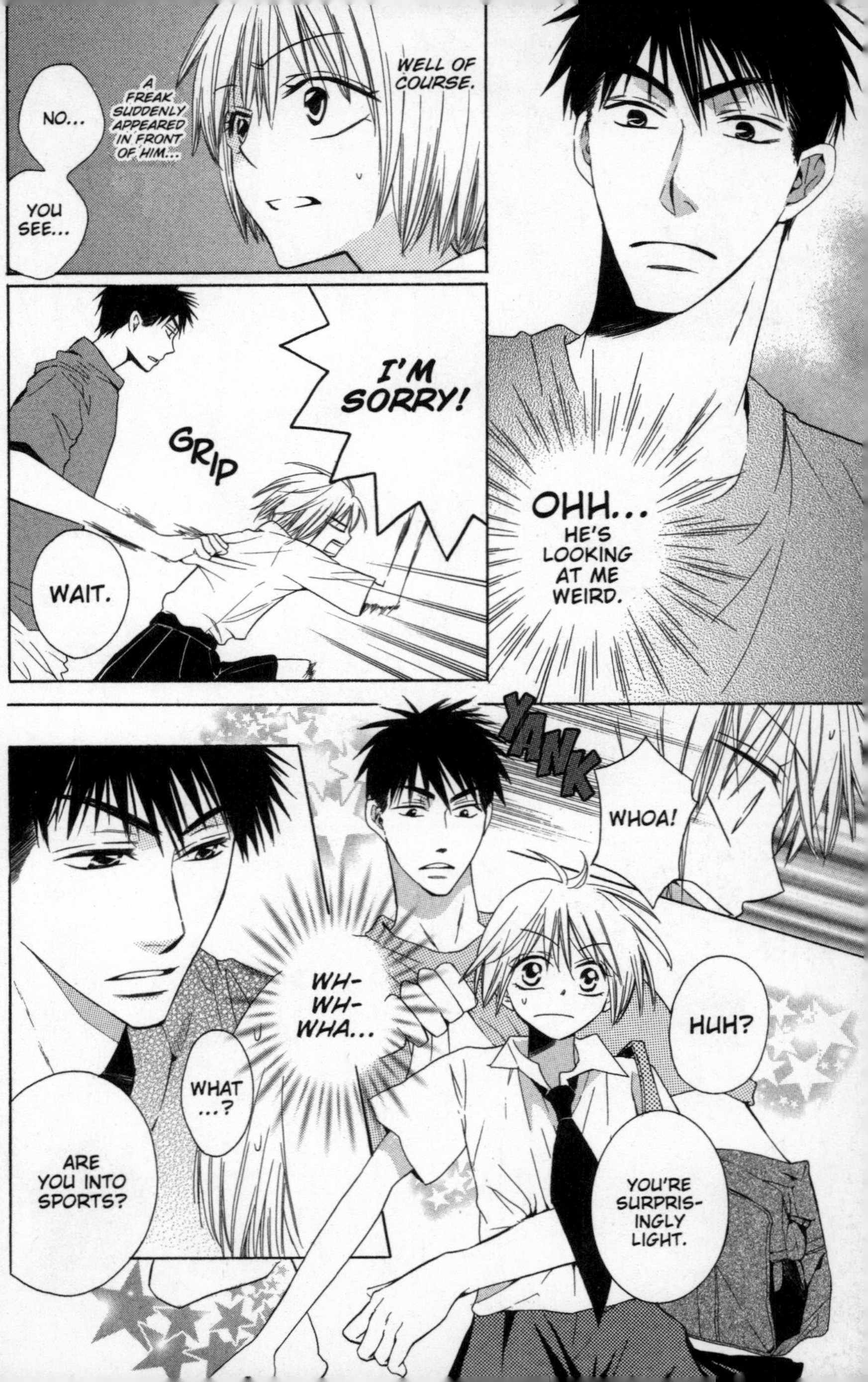
OHH... HE'S LOOKING AT ME WEIRD.
WELL OF COURSE.
A FREAK SUDDENLY APPEARED IN FRONT OF HIM...
NO... YOU SEE...
I'M SORRY!
GRIP
WAIT.
YANK
WHOA!
HUH?
WH-WH-WHA...
YOU'RE SURPRIS-INGLY LIGHT.
WHAT ...?
ARE YOU INTO SPORTS?

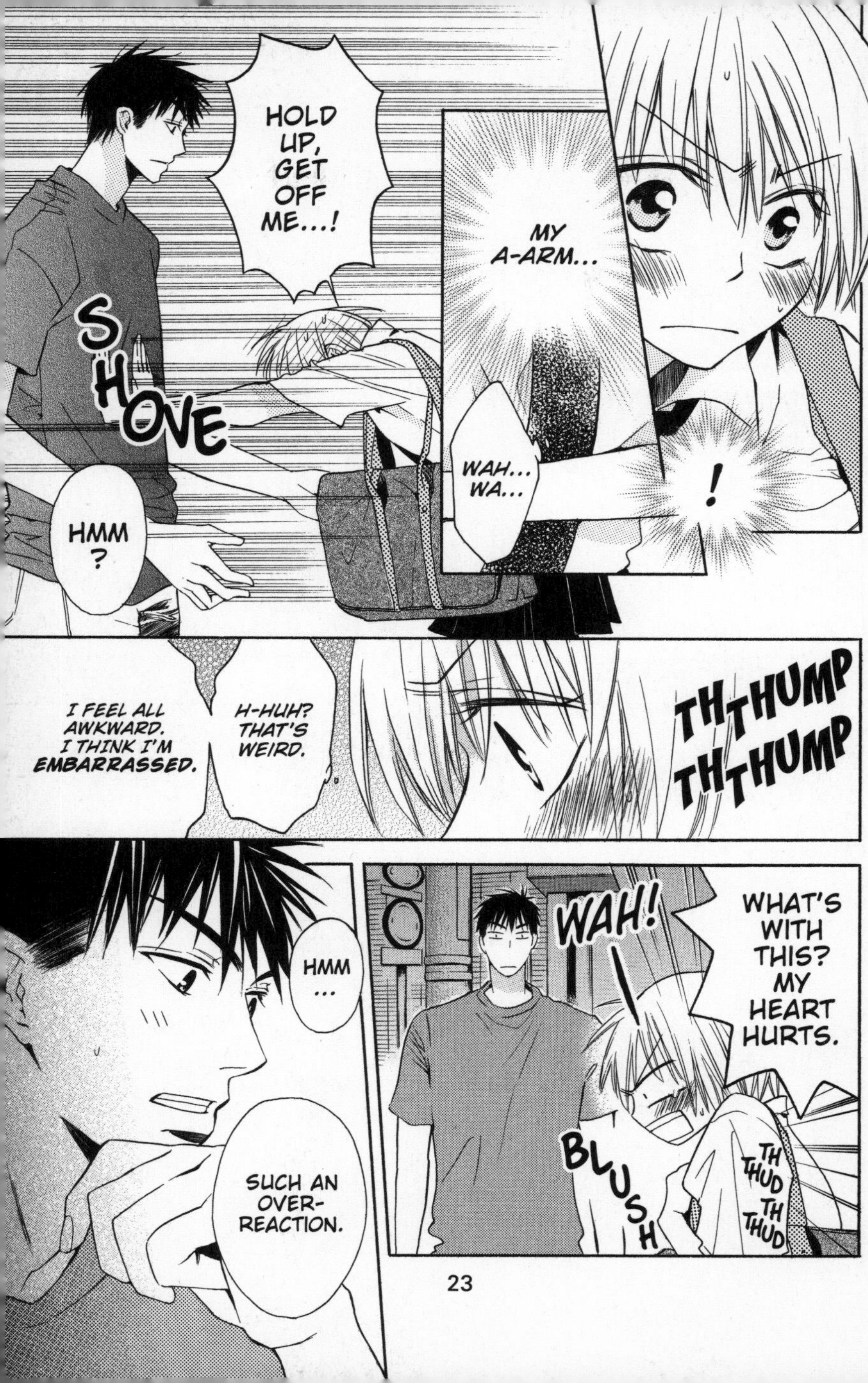
!
MY A-ARM...
WAH... WA...
HOLD UP, GET OFF ME...!
SHOVE
HMM?
THTHUMP THTHUMP
H-HUH? THAT'S WEIRD.
I FEEL ALL AWKWARD. I THINK I'M EMBARRASSED.
WHAT'S WITH THIS? MY HEART HURTS.
WAH!
BLUSH
TH THUD TH THUD
HMM...
SUCH AN OVER-REACTION.

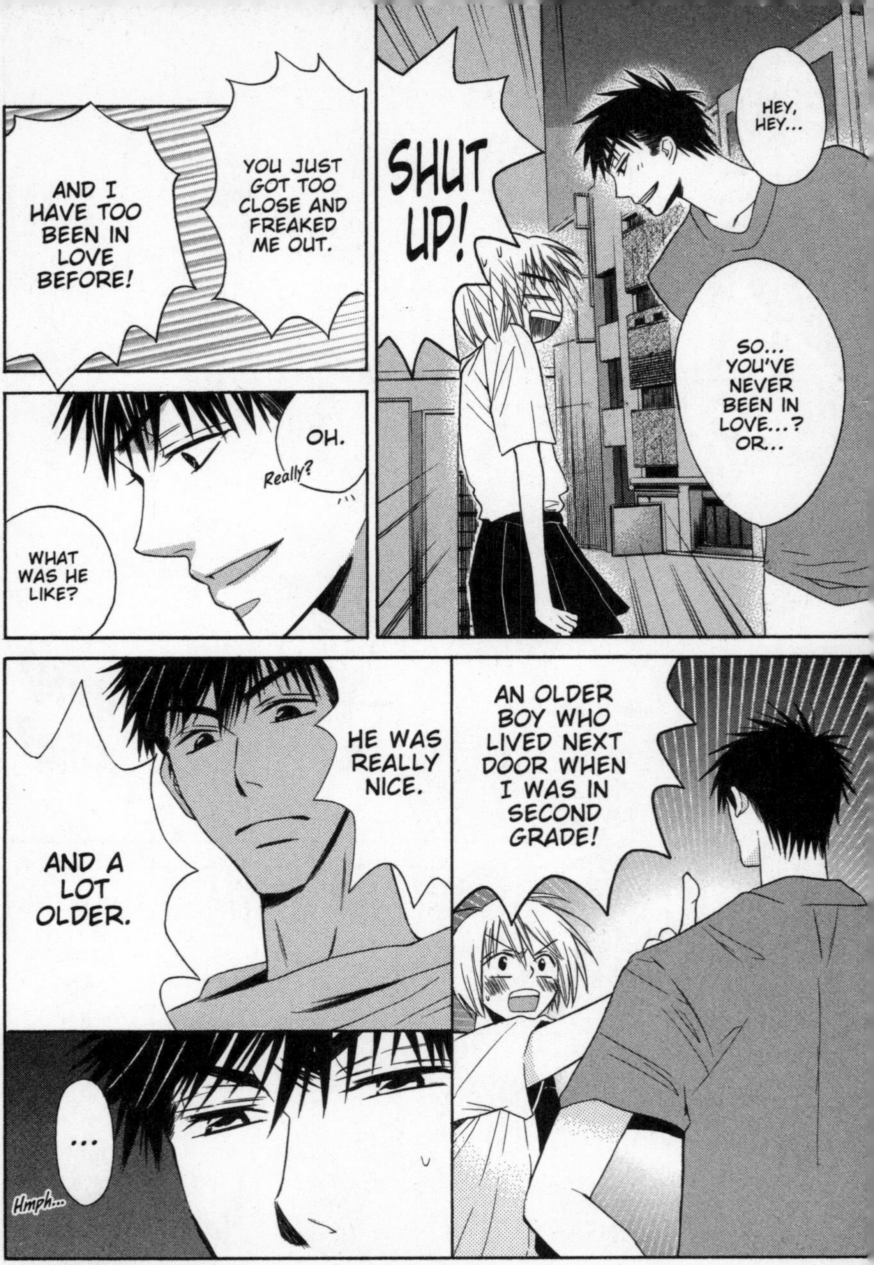
HEY, HEY...
SO... YOU'VE NEVER BEEN IN LOVE...? OR...
SHUT UP!
YOU JUST GOT TOO CLOSE AND FREAKED ME OUT.
AND I HAVE TOO BEEN IN LOVE BEFORE!
OH.
Really?
WHAT WAS HE LIKE?
AN OLDER BOY WHO LIVED NEXT DOOR WHEN I WAS IN SECOND GRADE!
HE WAS REALLY NICE.
AND A LOT OLDER.
...
Hmph...

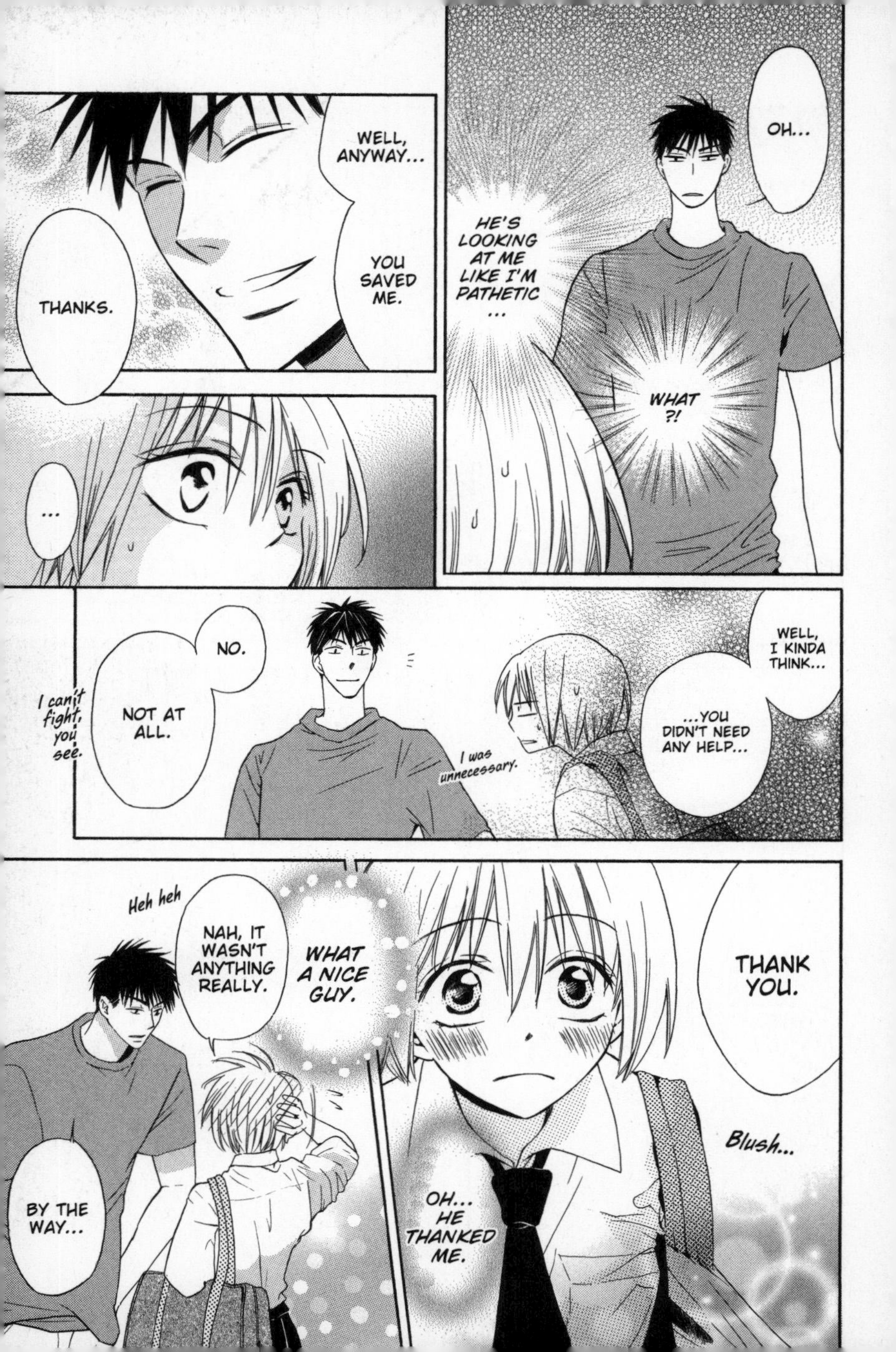
OH...
HE'S LOOKING AT ME LIKE I'M PATHETIC...
WHAT ?!
WELL, ANYWAY...
YOU SAVED ME.
THANKS.
...
WELL, I KINDA THINK...
...YOU DIDN'T NEED ANY HELP...
I was unnecessary.
NO.
NOT AT ALL.
I can't fight, you see.
THANK YOU.
Blush...
OH... HE THANKED ME.
WHAT A NICE GUY.
NAH, IT WASN'T ANYTHING REALLY.
Heh heh
BY THE WAY...

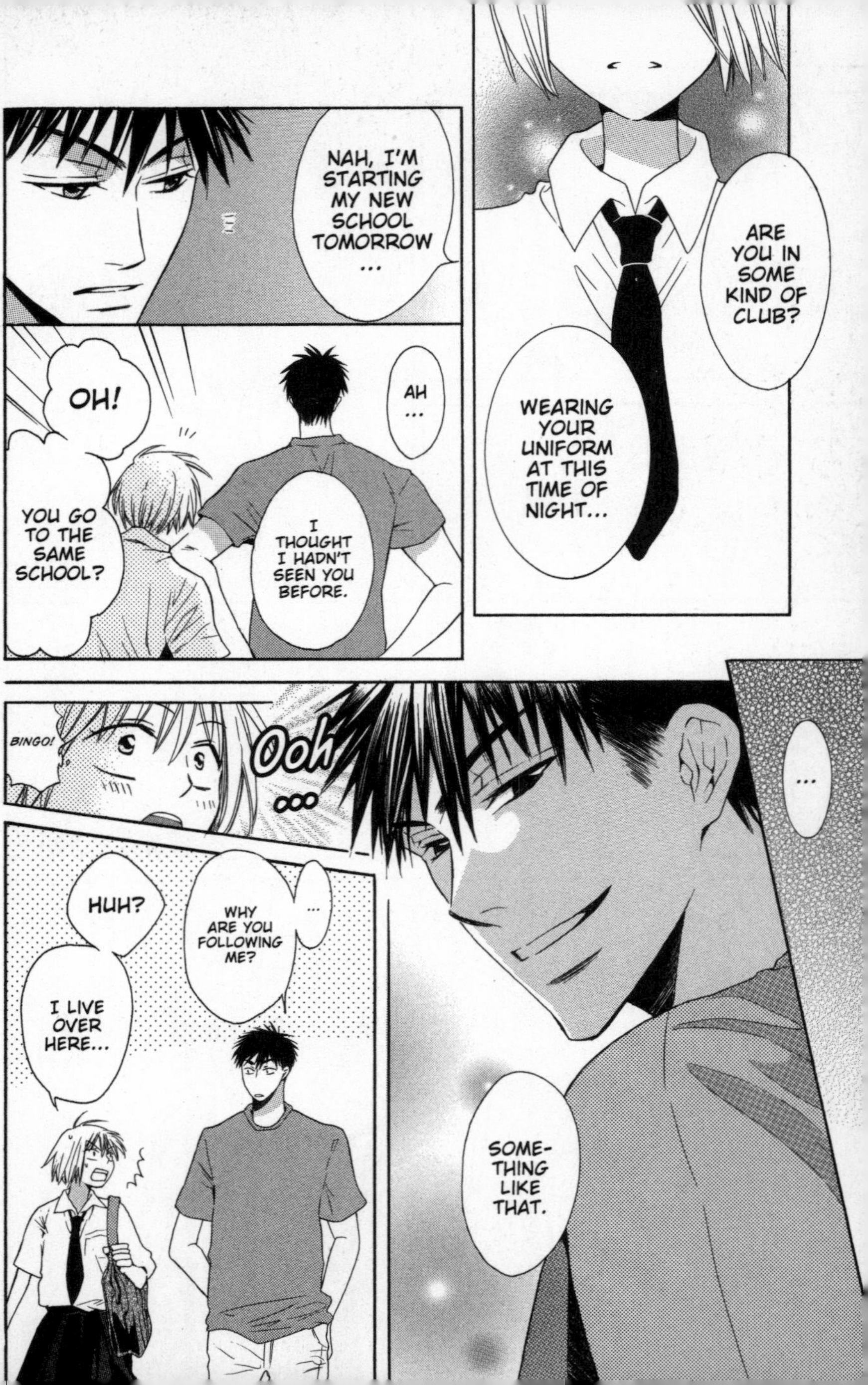
ARE YOU IN SOME KIND OF CLUB?
WEARING YOUR UNIFORM AT THIS TIME OF NIGHT...
NAH, I'M STARTING MY NEW SCHOOL TOMORROW...
AH...
I THOUGHT I HADN'T SEEN YOU BEFORE.
OH!
YOU GO TO THE SAME SCHOOL?
...
SOME-THING LIKE THAT.
Ooh ooo
BINGO!
...
WHY ARE YOU FOLLOWING ME?
HUH?
I LIVE OVER HERE...

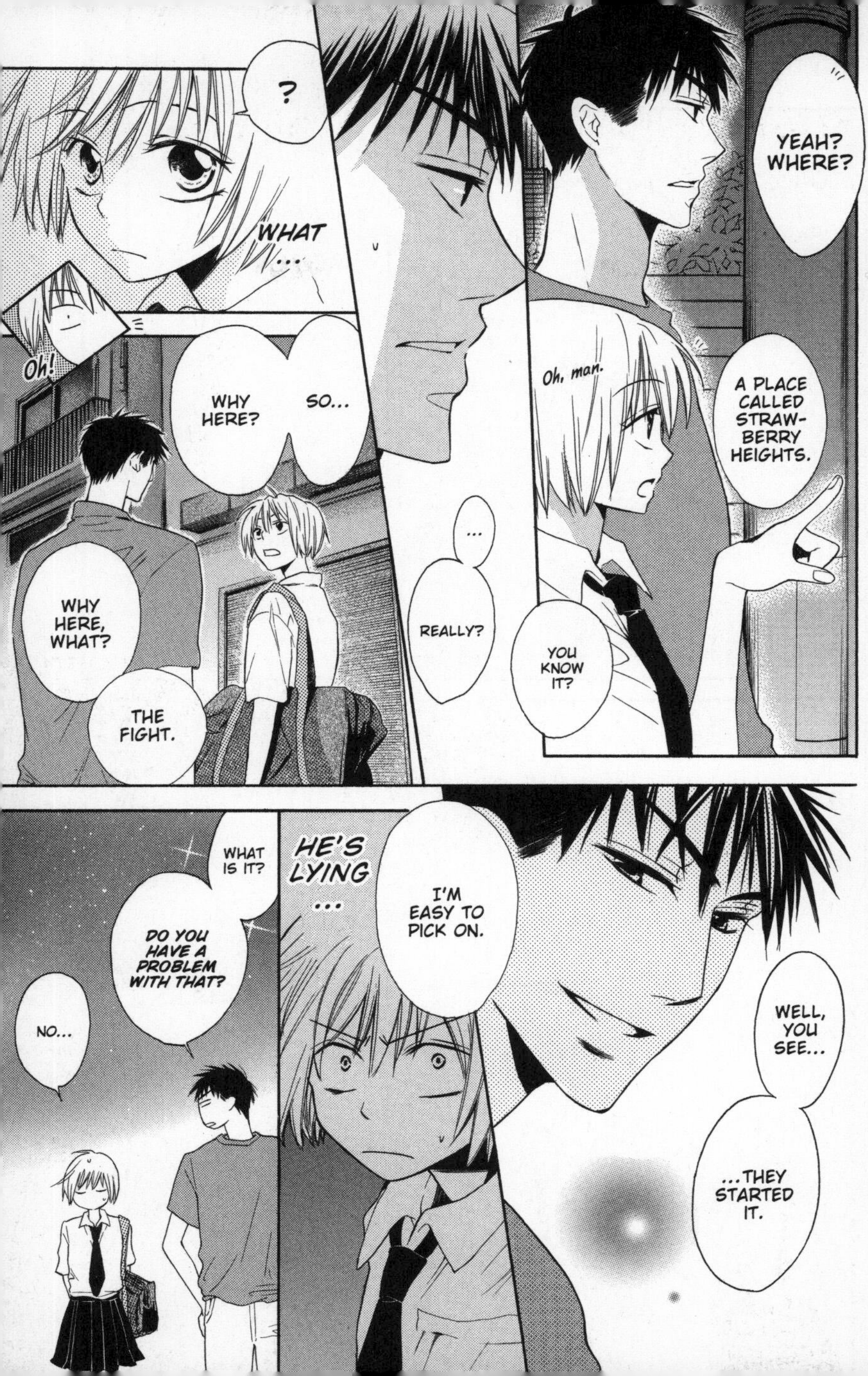
YEAH? WHERE?
A PLACE CALLED STRAWBERRY HEIGHTS.
Oh, man.
YOU KNOW IT?
...
REALLY?
?
WHAT...
Oh!
SO...
WHY HERE?
WHY HERE, WHAT?
THE FIGHT.
WELL, YOU SEE...
...THEY STARTED IT.
I'M EASY TO PICK ON.
HE'S LYING...
WHAT IS IT?
DO YOU HAVE A PROBLEM WITH THAT?
NO...

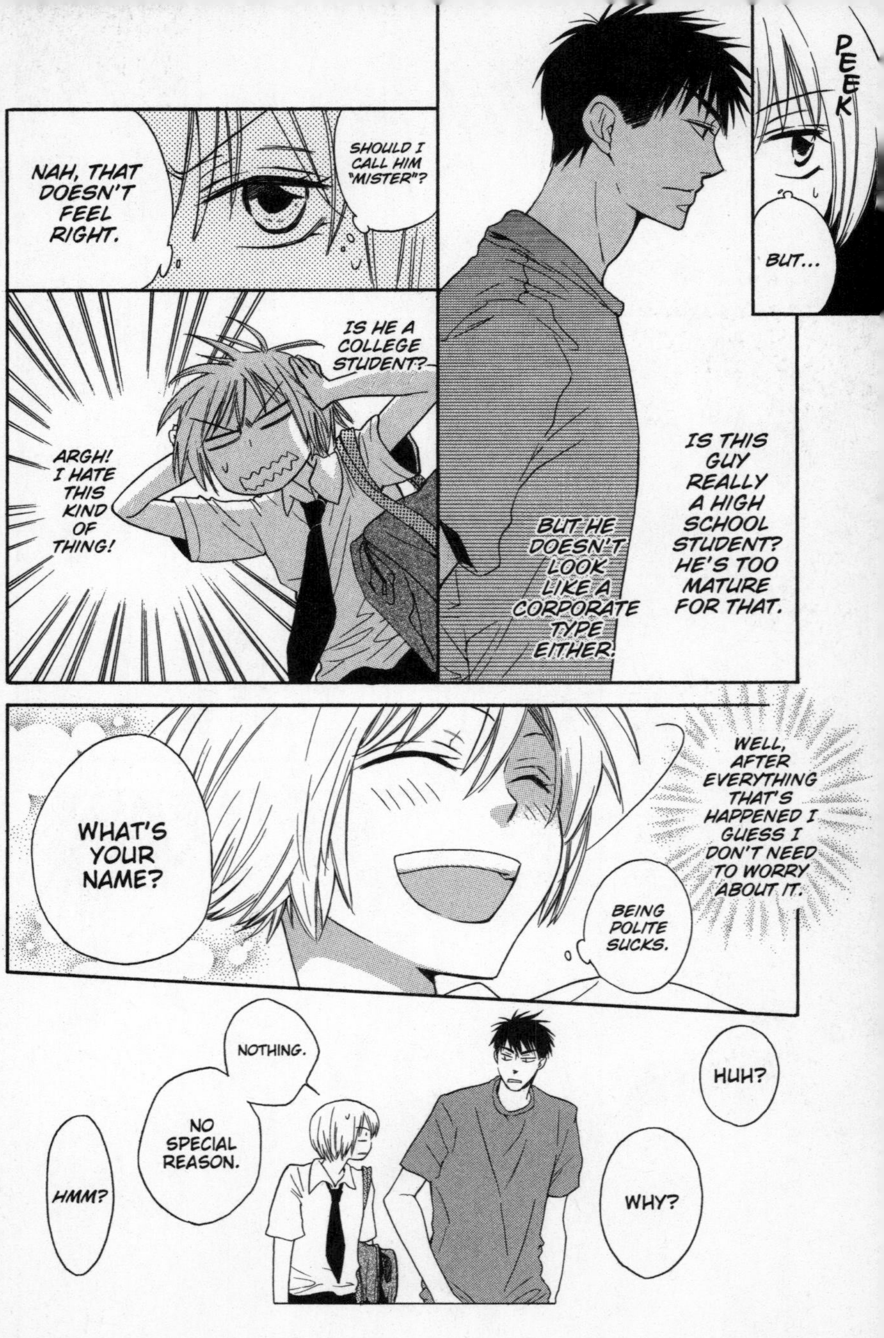
PEEK
BUT...
IS THIS GUY REALLY A HIGH SCHOOL STUDENT? HE'S TOO MATURE FOR THAT.
BUT HE DOESN'T LOOK LIKE A CORPORATE TYPE EITHER.
SHOULD I CALL HIM "MISTER"?
NAH, THAT DOESN'T FEEL RIGHT.
IS HE A COLLEGE STUDENT?
ARGH! I HATE THIS KIND OF THING!
WELL, AFTER EVERYTHING THAT'S HAPPENED I GUESS I DON'T NEED TO WORRY ABOUT IT.
BEING POLITE SUCKS.
WHAT'S YOUR NAME?
HUH?
WHY?
NOTHING.
NO SPECIAL REASON.
HMM?

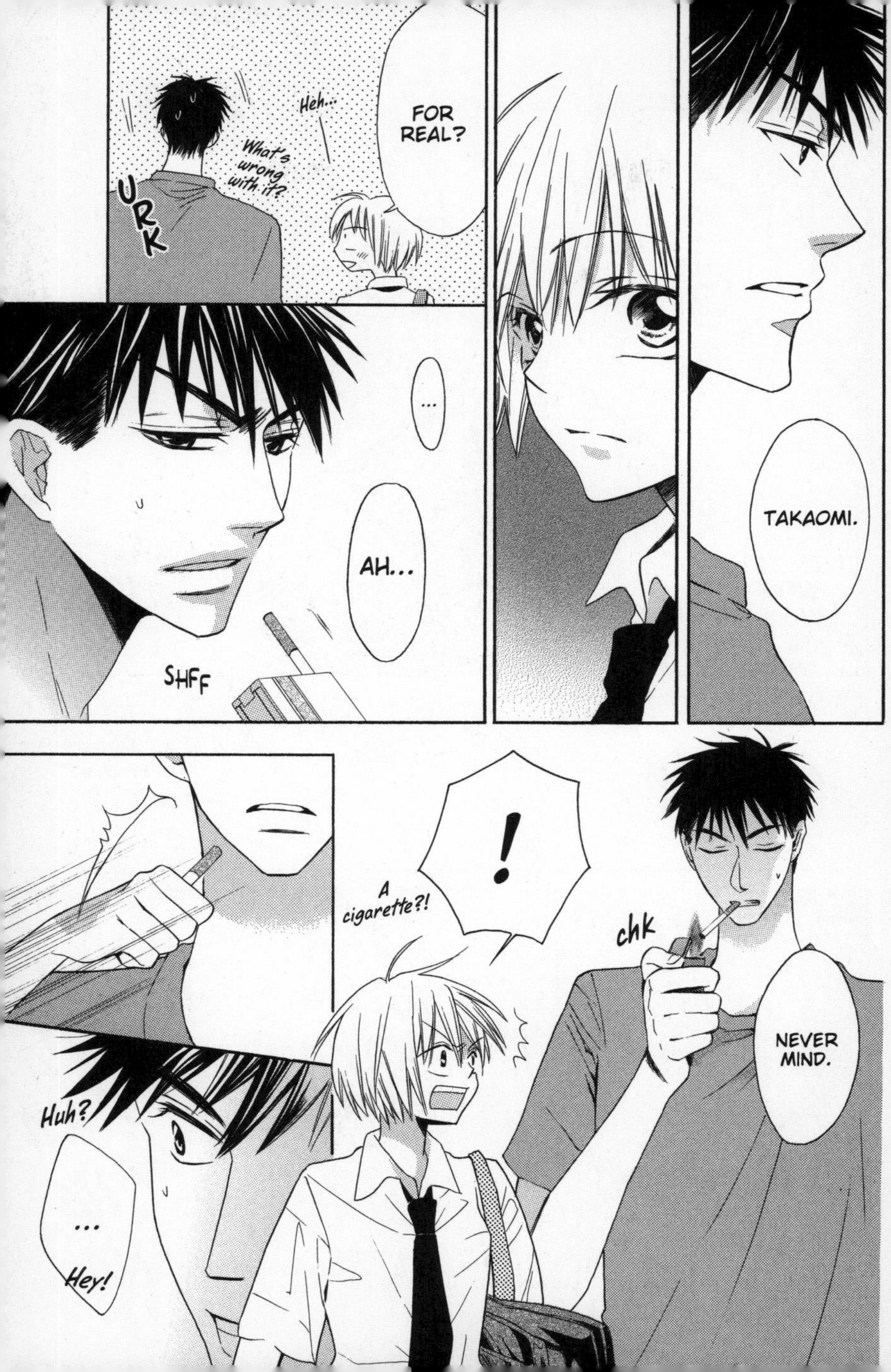

TAKAOMI.
FOR REAL?
Heh...
What's wrong with it?
URK
...
AH...
SHFF
NEVER MIND.
chk
!
A cigarette?!
Huh?
...
Hey!

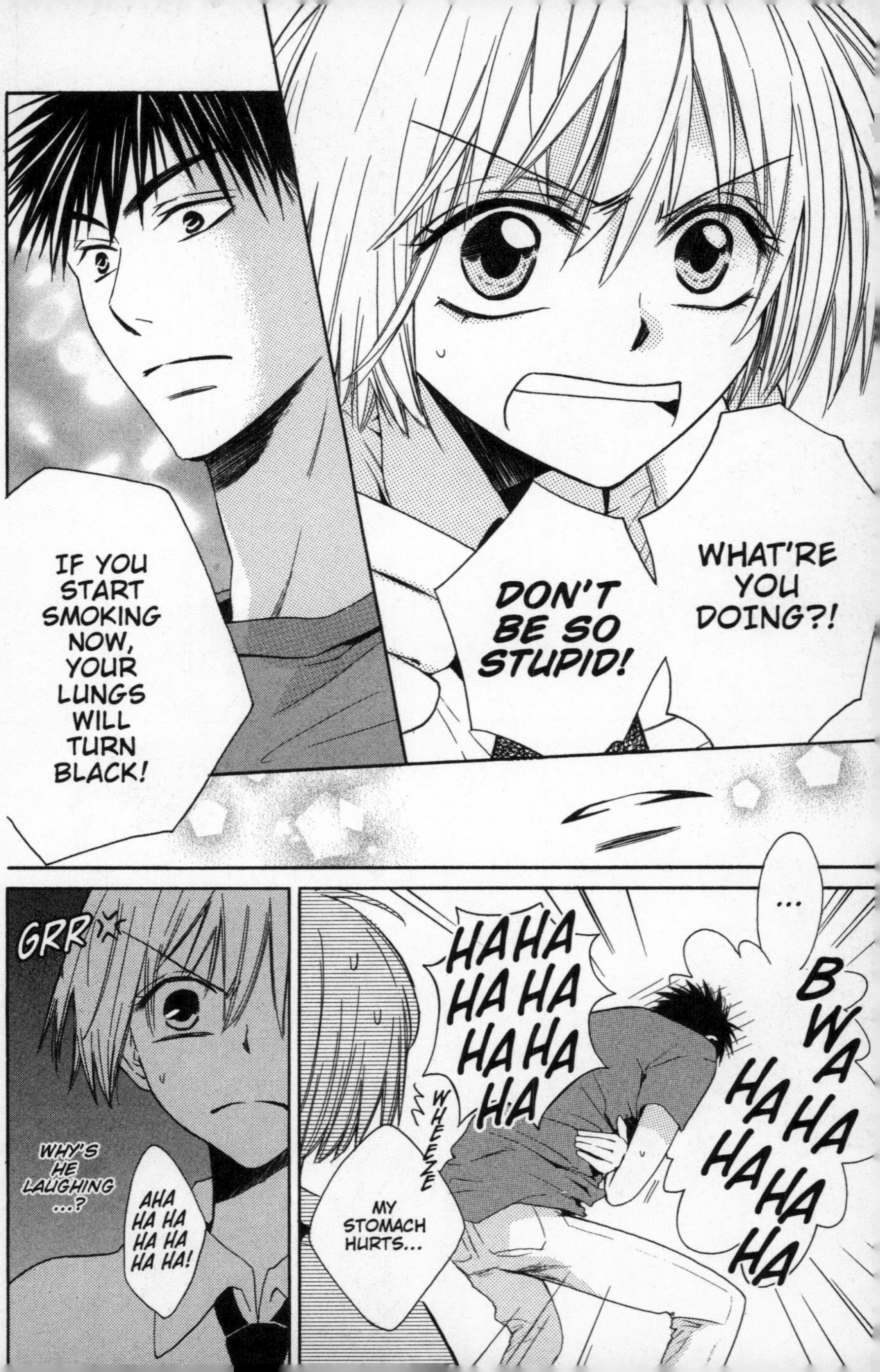

WHAT'RE YOU DOING?!
DON'T BE SO STUPID!
IF YOU START SMOKING NOW, YOUR LUNGS WILL TURN BLACK!
...
BWAHAHAHAHAHAHAHA
HAHAHAHAHAHAHAHA
WHEEZE
MY STOMACH HURTS...
GRR
WHY'S HE LAUGHING...?
AHA HA HA HA HA HA HA!

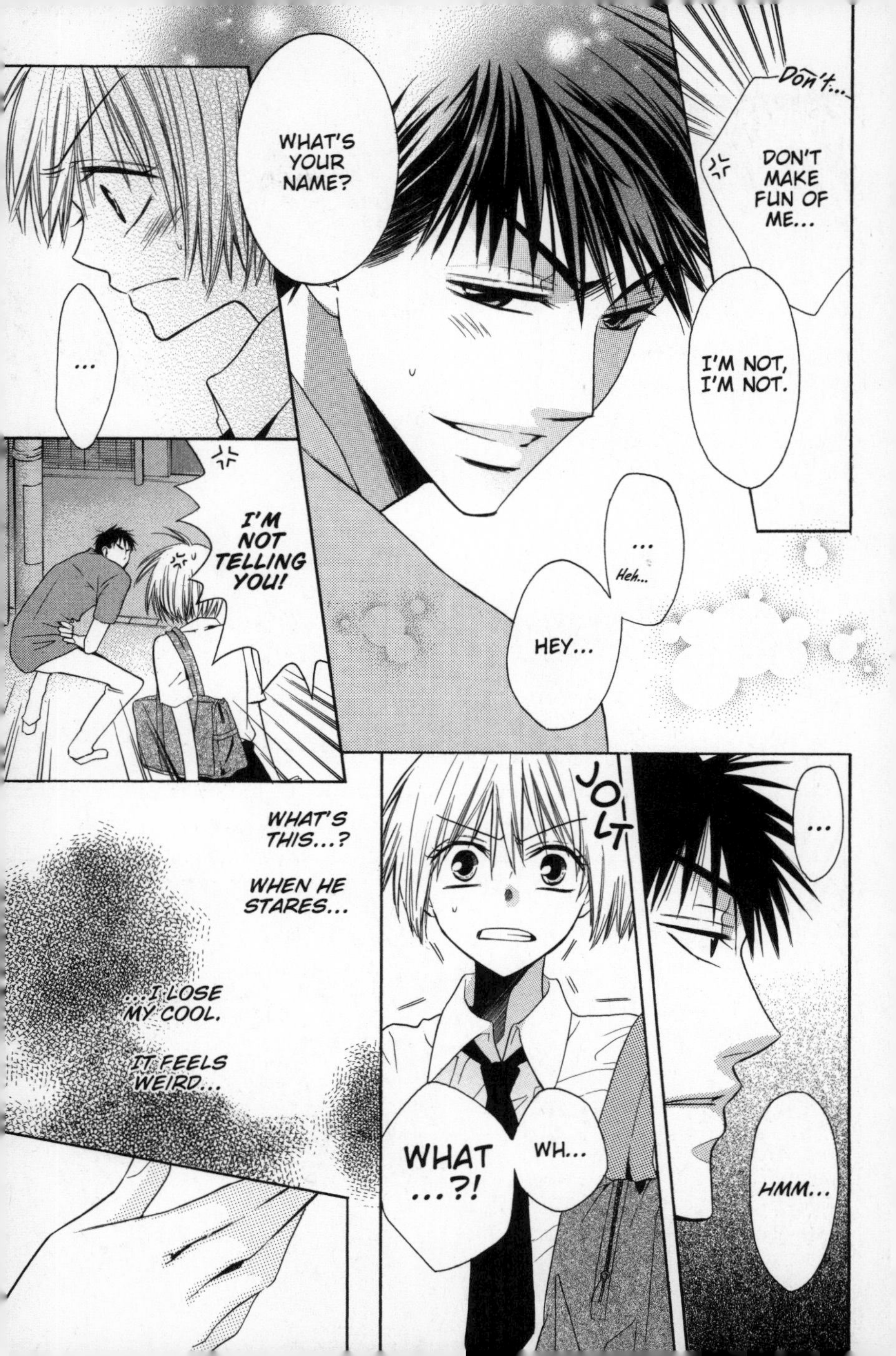

Don't...
DON'T MAKE FUN OF ME...
I'M NOT, I'M NOT.
... Heh...
HEY...
WHAT'S YOUR NAME?
...
I'M NOT TELLING YOU!
...
JOLT
HMM...
WH...
WHAT ...?!
WHAT'S THIS...?
WHEN HE STARES...
...I LOSE MY COOL.
IT FEELS WEIRD...

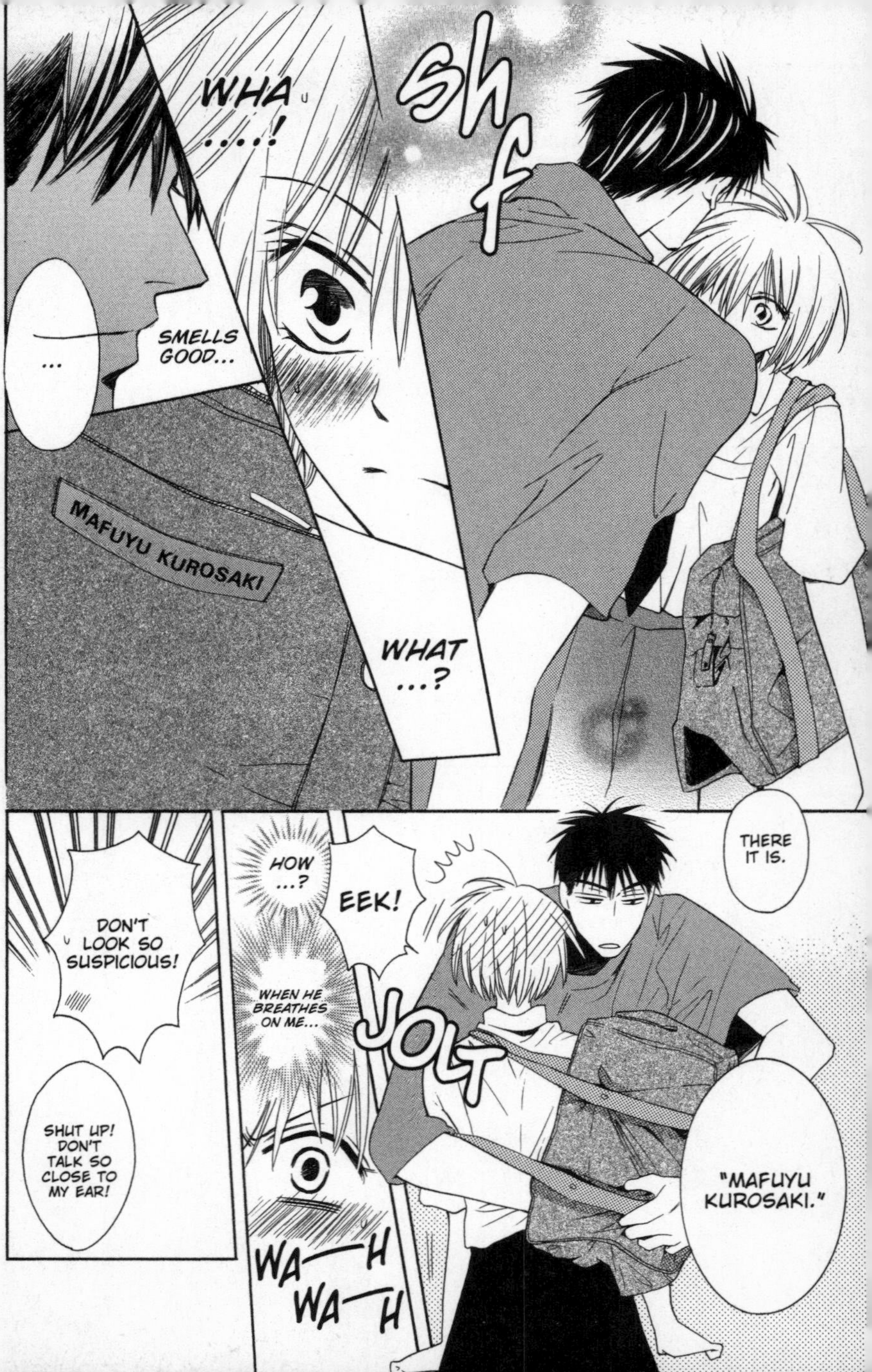
shf
WHA .....!
SMELLS GOOD...
MAFUYU KUROSAKI
WHAT ...?
...
THERE IT IS.
EEK!
HOW ...?
JOLT
WHEN HE BREATHES ON ME...
"MAFUYU KUROSAKI."
WA—H WA—H
DON'T LOOK SO SUSPICIOUS!
SHUT UP! DON'T TALK SO CLOSE TO MY EAR!

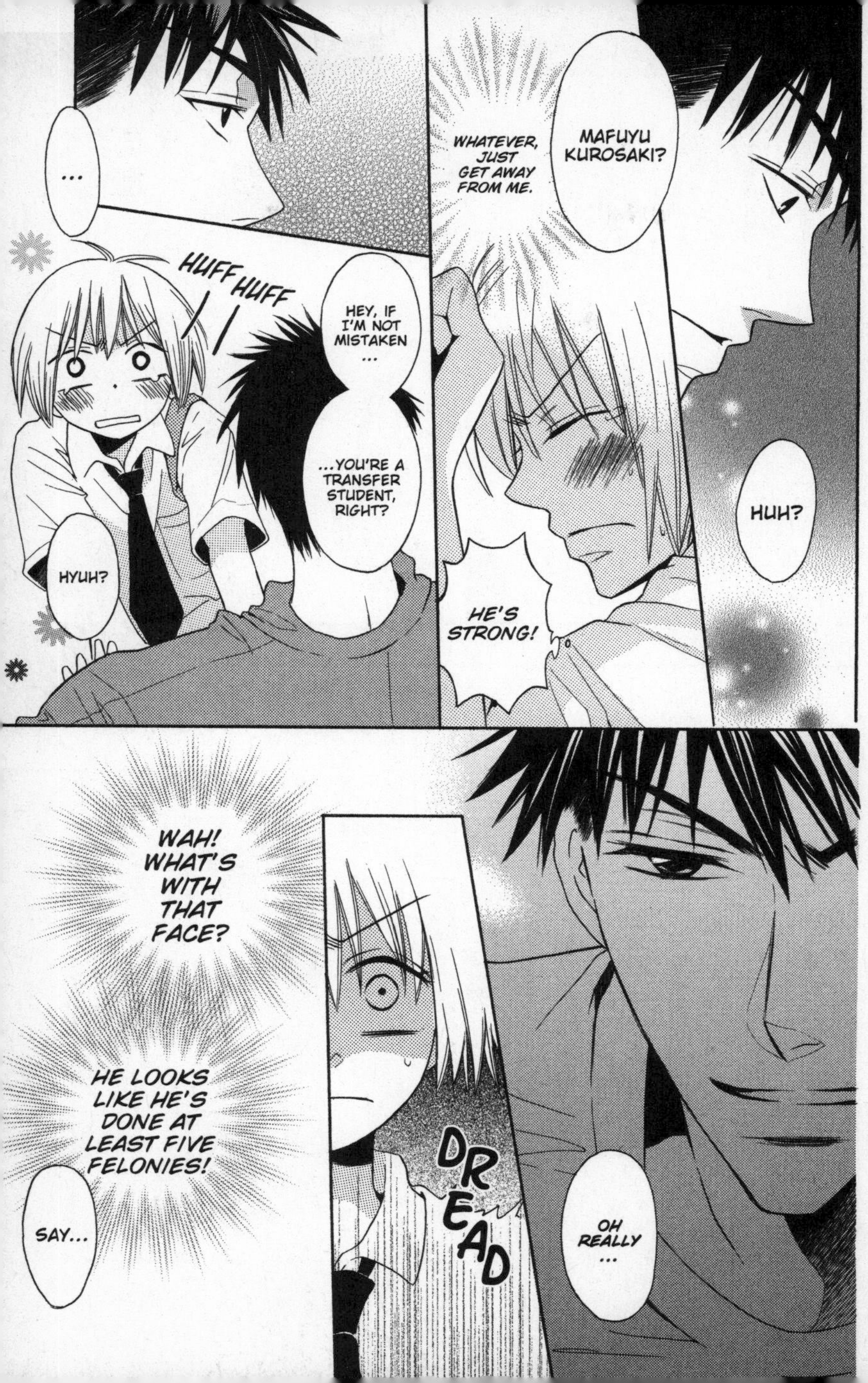
MAFUYU KUROSAKI?
WHATEVER, JUST GET AWAY FROM ME.
HUH?
HE'S STRONG!
...
HEY, IF I'M NOT MISTAKEN ...
...YOU'RE A TRANSFER STUDENT, RIGHT?
HUFF HUFF
HYUH?
OH REALLY ...
DREAD
WAH! WHAT'S WITH THAT FACE?
HE LOOKS LIKE HE'S DONE AT LEAST FIVE FELONIES!
SAY...

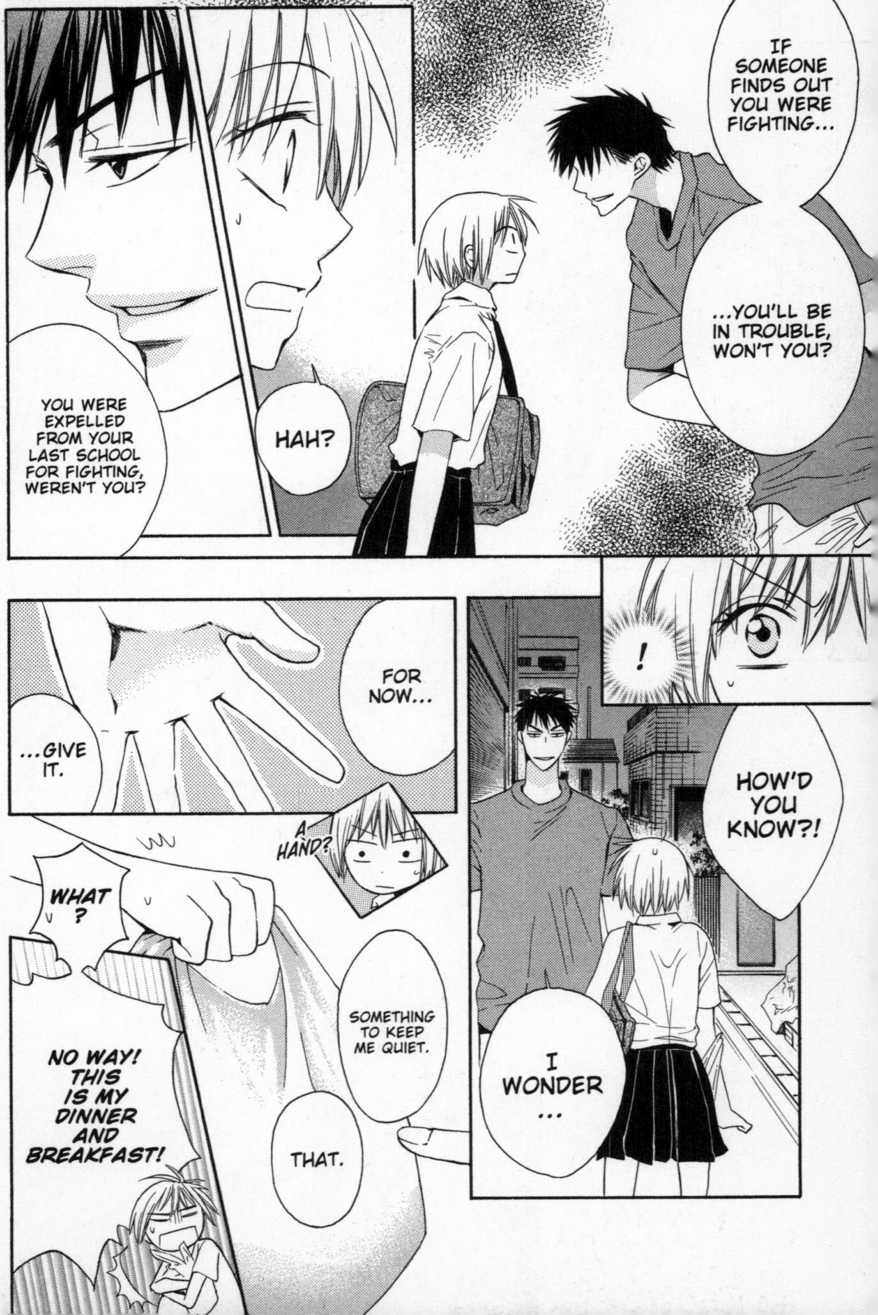
IF SOMEONE FINDS OUT YOU WERE FIGHTING...
...YOU'LL BE IN TROUBLE, WON'T YOU?
HAH?
YOU WERE EXPELLED FROM YOUR LAST SCHOOL FOR FIGHTING, WEREN'T YOU?
!
HOW'D YOU KNOW?!
I WONDER...
FOR NOW...
...GIVE IT.
A HAND?
WHAT ?
SOMETHING TO KEEP ME QUIET.
THAT.
NO WAY! THIS IS MY DINNER AND BREAKFAST!

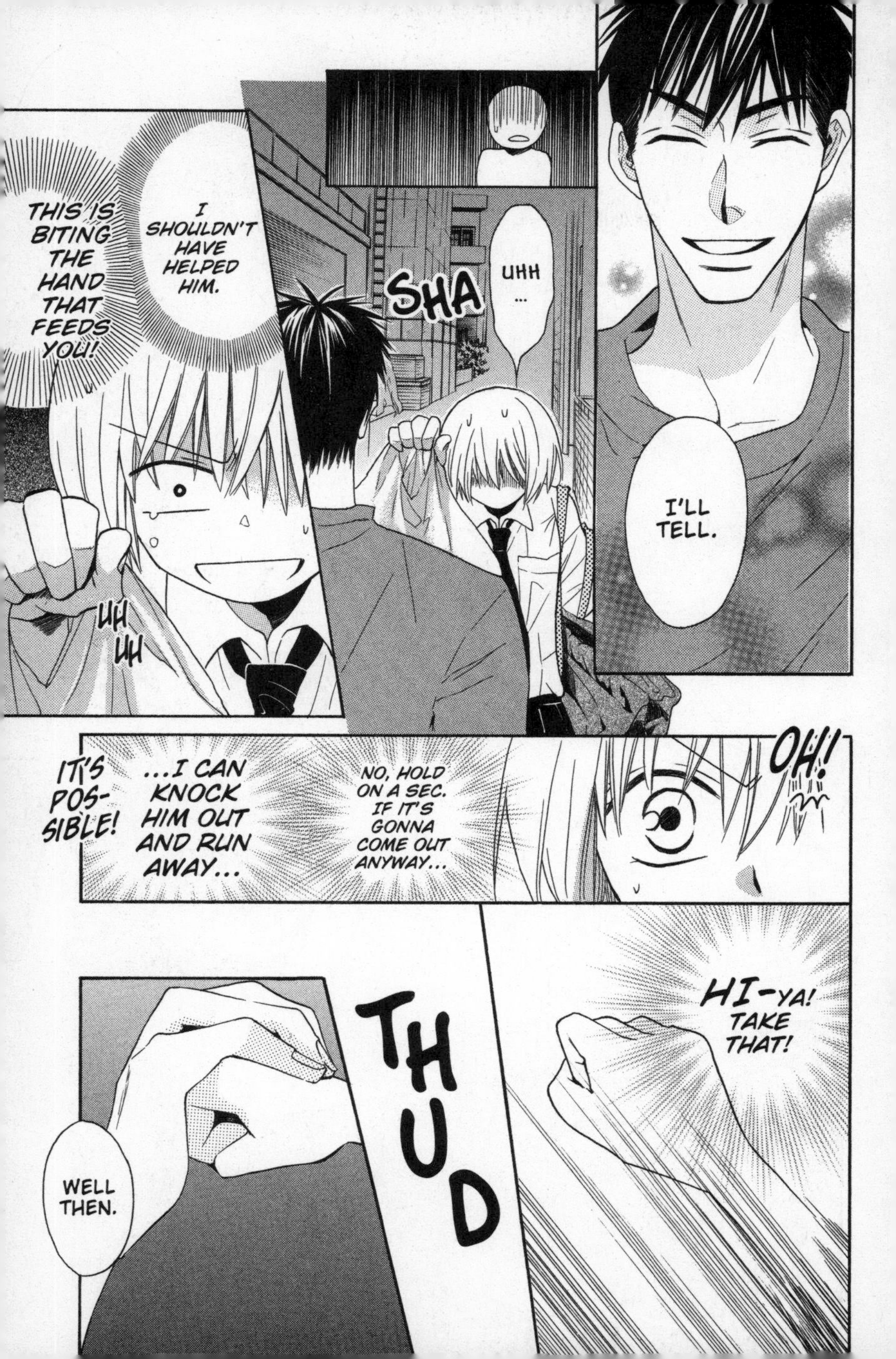
I'LL TELL.
UHH ...
SHA
I SHOULDN'T HAVE HELPED HIM.
THIS IS BITING THE HAND THAT FEEDS YOU!
UH UH
OH!
NO, HOLD ON A SEC. IF IT'S GONNA COME OUT ANYWAY...
...I CAN KNOCK HIM OUT AND RUN AWAY...
IT'S POS-SIBLE!
HI-YA! TAKE THAT!
THUD
WELL THEN.

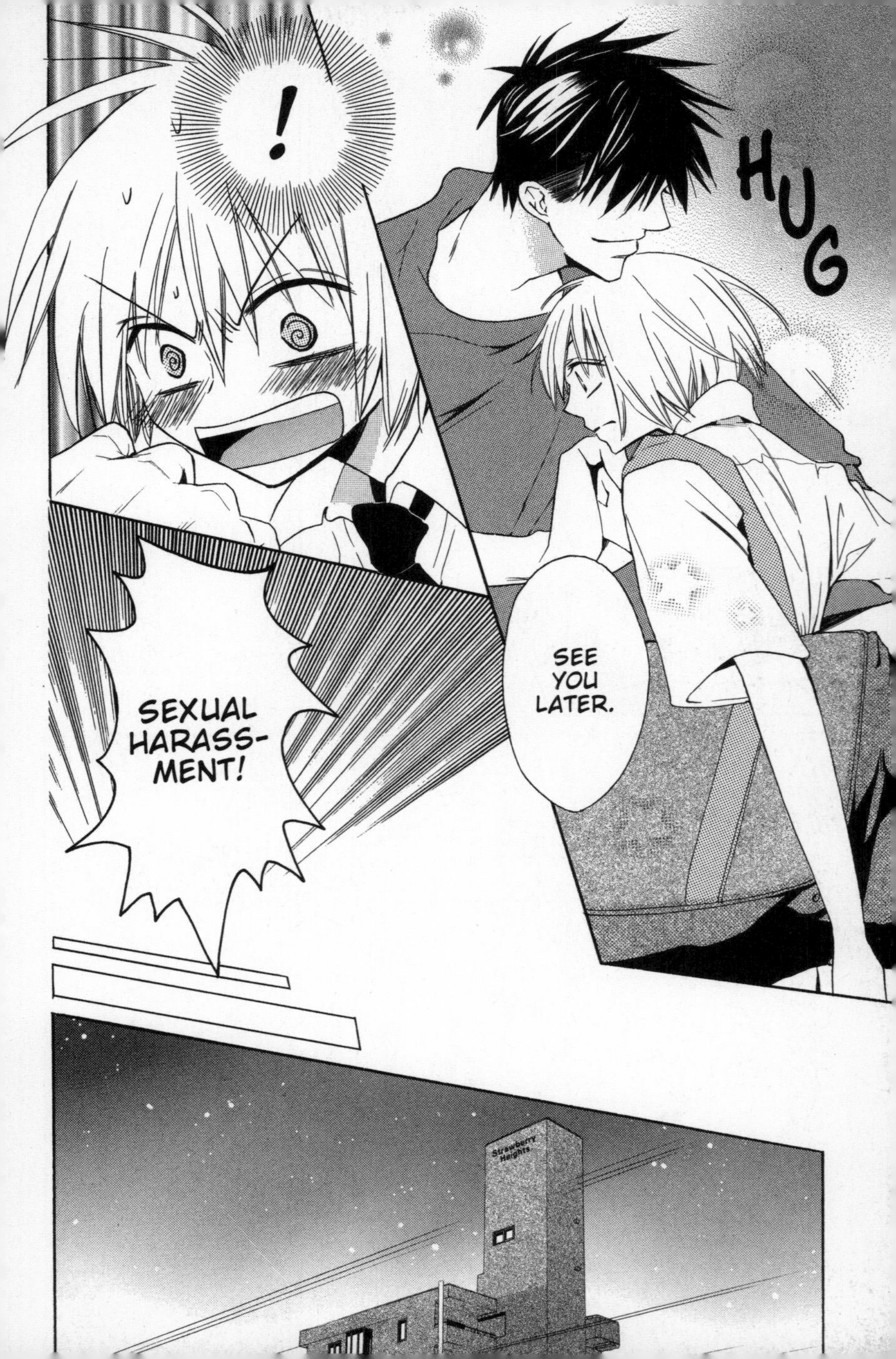
HUG
SEE YOU LATER.
!
SEXUAL HARASS-MENT!
Strawberry Heights

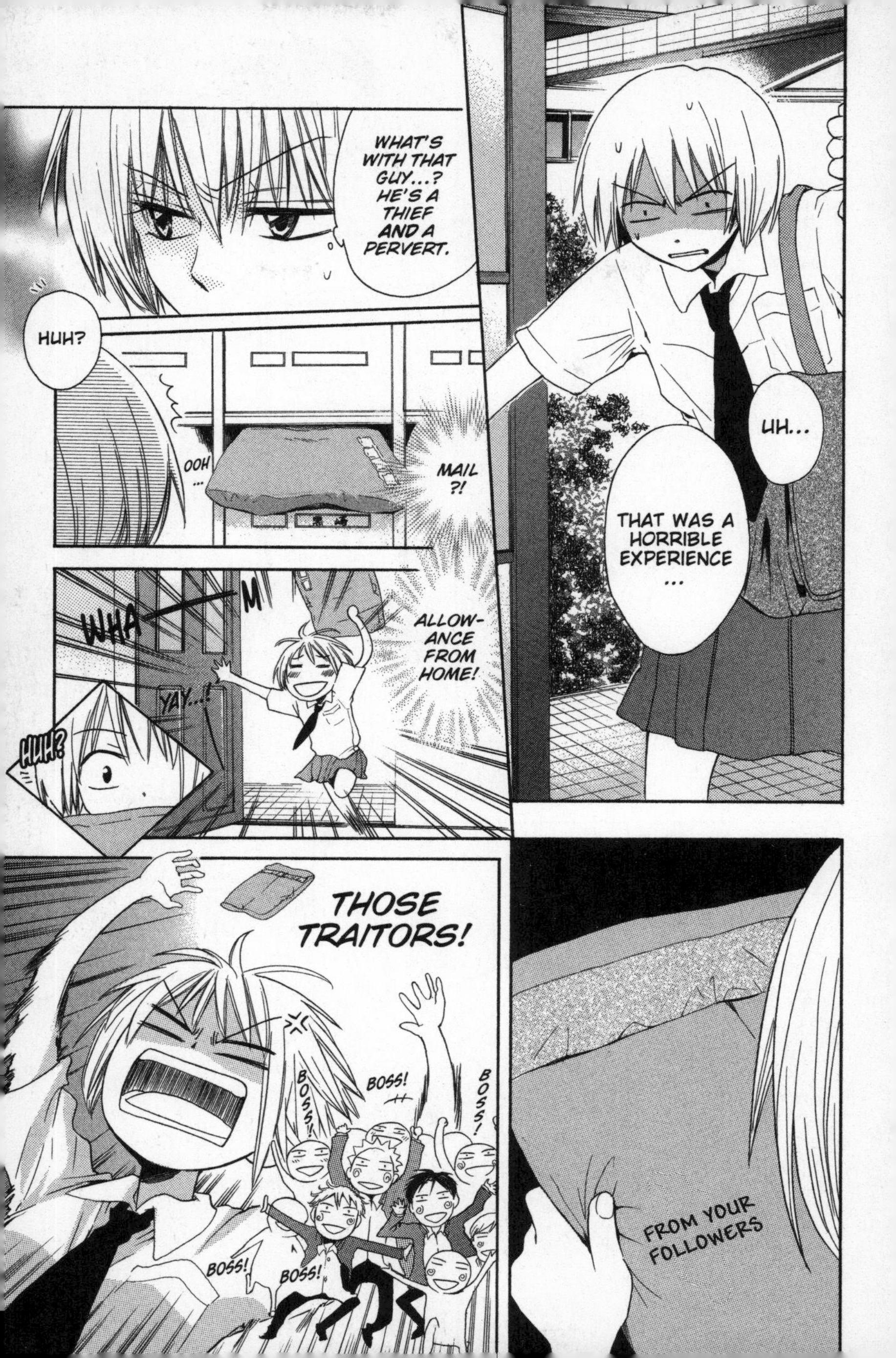
UH...
THAT WAS A HORRIBLE EXPERIENCE ...
WHAT'S WITH THAT GUY...? HE'S A THIEF AND A PERVERT.
HUH?
MAIL ?!
OOH ...
ALLOW-ANCE FROM HOME!
WHA—M
YAY...!
HUH?
FROM YOUR FOLLOWERS
THOSE TRAITORS!
BOSS!
BOSS!
BOSS!
BOSS!
BOSS!

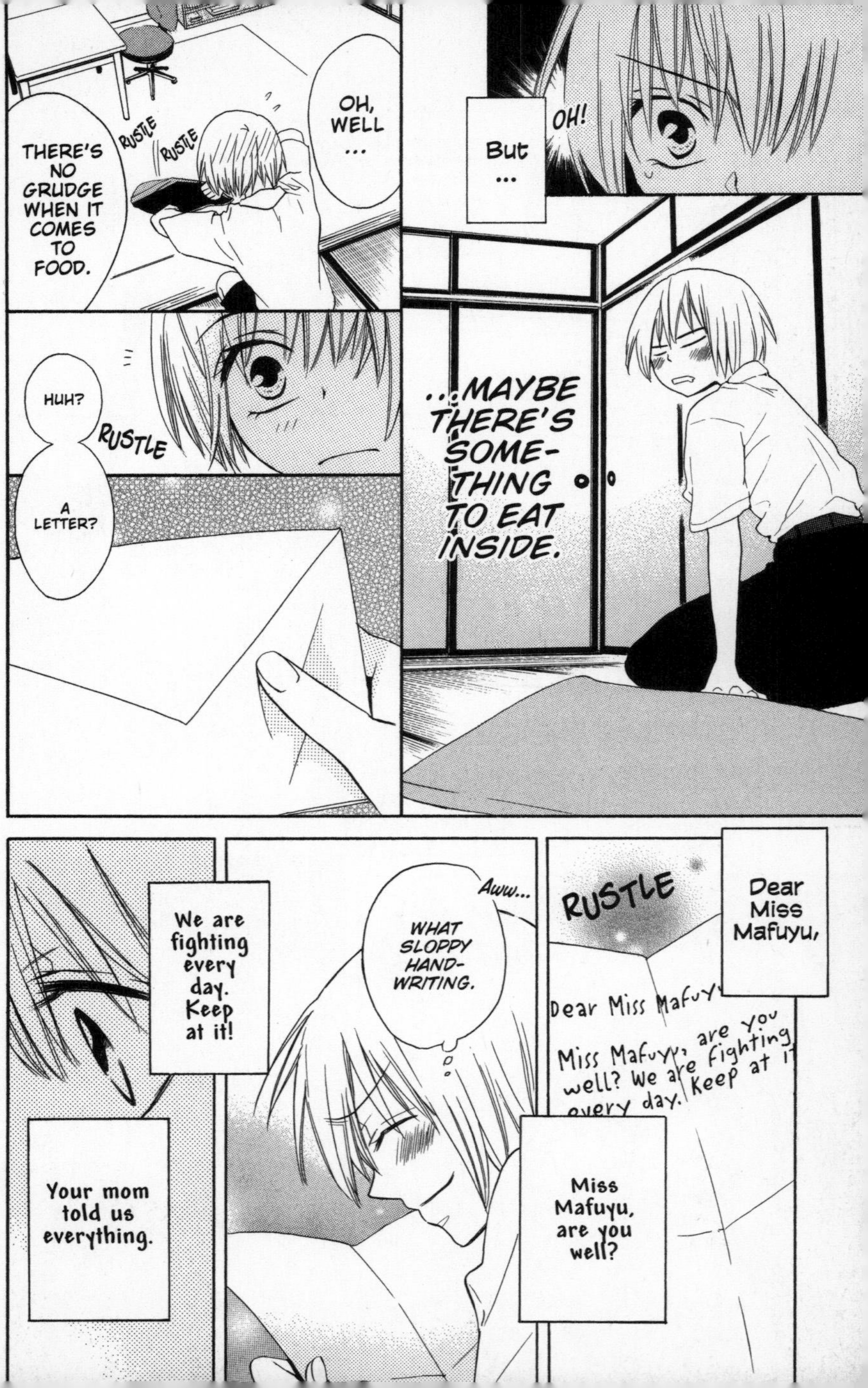
But...
OH!
...MAYBE THERE'S SOME-THING TO EAT INSIDE.
OH, WELL...
THERE'S NO GRUDGE WHEN IT COMES TO FOOD.
RUSTLE
RUSTLE
HUH?
RUSTLE
A LETTER?
Dear Miss Mafuyu,
RUSTLE
Dear Miss Mafuyu
Miss Mafuyu, are you
well? We are fighting
Keep at it
every day.
Miss Mafuyu, are you well?
Aww...
WHAT SLOPPY HAND-WRITING.
We are fighting every day. Keep at it!
Your mom told us everything.

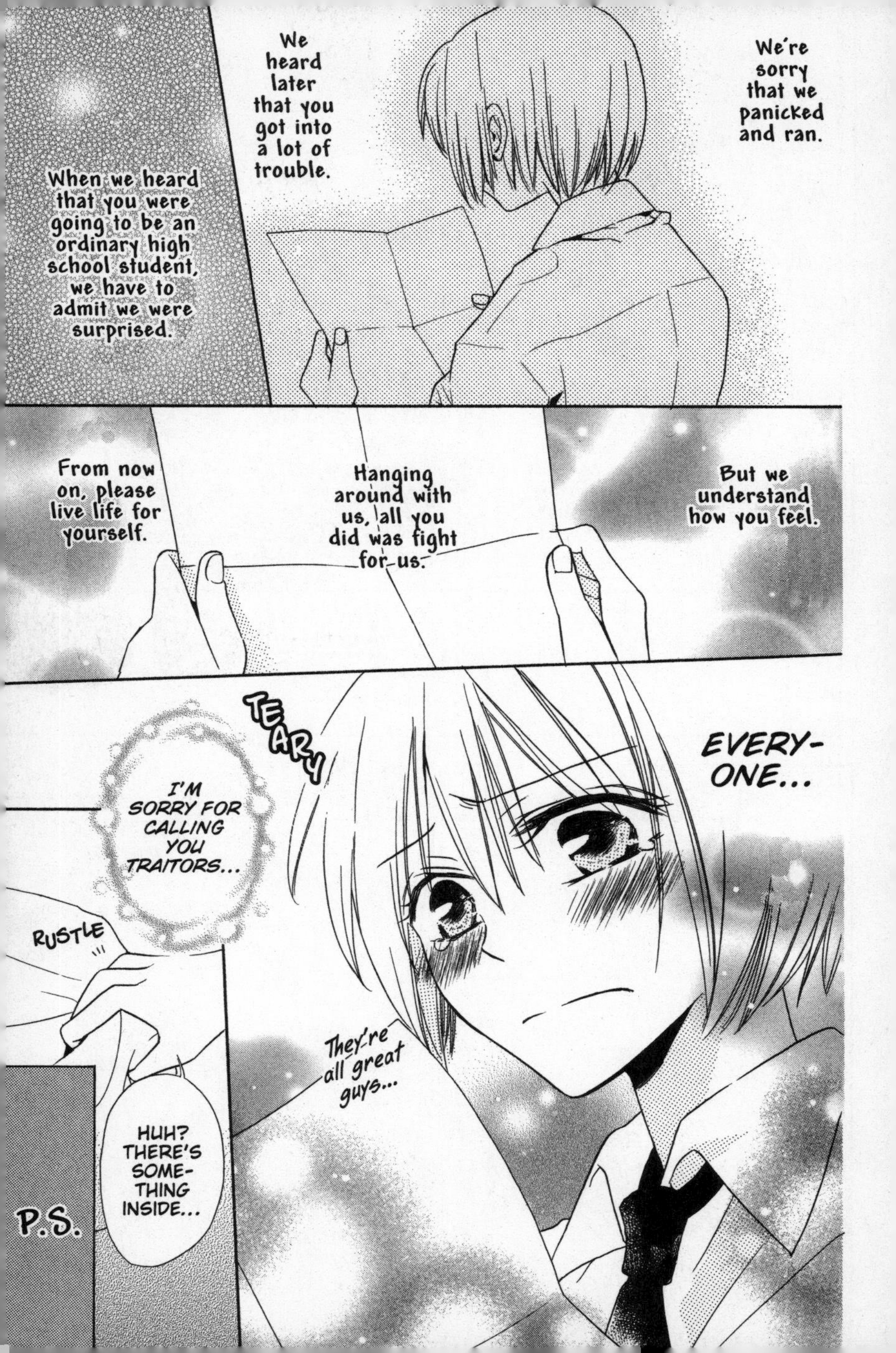
We're sorry that we panicked and ran.
We heard later that you got into a lot of trouble.
When we heard that you were going to be an ordinary high school student, we have to admit we were surprised.
But we understand how you feel.
Hanging around with us, all you did was fight for us.
From now on, please live life for yourself.
EVERY-ONE...
TEARY
I'M SORRY FOR CALLING YOU TRAITORS...
They're all great guys...
RUSTLE
HUH? THERE'S SOME-THING INSIDE...
P.S.

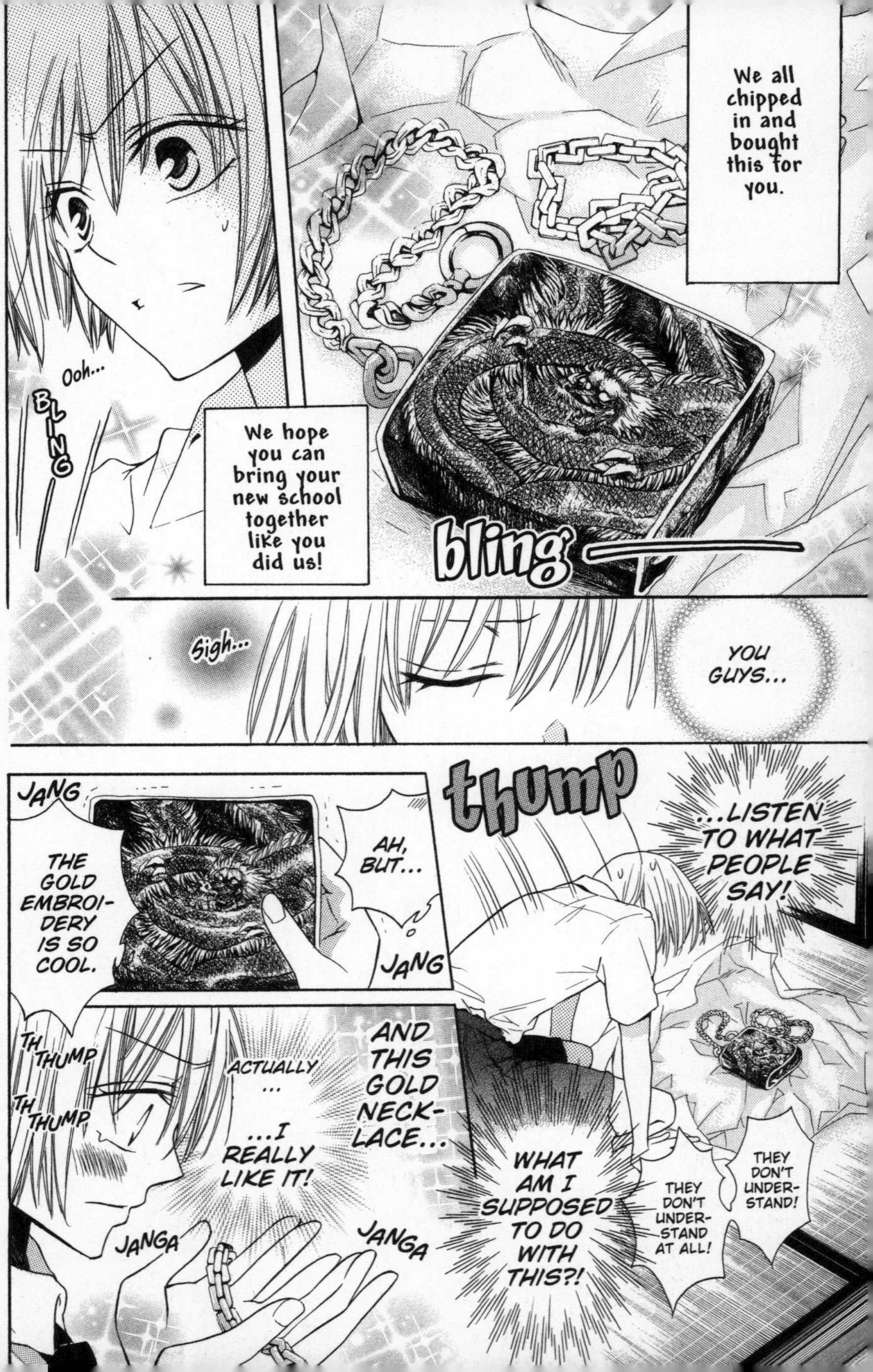
We all chipped in and bought this for you.
We hope you can bring your new school together like you did us!
bling
Ooh...
BLING
YOU GUYS...
Sigh...
thump
...LISTEN TO WHAT PEOPLE SAY!
THEY DON'T UNDERSTAND!
THEY DON'T UNDERSTAND AT ALL!
WHAT AM I SUPPOSED TO DO WITH THIS?!
JANG
AH, BUT...
THE GOLD EMBROIDERY IS SO COOL.
JANG
AND THIS GOLD NECKLACE...
ACTUALLY ...
...I REALLY LIKE IT!
TH THUMP
TH THUMP
JANGA
JANGA

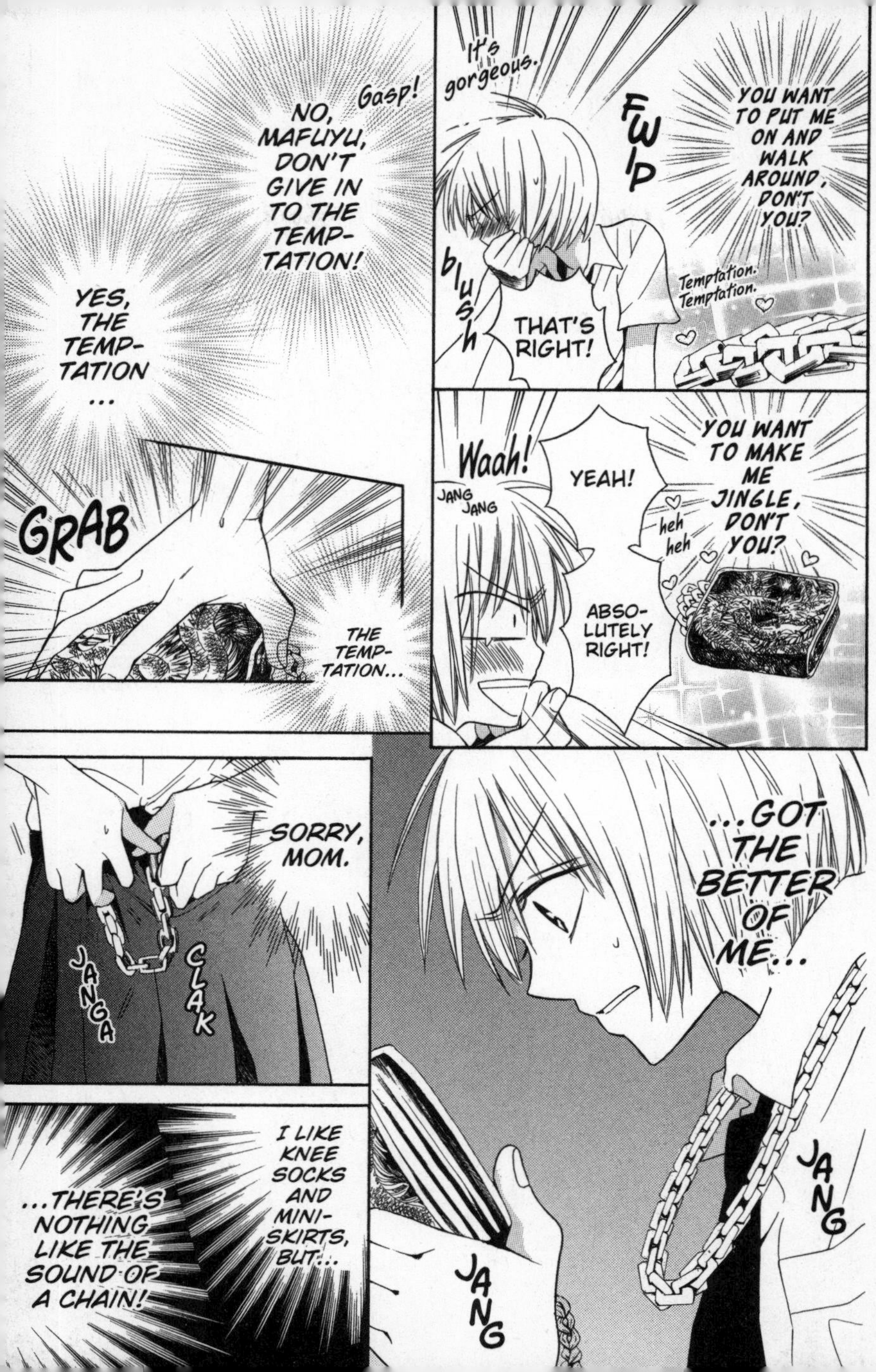
It's gorgeous.
FWIP
YOU WANT TO PUT ME ON AND WALK AROUND, DON'T YOU?
blush
THAT'S RIGHT!
Temptation. Temptation.
Gasp!
NO, MAFUYU, DON'T GIVE IN TO THE TEMPTATION!
YES, THE TEMPTATION...
Waah!
JANG JANG
YEAH!
YOU WANT TO MAKE ME JINGLE, DON'T YOU?
heh heh
ABSOLUTELY RIGHT!
GRAB
THE TEMPTATION...
...GOT THE BETTER OF ME...
JANG
JANG
SORRY, MOM.
CLAK
JANGA
I LIKE KNEE SOCKS AND MINI-SKIRTS, BUT...
...THERE'S NOTHING LIKE THE SOUND OF A CHAIN!

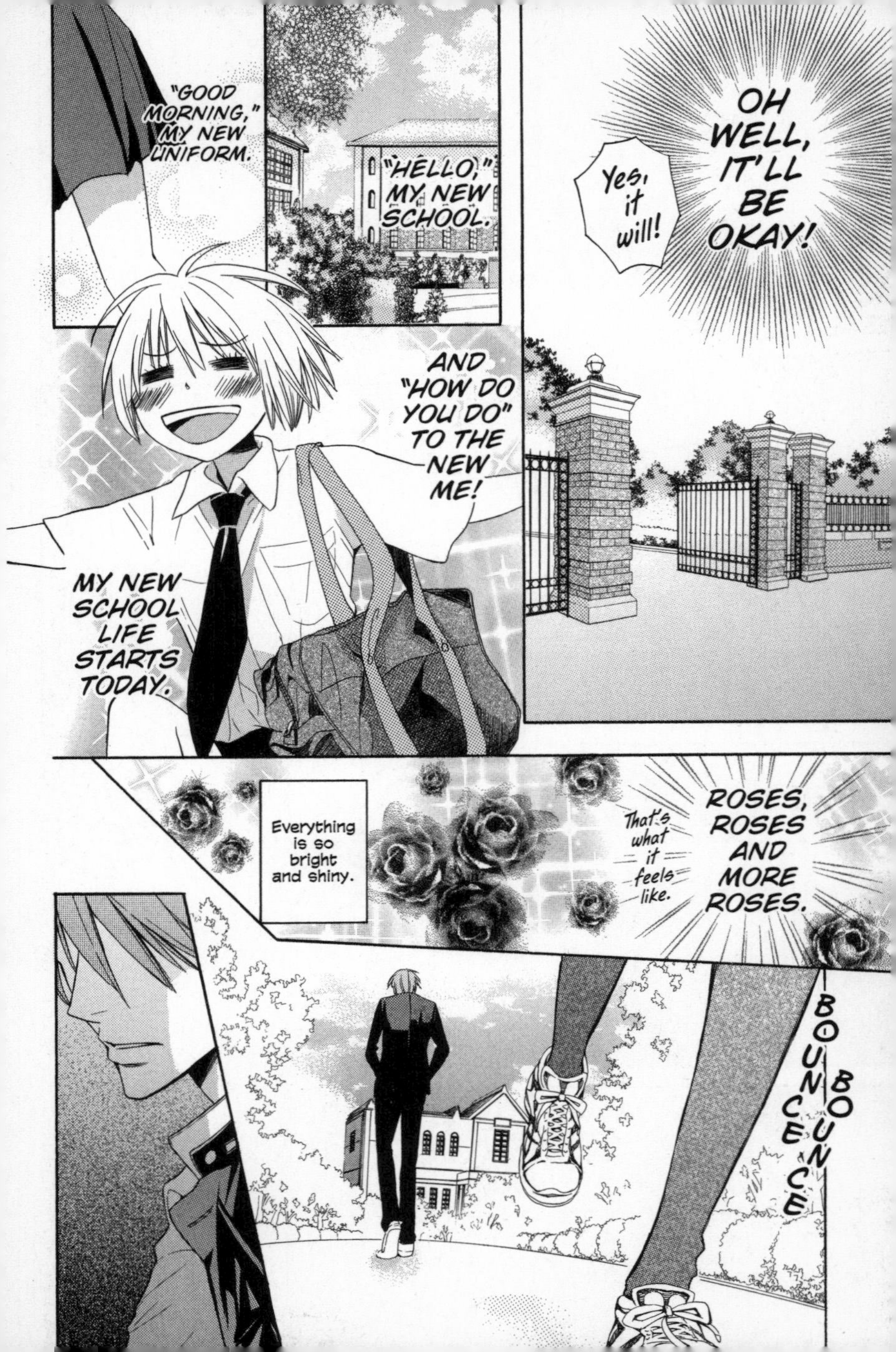
OH WELL, IT'LL BE OKAY!
Yes, it will!
"HELLO," MY NEW SCHOOL.
"GOOD MORNING," MY NEW UNIFORM.
AND "HOW DO YOU DO" TO THE NEW ME!
MY NEW SCHOOL LIFE STARTS TODAY.
ROSES, ROSES AND MORE ROSES.
That's what it feels like.
Everything is so bright and shiny.
BOUNCE
BOUNCE

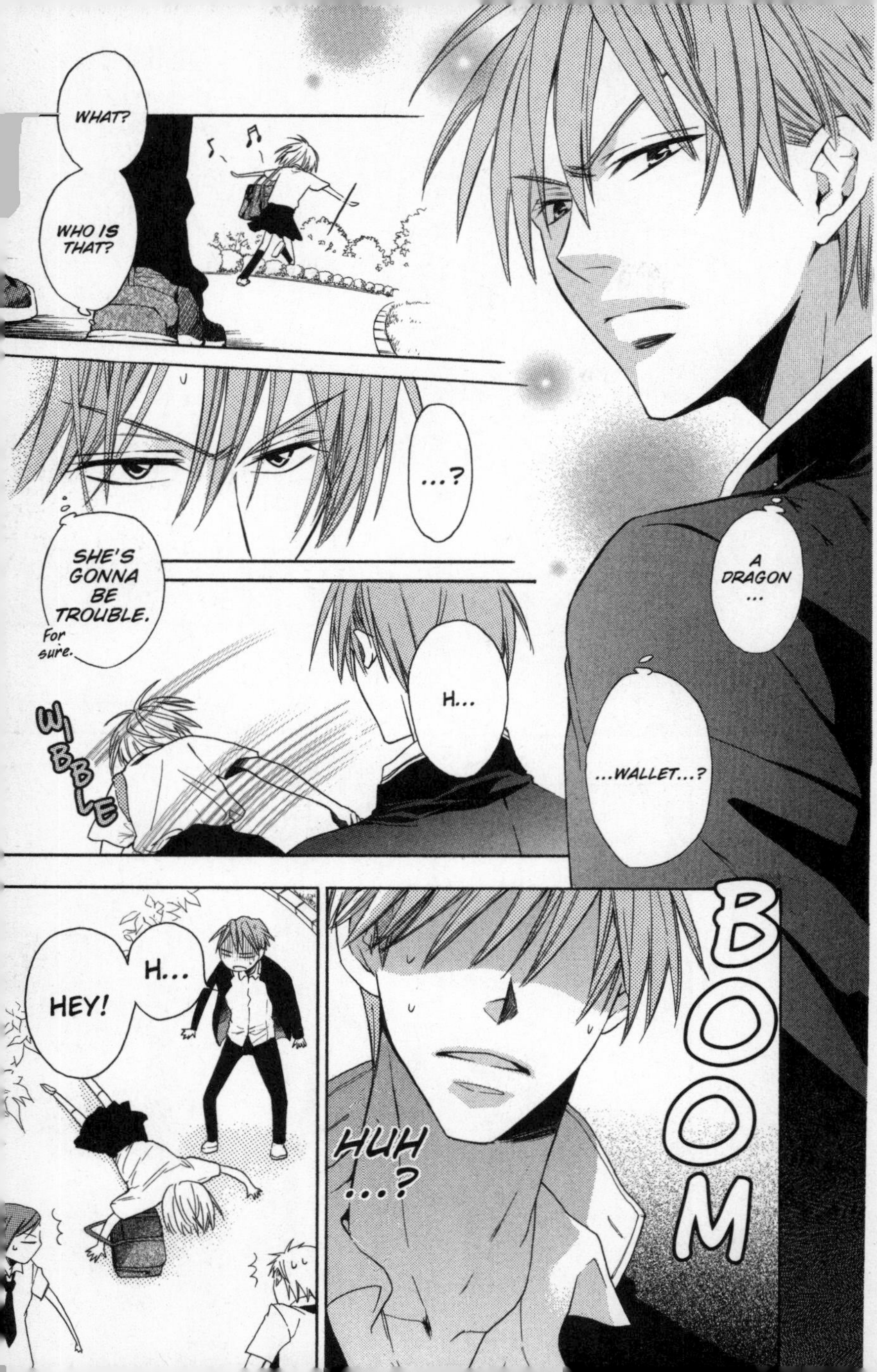
A DRAGON ...
...WALLET...?
WHAT?
WHO IS THAT?
...?
SHE'S GONNA BE TROUBLE.
For sure.
H...
WIBBLE
BOOM
HUH ...?
H...
HEY!

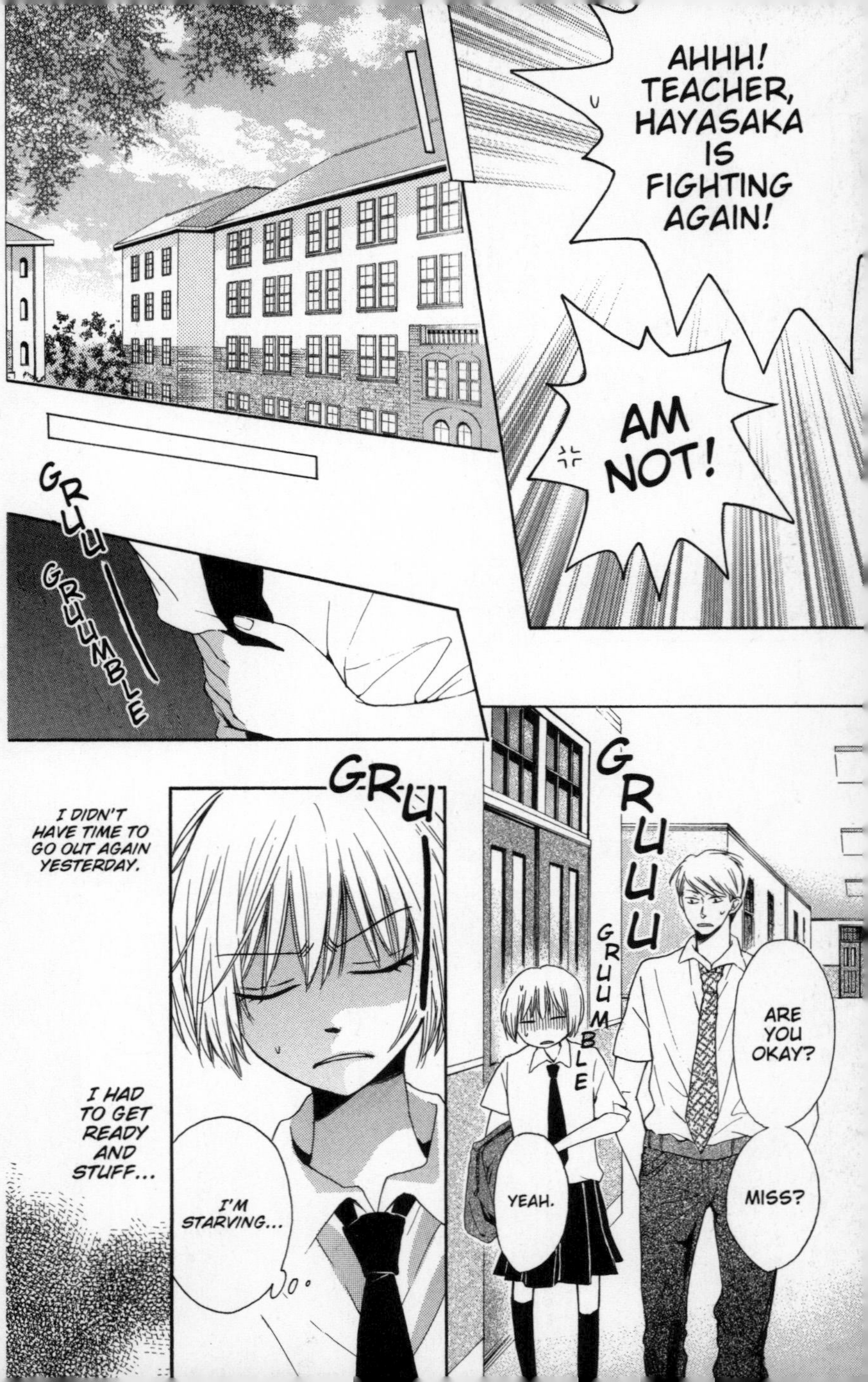
AHHH! TEACHER, HAYASAKA IS FIGHTING AGAIN!
AM NOT!
GRUU
GRUUMBLE
GRUUU
ARE YOU OKAY?
MISS?
GRUUMBLE
YEAH.
GRU
I DIDN'T HAVE TIME TO GO OUT AGAIN YESTERDAY.
I HAD TO GET READY AND STUFF...
I'M STARVING...

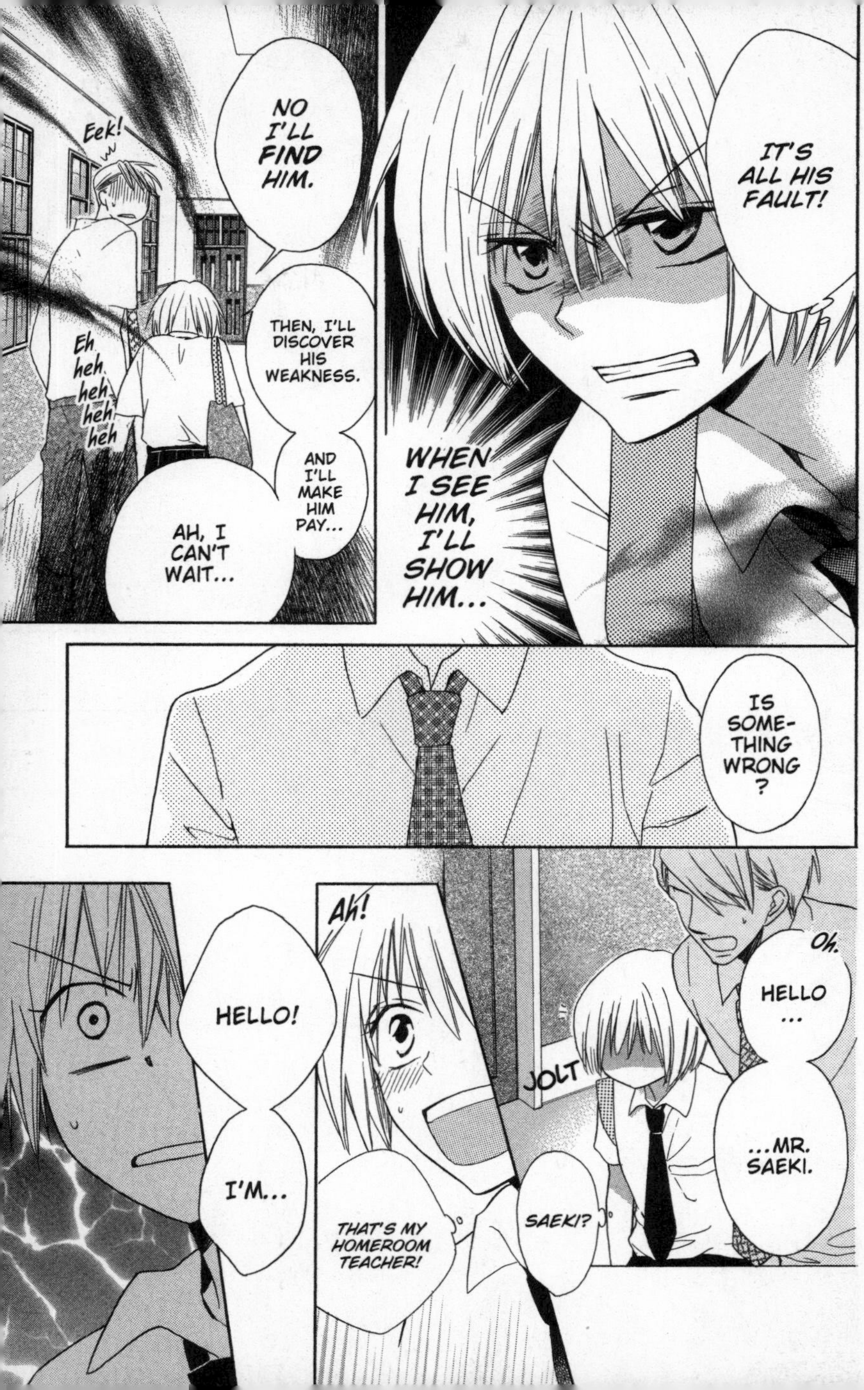

IT'S ALL HIS FAULT!
WHEN I SEE HIM, I'LL SHOW HIM...
Eek!
NO I'LL FIND HIM.
THEN, I'LL DISCOVER HIS WEAKNESS.
AND I'LL MAKE HIM PAY...
Eh heh heh heh heh
AH, I CAN'T WAIT...
IS SOMETHING WRONG?
Oh.
HELLO...
...MR. SAEKI.
JOLT
Ah!
SAEKI?
THAT'S MY HOMEROOM TEACHER!
HELLO!
I'M...

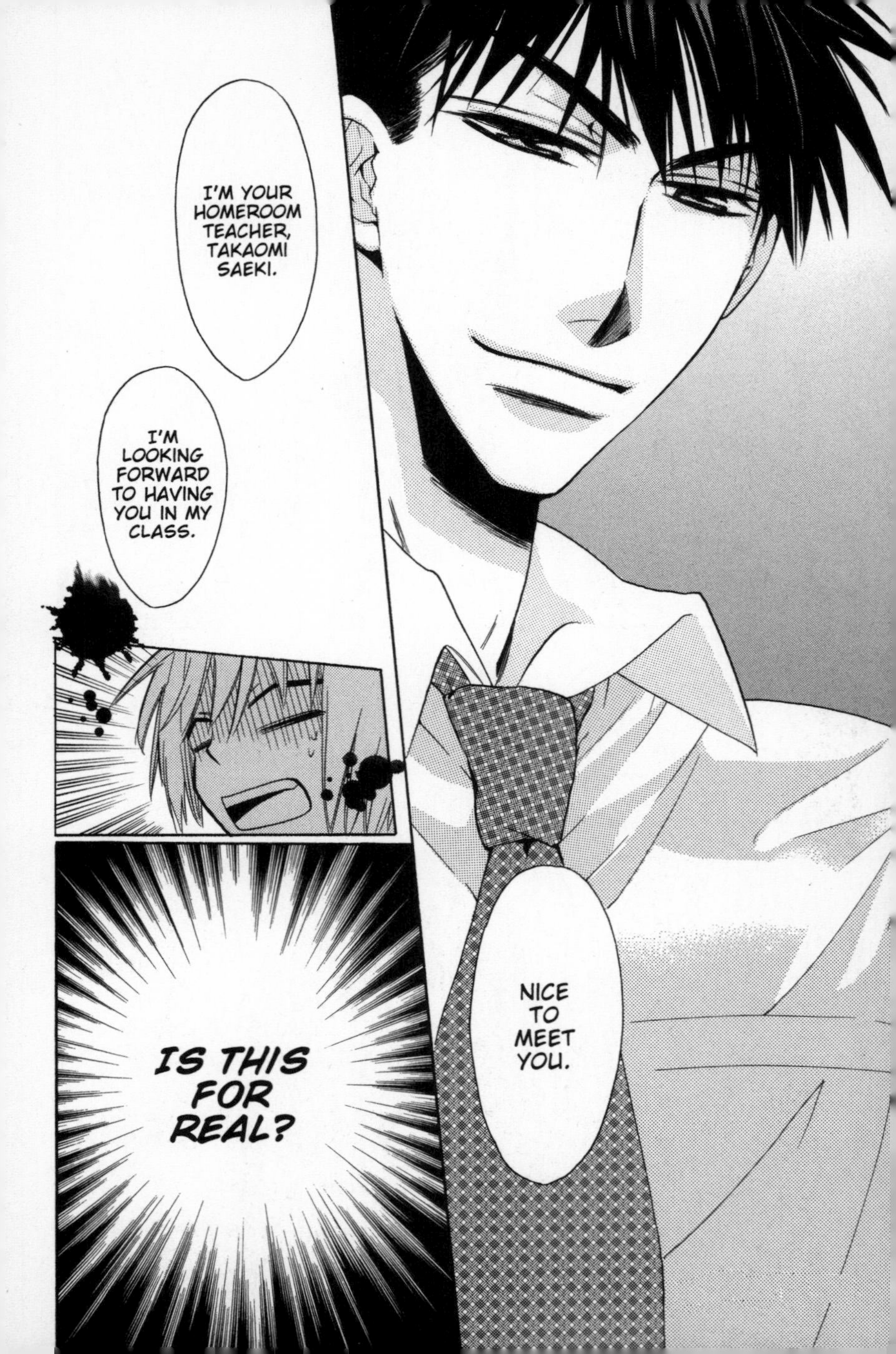
I'M YOUR HOMEROOM TEACHER, TAKAOMI SAEKI.
I'M LOOKING FORWARD TO HAVING YOU IN MY CLASS.
NICE TO MEET YOU.
IS THIS FOR REAL?

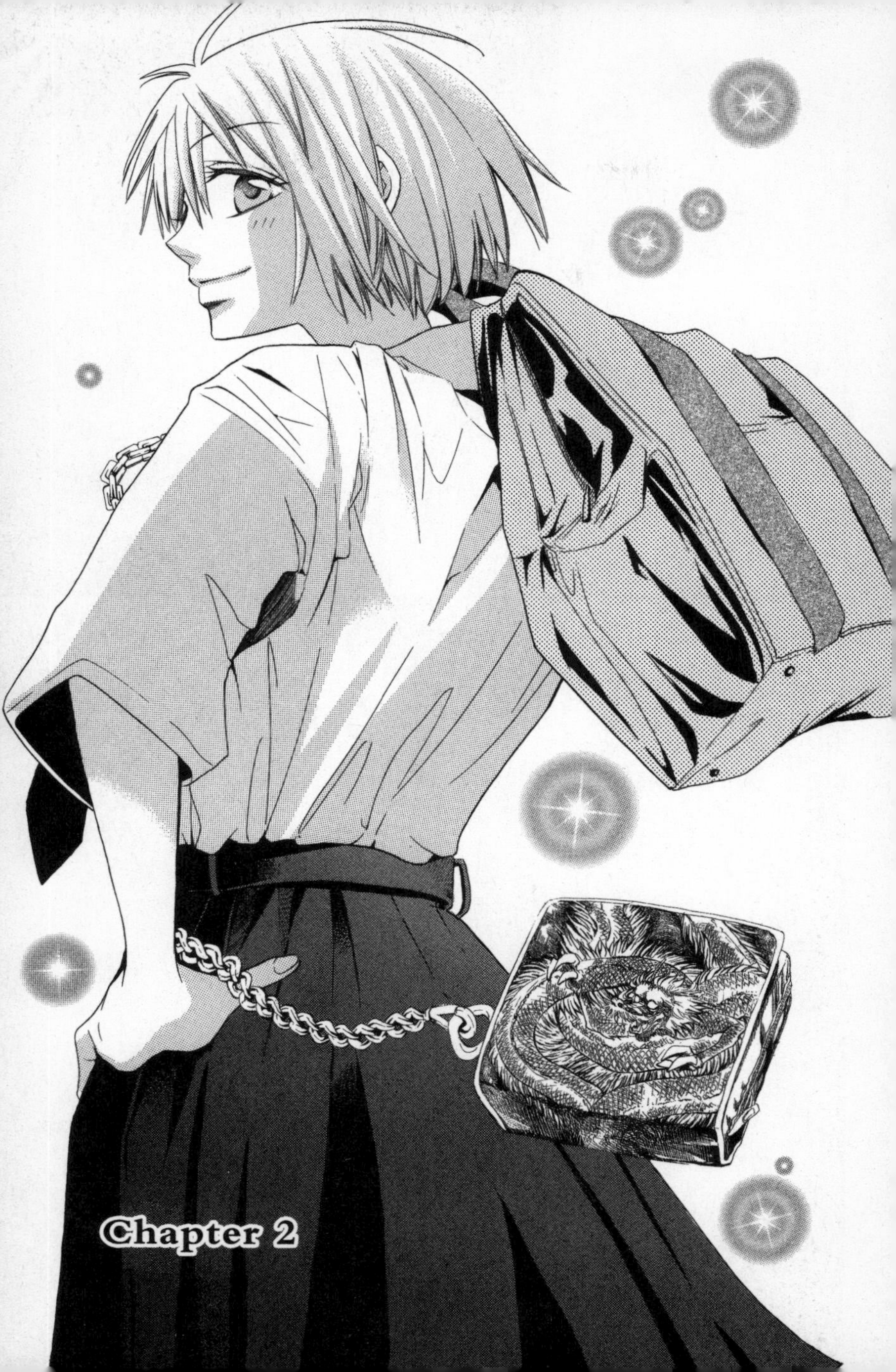
Chapter 2

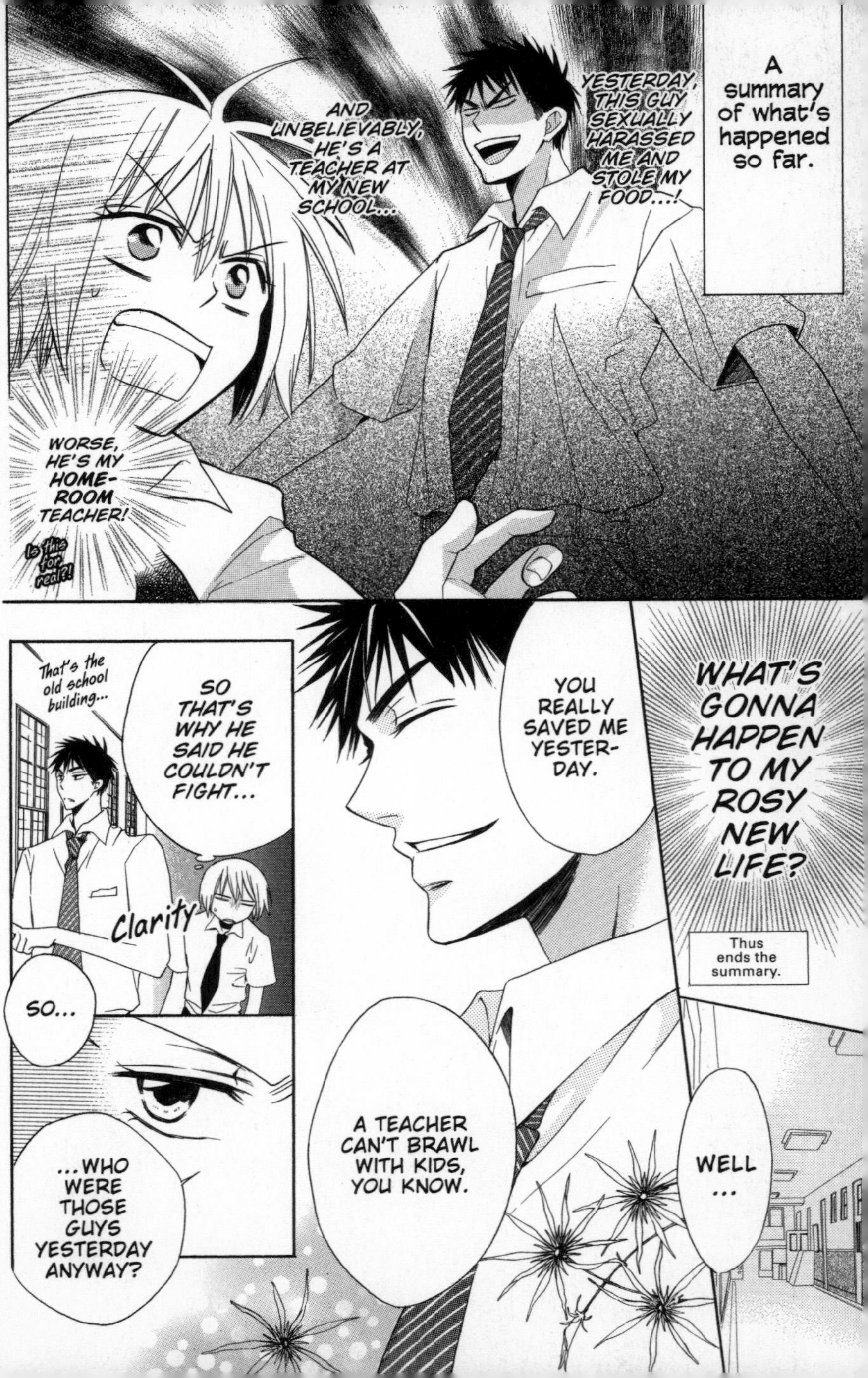
A summary of what's happened so far.
YESTERDAY, THIS GUY SEXUALLY HARASSED ME AND STOLE MY FOOD...!
AND UNBELIEVABLY, HE'S A TEACHER AT MY NEW SCHOOL...
WORSE, HE'S MY HOMEROOM TEACHER!
Is this for real?!
WHAT'S GONNA HAPPEN TO MY ROSY NEW LIFE?
Thus ends the summary.
YOU REALLY SAVED ME YESTERDAY.
WELL...
A TEACHER CAN'T BRAWL WITH KIDS, YOU KNOW.
SO THAT'S WHY HE SAID HE COULDN'T FIGHT...
That's the old school building...
Clarity
SO...
...WHO WERE THOSE GUYS YESTERDAY ANYWAY?

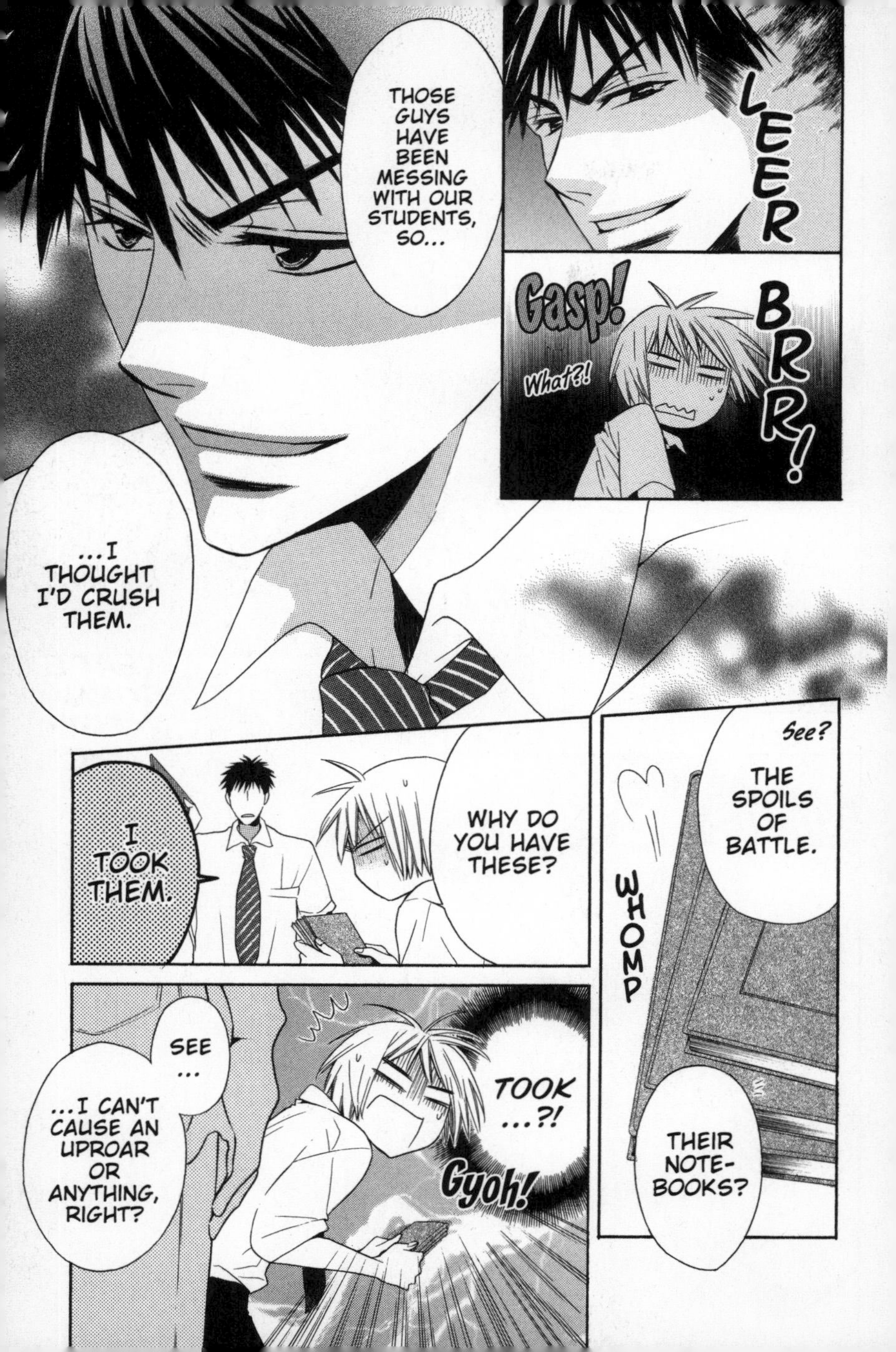
LEER
Gasp!
What?!
BRRR!
THOSE GUYS HAVE BEEN MESSING WITH OUR STUDENTS, SO...
...I THOUGHT I'D CRUSH THEM.
See?
THE SPOILS OF BATTLE.
WHOMP
THEIR NOTE-BOOKS?
WHY DO YOU HAVE THESE?
I TOOK THEM.
TOOK ...?!
Gyoh!
SEE ...
...I CAN'T CAUSE AN UPROAR OR ANYTHING, RIGHT?

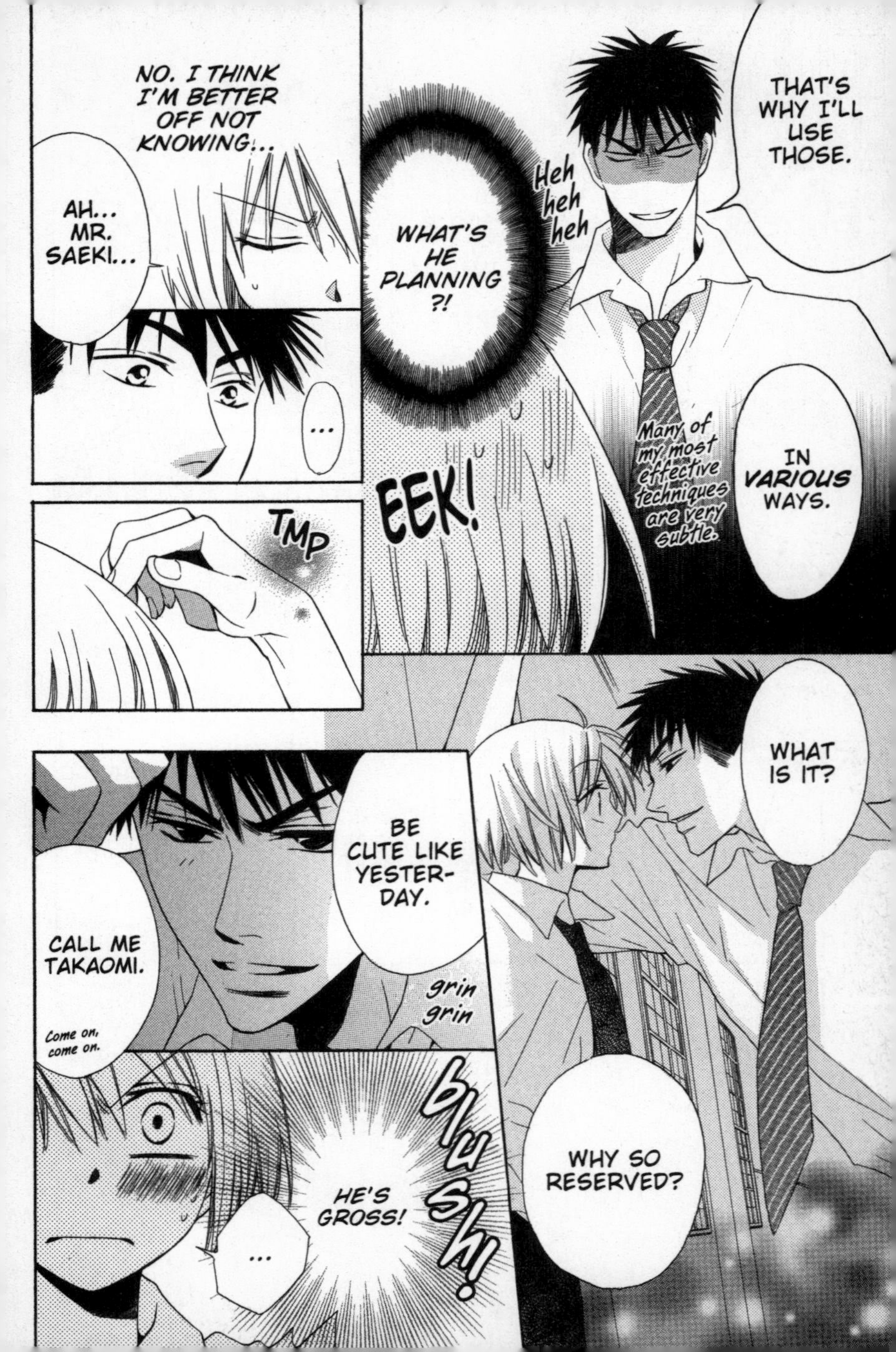
THAT'S WHY I'LL USE THOSE.
Heh heh heh
WHAT'S HE PLANNING?!
IN VARIOUS WAYS.
Many of my most effective techniques are very subtle.
EEK!
NO. I THINK I'M BETTER OFF NOT KNOWING...
AH... MR. SAEKI...
...
TMP
WHAT IS IT?
WHY SO RESERVED?
BE CUTE LIKE YESTERDAY.
CALL ME TAKAOMI.
grin grin
Come on, come on.
blush!
HE'S GROSS!
...

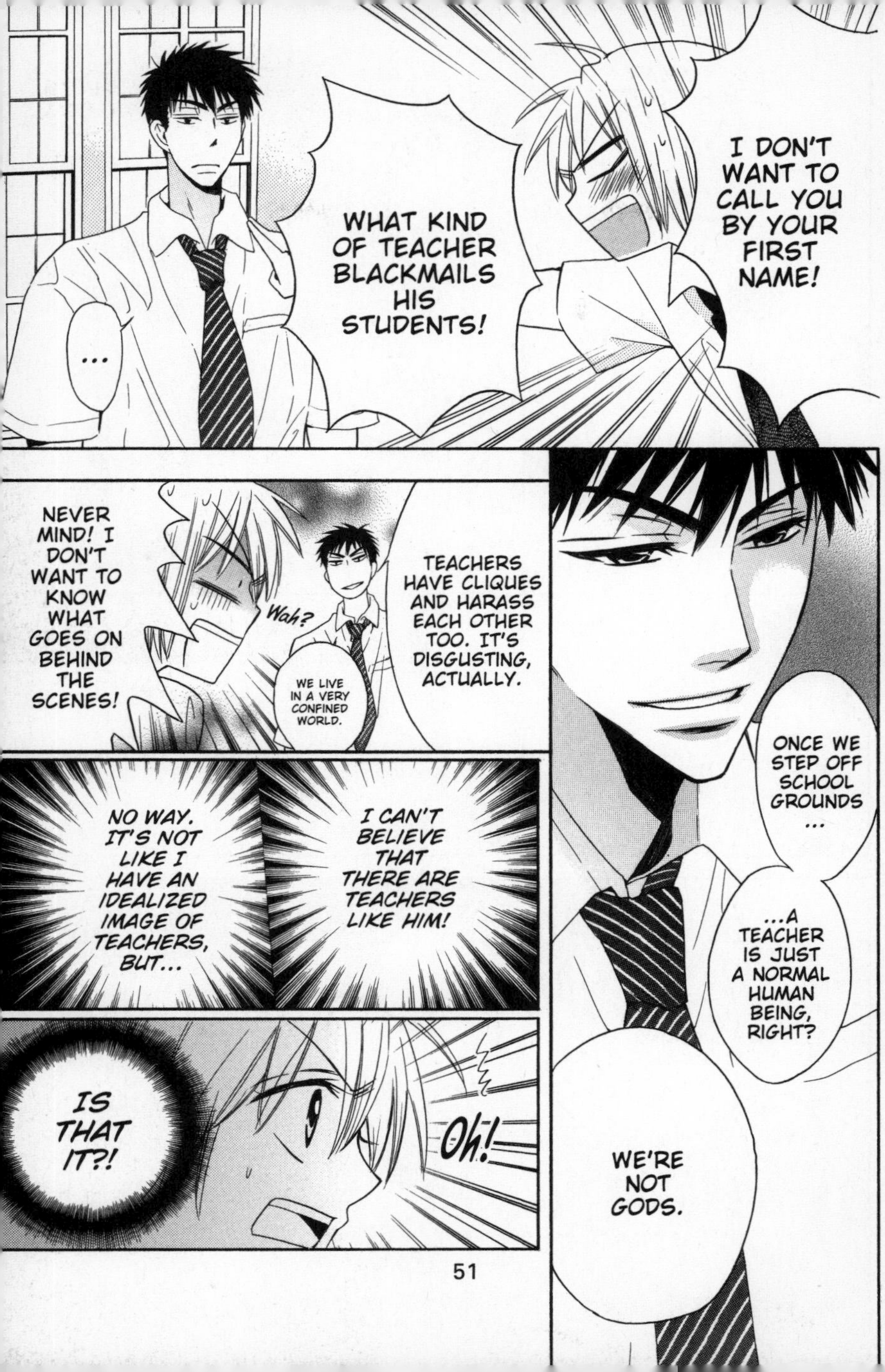
I DON'T WANT TO CALL YOU BY YOUR FIRST NAME!
WHAT KIND OF TEACHER BLACKMAILS HIS STUDENTS!
...
ONCE WE STEP OFF SCHOOL GROUNDS...
...A TEACHER IS JUST A NORMAL HUMAN BEING, RIGHT?
WE'RE NOT GODS.
TEACHERS HAVE CLIQUES AND HARASS EACH OTHER TOO. IT'S DISGUSTING, ACTUALLY.
WE LIVE IN A VERY CONFINED WORLD.
Wah?
NEVER MIND! I DON'T WANT TO KNOW WHAT GOES ON BEHIND THE SCENES!
I CAN'T BELIEVE THAT THERE ARE TEACHERS LIKE HIM!
NO WAY. IT'S NOT LIKE I HAVE AN IDEALIZED IMAGE OF TEACHERS, BUT...
Oh!
IS THAT IT?!

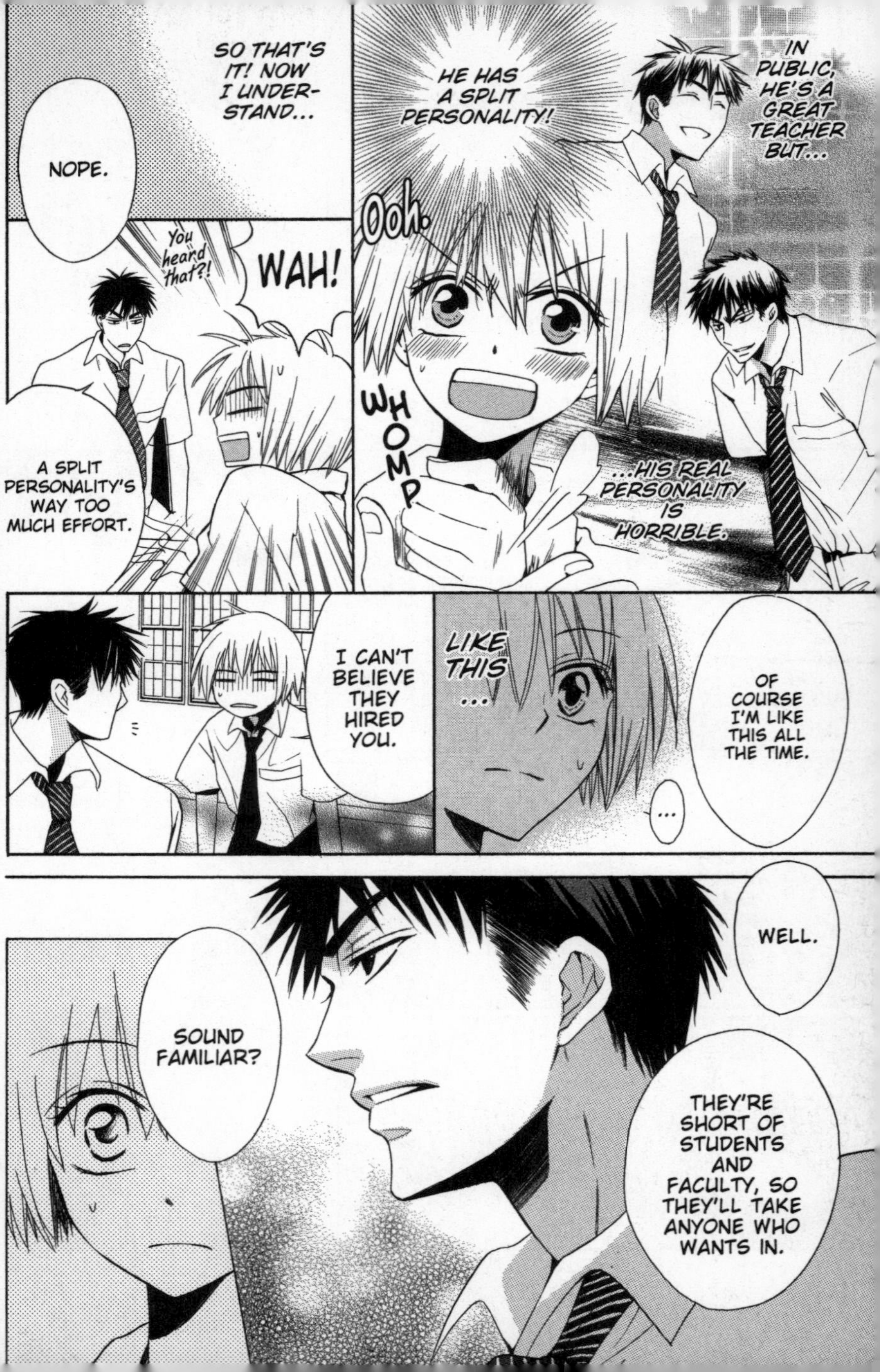
IN PUBLIC, HE'S A GREAT TEACHER BUT...
...HIS REAL PERSONALITY IS HORRIBLE.
HE HAS A SPLIT PERSONALITY!
Ooh.
WHOMP
SO THAT'S IT! NOW I UNDER-STAND...
NOPE.
WAH!
You heard that?!
A SPLIT PERSONALITY'S WAY TOO MUCH EFFORT.
OF COURSE I'M LIKE THIS ALL THE TIME.
...
LIKE THIS...
I CAN'T BELIEVE THEY HIRED YOU.
WELL.
THEY'RE SHORT OF STUDENTS AND FACULTY, SO THEY'LL TAKE ANYONE WHO WANTS IN.
SOUND FAMILIAR?

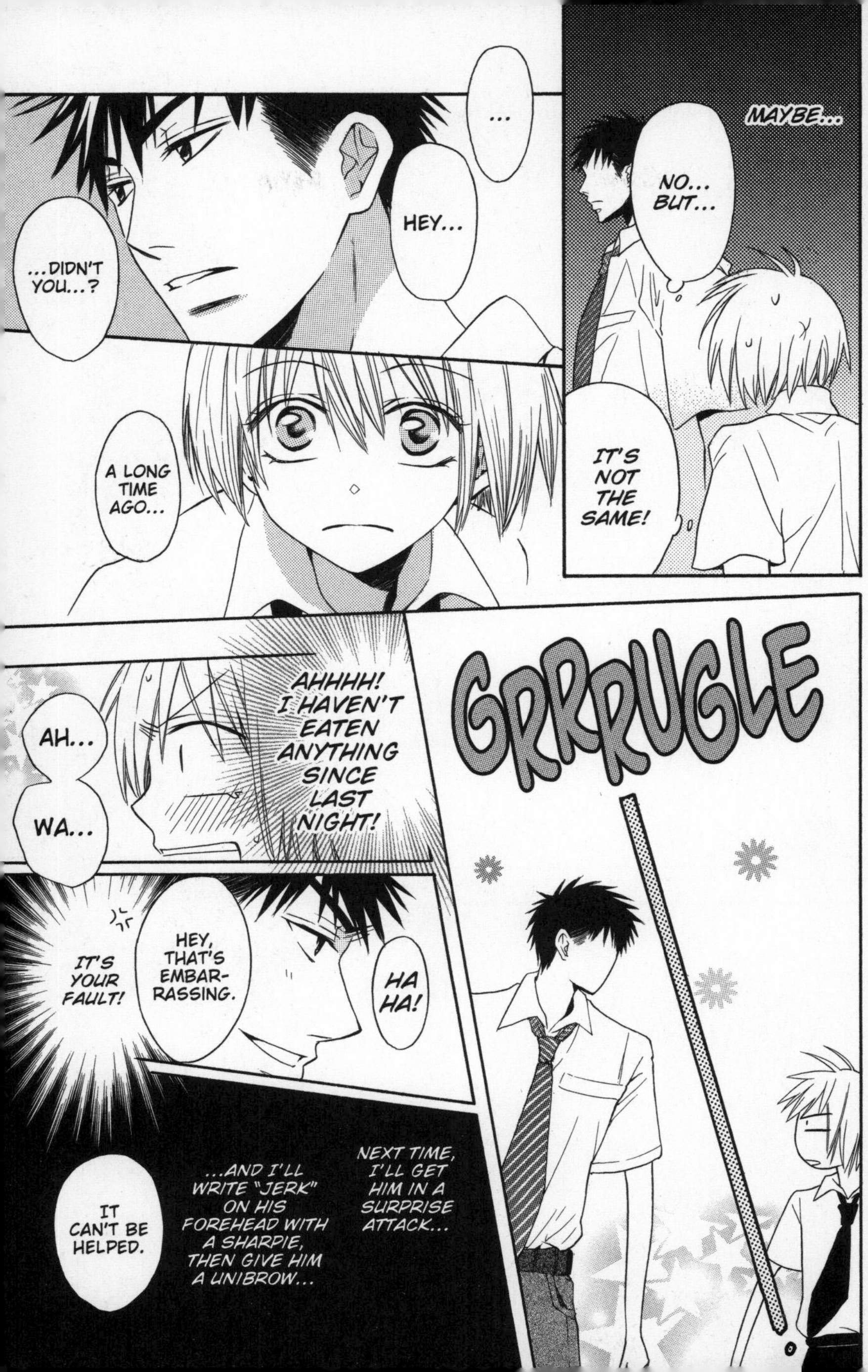
...
HEY...
...DIDN'T YOU...?
A LONG TIME AGO...
MAYBE...
NO... BUT...
IT'S NOT THE SAME!
GRRRUGLE
AHHHH! I HAVEN'T EATEN ANYTHING SINCE LAST NIGHT!
AH...
WA...
HA HA!
HEY, THAT'S EMBARRASSING.
IT'S YOUR FAULT!
NEXT TIME, I'LL GET HIM IN A SURPRISE ATTACK...
...AND I'LL WRITE "JERK" ON HIS FOREHEAD WITH A SHARPIE, THEN GIVE HIM A UNIBROW...
IT CAN'T BE HELPED.

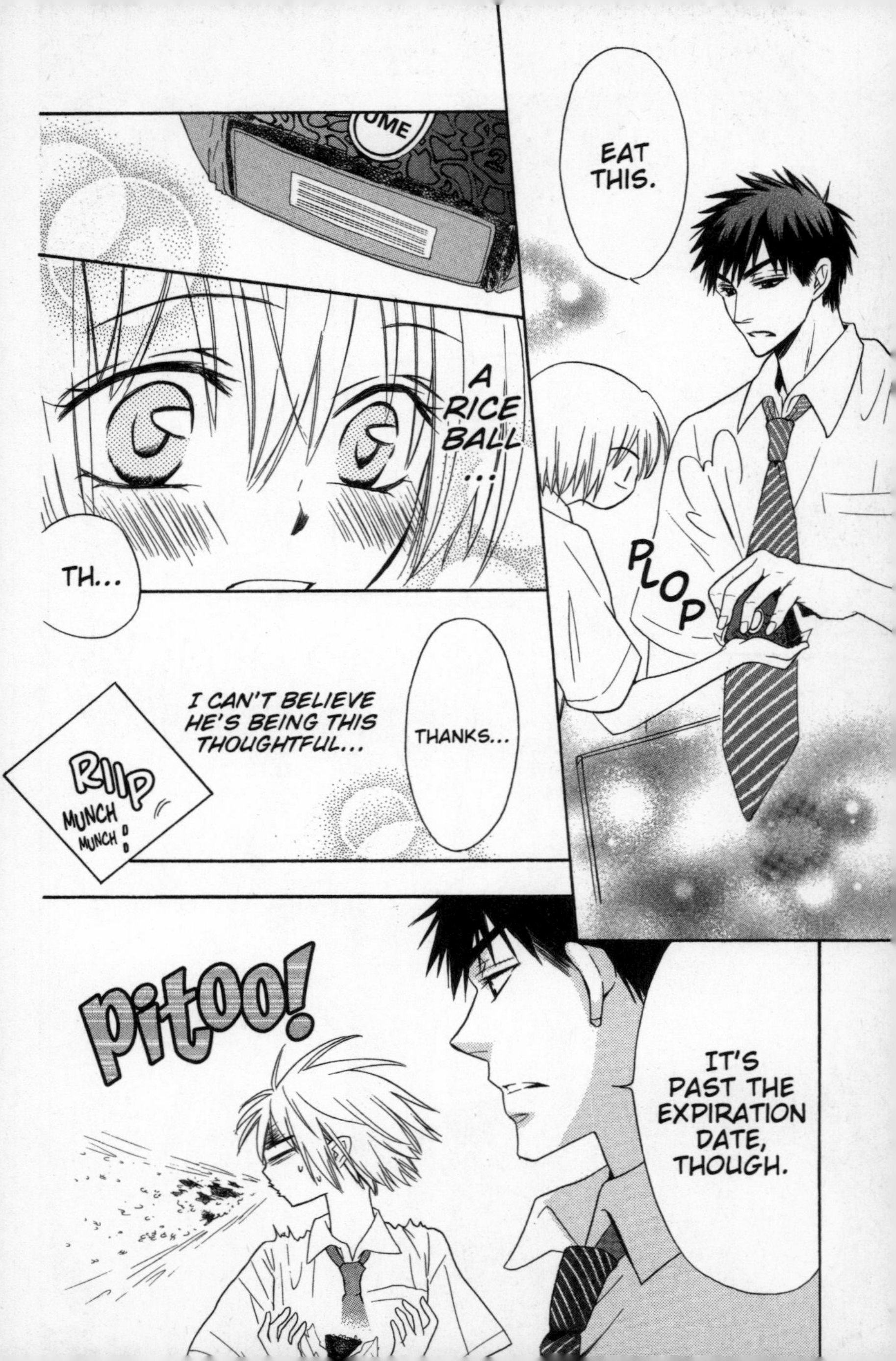
EAT THIS.
PLOP
UME
A RICE BALL...
TH...
THANKS...
I CAN'T BELIEVE HE'S BEING THIS THOUGHTFUL...
RIIP
MUNCH MUNCH
IT'S PAST THE EXPIRATION DATE, THOUGH.
pitoo!

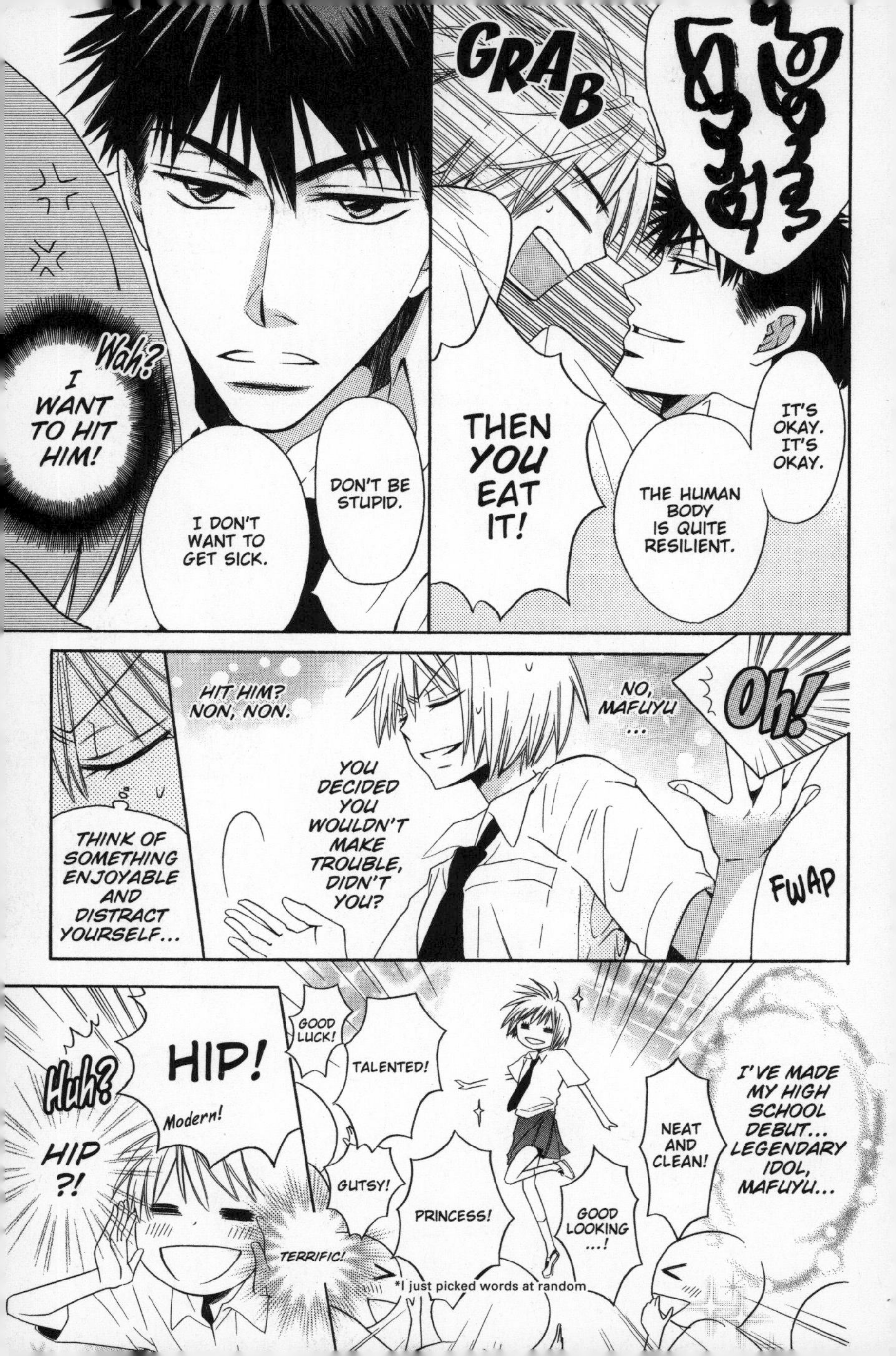
GRAB
IT'S OKAY. IT'S OKAY.
THE HUMAN BODY IS QUITE RESILIENT.
THEN YOU EAT IT!
DON'T BE STUPID.
I DON'T WANT TO GET SICK.
Wah?
I WANT TO HIT HIM!
Oh!
NO, MAFUYU ...
FWAP
HIT HIM? NON, NON.
YOU DECIDED YOU WOULDN'T MAKE TROUBLE, DIDN'T YOU?
THINK OF SOMETHING ENJOYABLE AND DISTRACT YOURSELF...
I'VE MADE MY HIGH SCHOOL DEBUT... LEGENDARY IDOL, MAFUYU...
NEAT AND CLEAN!
GOOD LOOKING ...!
PRINCESS!
TALENTED!
GOOD LUCK!
GUTSY!
TERRIFIC!
*I just picked words at random
HIP!
Huh?
Modern!
HIP ?!

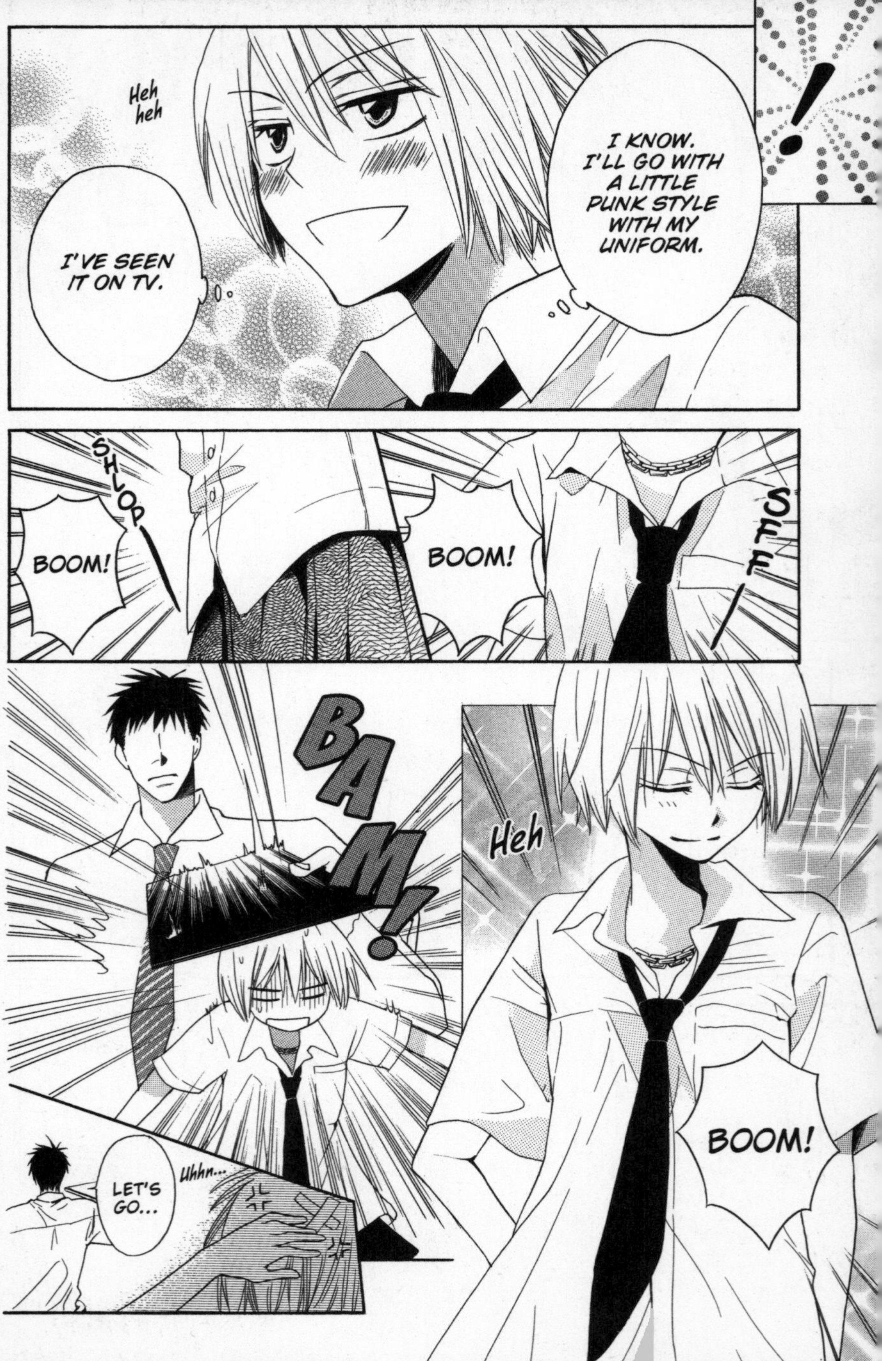
!
I KNOW. I'LL GO WITH A LITTLE PUNK STYLE WITH MY UNIFORM.
Heh heh
I'VE SEEN IT ON TV.
SFF
BOOM!
SHLOP
BOOM!
Heh
BOOM!
BAM!
Uhhn...
LET'S GO...

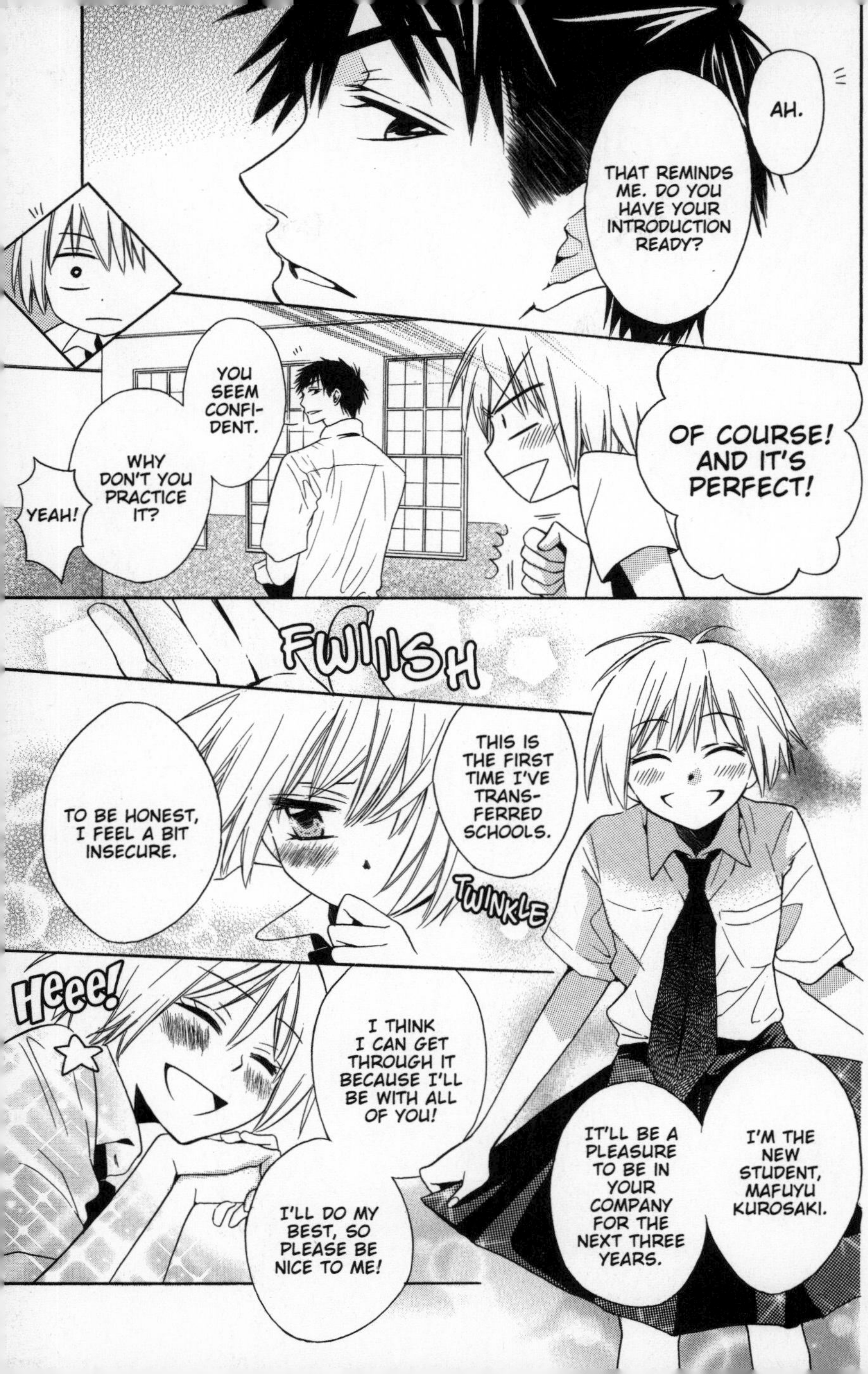
AH.
THAT REMINDS ME. DO YOU HAVE YOUR INTRODUCTION READY?
OF COURSE! AND IT'S PERFECT!
YOU SEEM CONFIDENT.
WHY DON'T YOU PRACTICE IT?
YEAH!
FWIIISH
THIS IS THE FIRST TIME I'VE TRANSFERRED SCHOOLS.
TWINKLE
TO BE HONEST, I FEEL A BIT INSECURE.
I'M THE NEW STUDENT, MAFUYU KUROSAKI.
IT'LL BE A PLEASURE TO BE IN YOUR COMPANY FOR THE NEXT THREE YEARS.
I THINK I CAN GET THROUGH IT BECAUSE I'LL BE WITH ALL OF YOU!
Heeee!
I'LL DO MY BEST, SO PLEASE BE NICE TO ME!

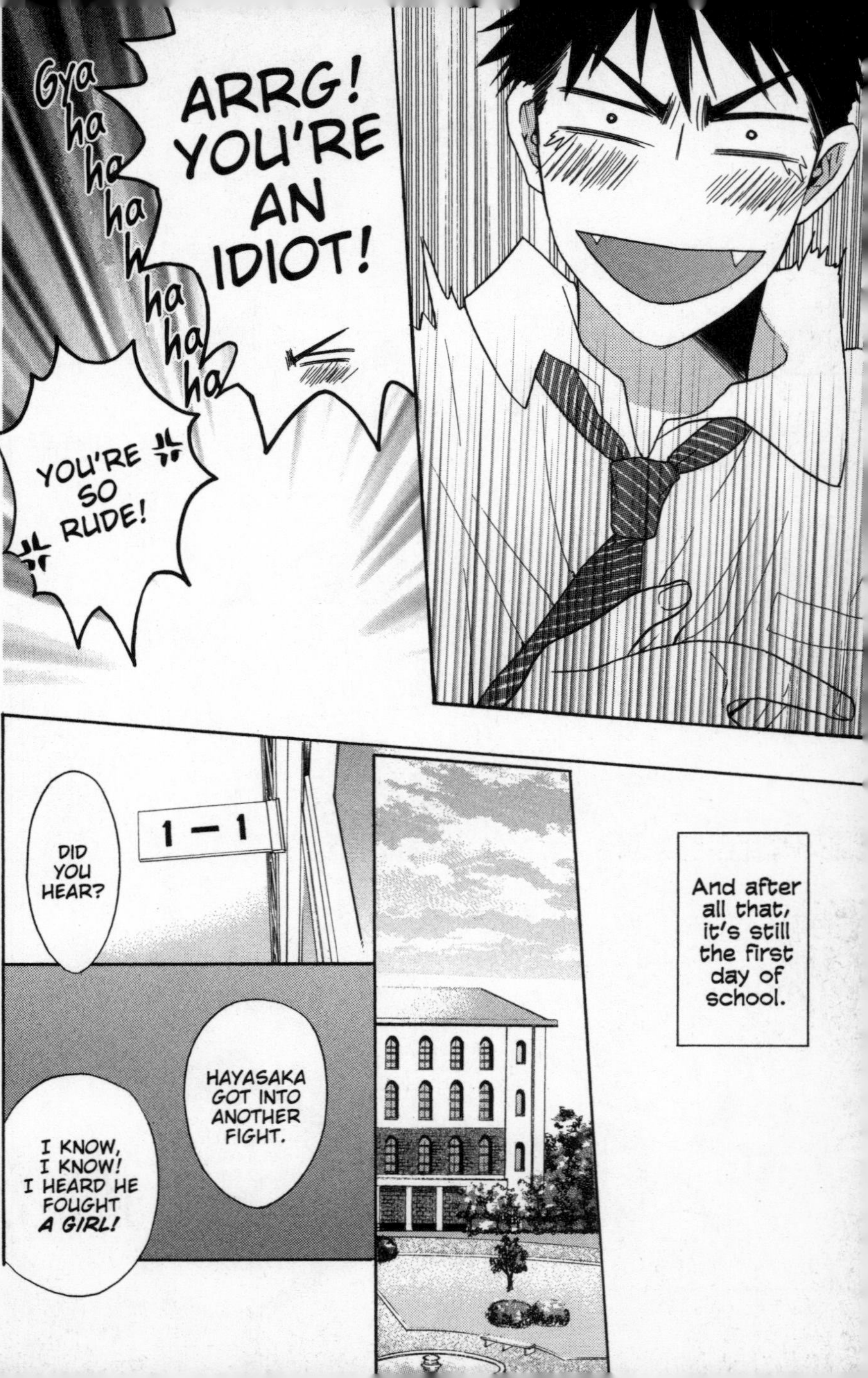
ARRG! YOU'RE AN IDIOT!
Gya ha ha ha ha ha ha ha ha
YOU'RE SO RUDE!
And after all that, it's still the first day of school.
1-1
DID YOU HEAR?
HAYASAKA GOT INTO ANOTHER FIGHT.
I KNOW, I KNOW! I HEARD HE FOUGHT *A GIRL!*

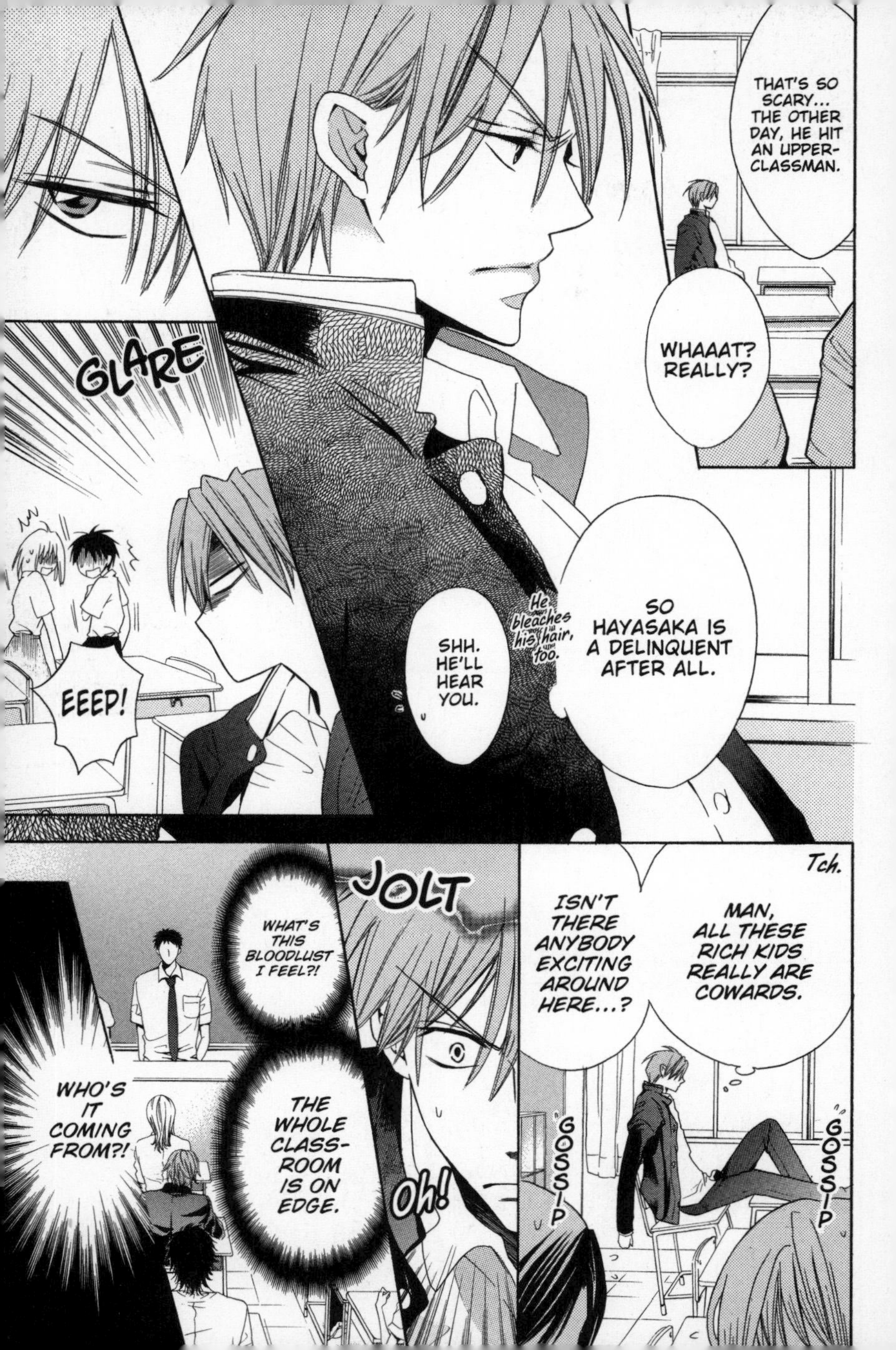
THAT'S SO SCARY... THE OTHER DAY, HE HIT AN UPPER-CLASSMAN.
WHAAAT? REALLY?
SO HAYASAKA IS A DELINQUENT AFTER ALL.
He bleaches his hair, too.
SHH. HE'LL HEAR YOU.
GLARE
EEEP!
Tch.
MAN, ALL THESE RICH KIDS REALLY ARE COWARDS.
ISN'T THERE ANYBODY EXCITING AROUND HERE...?
GOSSIP
GOSSIP
JOLT
WHAT'S THIS BLOODLUST I FEEL?!
THE WHOLE CLASSROOM IS ON EDGE.
Oh!
WHO'S IT COMING FROM?!

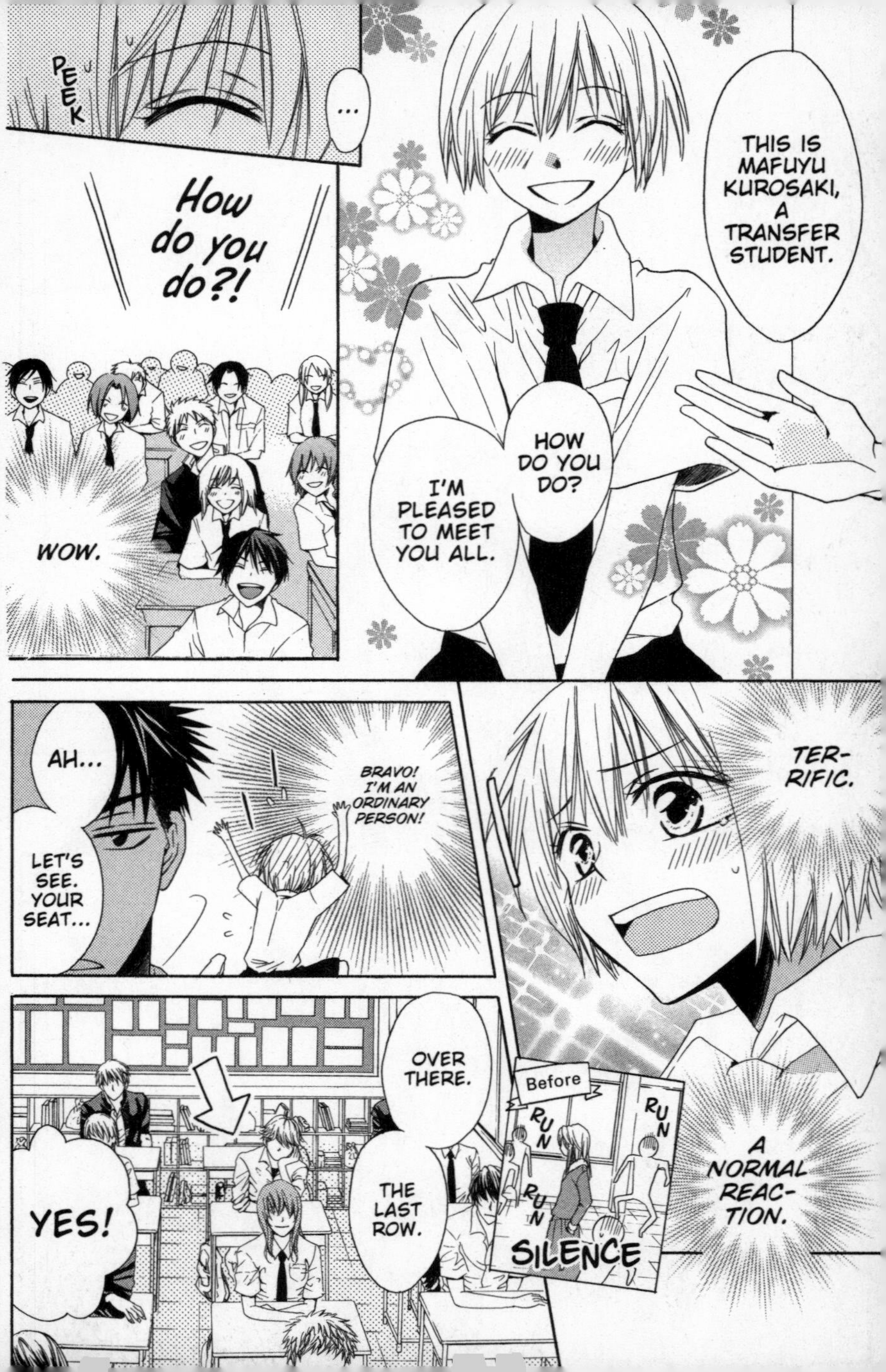
THIS IS MAFUYU KUROSAKI, A TRANSFER STUDENT.
HOW DO YOU DO?
I'M PLEASED TO MEET YOU ALL.
...
PEEK
How do you do?!
WOW.
TER-RIFIC.
A NORMAL REAC-TION.
Before
RUN
RUN
RUN
SILENCE
BRAVO! I'M AN ORDINARY PERSON!
AH...
LET'S SEE. YOUR SEAT...
OVER THERE.
THE LAST ROW.
YES!

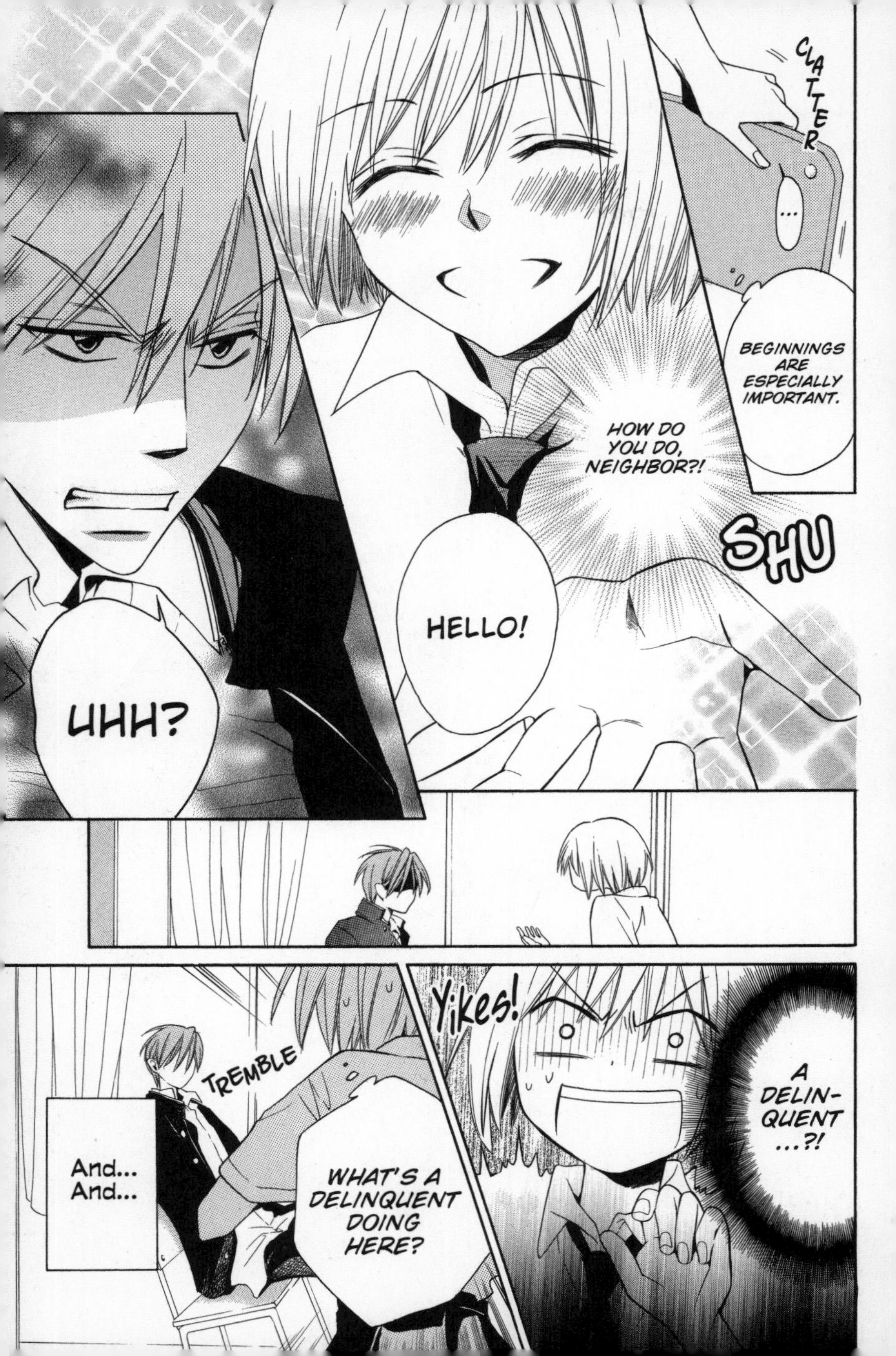
CLATTER
...
BEGINNINGS ARE ESPECIALLY IMPORTANT.
HOW DO YOU DO, NEIGHBOR?!
SHU
HELLO!
UHH?
Yikes!
A DELIN-QUENT ...?!
WHAT'S A DELINQUENT DOING HERE?
TREMBLE
And... And...

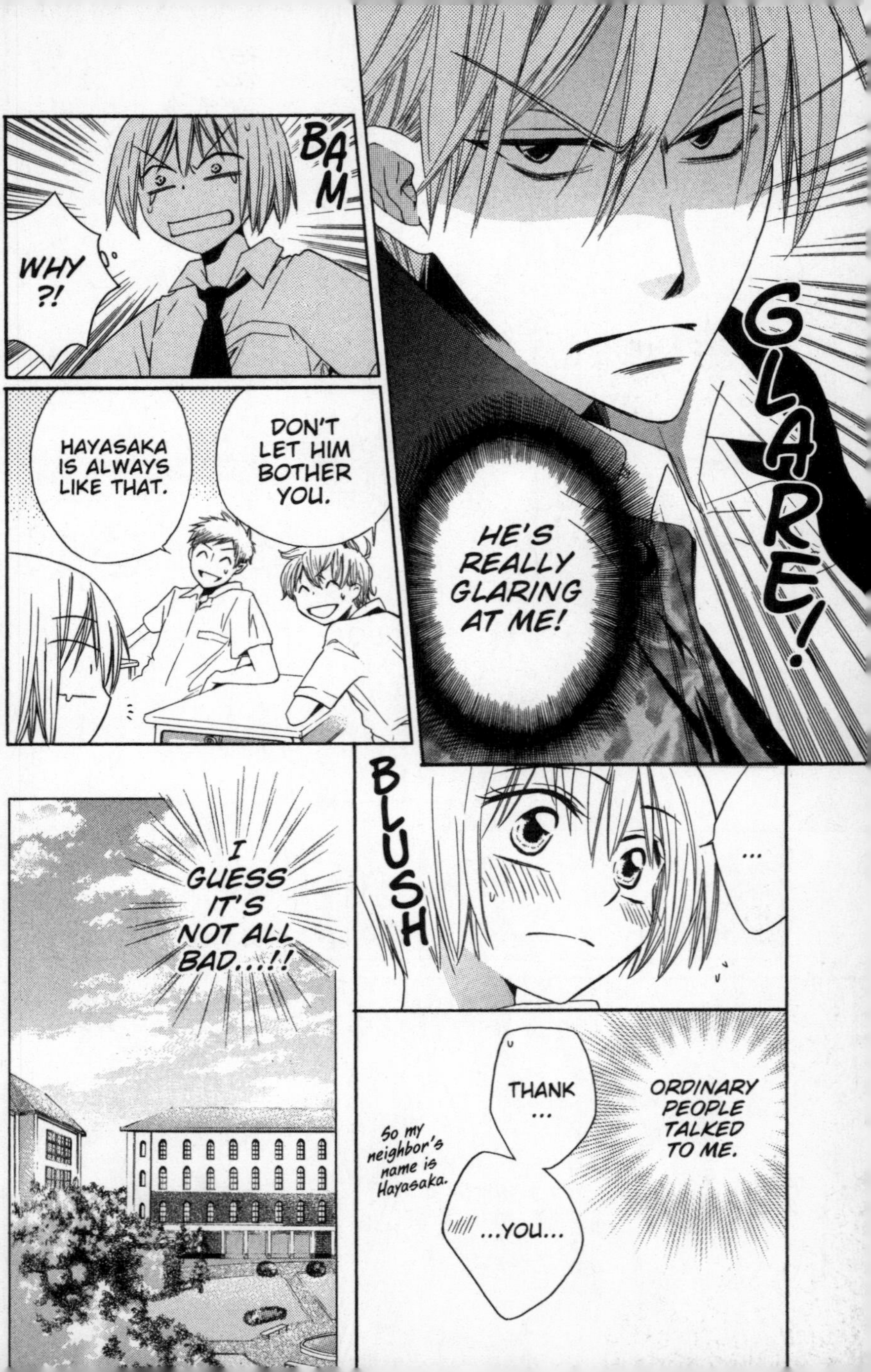
GLARE!
HE'S REALLY GLARING AT ME!
BAM
WHY?!
DON'T LET HIM BOTHER YOU.
HAYASAKA IS ALWAYS LIKE THAT.
BLUSH
...
ORDINARY PEOPLE TALKED TO ME.
THANK...
...YOU...
So my neighbor's name is Hayasaka.
I GUESS IT'S NOT ALL BAD...!!

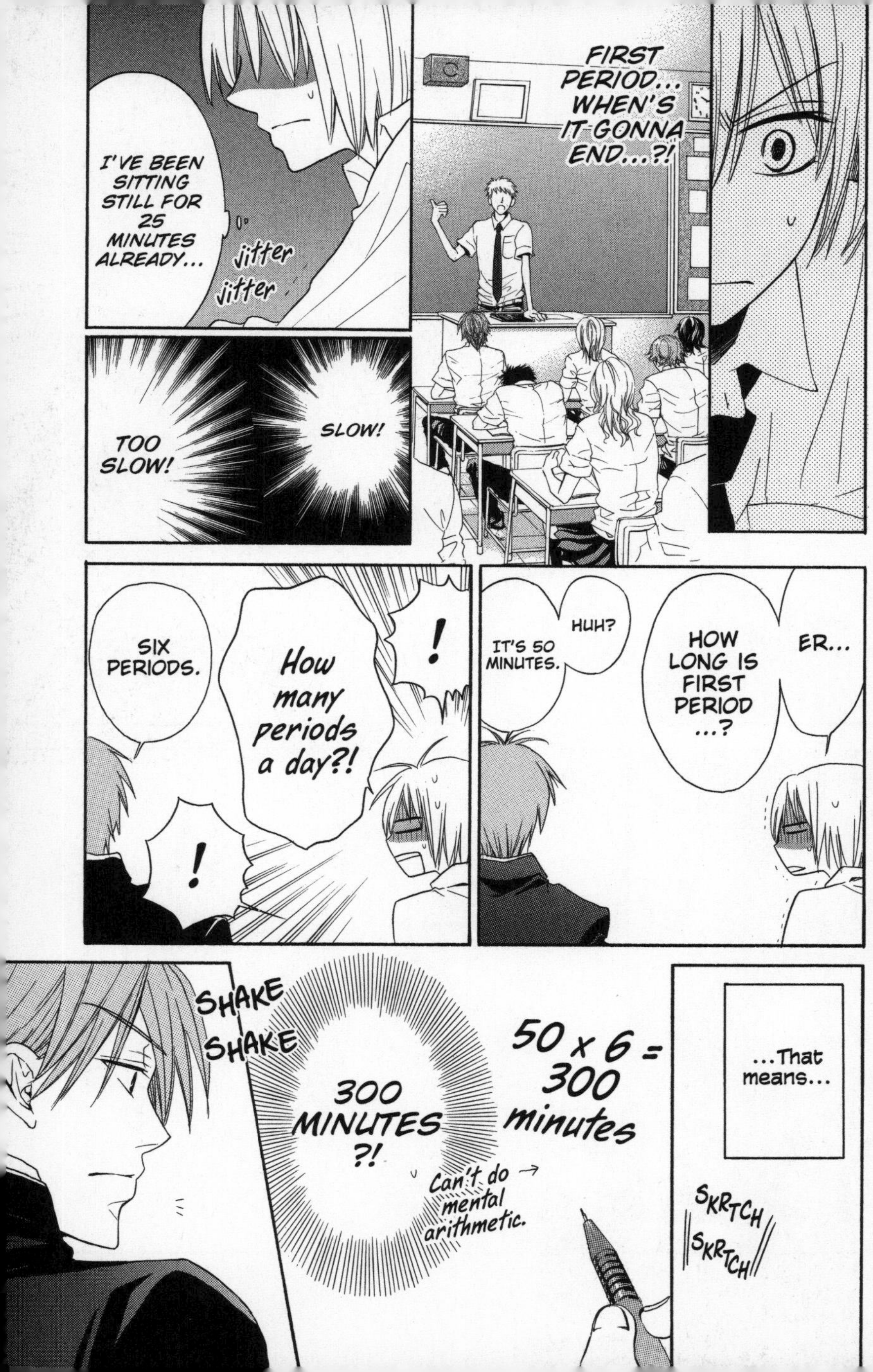

FIRST PERIOD... WHEN'S IT GONNA END...?!
I'VE BEEN SITTING STILL FOR 25 MINUTES ALREADY...
jitter jitter
SLOW!
TOO SLOW!
ER...
HOW LONG IS FIRST PERIOD...?
HUH?
IT'S 50 MINUTES.
!
How many periods a day?!
SIX PERIODS.
!
...That means...
SKRTCH SKRTCH
50 x 6 = 300 minutes
Can't do mental arithmetic.
300 MINUTES?!
SHAKE SHAKE

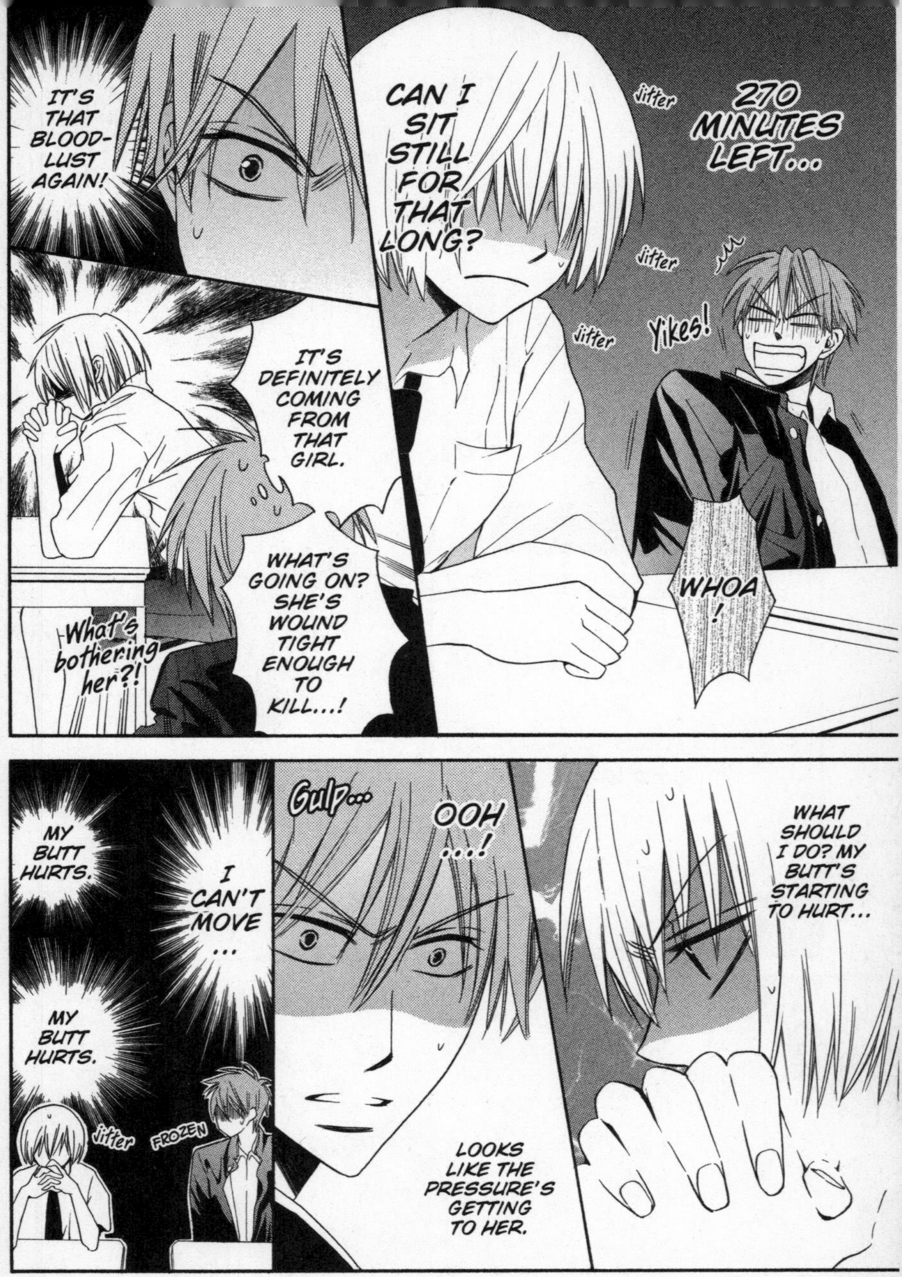
270 MINUTES LEFT...
jitter
CAN I SIT STILL FOR THAT LONG?
jitter
Yikes!
jitter
WHOA!
IT'S THAT BLOODLUST AGAIN!
IT'S DEFINITELY COMING FROM THAT GIRL.
WHAT'S GOING ON? SHE'S WOUND TIGHT ENOUGH TO KILL...!
What's bothering her?!
WHAT SHOULD I DO? MY BUTT'S STARTING TO HURT...
Gulp...
OOH ...!
LOOKS LIKE THE PRESSURE'S GETTING TO HER.
MY BUTT HURTS.
I CAN'T MOVE ...
MY BUTT HURTS.
jitter
FROZEN

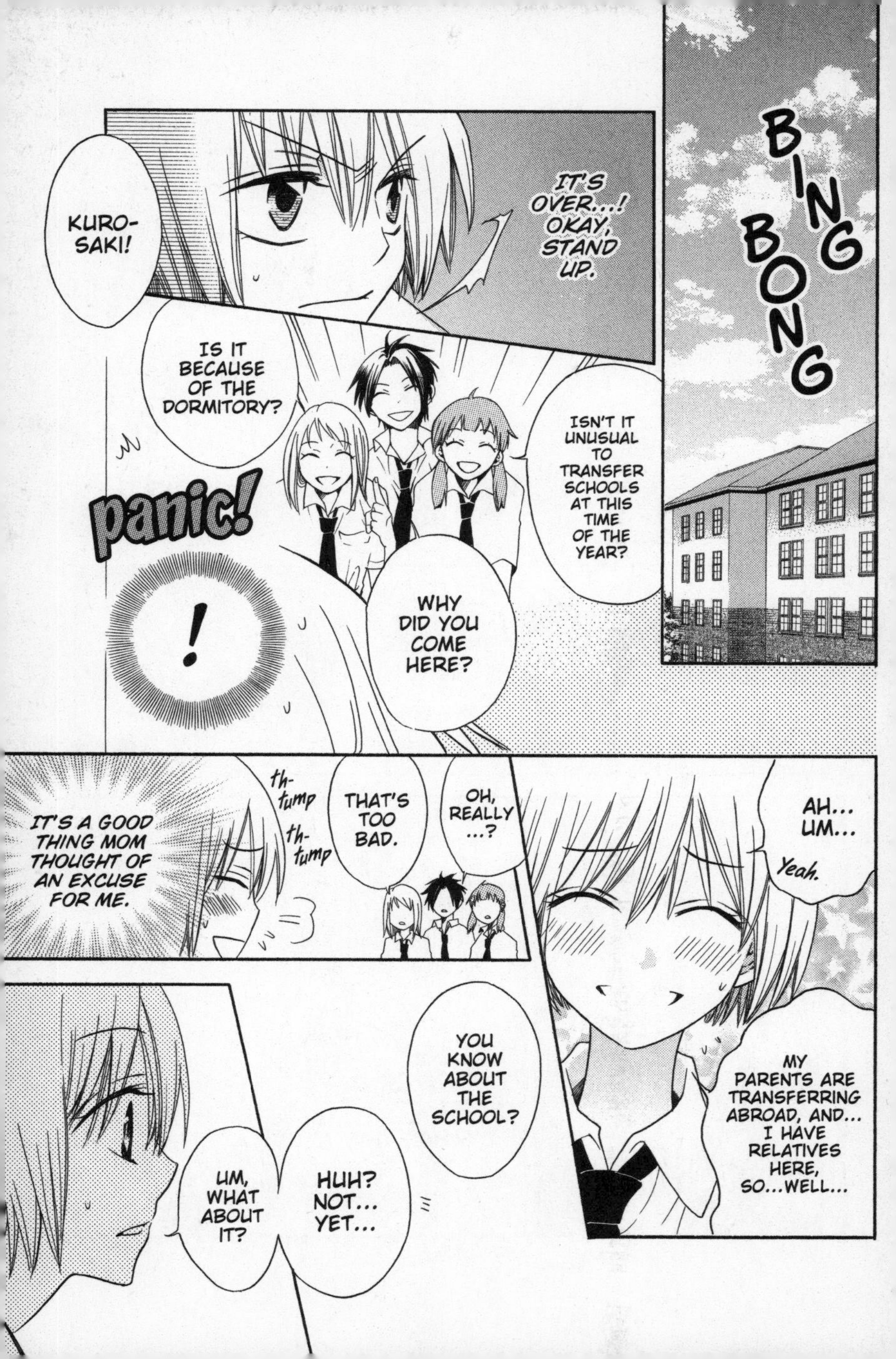
BING BONG
IT'S OVER...! OKAY, STAND UP.
KURO-SAKI!
ISN'T IT UNUSUAL TO TRANSFER SCHOOLS AT THIS TIME OF THE YEAR?
IS IT BECAUSE OF THE DORMITORY?
WHY DID YOU COME HERE?
panic!
!
AH... UM...
Yeah.
MY PARENTS ARE TRANSFERRING ABROAD, AND... I HAVE RELATIVES HERE, SO...WELL...
OH, REALLY ...?
THAT'S TOO BAD.
th-tump th-tump
IT'S A GOOD THING MOM THOUGHT OF AN EXCUSE FOR ME.
YOU KNOW ABOUT THE SCHOOL?
HUH? NOT... YET...
UM, WHAT ABOUT IT?

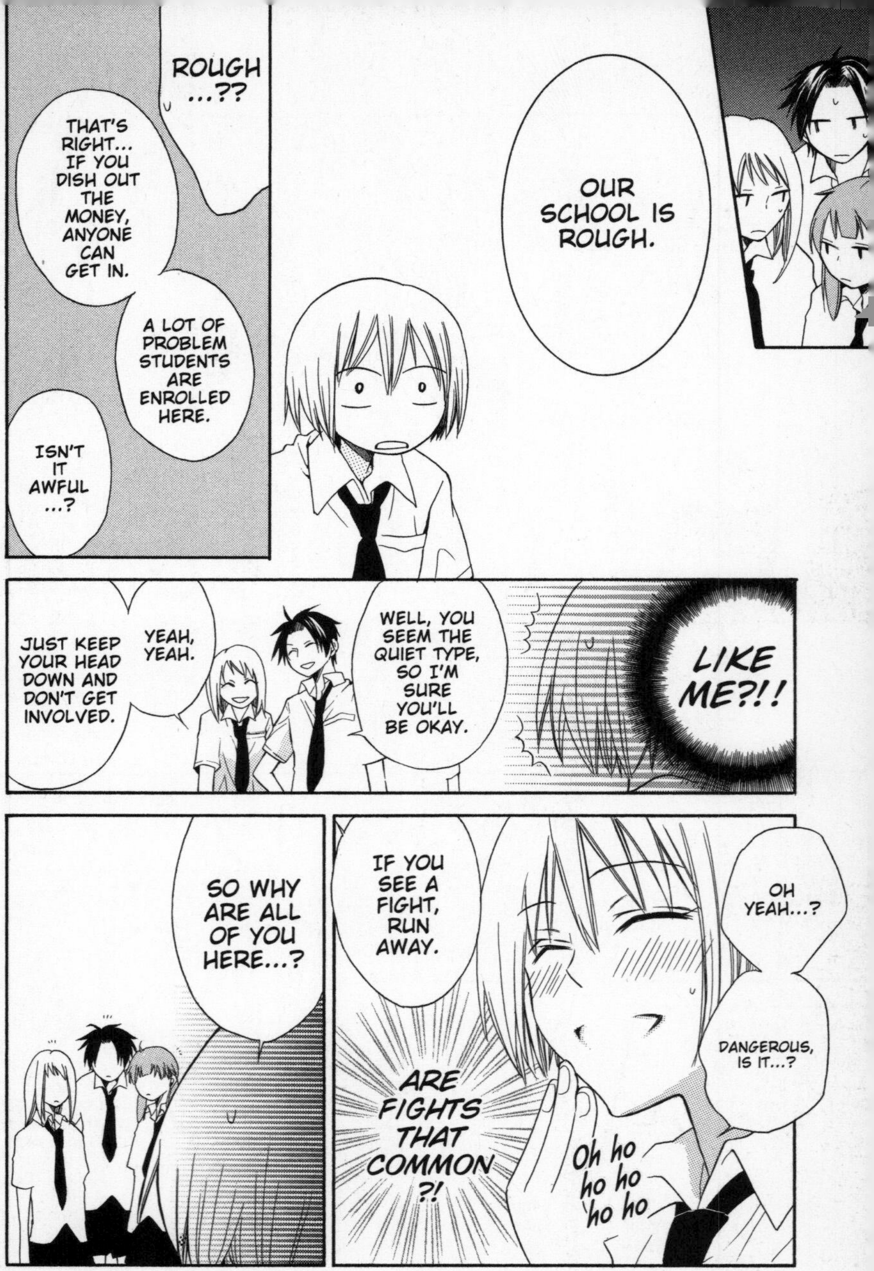
OUR SCHOOL IS ROUGH.
ROUGH ...??
THAT'S RIGHT... IF YOU DISH OUT THE MONEY, ANYONE CAN GET IN.
A LOT OF PROBLEM STUDENTS ARE ENROLLED HERE.
ISN'T IT AWFUL ...?
LIKE ME?!!
WELL, YOU SEEM THE QUIET TYPE, SO I'M SURE YOU'LL BE OKAY.
YEAH, YEAH.
JUST KEEP YOUR HEAD DOWN AND DON'T GET INVOLVED.
OH YEAH...?
IF YOU SEE A FIGHT, RUN AWAY.
DANGEROUS, IS IT...?
Oh ho ho ho ho ho
ARE FIGHTS THAT COMMON ?!
SO WHY ARE ALL OF YOU HERE...?

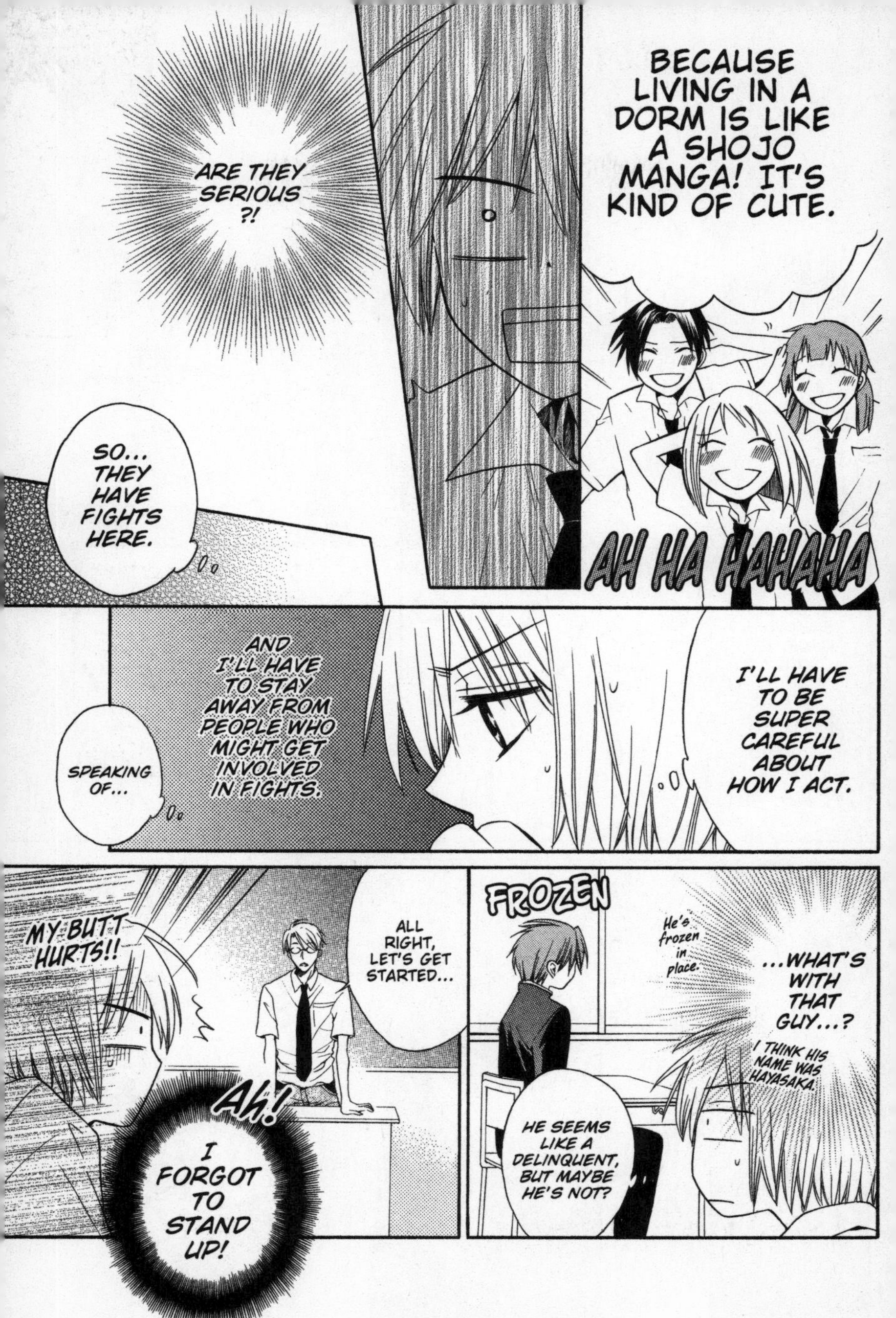
BECAUSE LIVING IN A DORM IS LIKE A SHOJO MANGA! IT'S KIND OF CUTE.
AH HA HAHAHA
ARE THEY SERIOUS?!
SO... THEY HAVE FIGHTS HERE.
I'LL HAVE TO BE SUPER CAREFUL ABOUT HOW I ACT.
AND I'LL HAVE TO STAY AWAY FROM PEOPLE WHO MIGHT GET INVOLVED IN FIGHTS.
SPEAKING OF...
FROZEN
...WHAT'S WITH THAT GUY...?
He's frozen in place.
I THINK HIS NAME WAS HAYASAKA.
HE SEEMS LIKE A DELINQUENT, BUT MAYBE HE'S NOT?
ALL RIGHT, LET'S GET STARTED...
MY BUTT HURTS!!
Ah!
I FORGOT TO STAND UP!

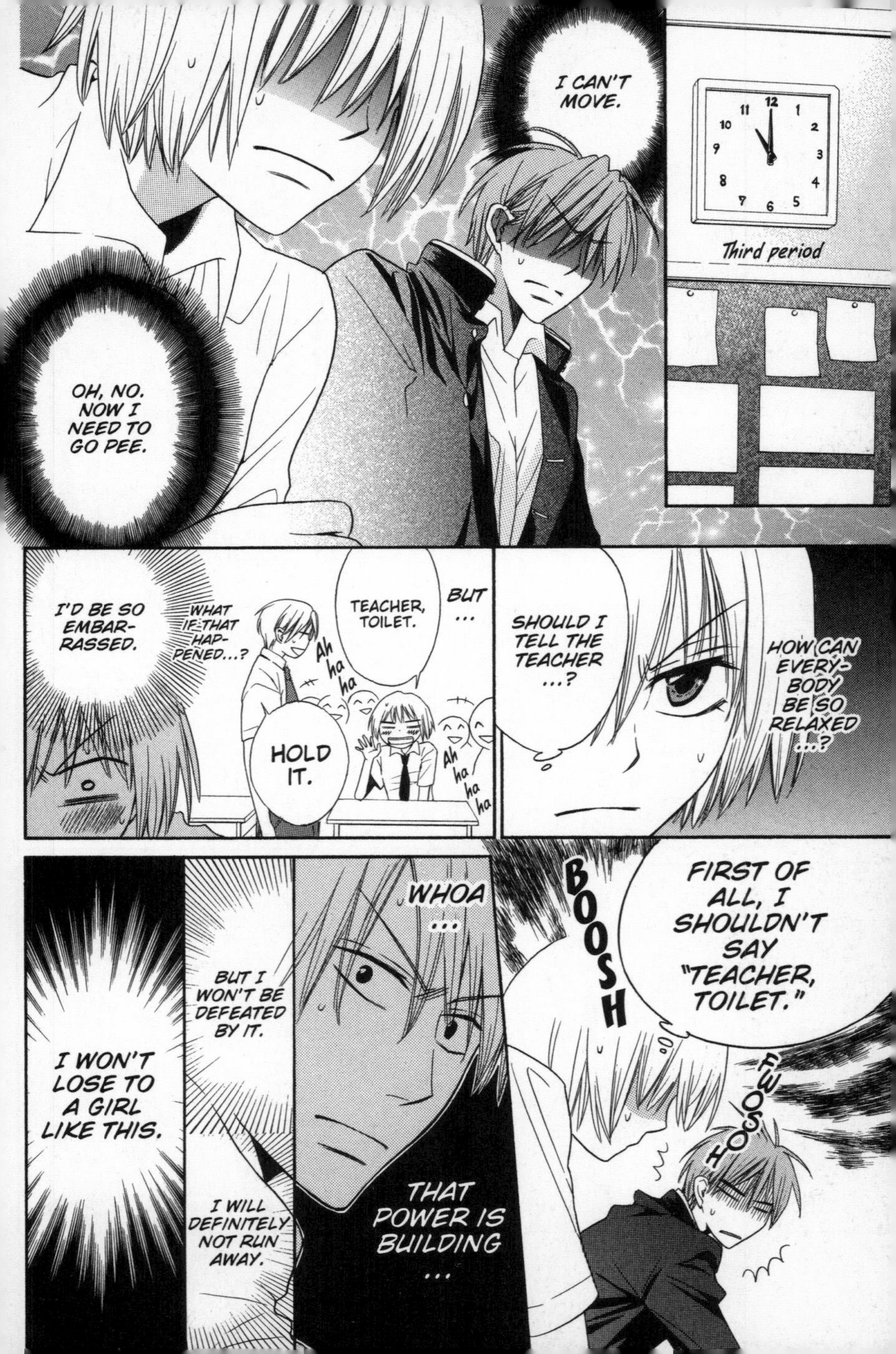

Third period
I CAN'T MOVE.
OH, NO. NOW I NEED TO GO PEE.
HOW CAN EVERYBODY BE SO RELAXED ...?
SHOULD I TELL THE TEACHER ...?
BUT ...
TEACHER, TOILET.
Ah ha ha
HOLD IT.
Ah ha ha ha
WHAT IF THAT HAPPENED...?
I'D BE SO EMBARRASSED.
FIRST OF ALL, I SHOULDN'T SAY "TEACHER, TOILET."
BOOSH
FWOOSH
WHOA ...
THAT POWER IS BUILDING ...
BUT I WON'T BE DEFEATED BY IT.
I WILL DEFINITELY NOT RUN AWAY.
I WON'T LOSE TO A GIRL LIKE THIS.

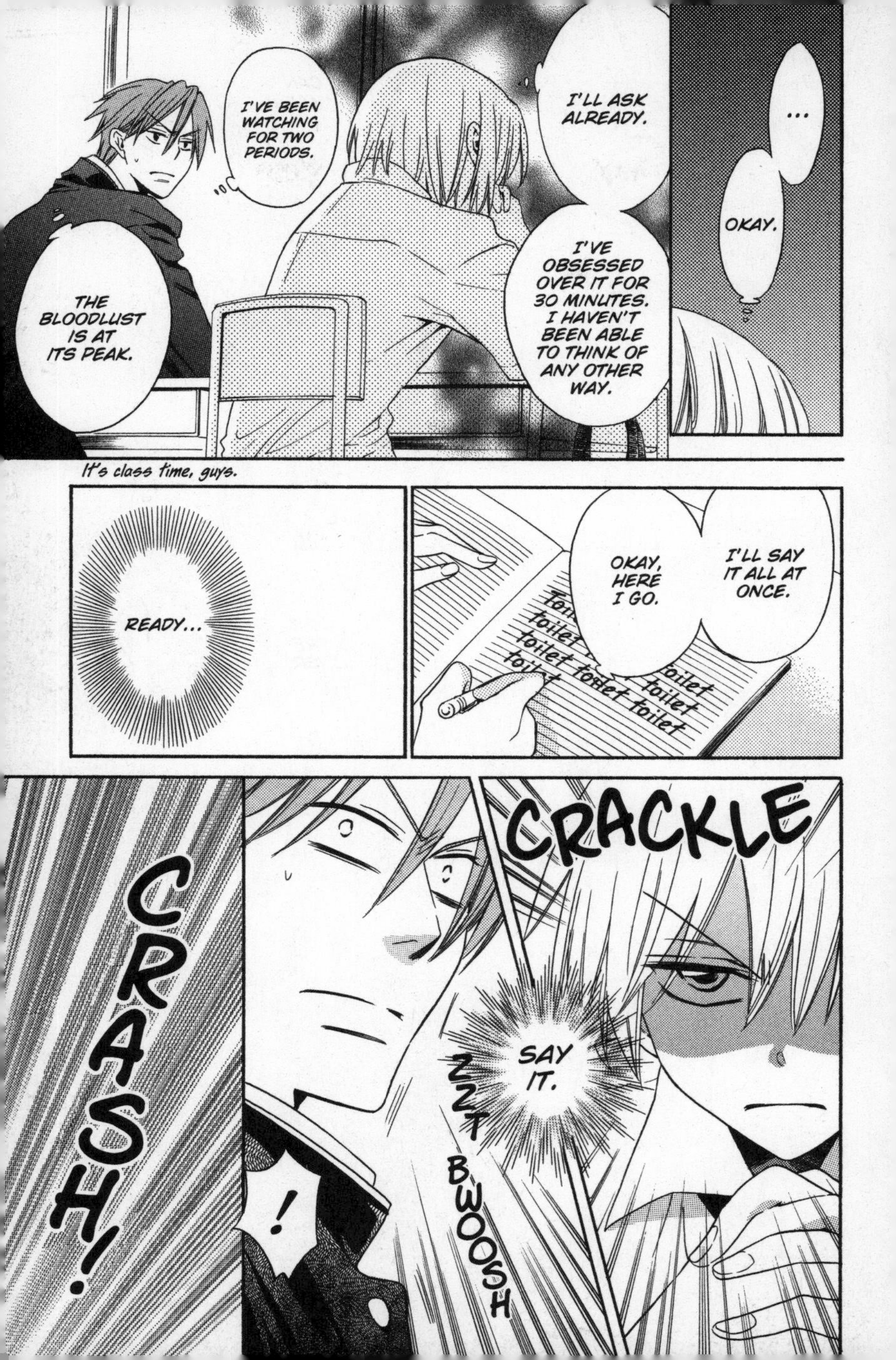
...
OKAY.
I'LL ASK ALREADY.
I'VE OBSESSED OVER IT FOR 30 MINUTES. I HAVEN'T BEEN ABLE TO THINK OF ANY OTHER WAY.
I'VE BEEN WATCHING FOR TWO PERIODS.
THE BLOODLUST IS AT ITS PEAK.
It's class time, guys.
I'LL SAY IT ALL AT ONCE.
OKAY, HERE I GO.
READY...
CRACKLE
SAY IT.
ZZZT
BWOOSH
!
CRASH!

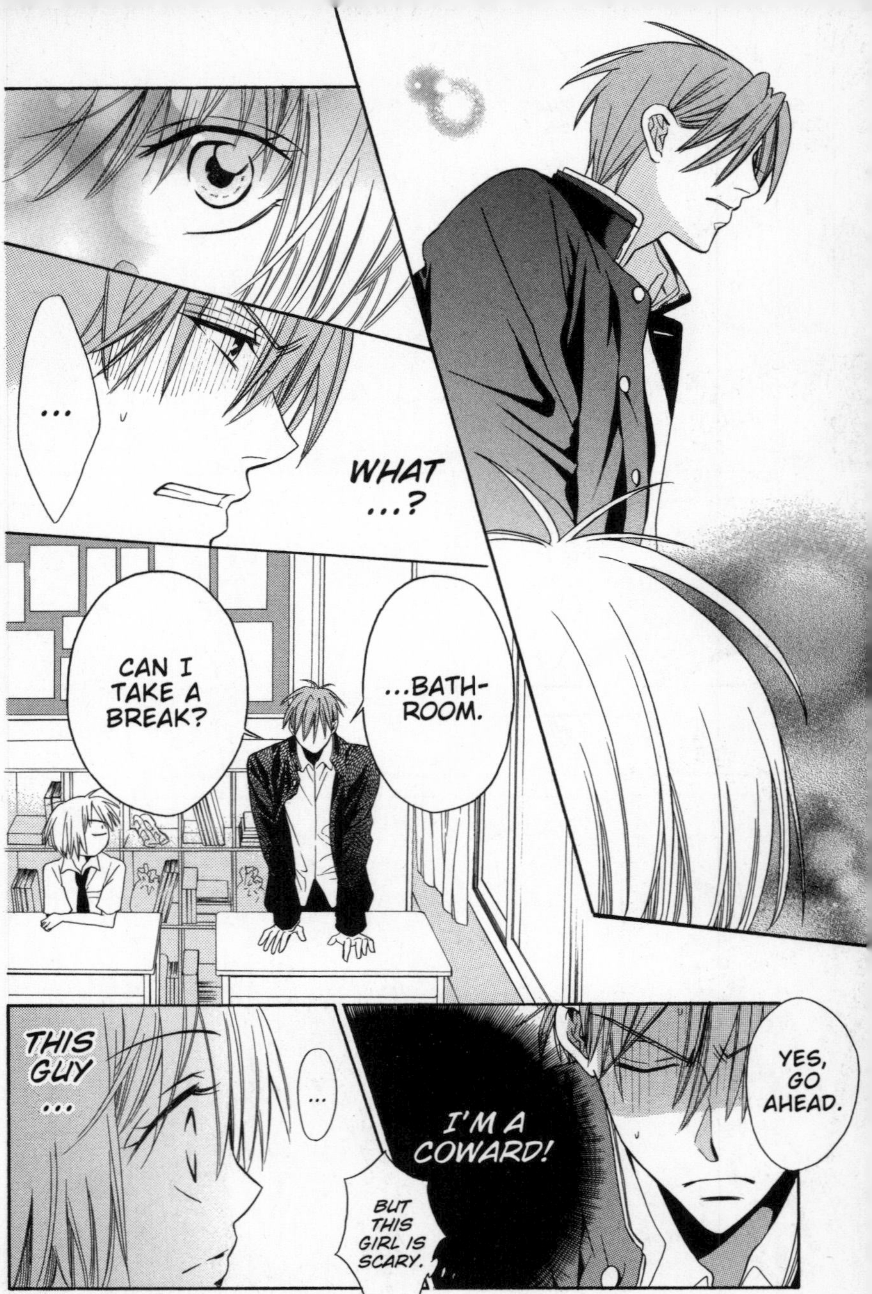
...
WHAT ...?
CAN I TAKE A BREAK?
...BATH-ROOM.
YES, GO AHEAD.
I'M A COWARD!
BUT THIS GIRL IS SCARY.
...
THIS GUY ...

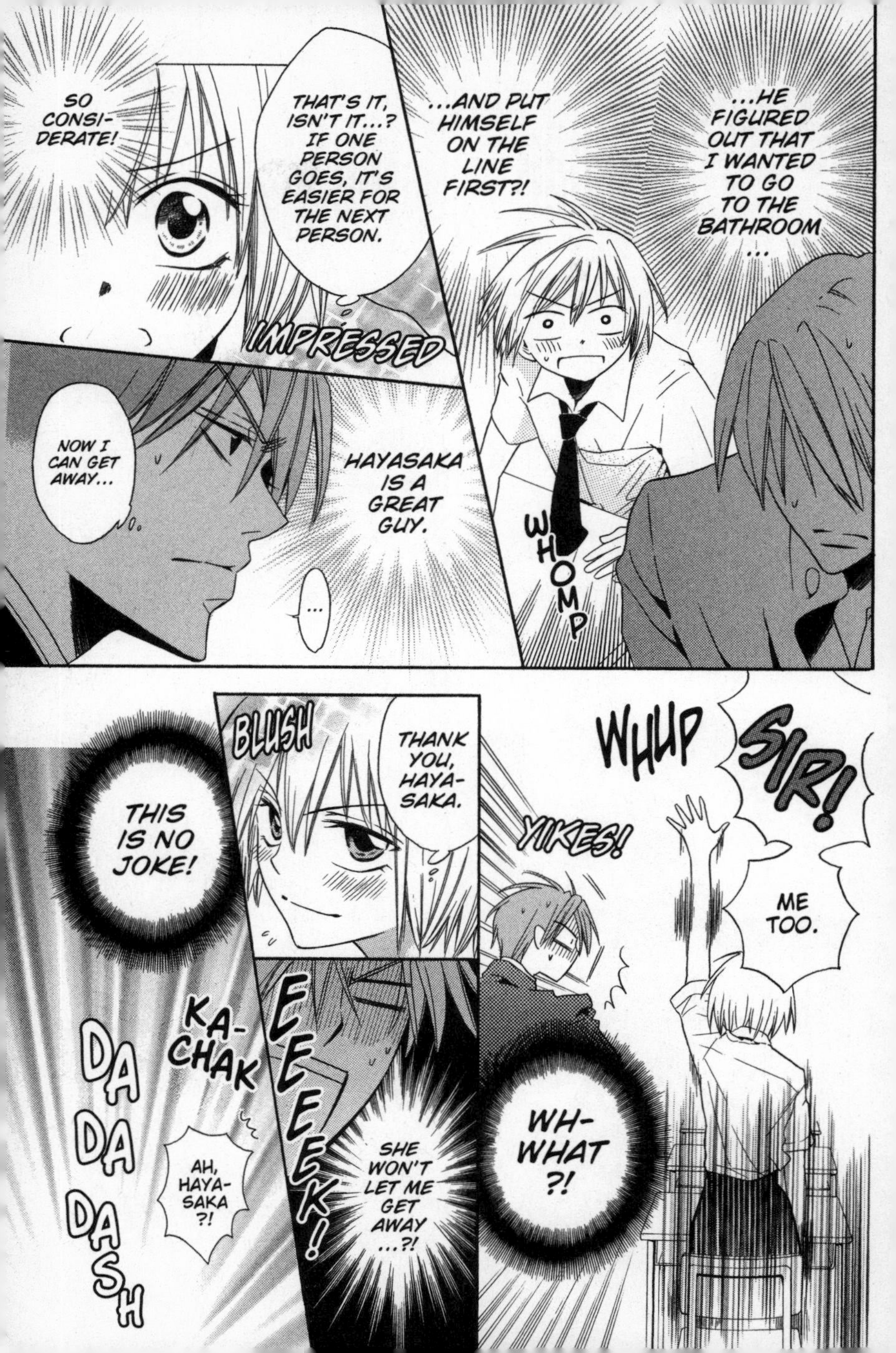
...HE FIGURED OUT THAT I WANTED TO GO TO THE BATHROOM...
...AND PUT HIMSELF ON THE LINE FIRST?!
WHOMP
THAT'S IT, ISN'T IT...? IF ONE PERSON GOES, IT'S EASIER FOR THE NEXT PERSON.
SO CONSIDERATE!
IMPRESSED
HAYASAKA IS A GREAT GUY.
NOW I CAN GET AWAY...
...
SIR!
WHUP
ME TOO.
YIKES!
WH-WHAT?!
THANK YOU, HAYA-SAKA.
BLUSH
THIS IS NO JOKE!
EEEEEK!
SHE WON'T LET ME GET AWAY...?!
AH, HAYA-SAKA?!
KA-CHAK
DA DA DA DASH

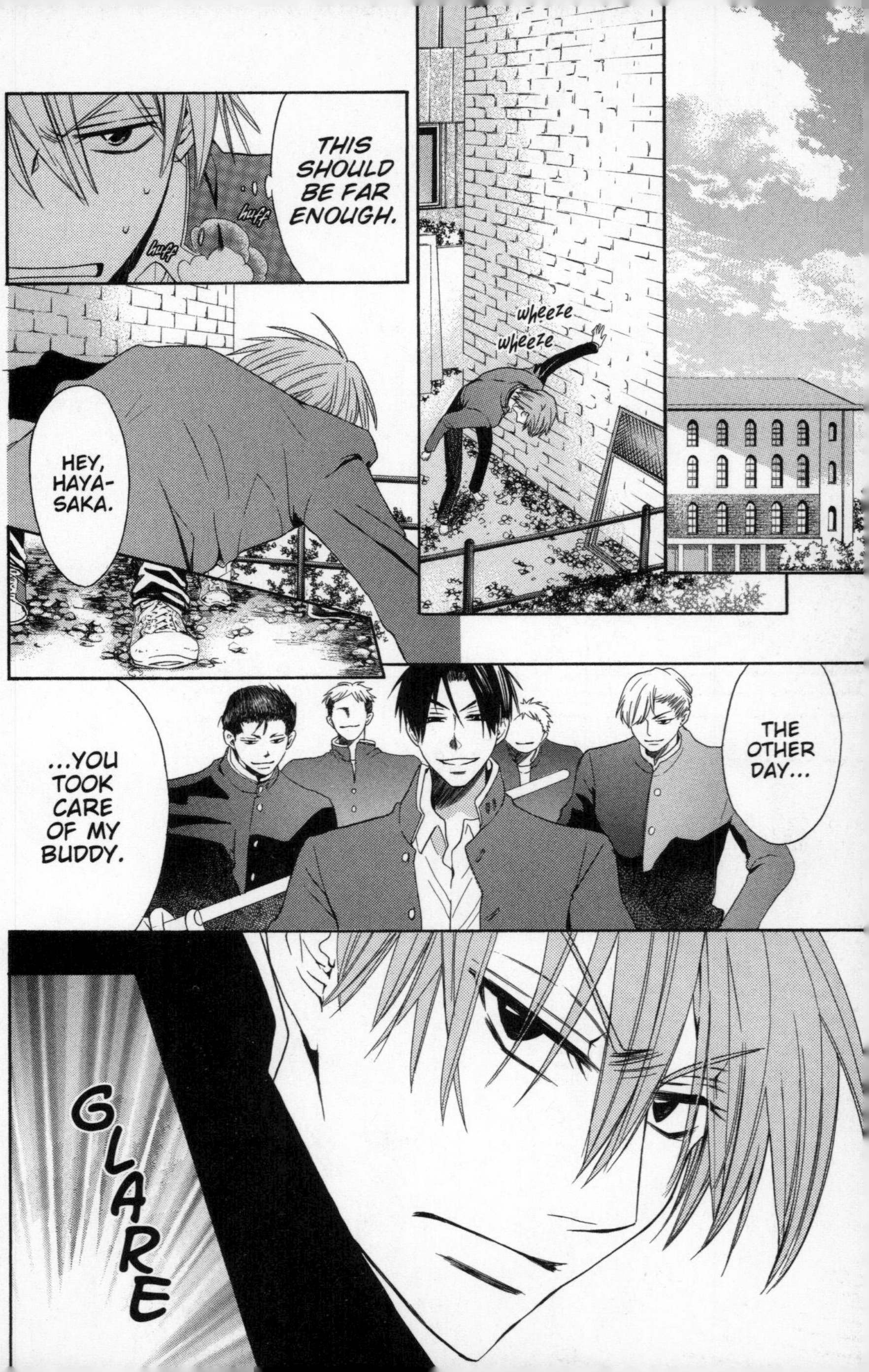
wheeze
wheeze
THIS SHOULD BE FAR ENOUGH.
huff
huff
HEY, HAYA-SAKA.
THE OTHER DAY...
...YOU TOOK CARE OF MY BUDDY.
GLARE

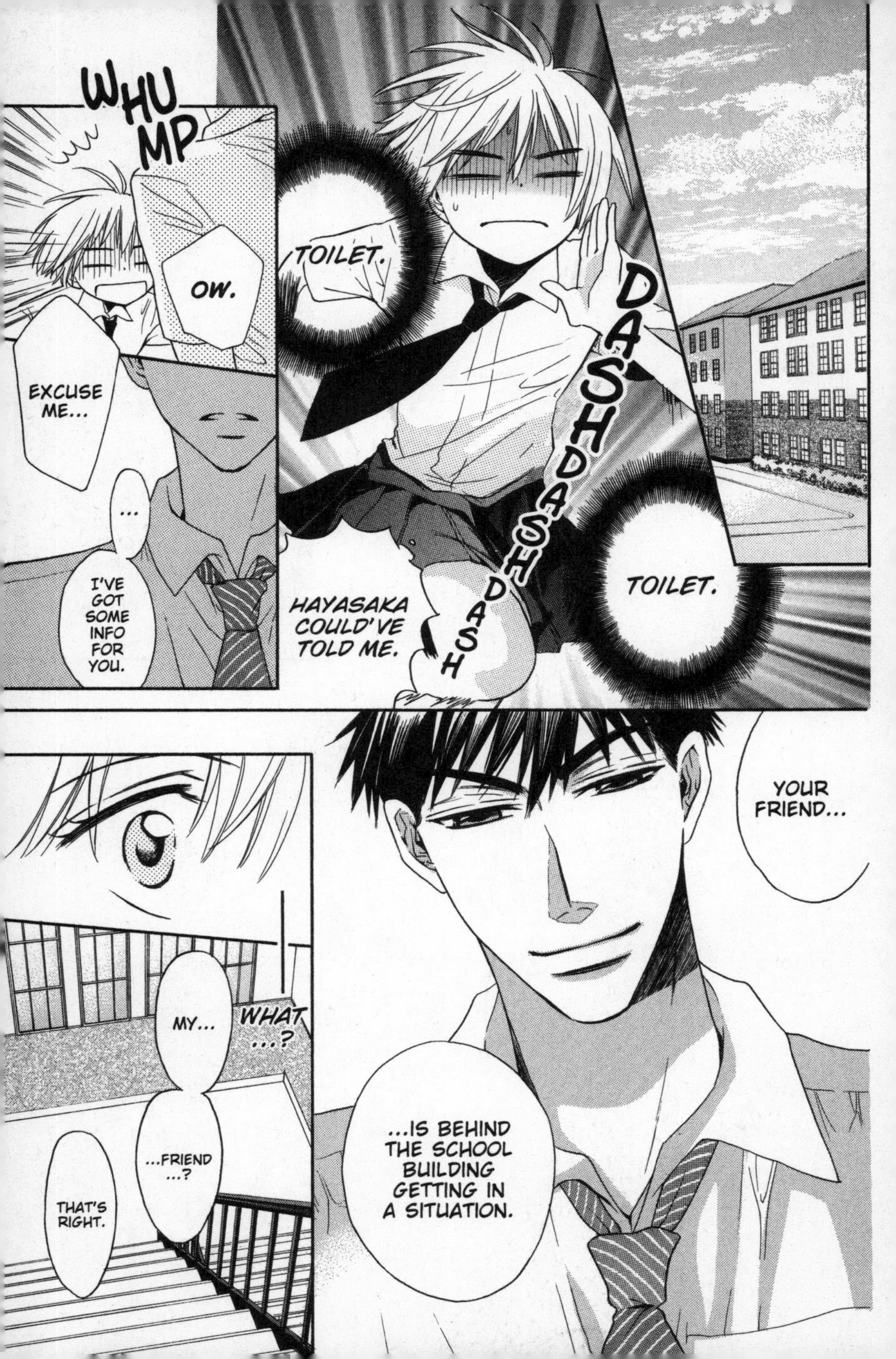
TOILET.
TOILET.
DASHDASHDASH
HAYASAKA COULD'VE TOLD ME.
WHUMP
OW.
EXCUSE ME...
...
I'VE GOT SOME INFO FOR YOU.
YOUR FRIEND...
...IS BEHIND THE SCHOOL BUILDING GETTING IN A SITUATION.
WHAT ...?
MY...
...FRIEND ...?
THAT'S RIGHT.

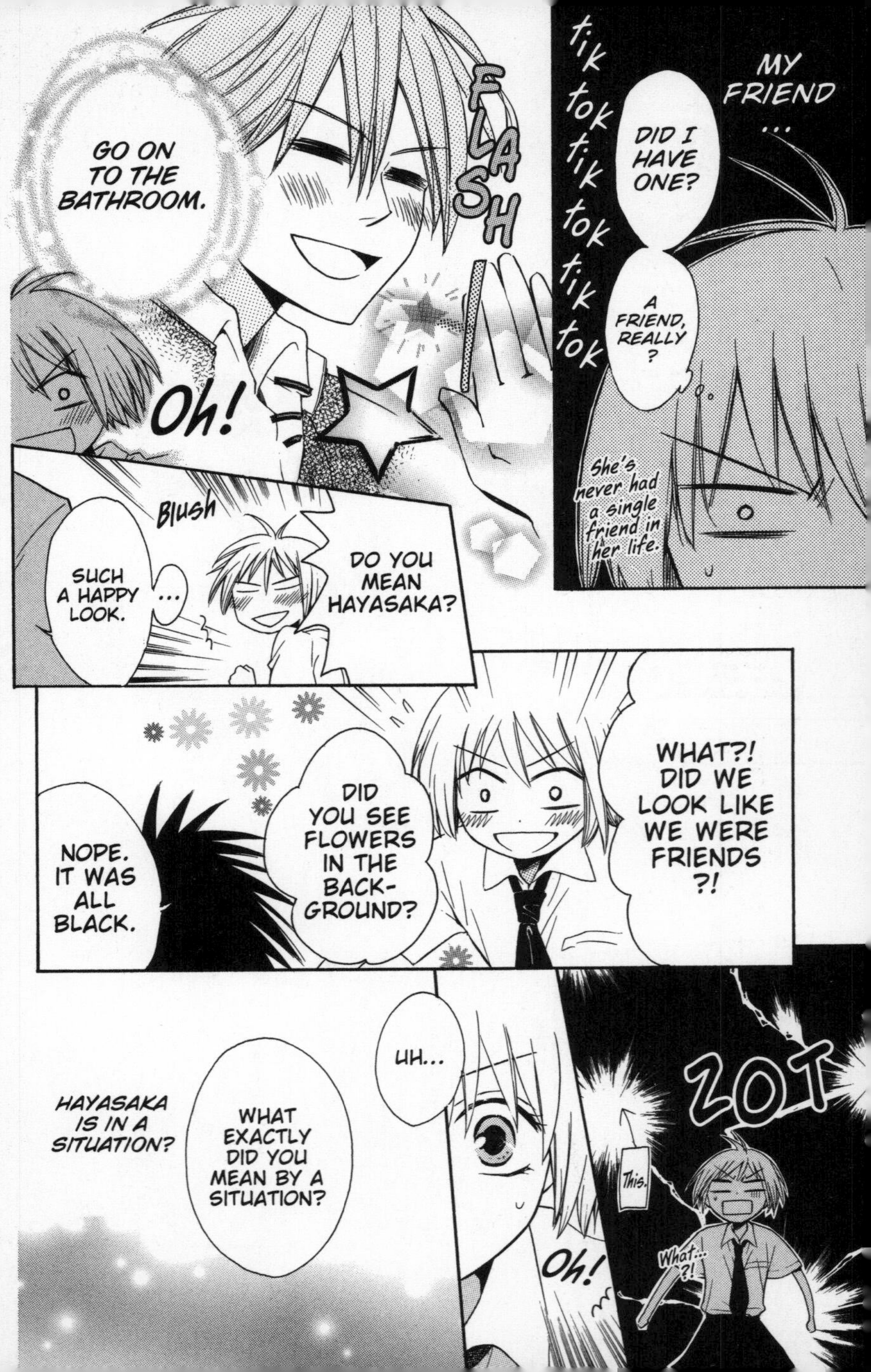
MY FRIEND ...
tik tok tik tok tik tok
DID I HAVE ONE?
A FRIEND, REALLY ?
She's never had a single friend in her life.
GO ON TO THE BATHROOM.
FLASH
Oh!
Blush
DO YOU MEAN HAYASAKA?
...
SUCH A HAPPY LOOK.
WHAT?! DID WE LOOK LIKE WE WERE FRIENDS ?!
DID YOU SEE FLOWERS IN THE BACK-GROUND?
NOPE. IT WAS ALL BLACK.
ZOT
This.
What... ?!
Oh!
UH...
WHAT EXACTLY DID YOU MEAN BY A SITUATION?
HAYASAKA IS IN A SITUATION?

Oresama Teacher

◎ "How do you do," or "Hello." This is a new series. It's a teacher story. A total change of pace. I will do my best! Regards.

◎ Now, about the title, **Oresama Teacher**... My editor thought of it. ...There were a lot of choices, but they were all rejected. Wah wah!

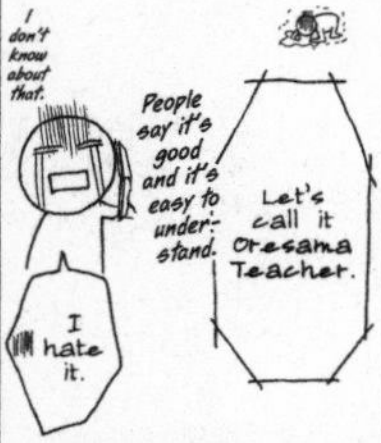

I don't know about that.
People say it's good and it's easy to understand.
Let's call it Oresama Teacher.
I hate it.

I argued for four hours, but I was overruled. At least they let me use the kanji. I'm so happy about the kanji...!

◎ This time love is not the central theme, so I can draw other things, which is fun. No one tells me to make the illustrations and the dialogue "lovey-dovey" or other harsh things, so I'm glad. The storyboard and drawings take a lot of time, so each time I feel like it will kill me, but if you find it even a little entertaining, I will be very happy.

◎ Recently, I realized there is one thing I refuse to back down on.

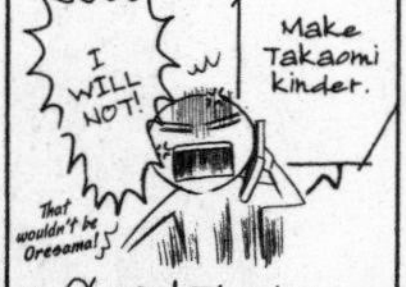

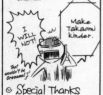

Make Takaomi kinder.
I WILL NOT!
That wouldn't be Oresama!

◎ Special Thanks

To my sister, family, Toya-sama, Pochi-sama, my editor, and to you readers.

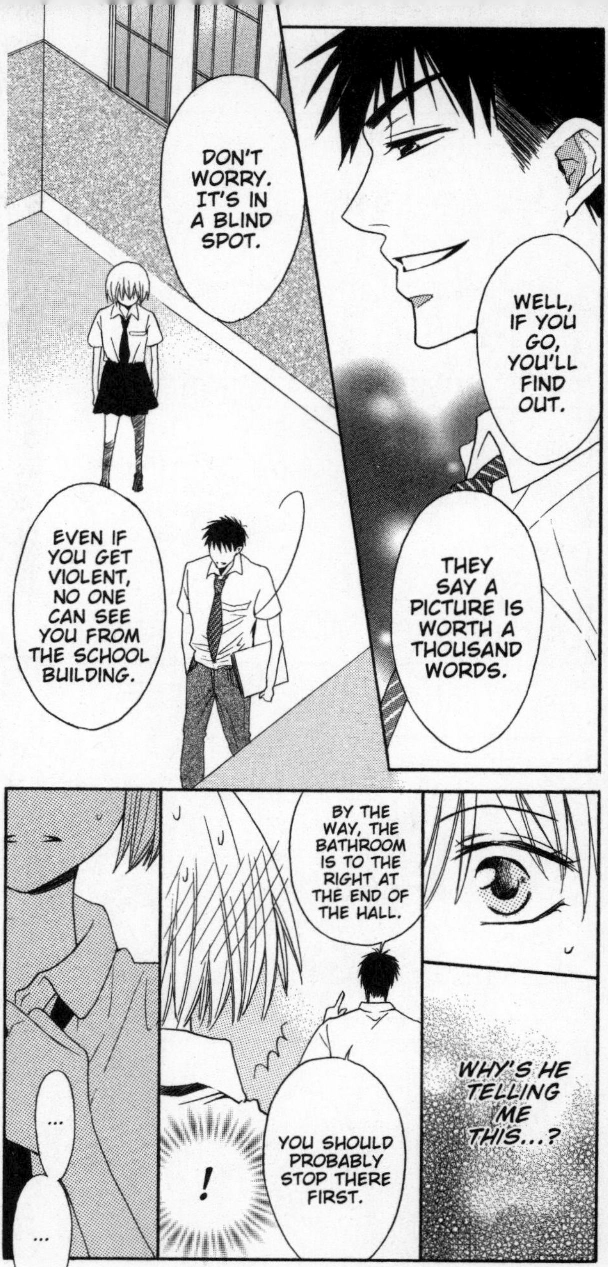

DON'T WORRY. IT'S IN A BLIND SPOT.
EVEN IF YOU GET VIOLENT, NO ONE CAN SEE YOU FROM THE SCHOOL BUILDING.
WELL, IF YOU GO, YOU'LL FIND OUT.
THEY SAY A PICTURE IS WORTH A THOUSAND WORDS.
WHY'S HE TELLING ME THIS...?
BY THE WAY, THE BATHROOM IS TO THE RIGHT AT THE END OF THE HALL.
YOU SHOULD PROBABLY STOP THERE FIRST.
!
...
...

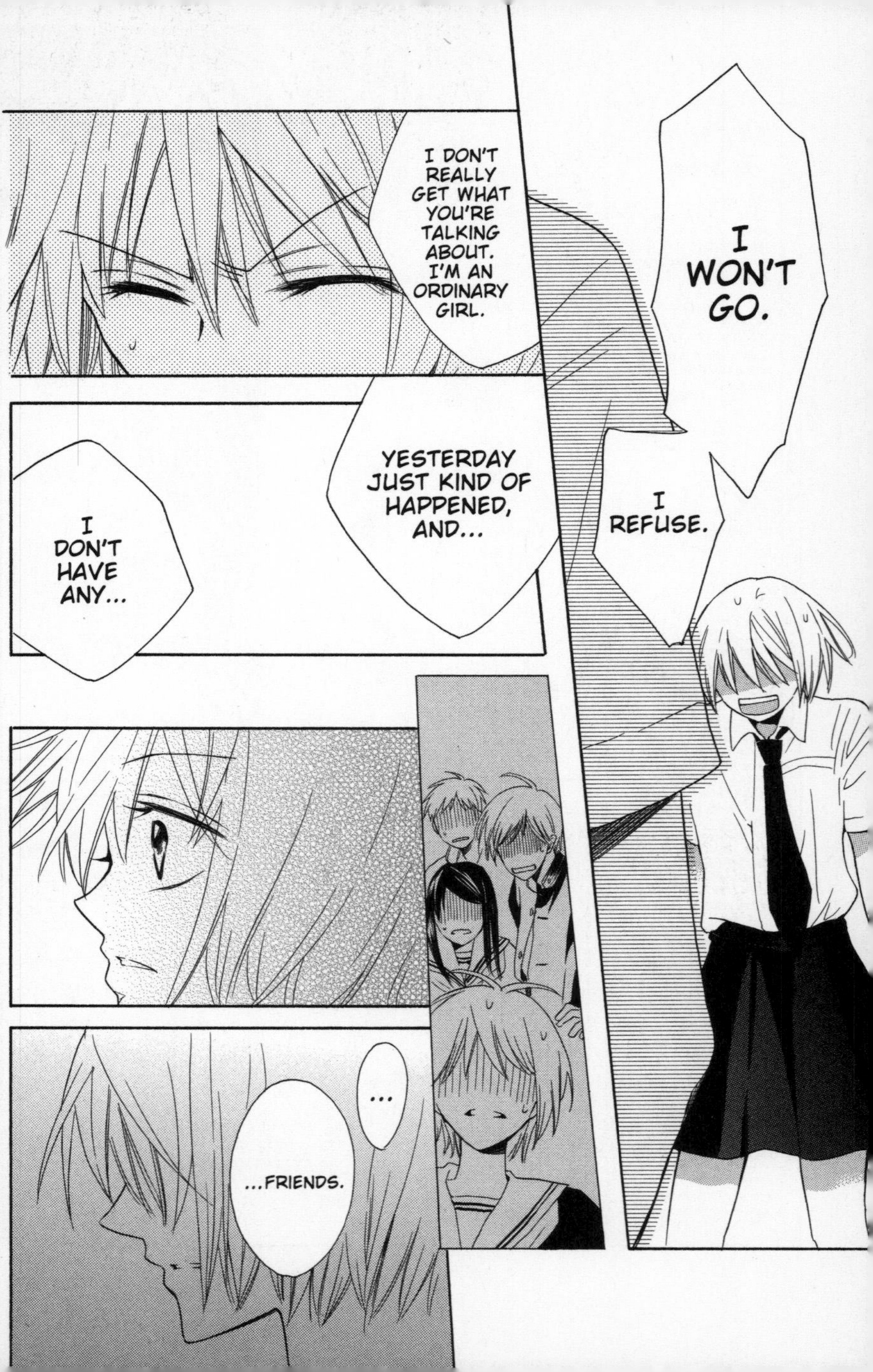

I WON'T GO.
I REFUSE.
I DON'T REALLY GET WHAT YOU'RE TALKING ABOUT. I'M AN ORDINARY GIRL.
YESTERDAY JUST KIND OF HAPPENED, AND...
I DON'T HAVE ANY...
...
...FRIENDS.

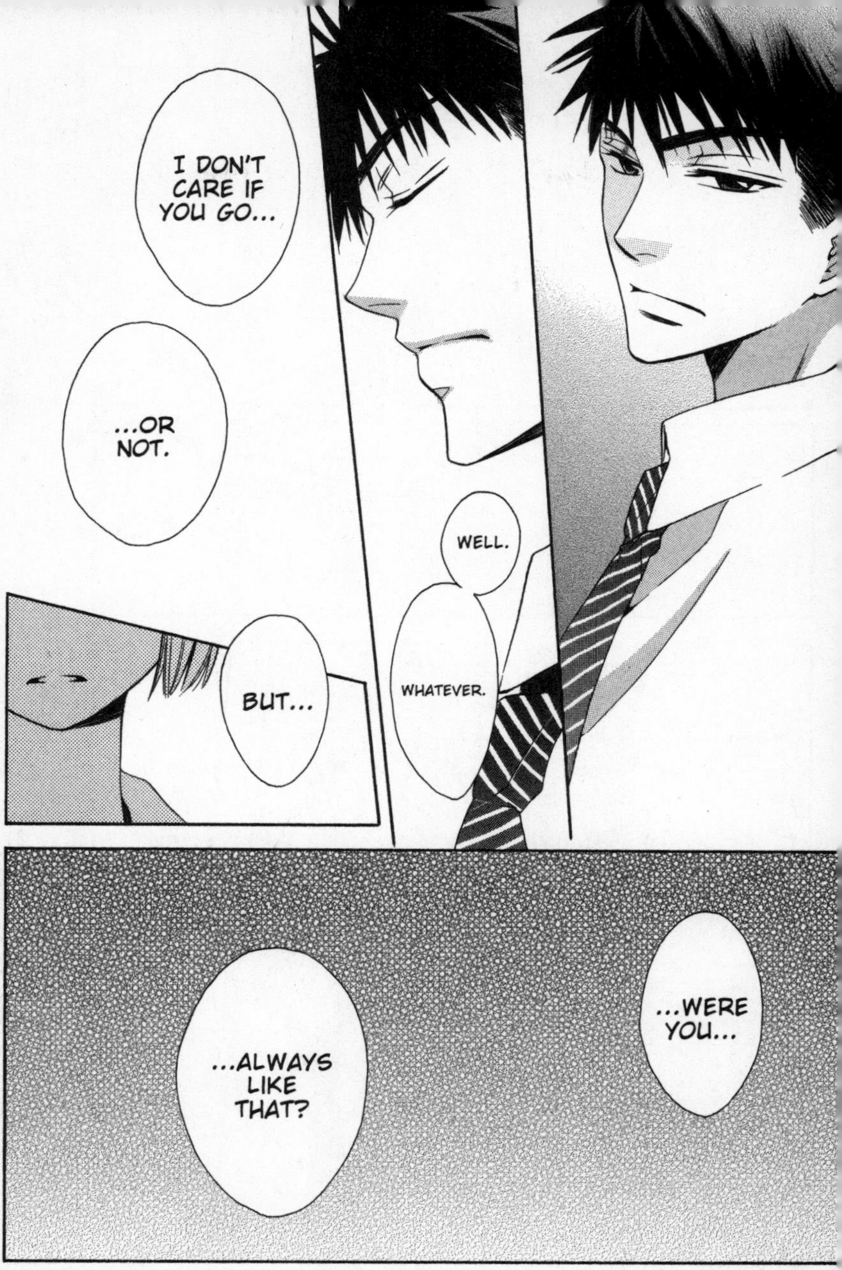
I DON'T CARE IF YOU GO...
...OR NOT.
WELL.
WHATEVER.
BUT...
...WERE YOU...
...ALWAYS LIKE THAT?

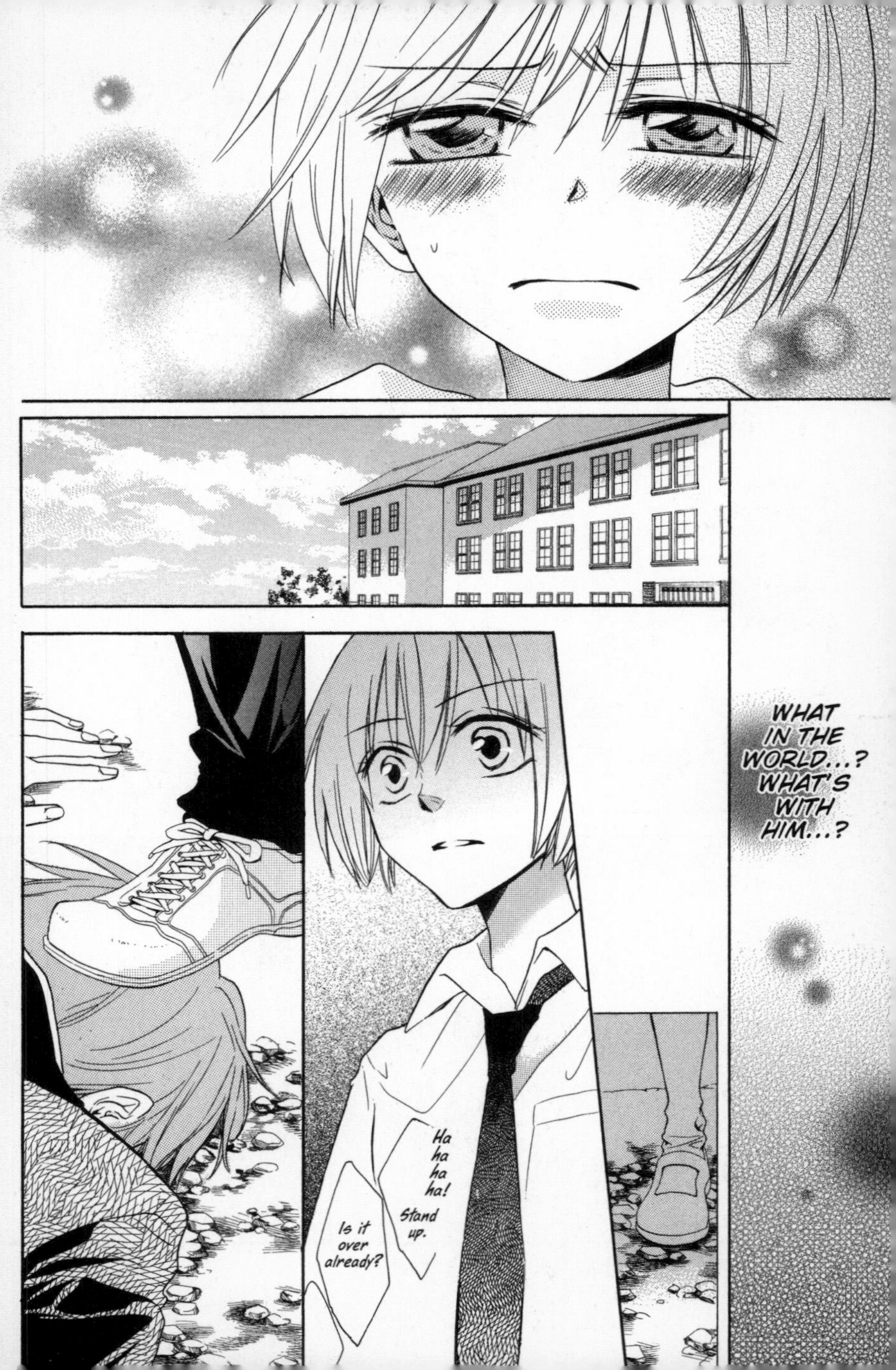
WHAT IN THE WORLD...? WHAT'S WITH HIM...?
Ha ha ha ha!
Stand up.
Is it over already?

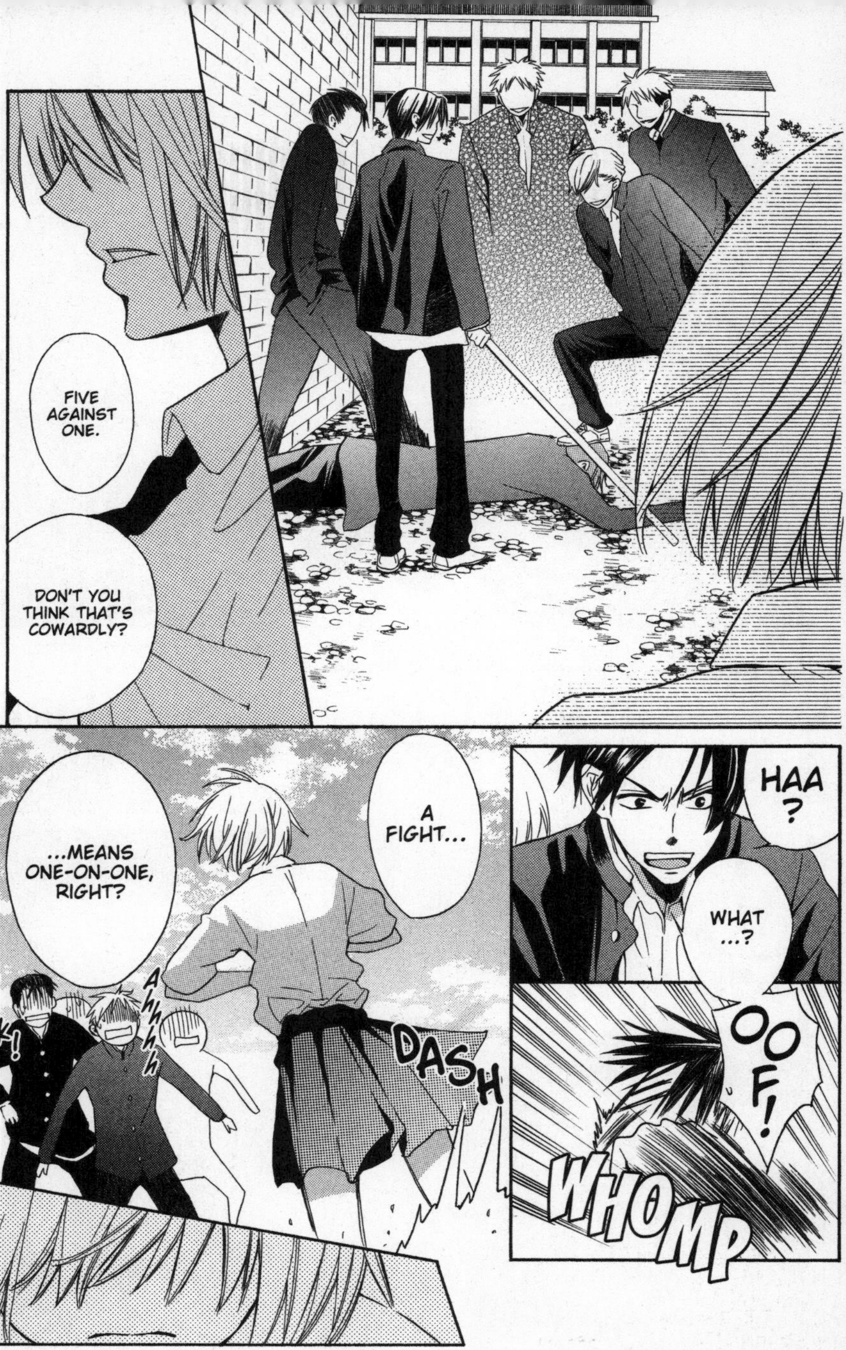
FIVE AGAINST ONE.
DON'T YOU THINK THAT'S COWARDLY?
HAA?
WHAT...?
OOF!
WHOMP
A FIGHT...
...MEANS ONE-ON-ONE, RIGHT?
Eeeek!
Ahhhh
DASH

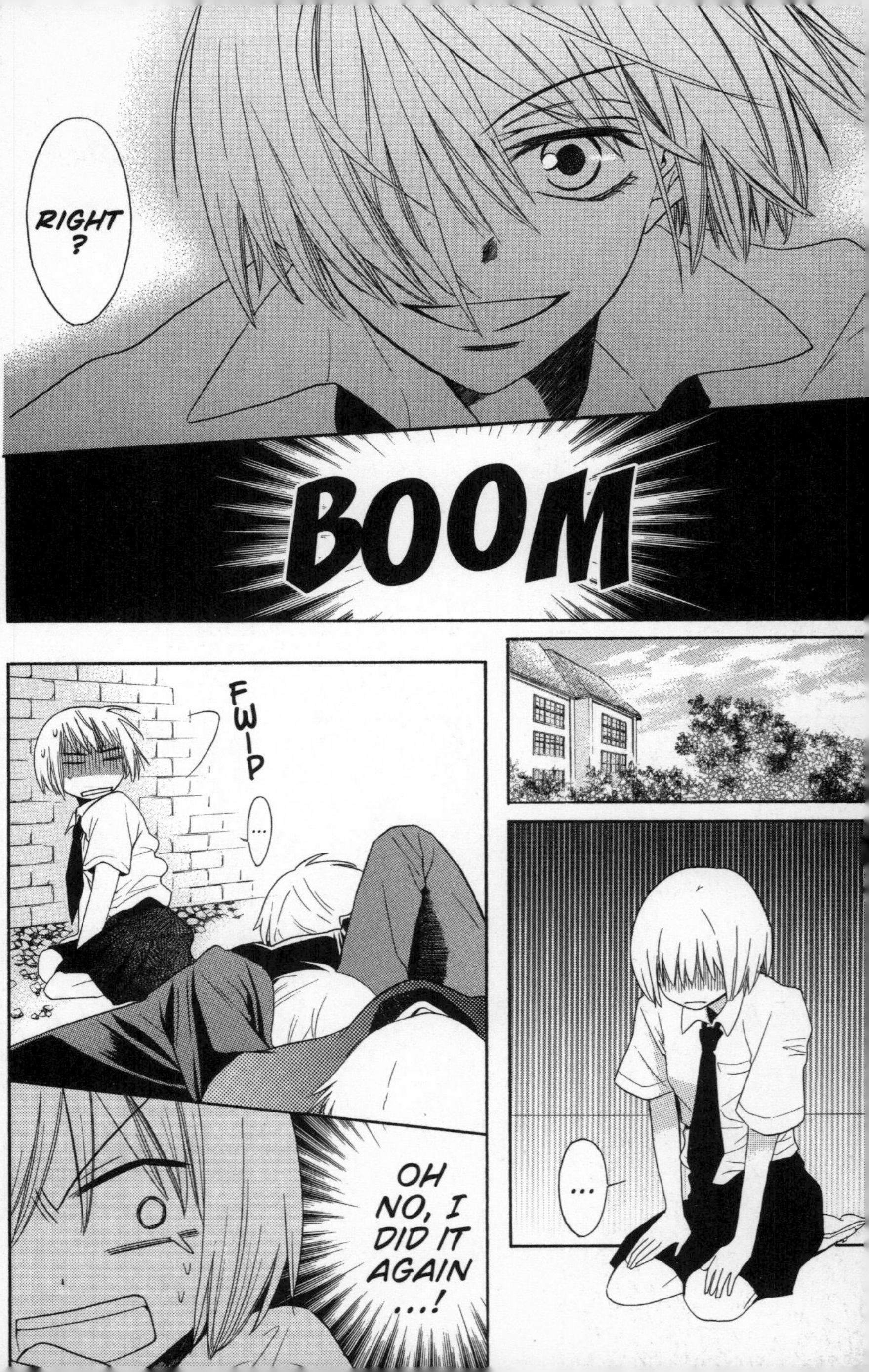
RIGHT?
BOOM
...
FWIP
...
OH NO, I DID IT AGAIN ...!

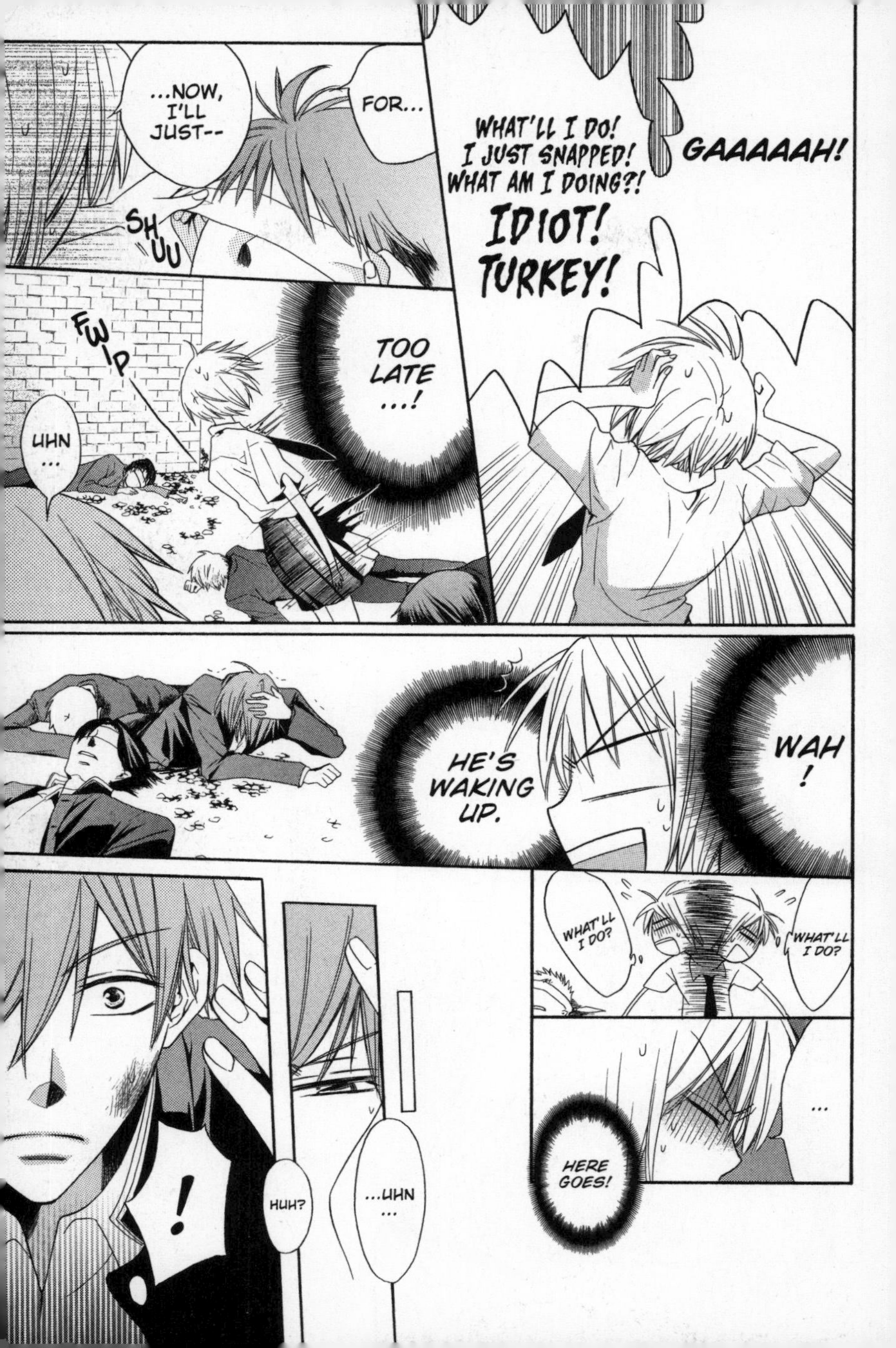
GAAAAAH!
WHAT'LL I DO! I JUST SNAPPED! WHAT AM I DOING?!
IDIOT! TURKEY!
FOR...
...NOW, I'LL JUST--
SHUU
TOO LATE...!
FWIP
UHN...
WAH!
HE'S WAKING UP.
WHAT'LL I DO?
WHAT'LL I DO?
...
HERE GOES!
...UHN...
HUH?
!

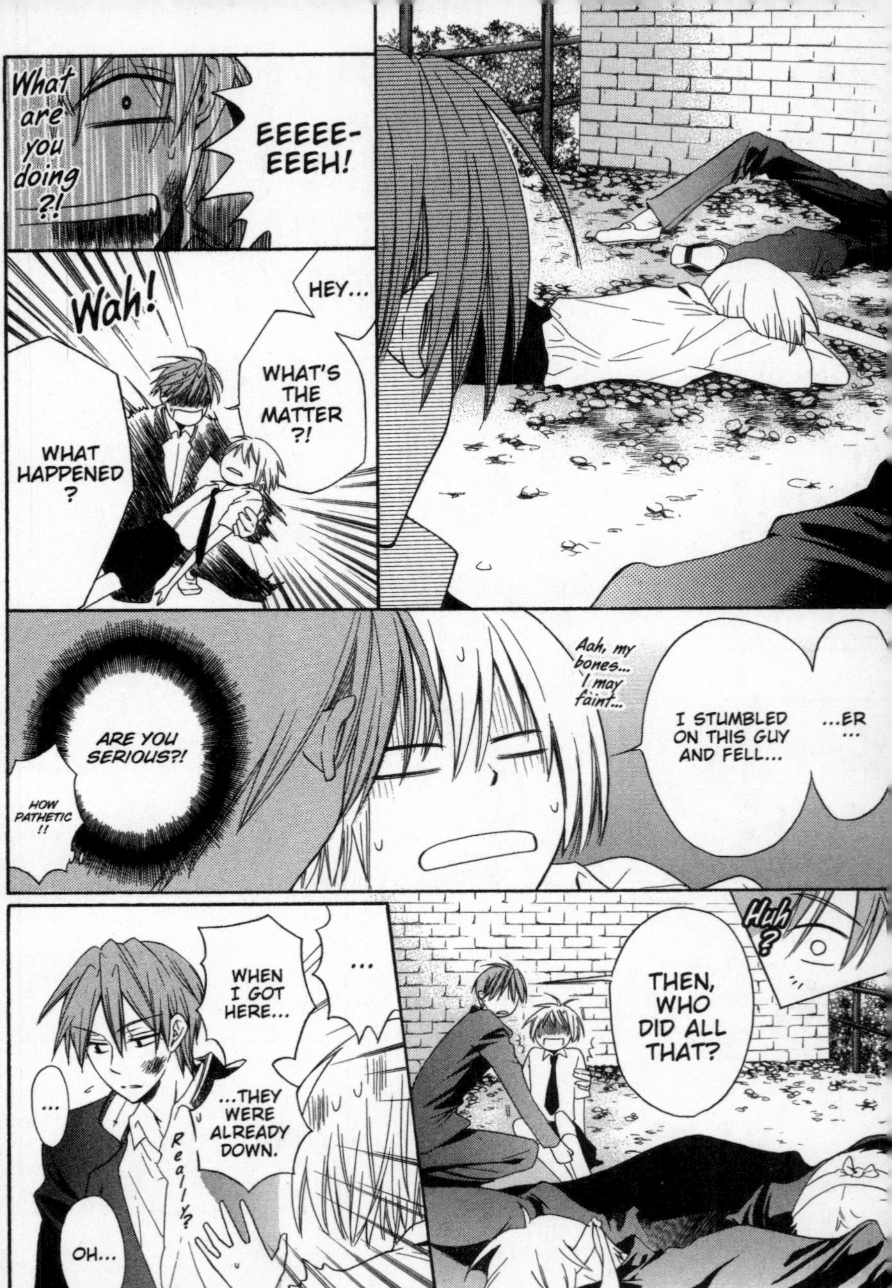
EEEEE-EEEH!
What are you doing?!
HEY...
WHAT'S THE MATTER?!
Wah!
WHAT HAPPENED?
...ER...
I STUMBLED ON THIS GUY AND FELL...
Aah, my bones... I may faint...
ARE YOU SERIOUS?!
HOW PATHETIC!!
Huh?
THEN, WHO DID ALL THAT?
...
WHEN I GOT HERE...
...THEY WERE ALREADY DOWN.
Really?
...
OH...

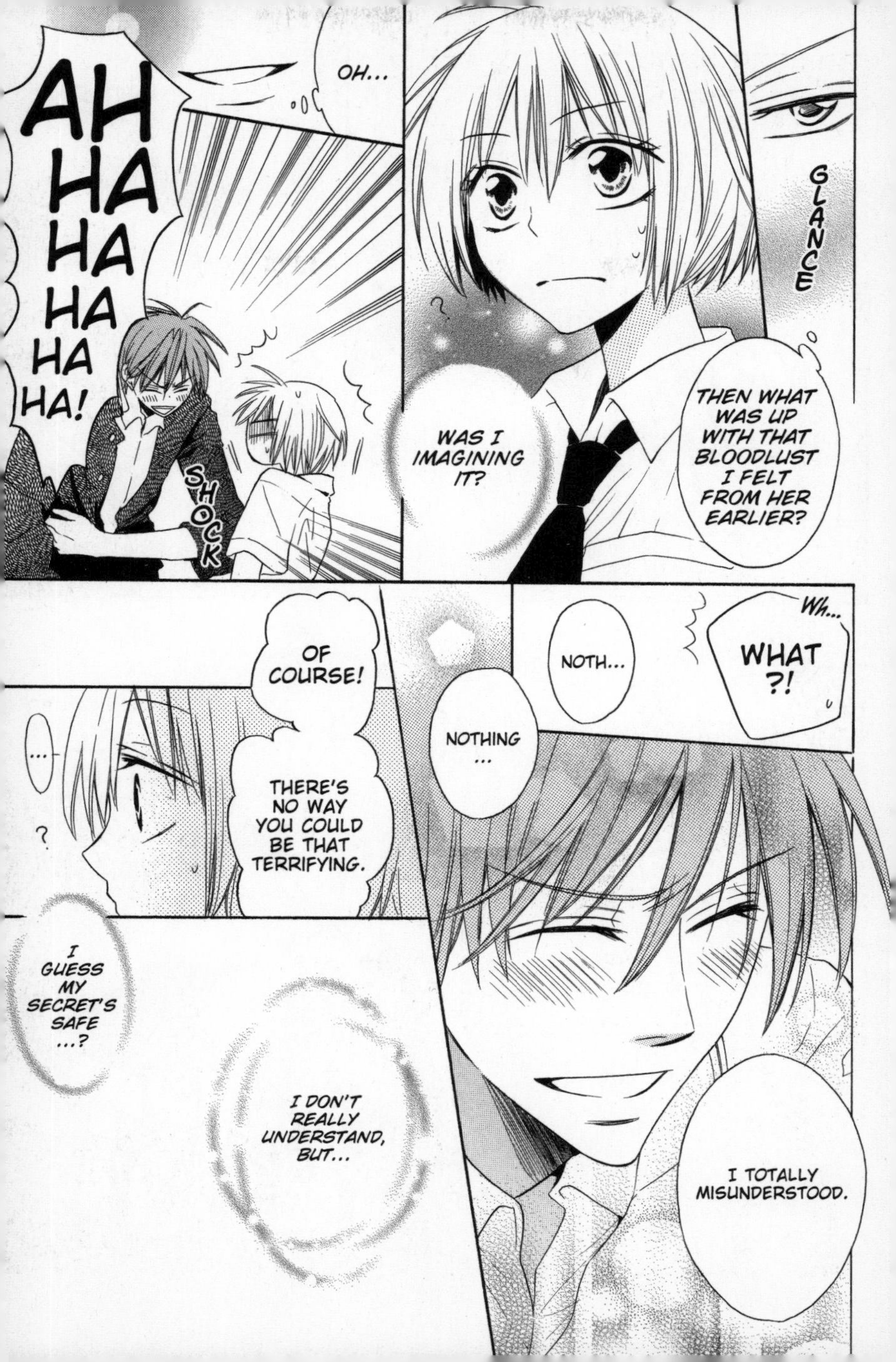
GLANCE
THEN WHAT WAS UP WITH THAT BLOODLUST I FELT FROM HER EARLIER?
WAS I IMAGINING IT?
OH...
AH HA HA HA HA HA!
SHOCK
Wh... WHAT?!
NOTH...
NOTHING ...
OF COURSE!
THERE'S NO WAY YOU COULD BE THAT TERRIFYING.
...
?
I TOTALLY MISUNDERSTOOD.
I GUESS MY SECRET'S SAFE ...?
I DON'T REALLY UNDERSTAND, BUT...

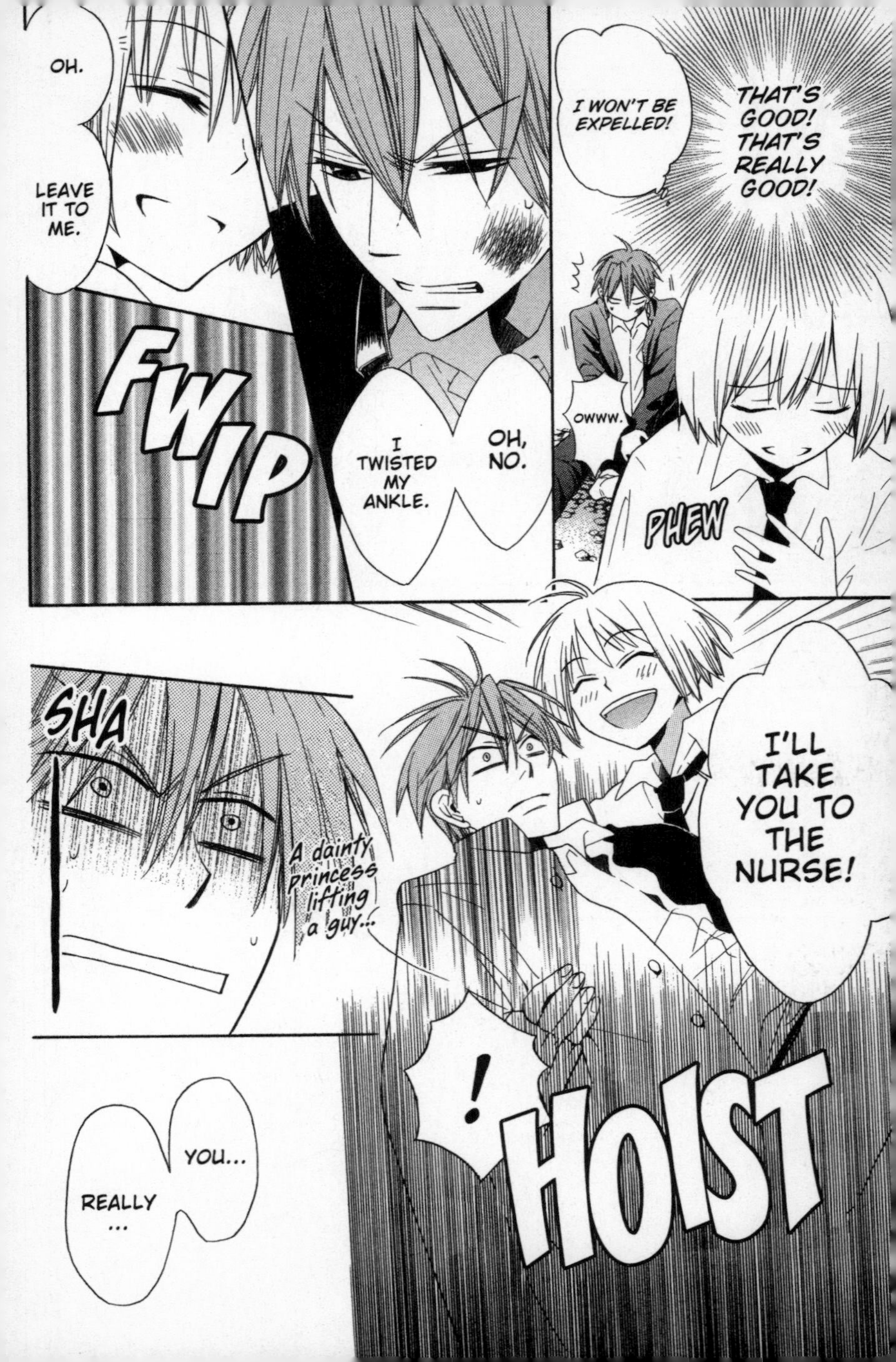
THAT'S GOOD! THAT'S REALLY GOOD!
I WON'T BE EXPELLED!
OWWW.
PHEW
OH, NO.
I TWISTED MY ANKLE.
OH.
LEAVE IT TO ME.
FWIP
I'LL TAKE YOU TO THE NURSE!
!
HOIST
SHA
A dainty princess lifting a guy...
YOU...
REALLY ...

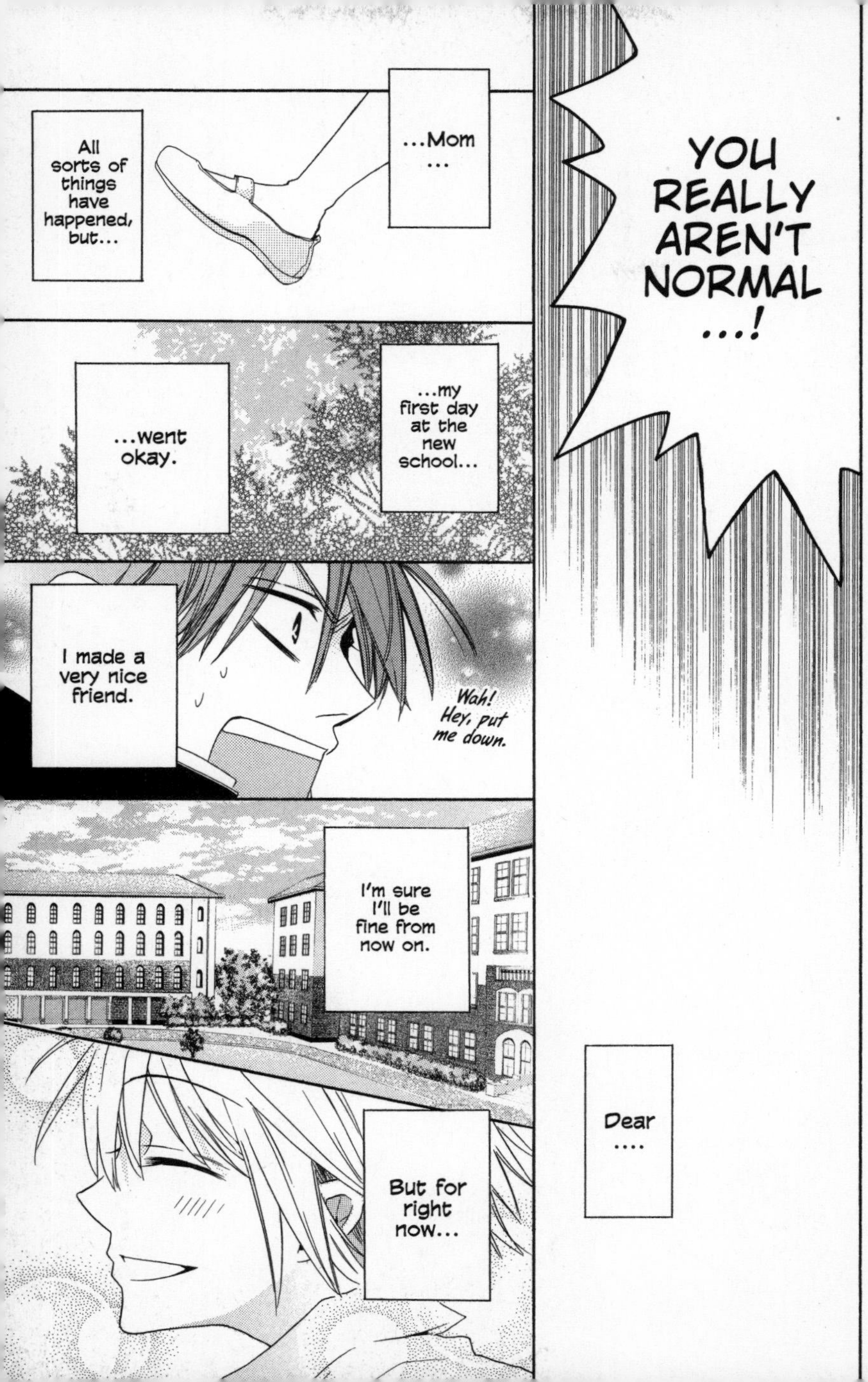
YOU REALLY AREN'T NORMAL ...!
Dear ....
...Mom ...
All sorts of things have happened, but...
...my first day at the new school...
...went okay.
Wah! Hey, put me down.
I made a very nice friend.
I'm sure I'll be fine from now on.
But for right now...

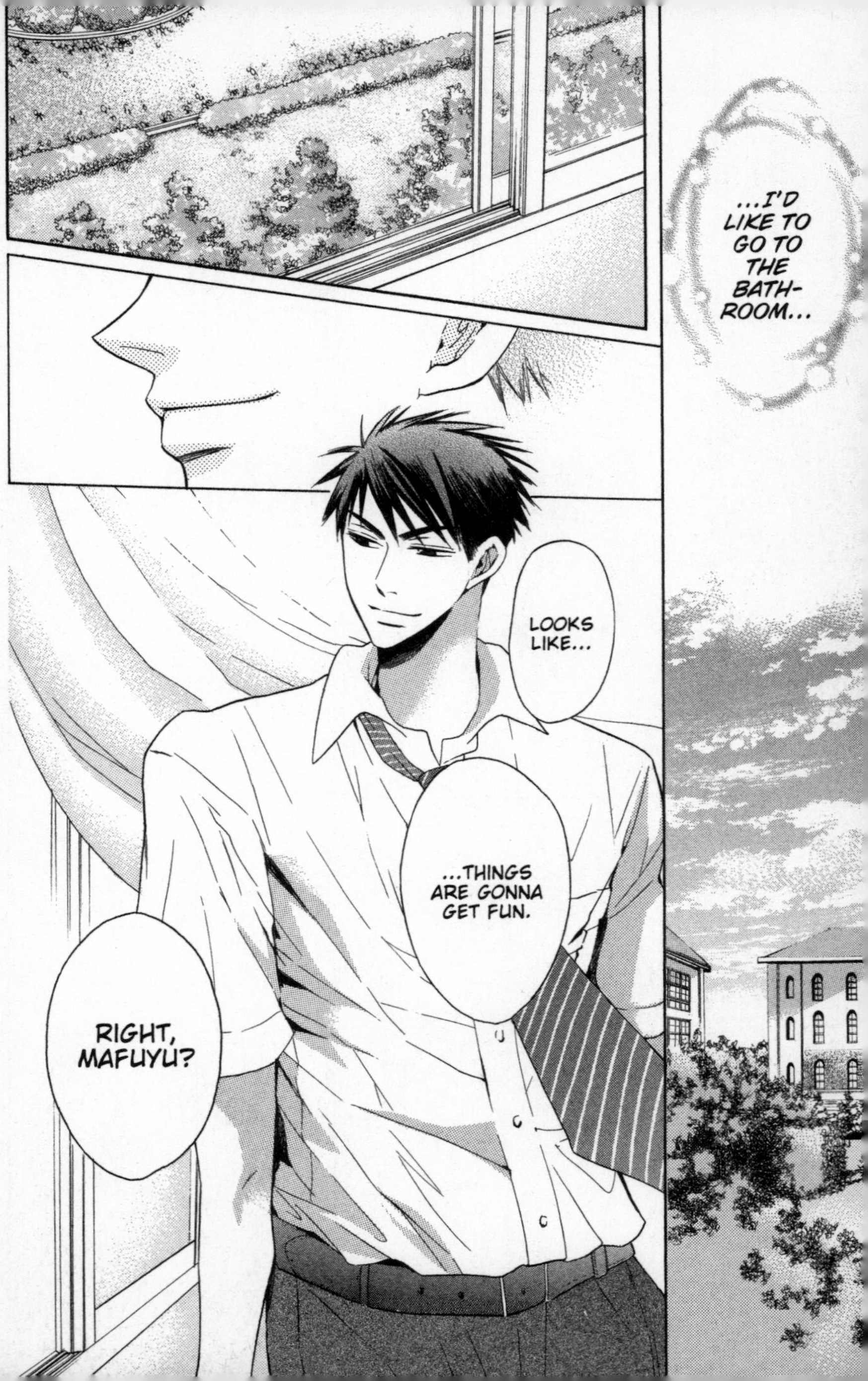
...I'D LIKE TO GO TO THE BATH-ROOM...
LOOKS LIKE...
...THINGS ARE GONNA GET FUN.
RIGHT, MAFUYU?

Chapter 3

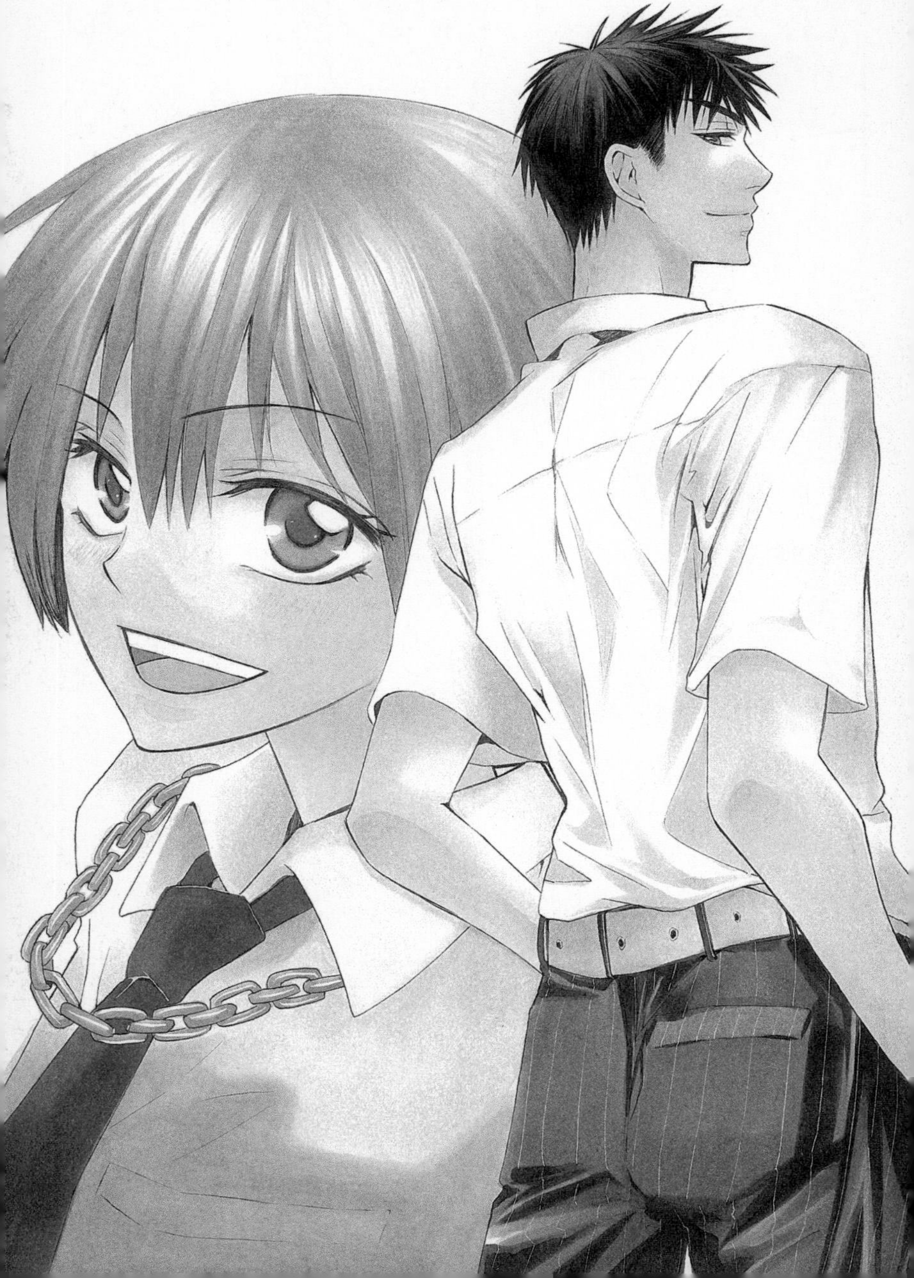

Oresama Teacher: Road to Completion

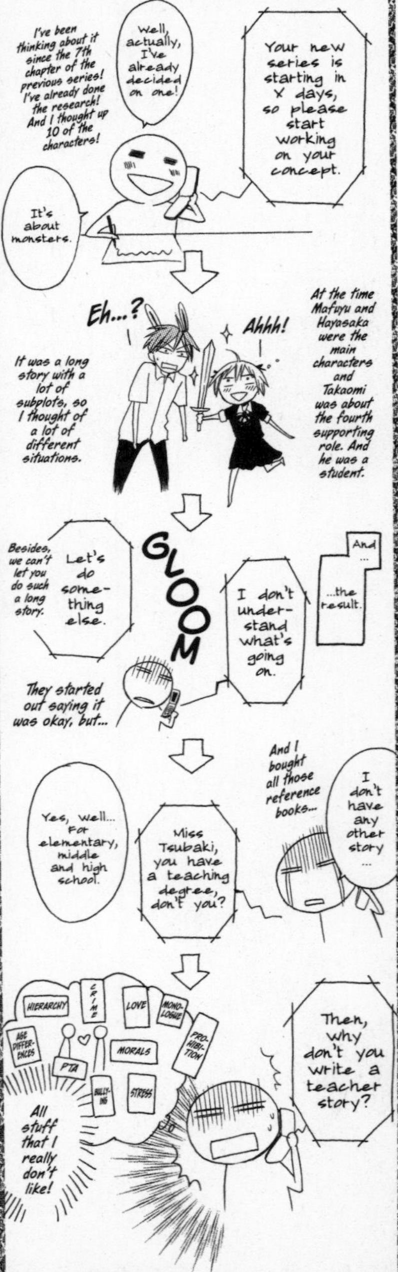

Your new series is starting in X days, so please start working on your concept.
Well, actually, I've already decided on one!
I've been thinking about it since the 7th chapter of the previous series! I've already done the research! And I thought up 10 of the characters!
It's about monsters.
At the time Mafuyu and Hayasaka were the main characters and Takaomi was about the fourth supporting role. And he was a student.
Ahhh!
Eh...?
It was a long story with a lot of subplots, so I thought of a lot of different situations.
And...
...the result.
I don't understand what's going on.
GLOOM
Let's do something else.
Besides, we can't let you do such a long story.
They started out saying it was okay, but...
I don't have any other story...
And I bought all those reference books...
Miss Tsubaki, you have a teaching degree, don't you?
Yes, well... For elementary, middle and high school.
Then, why don't you write a teacher story?
HIERARCHY
CRIME
LOVE
MONOLOGUE
AGE DIFFERENCES
PTA
MORALS
PROHIBITION
BULLYING
STRESS
All stuff that I really don't like!

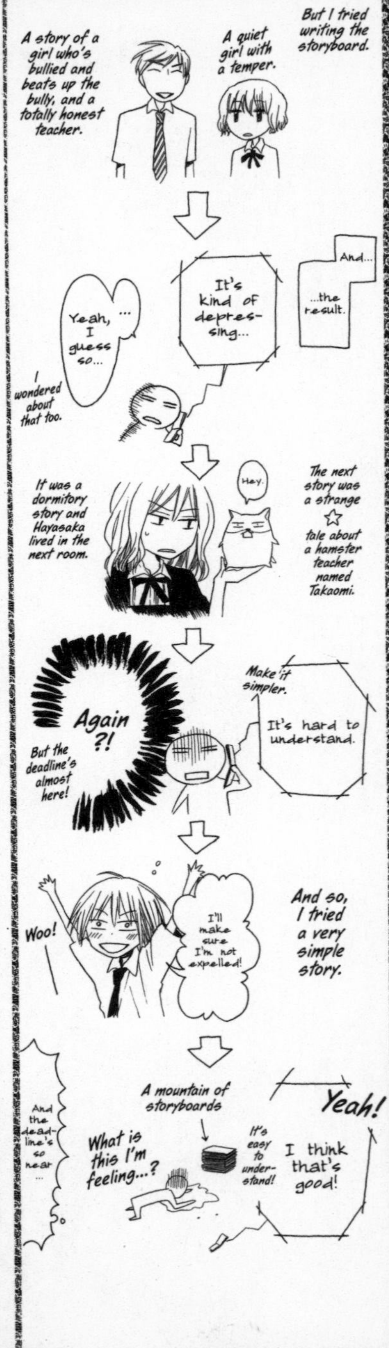

But I tried writing the storyboard.
A quiet girl with a temper.
A story of a girl who's bullied and beats up the bully, and a totally honest teacher.
And...
...the result.
It's kind of depressing...
...
Yeah, I guess so...
I wondered about that too.
The next story was a strange ☆ tale about a hamster teacher named Takaomi.
Hey.
It was a dormitory story and Hayasaka lived in the next room.
Make it simpler.
It's hard to understand.
Again?!
But the deadline's almost here!
And so, I tried a very simple story.
I'll make sure I'm not expelled!
Woo!
Yeah!
I think that's good!
It's easy to understand!
A mountain of storyboards
What is this I'm feeling...?
And the deadline's so near...

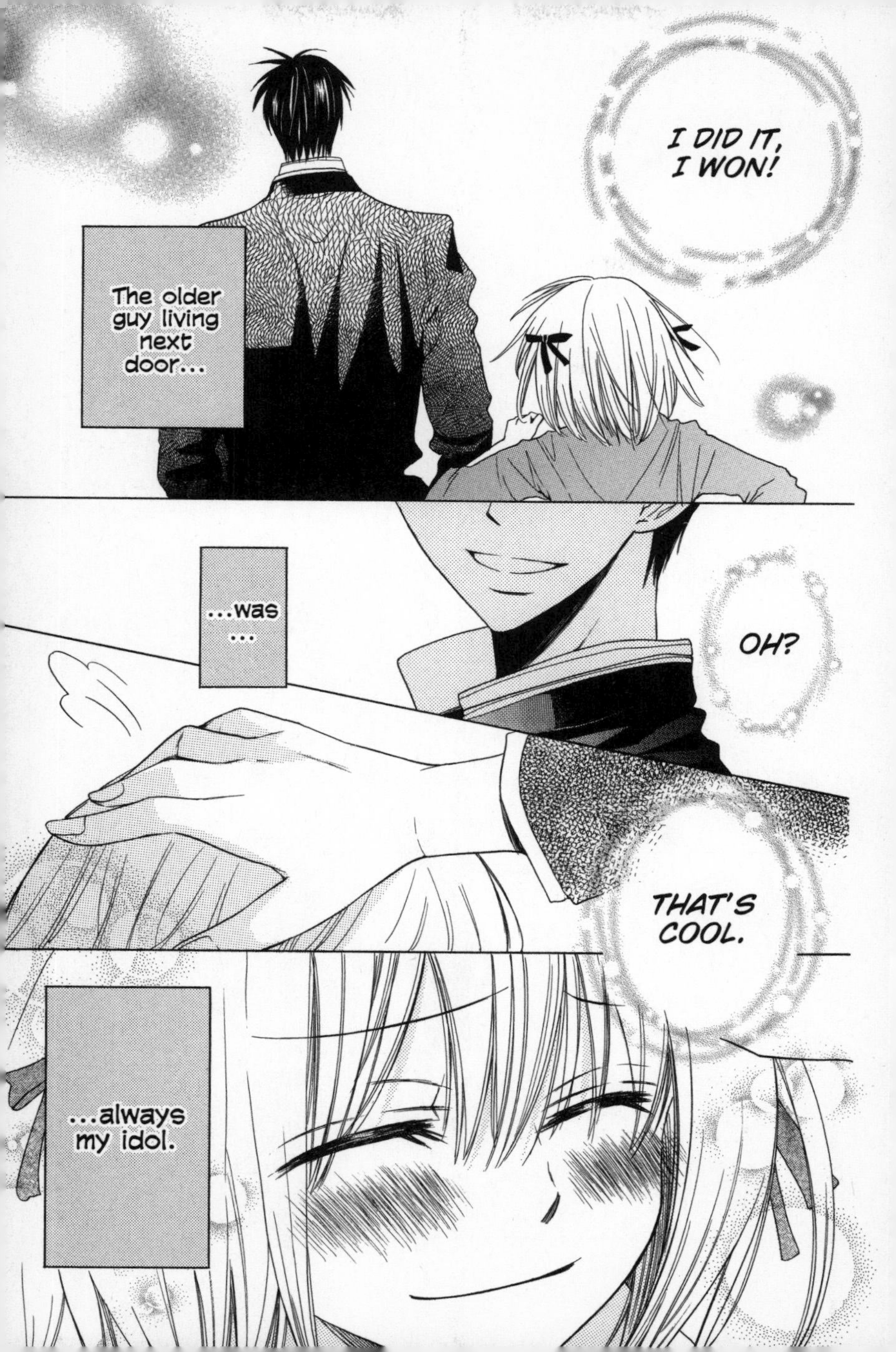
I DID IT, I WON!
The older guy living next door...
OH?
...was...
THAT'S COOL.
...always my idol.

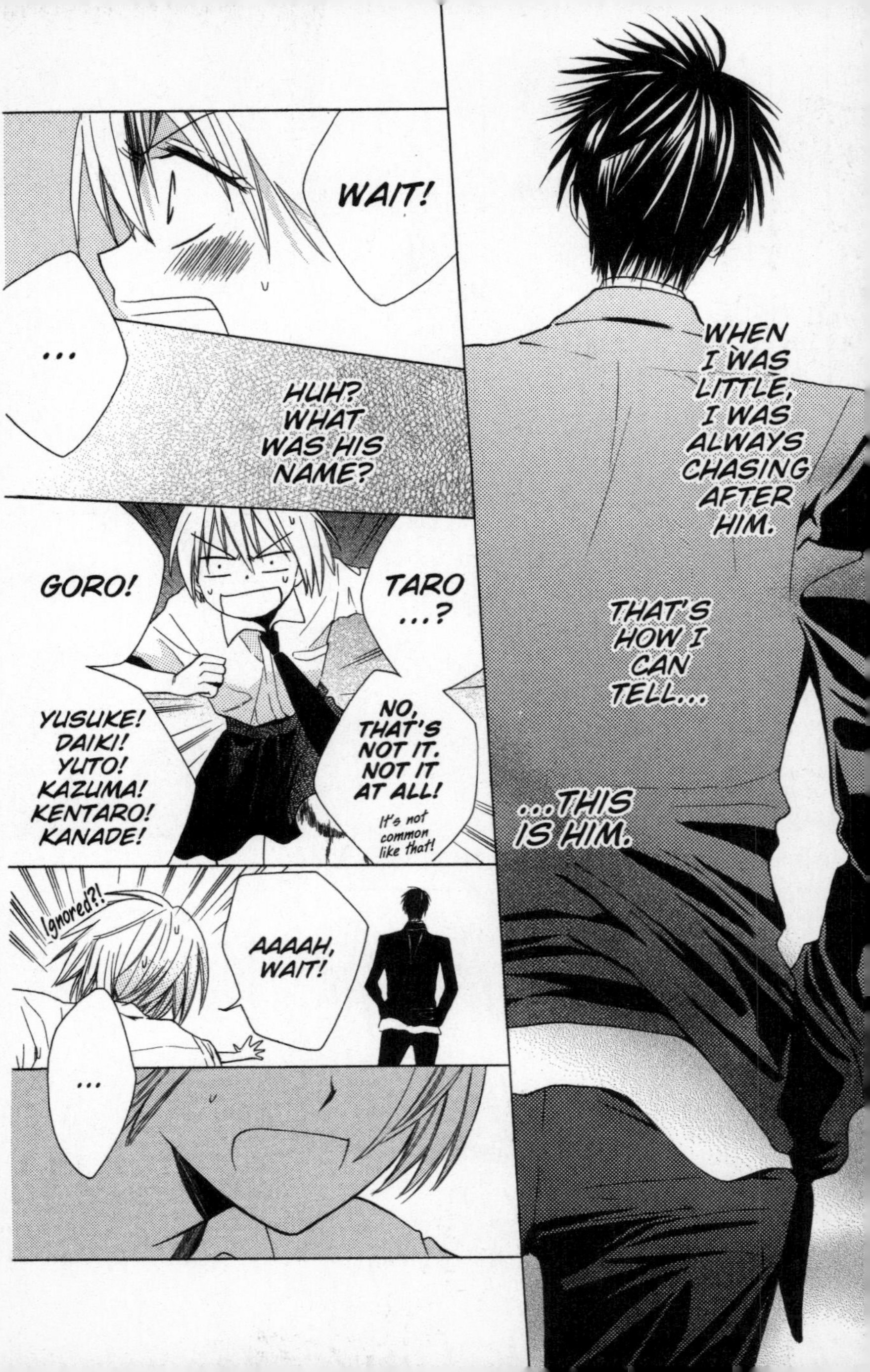
WHEN I WAS LITTLE, I WAS ALWAYS CHASING AFTER HIM.
THAT'S HOW I CAN TELL...
...THIS IS HIM.
WAIT!
...
HUH? WHAT WAS HIS NAME?
TARO ...?
GORO!
NO, THAT'S NOT IT. NOT IT AT ALL!
It's not common like that!
YUSUKE! DAIKI! YUTO! KAZUMA! KENTARO! KANADE!
AAAAH, WAIT!
Ignored?!
...

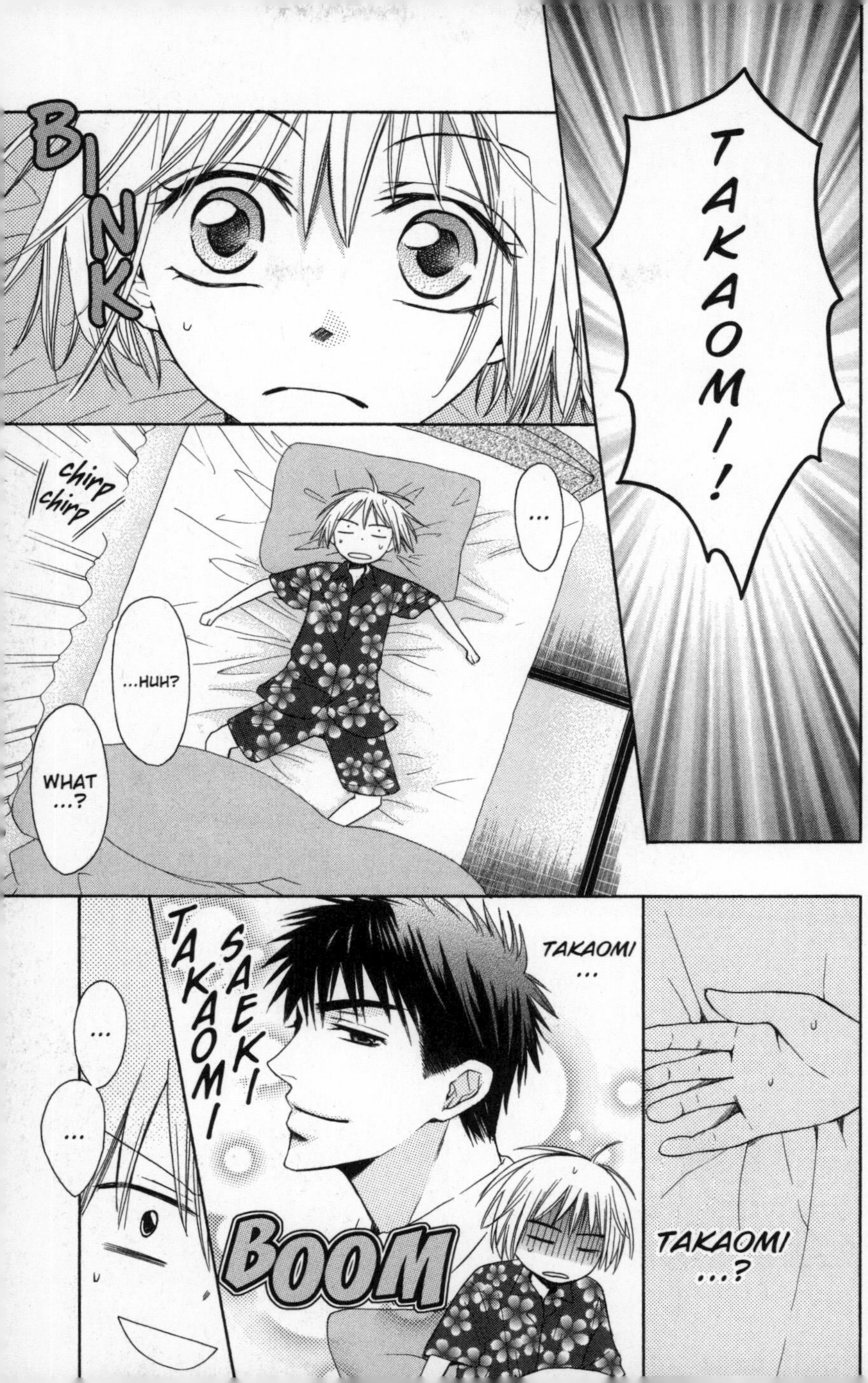
TAKAOMI!!
BLINK
...
chirp chirp
...HUH?
WHAT ...?
TAKAOMI ...?
TAKAOMI ...
SAEKI TAKAOMI
BOOM
...
...

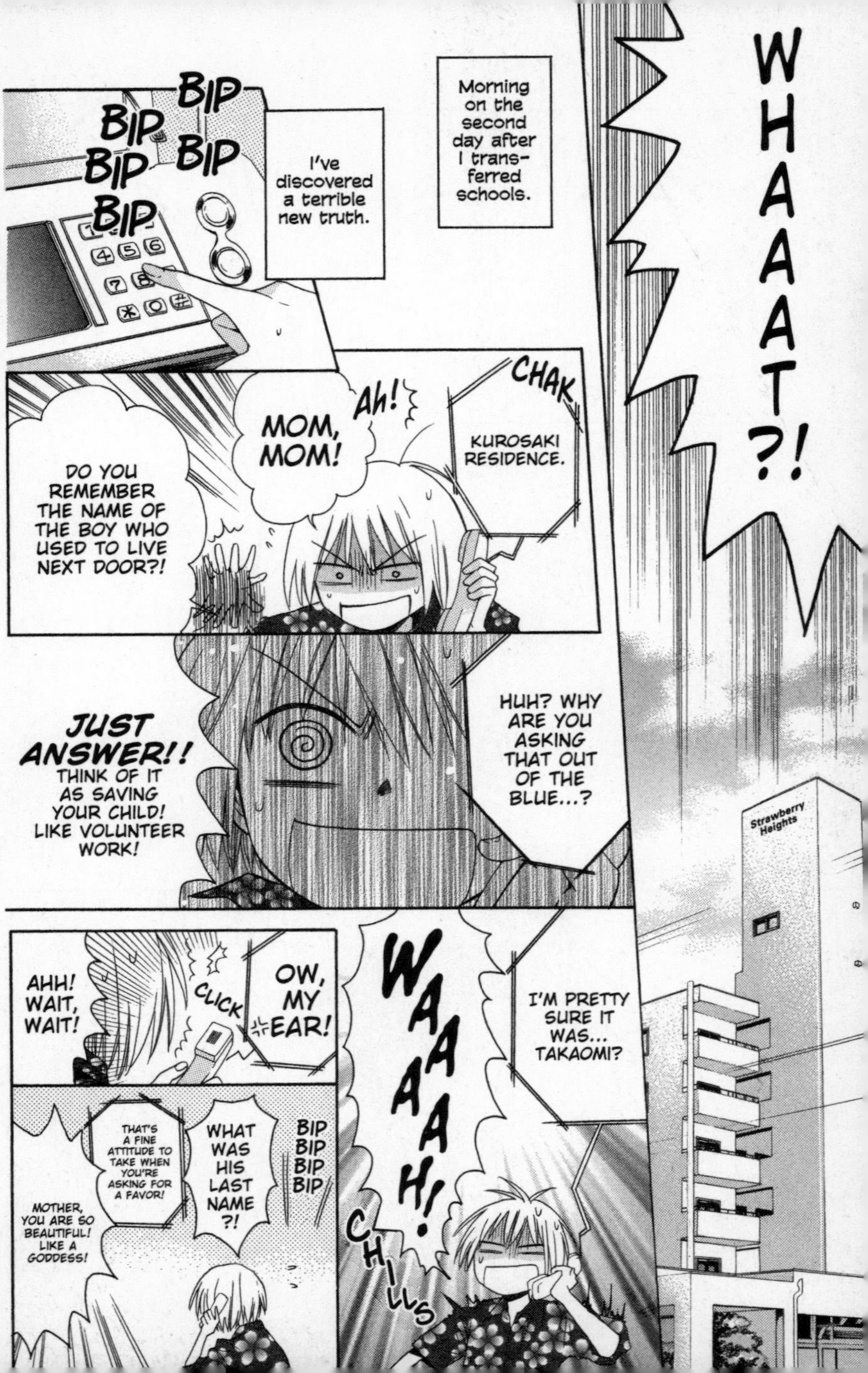
WHAAAT?!
Strawberry Heights
Morning on the second day after I transferred schools.
I've discovered a terrible new truth.
BIP BIP BIP BIP BIP
CHAK
KUROSAKI RESIDENCE.
Ah!
MOM, MOM!
DO YOU REMEMBER THE NAME OF THE BOY WHO USED TO LIVE NEXT DOOR?!
HUH? WHY ARE YOU ASKING THAT OUT OF THE BLUE...?
JUST ANSWER!!
THINK OF IT AS SAVING YOUR CHILD! LIKE VOLUNTEER WORK!
I'M PRETTY SURE IT WAS... TAKAOMI?
WAAAAAH!
CHILLS
OW, MY EAR!
CLICK
AHH! WAIT, WAIT!
BIP BIP BIP BIP
WHAT WAS HIS LAST NAME?!
THAT'S A FINE ATTITUDE TO TAKE WHEN YOU'RE ASKING FOR A FAVOR!
MOTHER, YOU ARE SO BEAUTIFUL! LIKE A GODDESS!

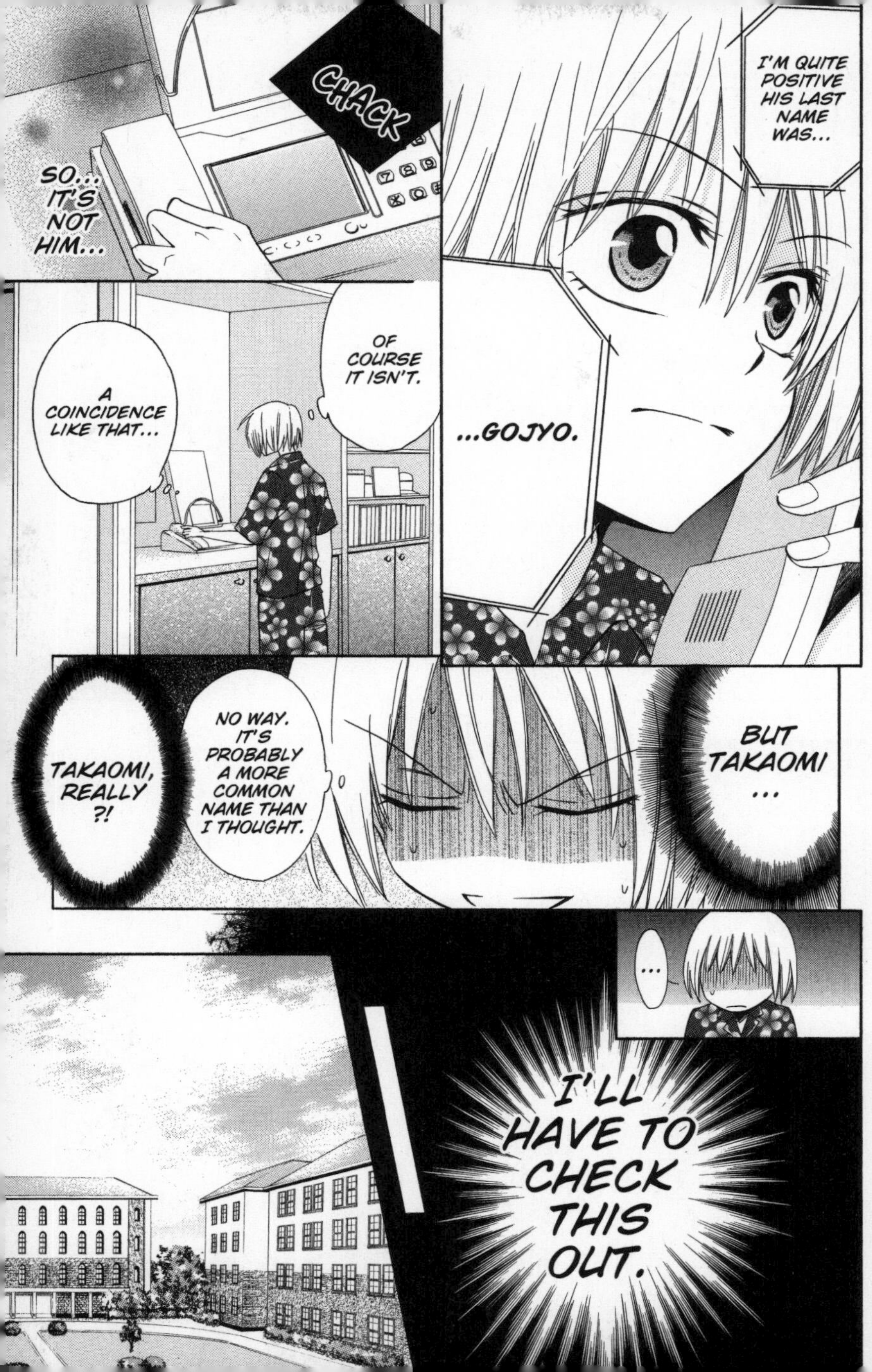
I'M QUITE POSITIVE HIS LAST NAME WAS...
...GOJYO.
CHACK
SO... IT'S NOT HIM...
OF COURSE IT ISN'T.
A COINCIDENCE LIKE THAT...
BUT TAKAOMI...
NO WAY. IT'S PROBABLY A MORE COMMON NAME THAN I THOUGHT.
TAKAOMI, REALLY?!
...
I'LL HAVE TO CHECK THIS OUT.

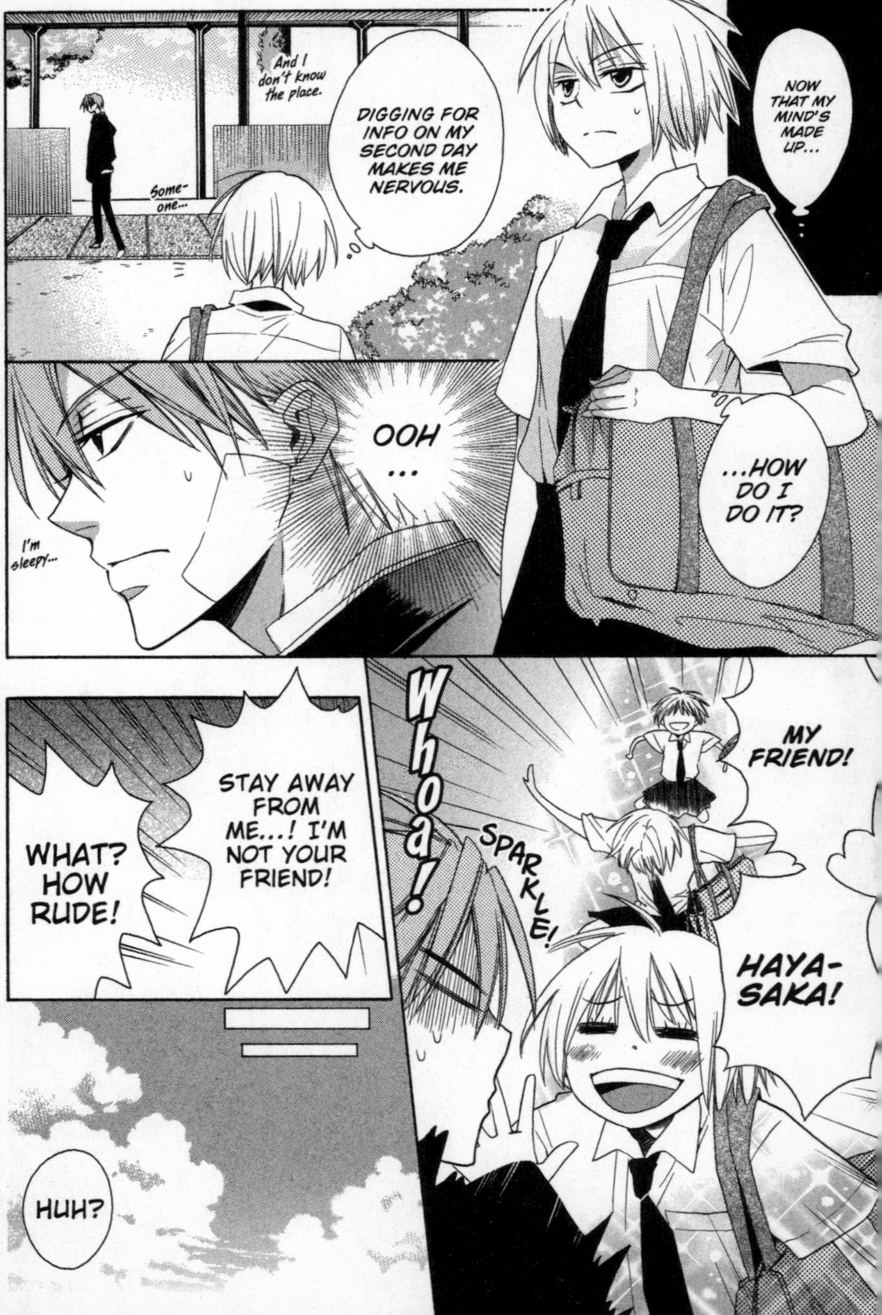
NOW THAT MY MIND'S MADE UP...
...HOW DO I DO IT?
DIGGING FOR INFO ON MY SECOND DAY MAKES ME NERVOUS.
And I don't know the place.
Some-one...
OOH ...
I'm sleepy...
MY FRIEND!
Whoa!
SPARKLE!
HAYA-SAKA!
STAY AWAY FROM ME...! I'M NOT YOUR FRIEND!
WHAT? HOW RUDE!
HUH?

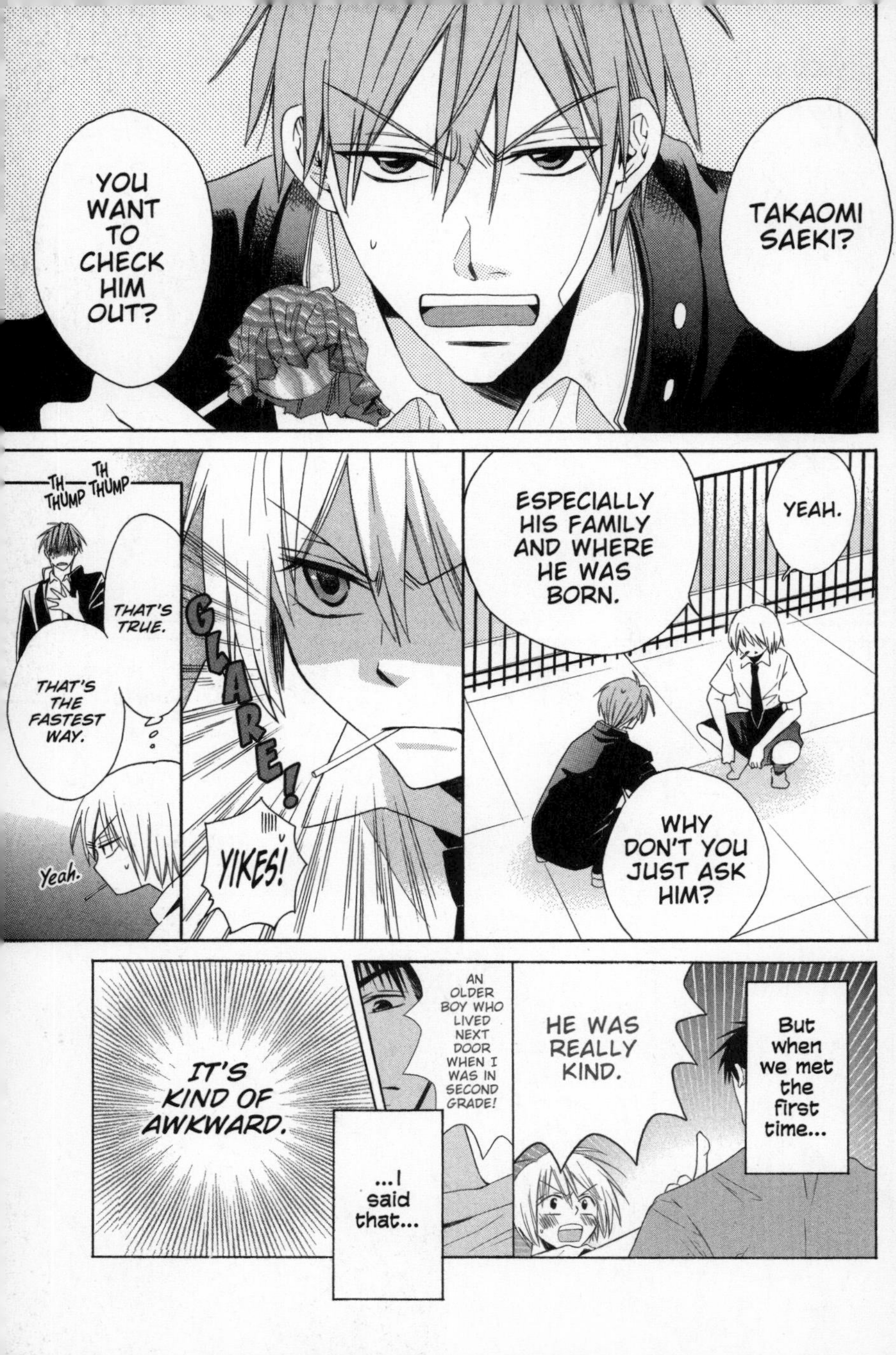
TAKAOMI SAEKI?
YOU WANT TO CHECK HIM OUT?
YEAH.
ESPECIALLY HIS FAMILY AND WHERE HE WAS BORN.
WHY DON'T YOU JUST ASK HIM?
GLARE!
YIKES!
TH THUMP TH THUMP
THAT'S TRUE.
THAT'S THE FASTEST WAY.
Yeah.
But when we met the first time...
HE WAS REALLY KIND.
AN OLDER BOY WHO LIVED NEXT DOOR WHEN I WAS IN SECOND GRADE!
...I said that...
IT'S KIND OF AWKWARD.

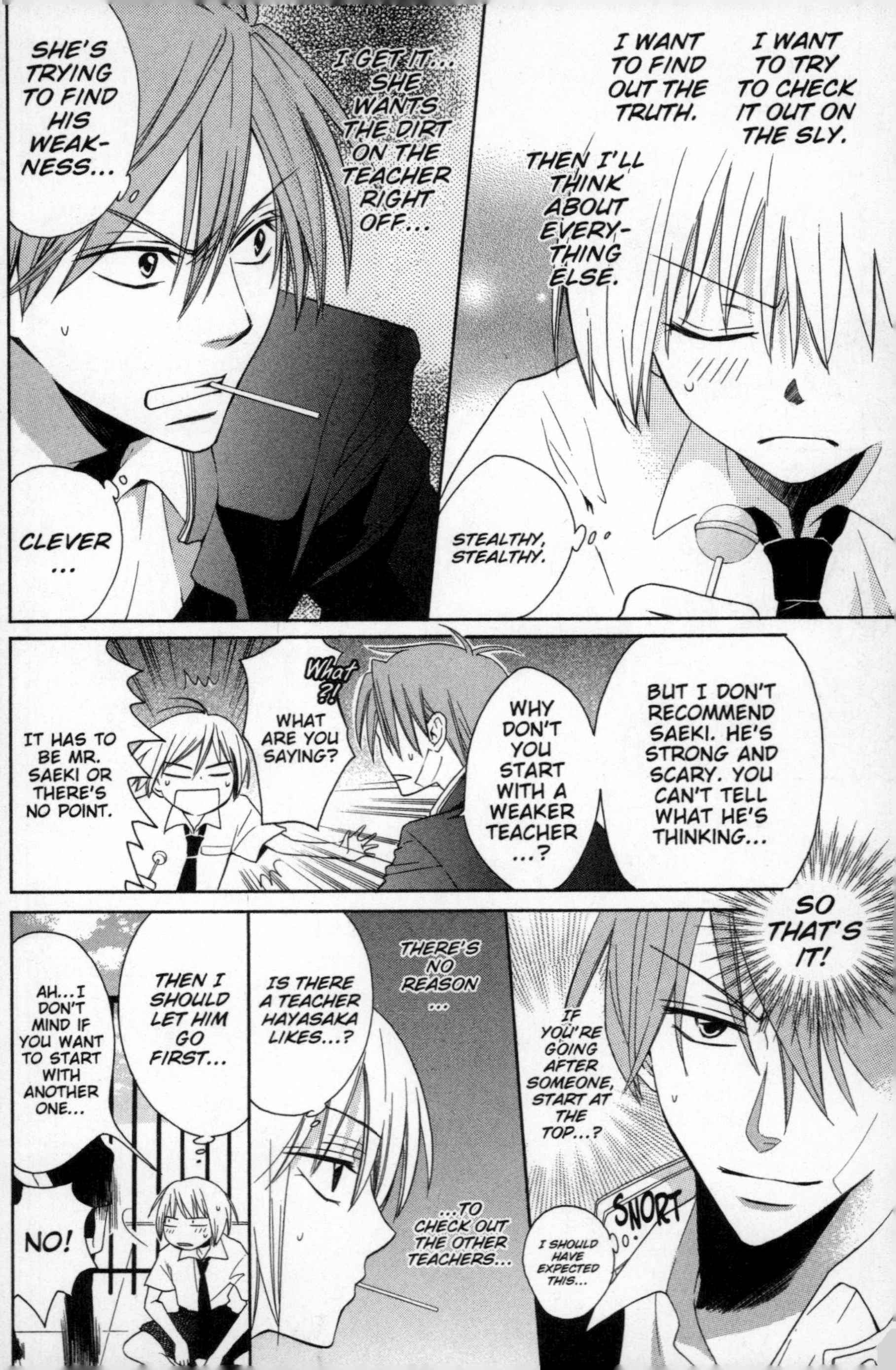
I WANT TO TRY TO CHECK IT OUT ON THE SLY.
I WANT TO FIND OUT THE TRUTH.
THEN I'LL THINK ABOUT EVERYTHING ELSE.
STEALTHY, STEALTHY.
I GET IT... SHE WANTS THE DIRT ON THE TEACHER RIGHT OFF...
SHE'S TRYING TO FIND HIS WEAKNESS...
CLEVER...
BUT I DON'T RECOMMEND SAEKI. HE'S STRONG AND SCARY. YOU CAN'T TELL WHAT HE'S THINKING...
WHY DON'T YOU START WITH A WEAKER TEACHER...?
What?!
WHAT ARE YOU SAYING?
IT HAS TO BE MR. SAEKI OR THERE'S NO POINT.
SO THAT'S IT!
IF YOU'RE GOING AFTER SOMEONE, START AT THE TOP...?
SNORT
I SHOULD HAVE EXPECTED THIS...
THERE'S NO REASON...
...TO CHECK OUT THE OTHER TEACHERS...
IS THERE A TEACHER HAYASAKA LIKES...?
THEN I SHOULD LET HIM GO FIRST...
AH...I DON'T MIND IF YOU WANT TO START WITH ANOTHER ONE...
NO!

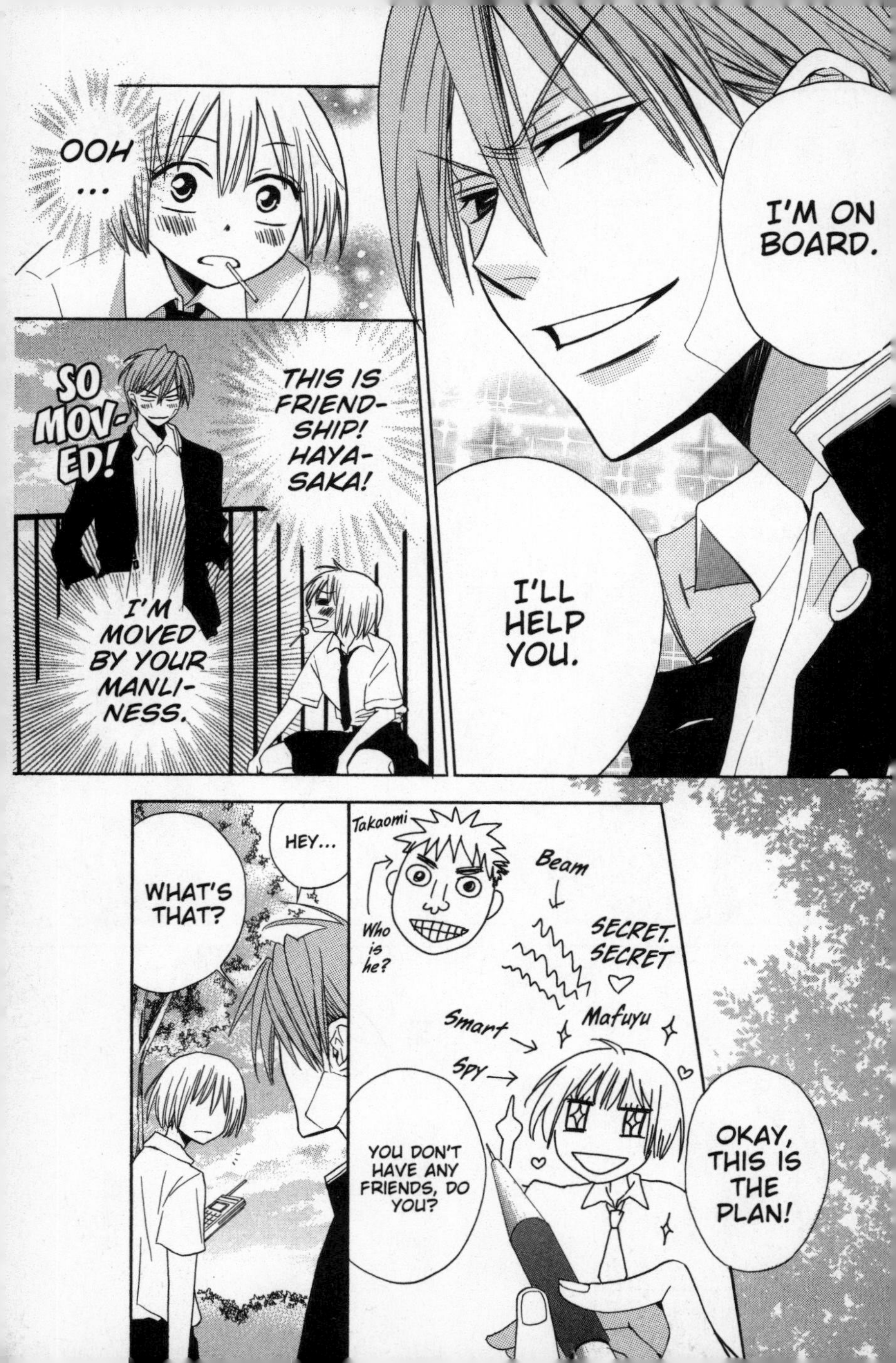
I'M ON BOARD.
I'LL HELP YOU.
OOH ...
THIS IS FRIEND-SHIP! HAYA-SAKA!
SO MOV-ED!
I'M MOVED BY YOUR MANLI-NESS.
OKAY, THIS IS THE PLAN!
Takaomi
Who is he?
Beam
SECRET. SECRET
Mafuyu
Smart
Spy
YOU DON'T HAVE ANY FRIENDS, DO YOU?
HEY...
WHAT'S THAT?

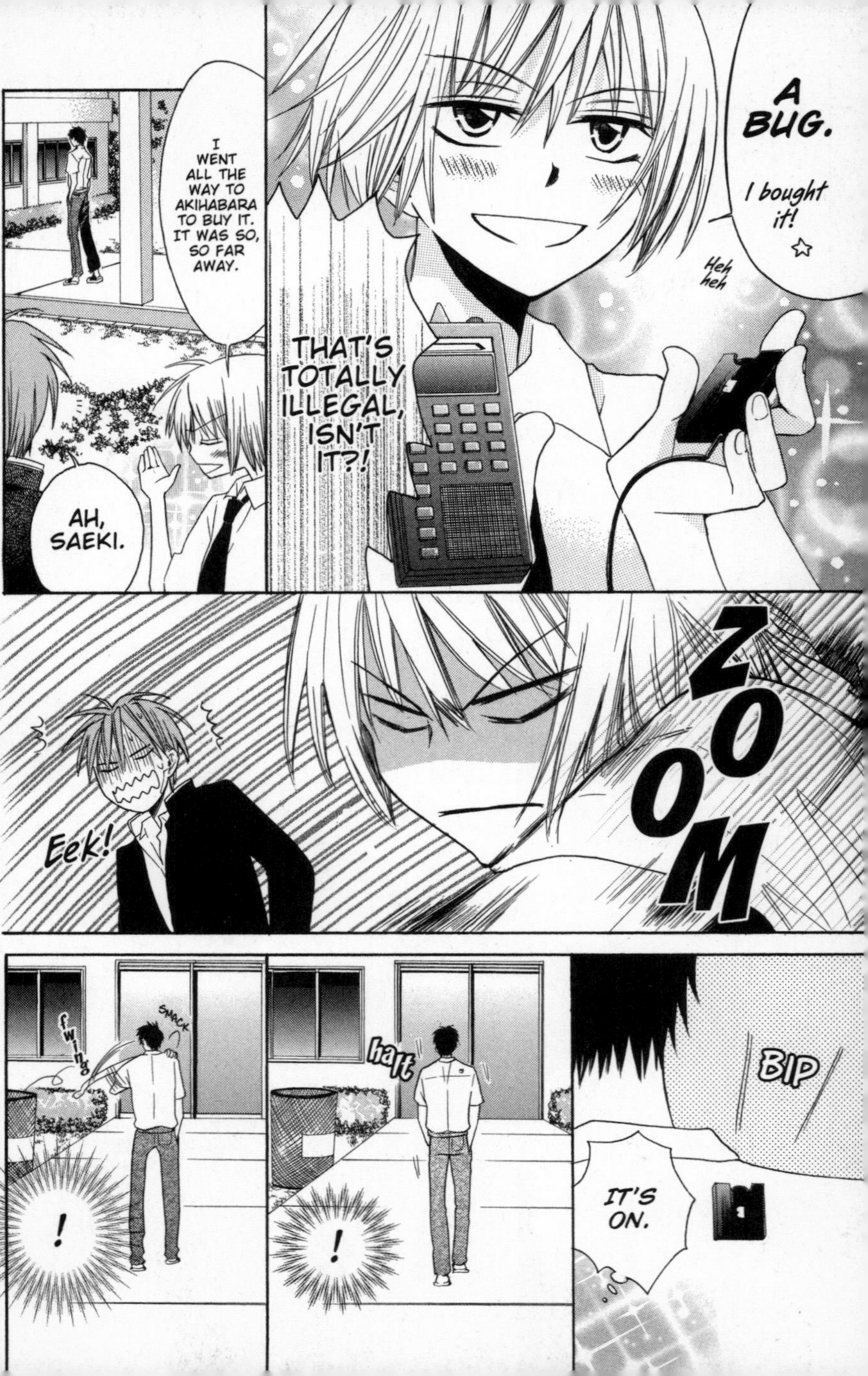
A BUG.
I bought it! ☆
Heh heh
THAT'S TOTALLY ILLEGAL, ISN'T IT?!
I WENT ALL THE WAY TO AKIHABARA TO BUY IT. IT WAS SO, SO FAR AWAY.
AH, SAEKI.
ZOOM
Eek!
BIP
IT'S ON.
halt
!
SMACK
fwing
!

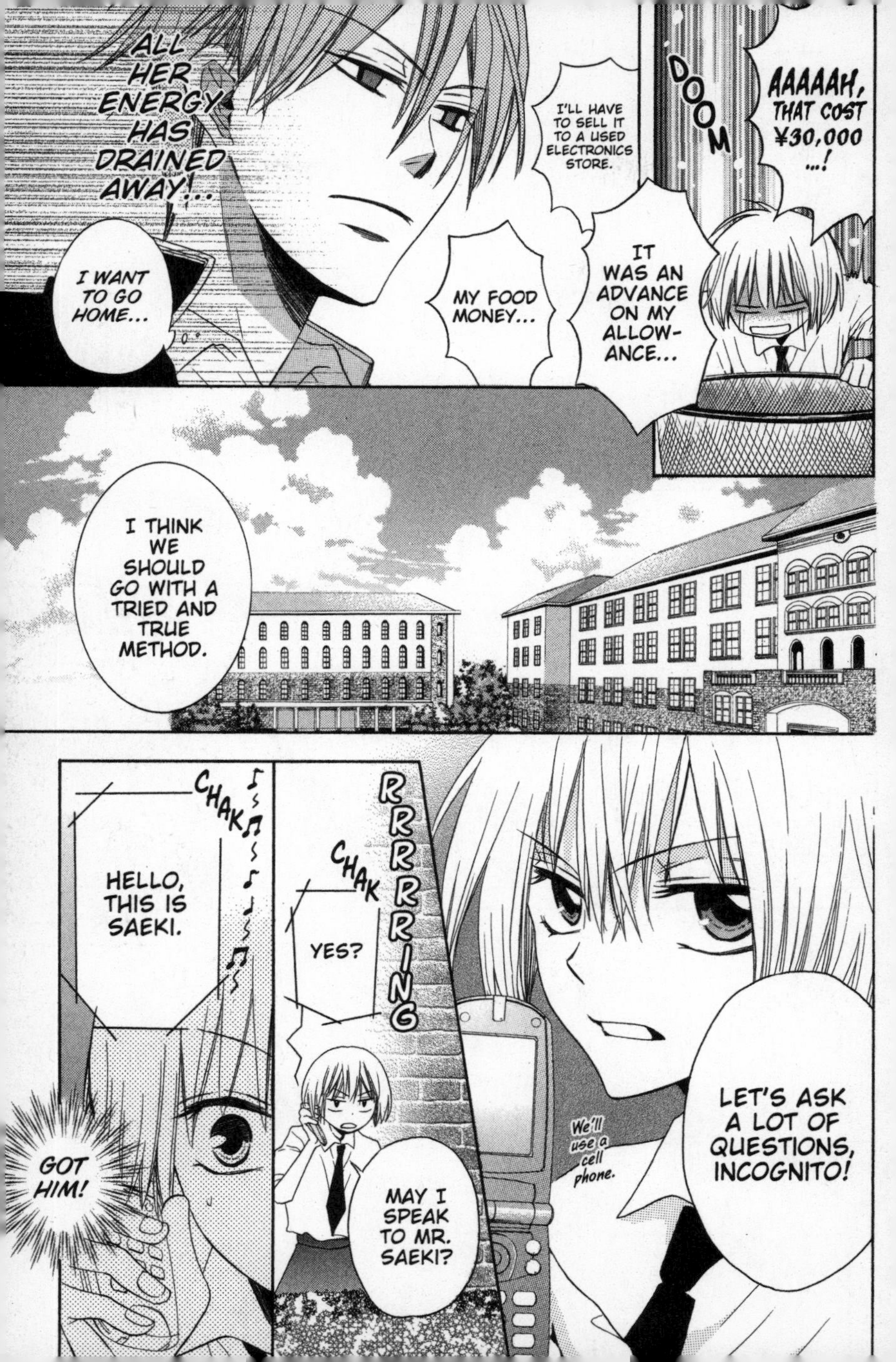
AAAAAH, THAT COST ¥30,000 ...!
DOOM
IT WAS AN ADVANCE ON MY ALLOWANCE...
I'LL HAVE TO SELL IT TO A USED ELECTRONICS STORE.
MY FOOD MONEY...
ALL HER ENERGY HAS DRAINED AWAY!...
I WANT TO GO HOME...
I THINK WE SHOULD GO WITH A TRIED AND TRUE METHOD.
LET'S ASK A LOT OF QUESTIONS, INCOGNITO!
We'll use a cell phone.
RRRRRING
CHAK
YES?
MAY I SPEAK TO MR. SAEKI?
CHAK
HELLO, THIS IS SAEKI.
GOT HIM!

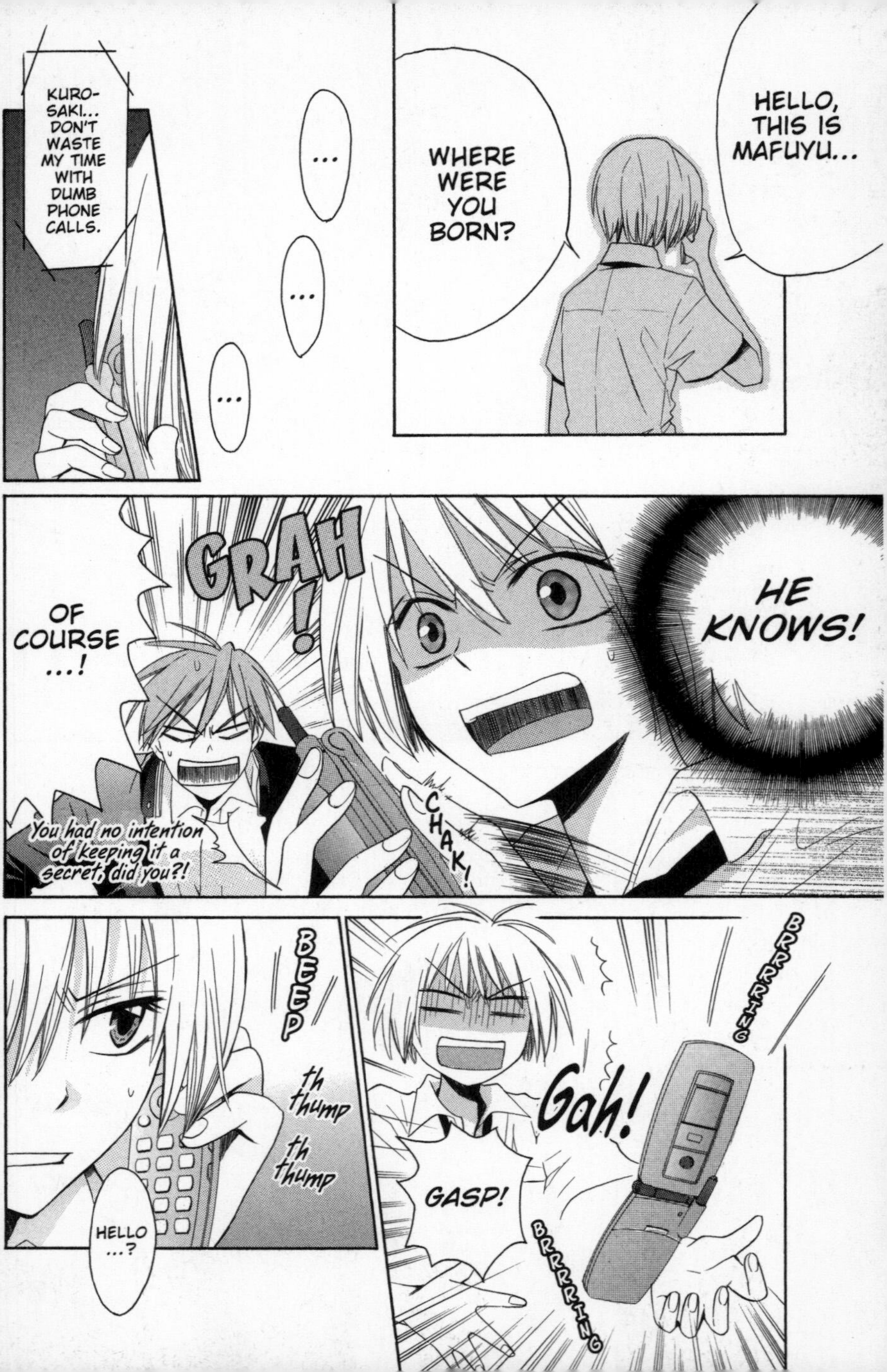
HELLO, THIS IS MAFUYU...
WHERE WERE YOU BORN?
...
...
...
KURO-SAKI... DON'T WASTE MY TIME WITH DUMB PHONE CALLS.
HE KNOWS!
GRAH!
OF COURSE ...!
CHAK!
You had no intention of keeping it a secret, did you?!
BRRRRING
Gah!
GASP!
BRRRRING
BEEEP
th thump
th thump
HELLO ...?

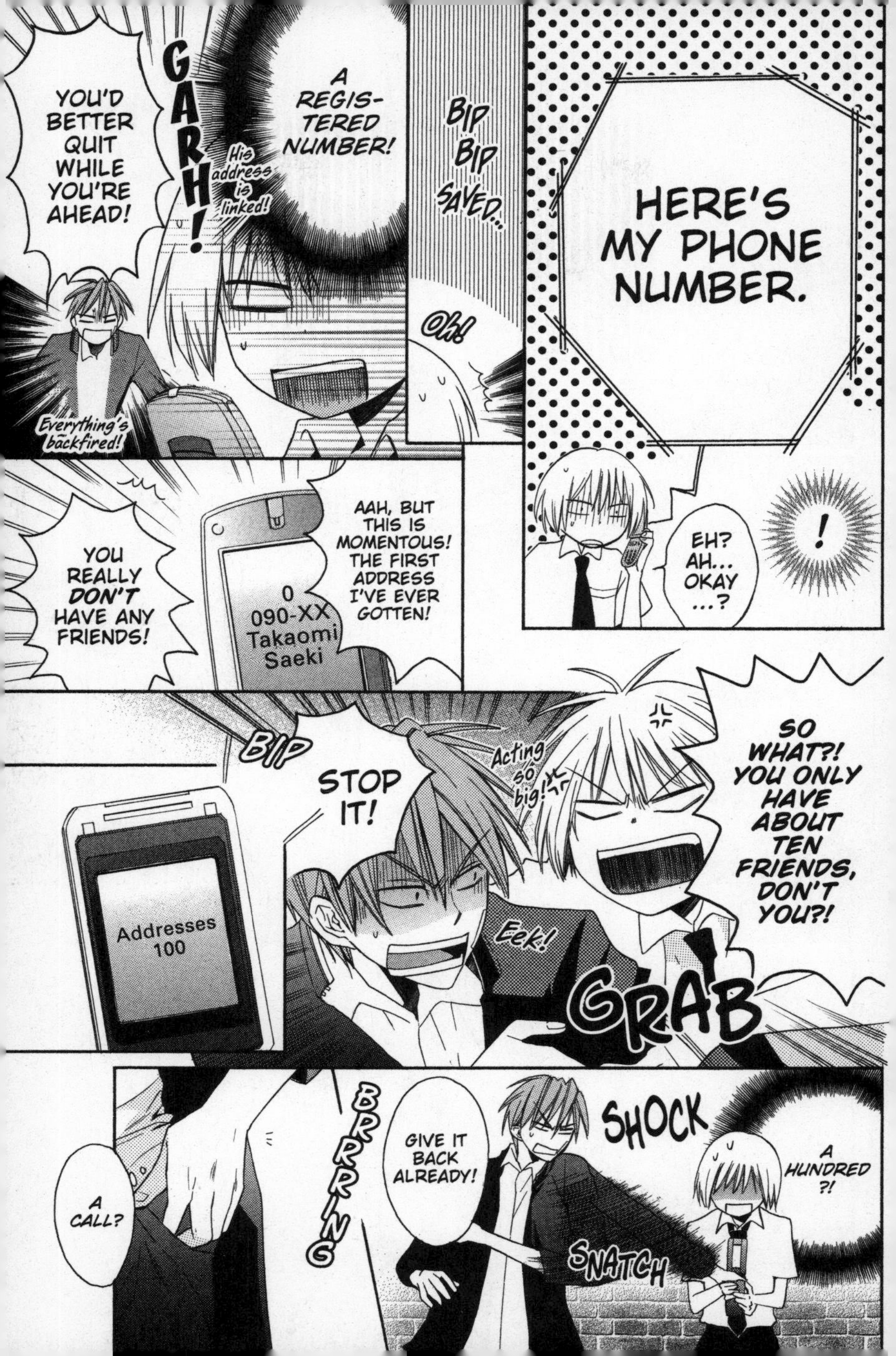
HERE'S MY PHONE NUMBER.
!
EH? AH... OKAY ...?
BIP BIP SAVED...
Oh!
A REGIS-TERED NUMBER!
GARH!
His address is linked!
YOU'D BETTER QUIT WHILE YOU'RE AHEAD!
Everything's backfired!
AAH, BUT THIS IS MOMENTOUS! THE FIRST ADDRESS I'VE EVER GOTTEN!
0
090-XX
Takaomi
Saeki
YOU REALLY DON'T HAVE ANY FRIENDS!
SO WHAT?! YOU ONLY HAVE ABOUT TEN FRIENDS, DON'T YOU?!
Acting so big!
GRAB
Eek!
STOP IT!
BIP
Addresses
100
A HUNDRED ?!
SHOCK
SNATCH
GIVE IT BACK ALREADY!
BRRRING
A CALL?

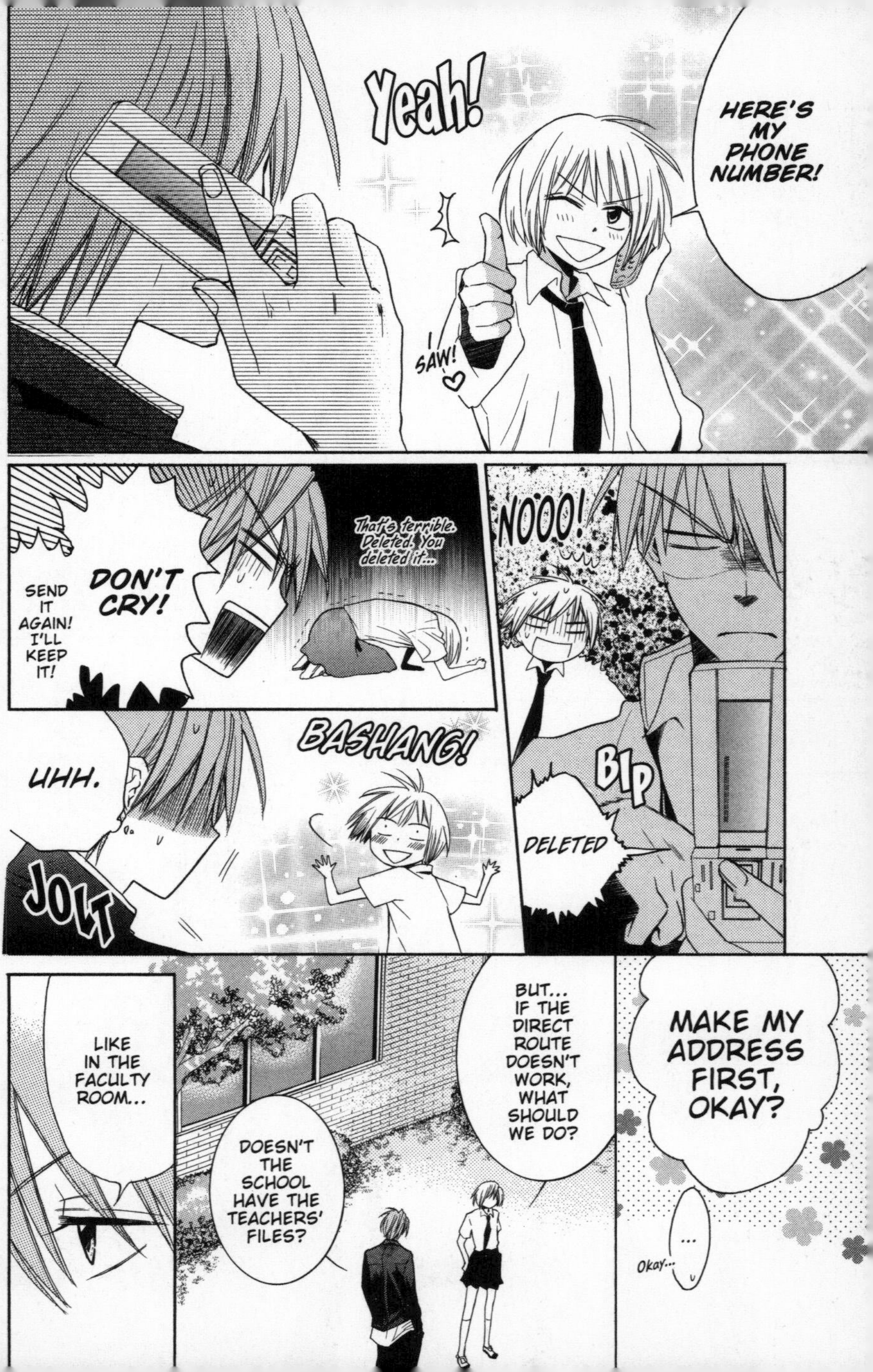
HERE'S MY PHONE NUMBER!
Yeah!
I SAW! ♡
NOOO!
BIP
DELETED
That's terrible. Deleted. You deleted it...
DON'T CRY!
SEND IT AGAIN! I'LL KEEP IT!
BASHANG!
UHH.
JOLT
MAKE MY ADDRESS FIRST, OKAY?
...
Okay...
BUT... IF THE DIRECT ROUTE DOESN'T WORK, WHAT SHOULD WE DO?
DOESN'T THE SCHOOL HAVE THE TEACHERS' FILES?
LIKE IN THE FACULTY ROOM...

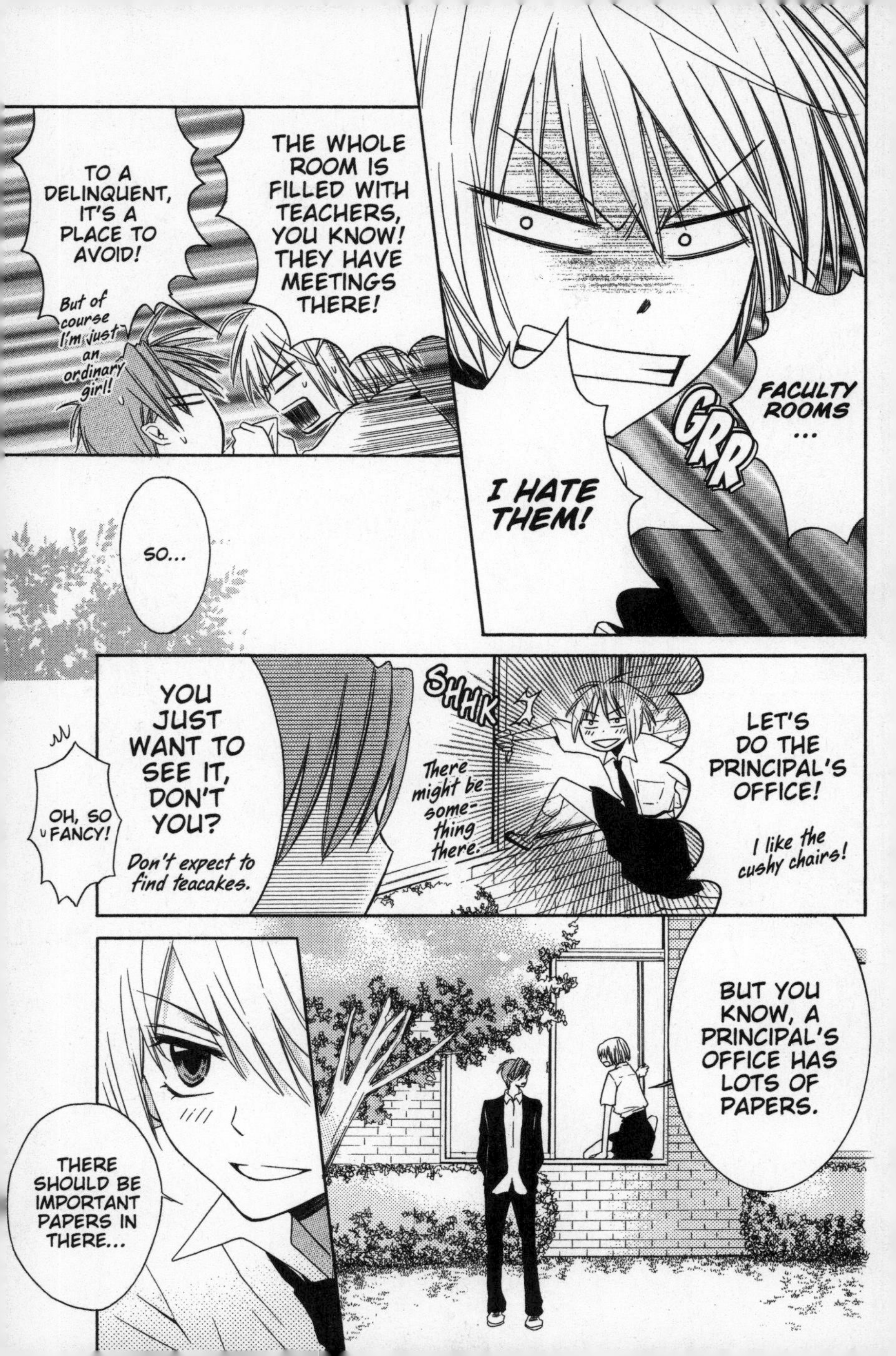
FACULTY ROOMS ...
GRR
I HATE THEM!
THE WHOLE ROOM IS FILLED WITH TEACHERS, YOU KNOW! THEY HAVE MEETINGS THERE!
TO A DELINQUENT, IT'S A PLACE TO AVOID!
But of course I'm just an ordinary girl!
SO...
LET'S DO THE PRINCIPAL'S OFFICE!
I like the cushy chairs!
SHHK
There might be some-thing there.
YOU JUST WANT TO SEE IT, DON'T YOU?
Don't expect to find teacakes.
OH, SO FANCY!
BUT YOU KNOW, A PRINCIPAL'S OFFICE HAS LOTS OF PAPERS.
THERE SHOULD BE IMPORTANT PAPERS IN THERE...

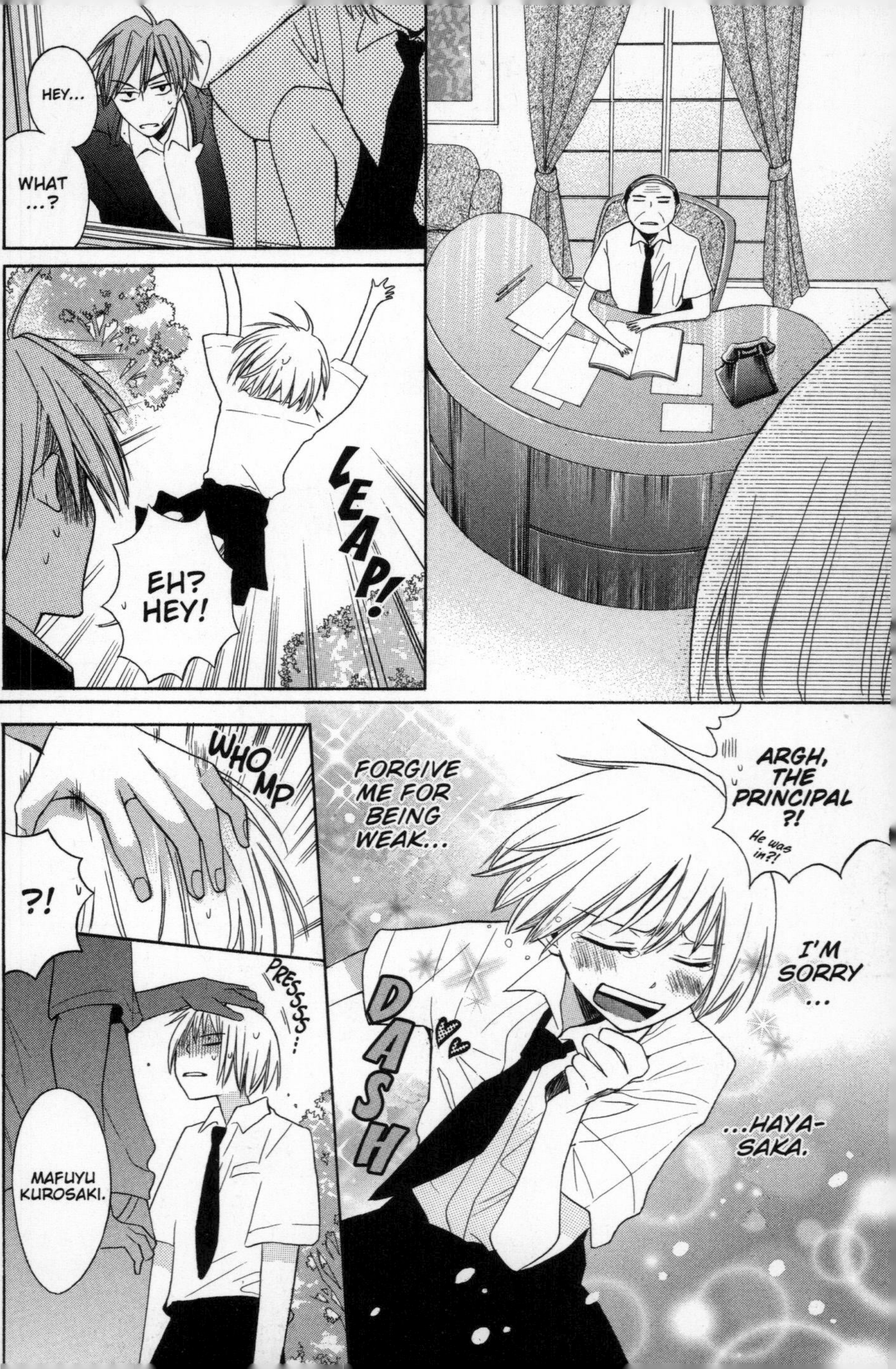
HEY...
WHAT ...?
LEAP!
EH? HEY!
ARGH, THE PRINCIPAL ?!
He was in?!
FORGIVE ME FOR BEING WEAK...
I'M SORRY ...
DASH
...HAYA-SAKA.
WHOMP
?!
PRESSSS...
MAFUYU KUROSAKI.

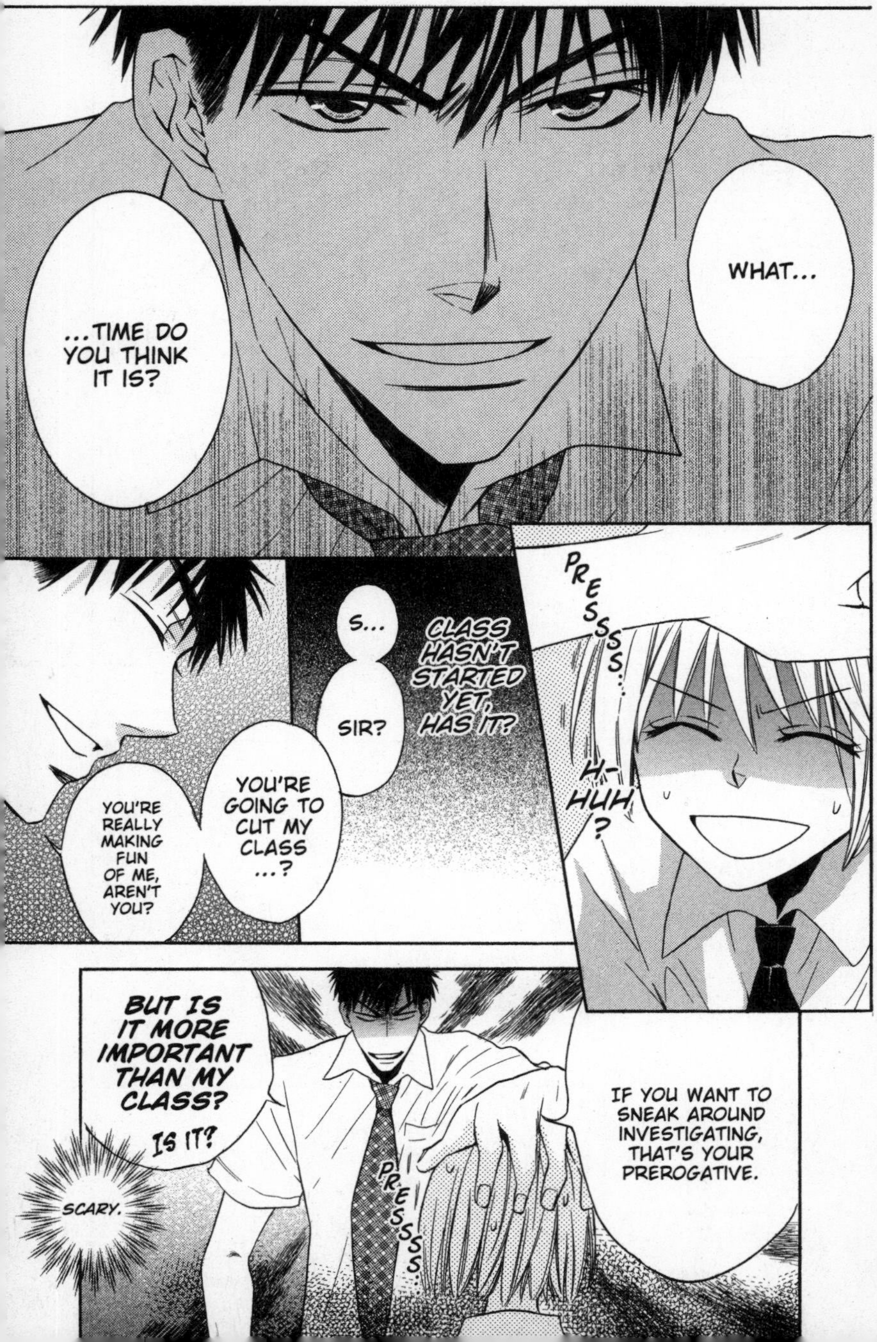
WHAT...
...TIME DO YOU THINK IT IS?
PRESSSS...
H-HUH?
S...
SIR?
CLASS HASN'T STARTED YET, HAS IT?
YOU'RE GOING TO CUT MY CLASS ...?
YOU'RE REALLY MAKING FUN OF ME, AREN'T YOU?
IF YOU WANT TO SNEAK AROUND INVESTIGATING, THAT'S YOUR PREROGATIVE.
PRESSSS...
BUT IS IT MORE IMPORTANT THAN MY CLASS?
IS IT?
SCARY.

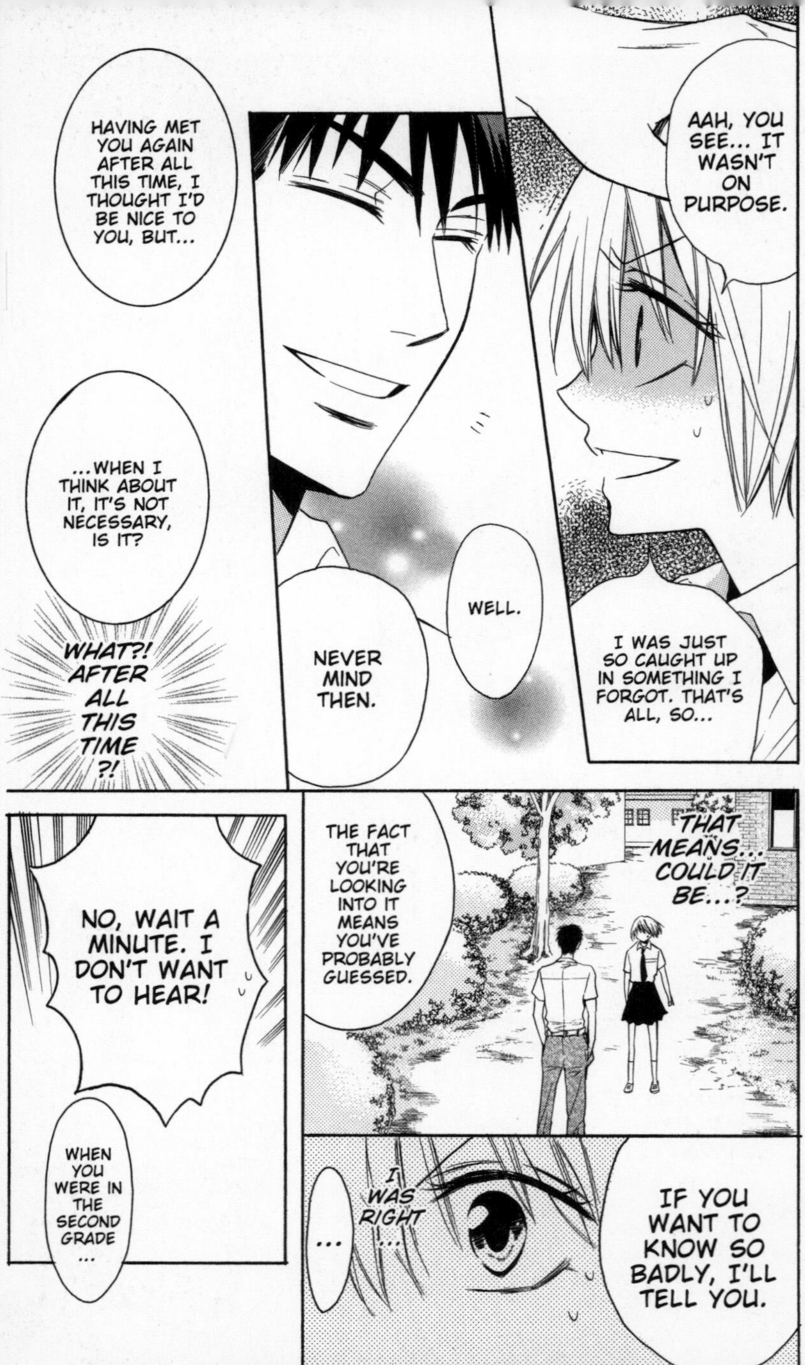
AAH, YOU SEE... IT WASN'T ON PURPOSE.
I WAS JUST SO CAUGHT UP IN SOMETHING I FORGOT. THAT'S ALL, SO...
WELL.
NEVER MIND THEN.
HAVING MET YOU AGAIN AFTER ALL THIS TIME, I THOUGHT I'D BE NICE TO YOU, BUT...
...WHEN I THINK ABOUT IT, IT'S NOT NECESSARY, IS IT?
WHAT?! AFTER ALL THIS TIME?!
THAT MEANS... COULD IT BE...?
THE FACT THAT YOU'RE LOOKING INTO IT MEANS YOU'VE PROBABLY GUESSED.
IF YOU WANT TO KNOW SO BADLY, I'LL TELL YOU.
I WAS RIGHT...
...
NO, WAIT A MINUTE. I DON'T WANT TO HEAR!
WHEN YOU WERE IN THE SECOND GRADE...

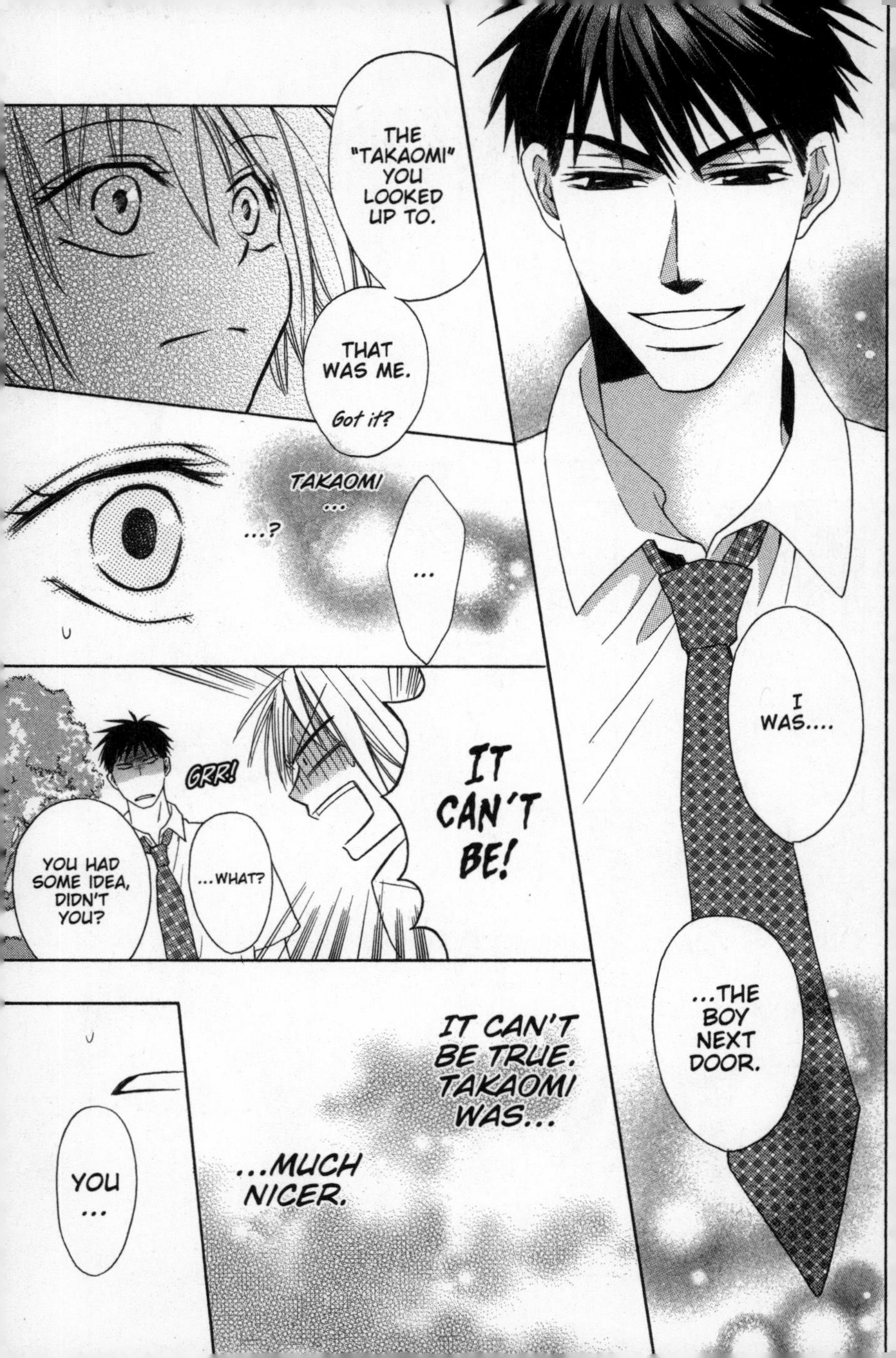
I WAS....
...THE BOY NEXT DOOR.
THE "TAKAOMI" YOU LOOKED UP TO.
THAT WAS ME.
Got it?
...
TAKAOMI ...
...?
IT CAN'T BE!
GRR!
...WHAT?
YOU HAD SOME IDEA, DIDN'T YOU?
IT CAN'T BE TRUE. TAKAOMI WAS...
...MUCH NICER.
YOU ...

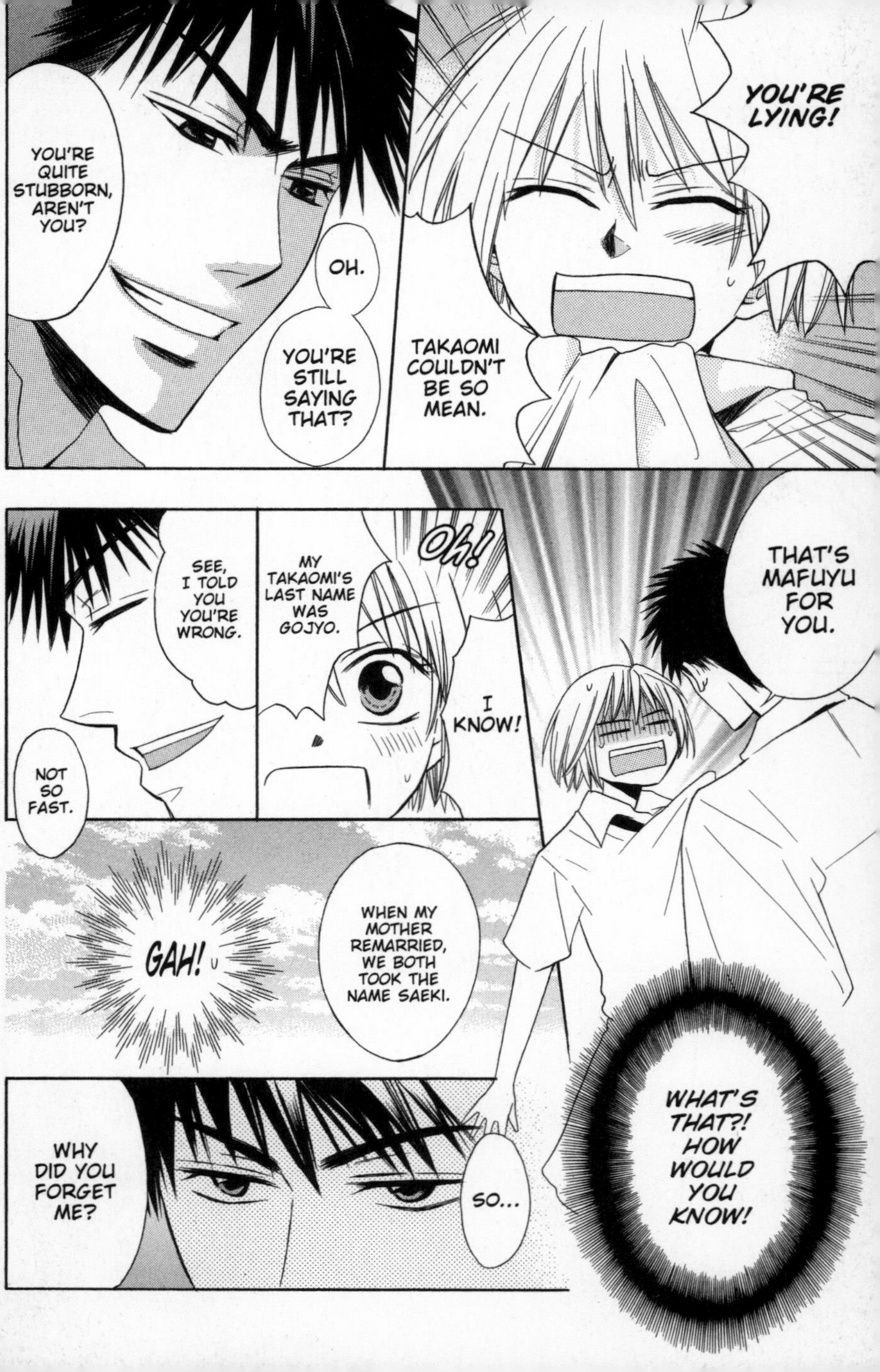
YOU'RE LYING!
TAKAOMI COULDN'T BE SO MEAN.
OH.
YOU'RE STILL SAYING THAT?
YOU'RE QUITE STUBBORN, AREN'T YOU?
THAT'S MAFUYU FOR YOU.
WHAT'S THAT?! HOW WOULD YOU KNOW!
Oh!
MY TAKAOMI'S LAST NAME WAS GOJYO.
I KNOW!
SEE, I TOLD YOU YOU'RE WRONG.
NOT SO FAST.
WHEN MY MOTHER REMARRIED, WE BOTH TOOK THE NAME SAEKI.
GAH!
SO...
WHY DID YOU FORGET ME?

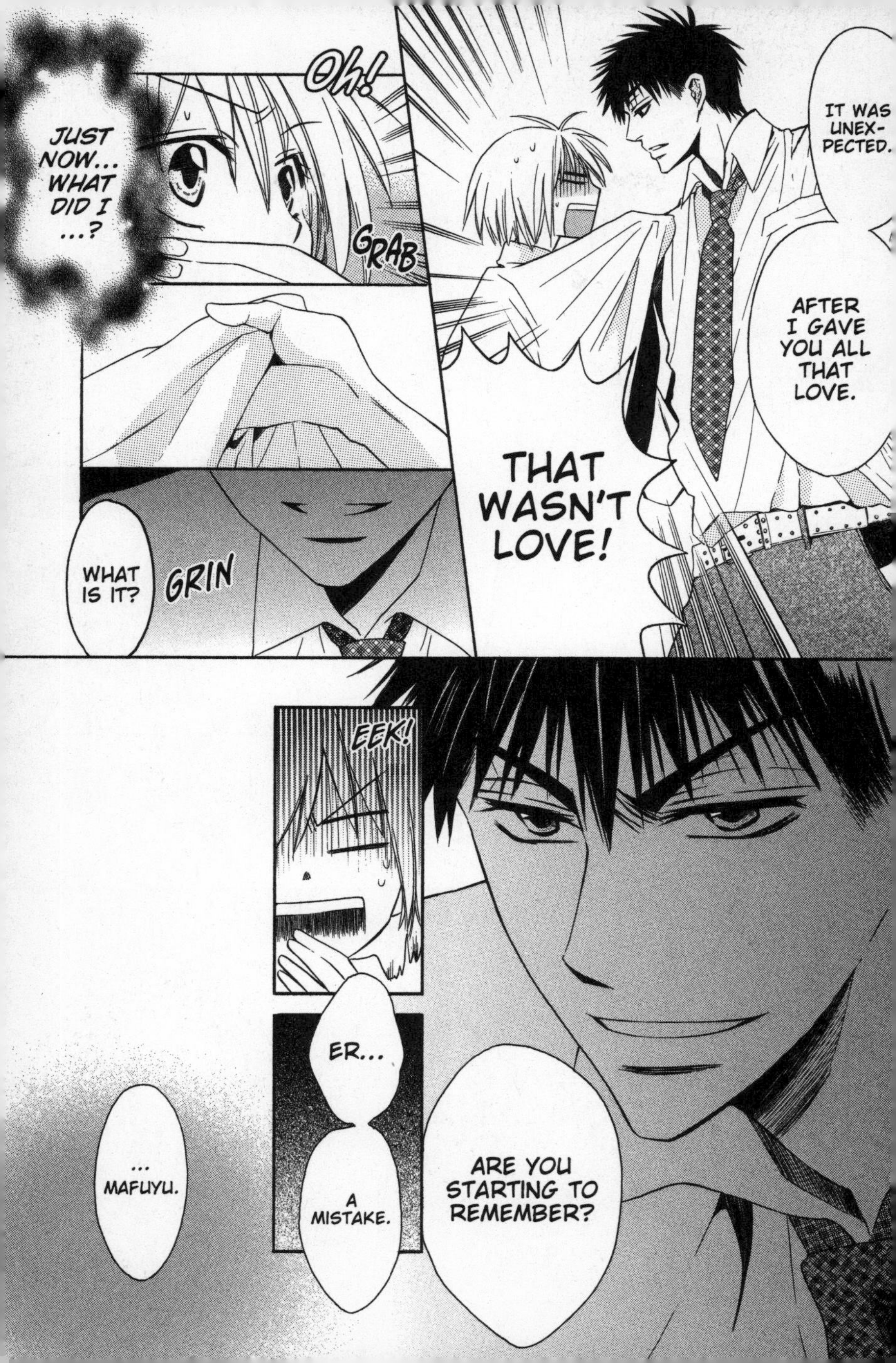
IT WAS UNEXPECTED.
AFTER I GAVE YOU ALL THAT LOVE.
THAT WASN'T LOVE!
Oh!
JUST NOW... WHAT DID I ...?
GRAB
GRIN
WHAT IS IT?
ARE YOU STARTING TO REMEMBER?
EEK!
ER...
A MISTAKE.
... MAFUYU.

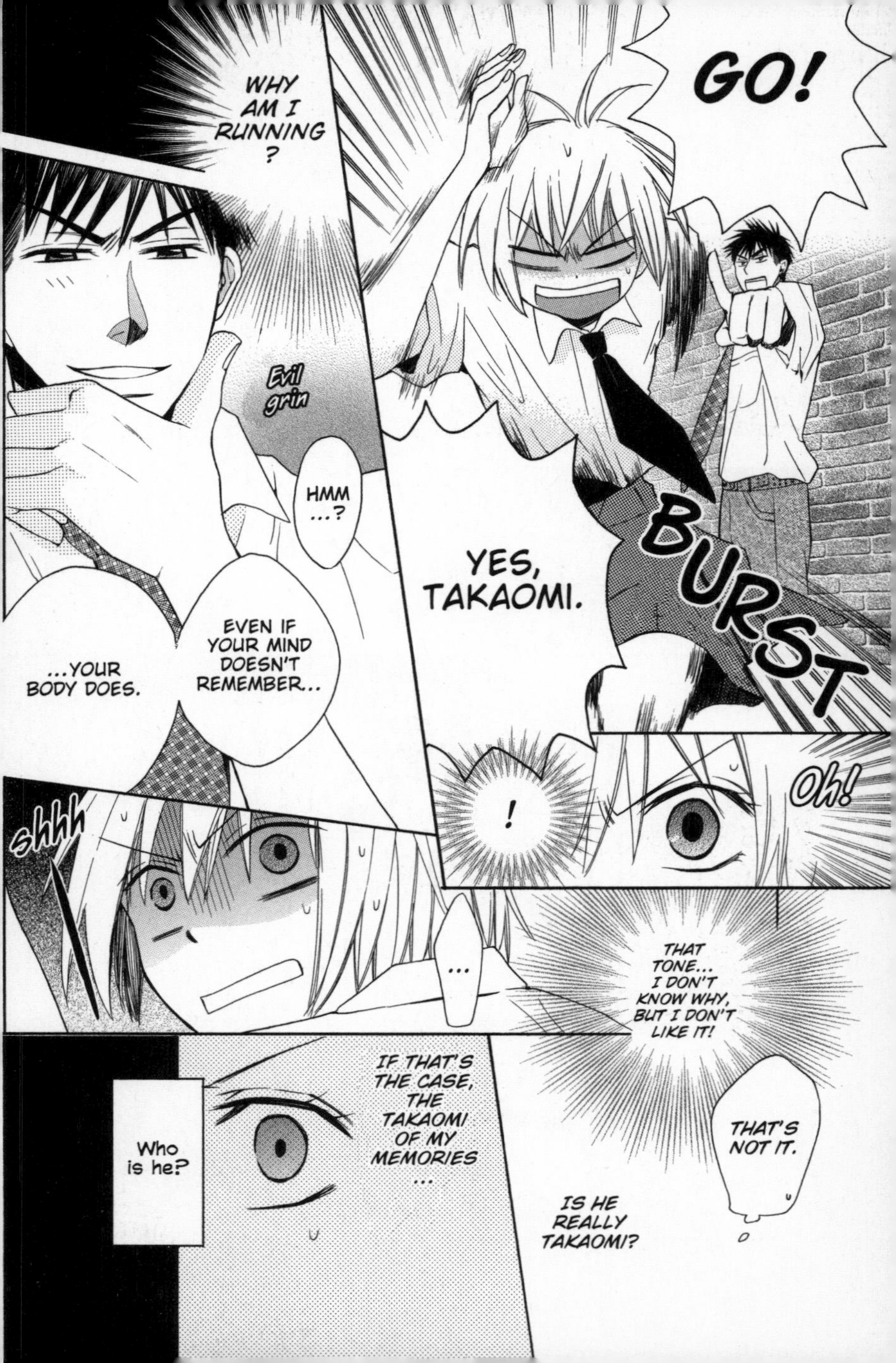
GO!
BURST
YES, TAKAOMI.
WHY AM I RUNNING?
Evil grin
HMM ...?
EVEN IF YOUR MIND DOESN'T REMEMBER...
...YOUR BODY DOES.
Oh!
!
shhh
...
THAT TONE... I DON'T KNOW WHY, BUT I DON'T LIKE IT!
THAT'S NOT IT.
IS HE REALLY TAKAOMI?
IF THAT'S THE CASE, THE TAKAOMI OF MY MEMORIES ...
Who is he?

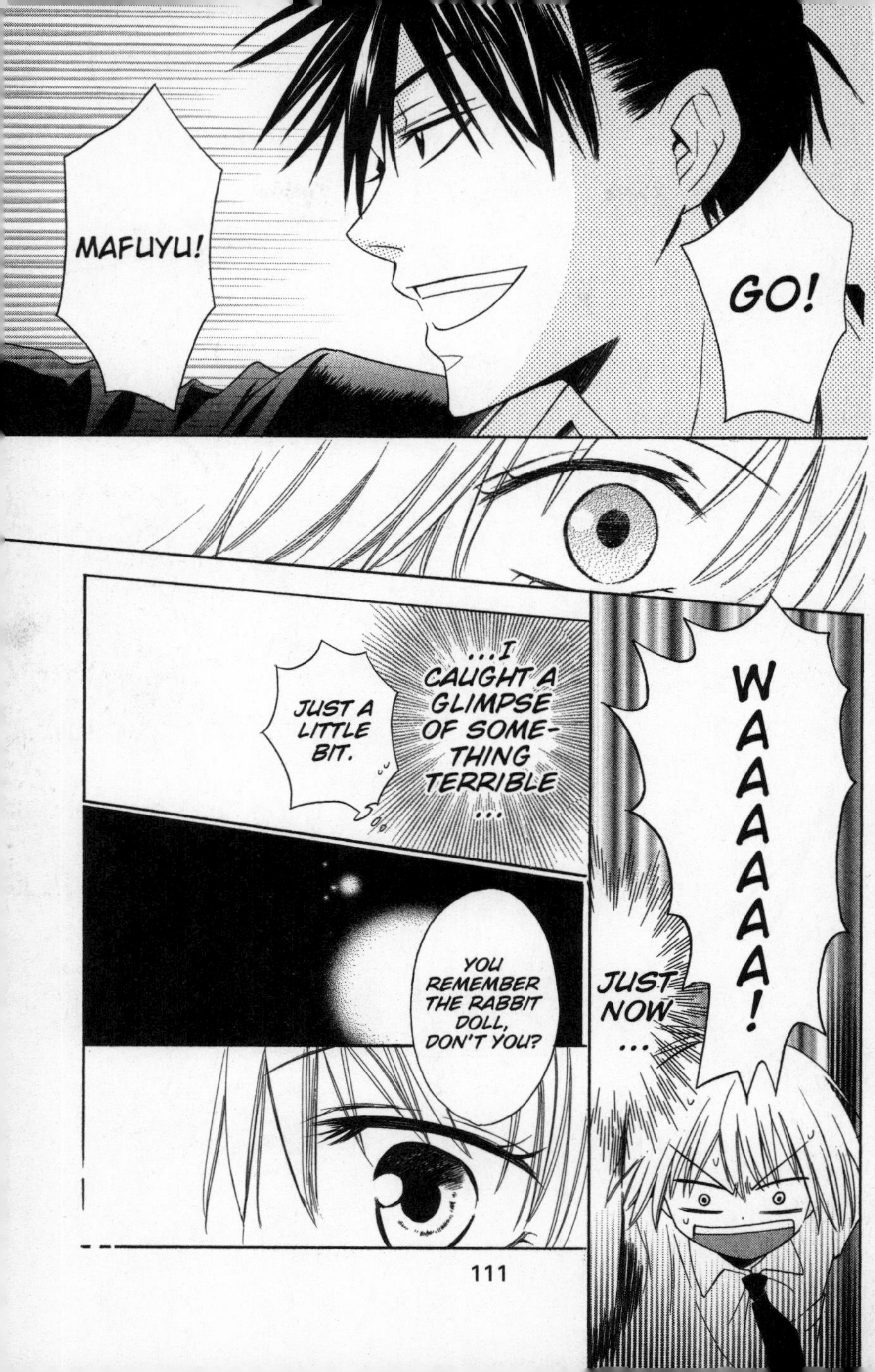

MAFUYU!
GO!
WAAAAAAA!
JUST NOW...
...I CAUGHT A GLIMPSE OF SOMETHING TERRIBLE...
JUST A LITTLE BIT.
YOU REMEMBER THE RABBIT DOLL, DON'T YOU?

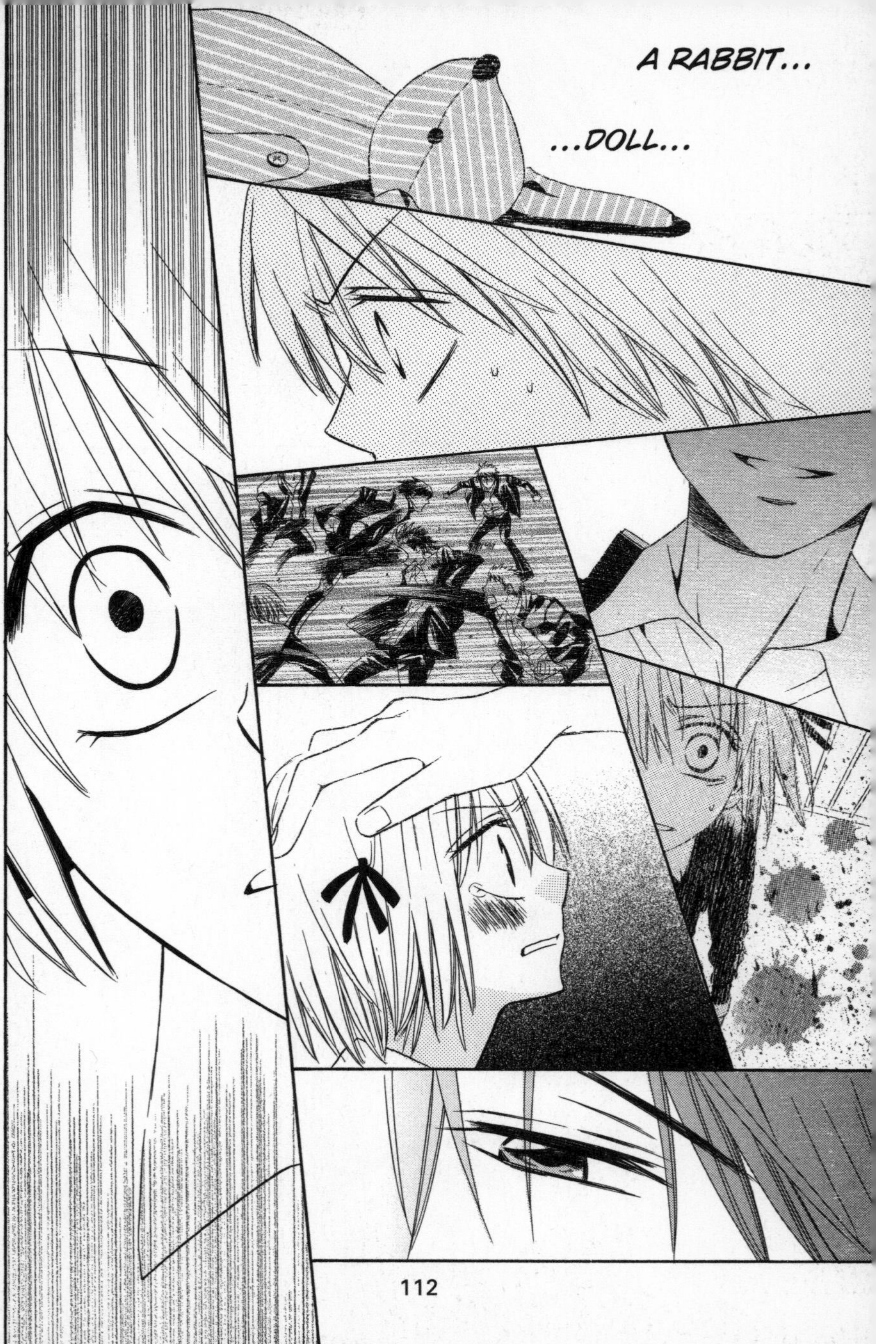
A RABBIT...
...DOLL...

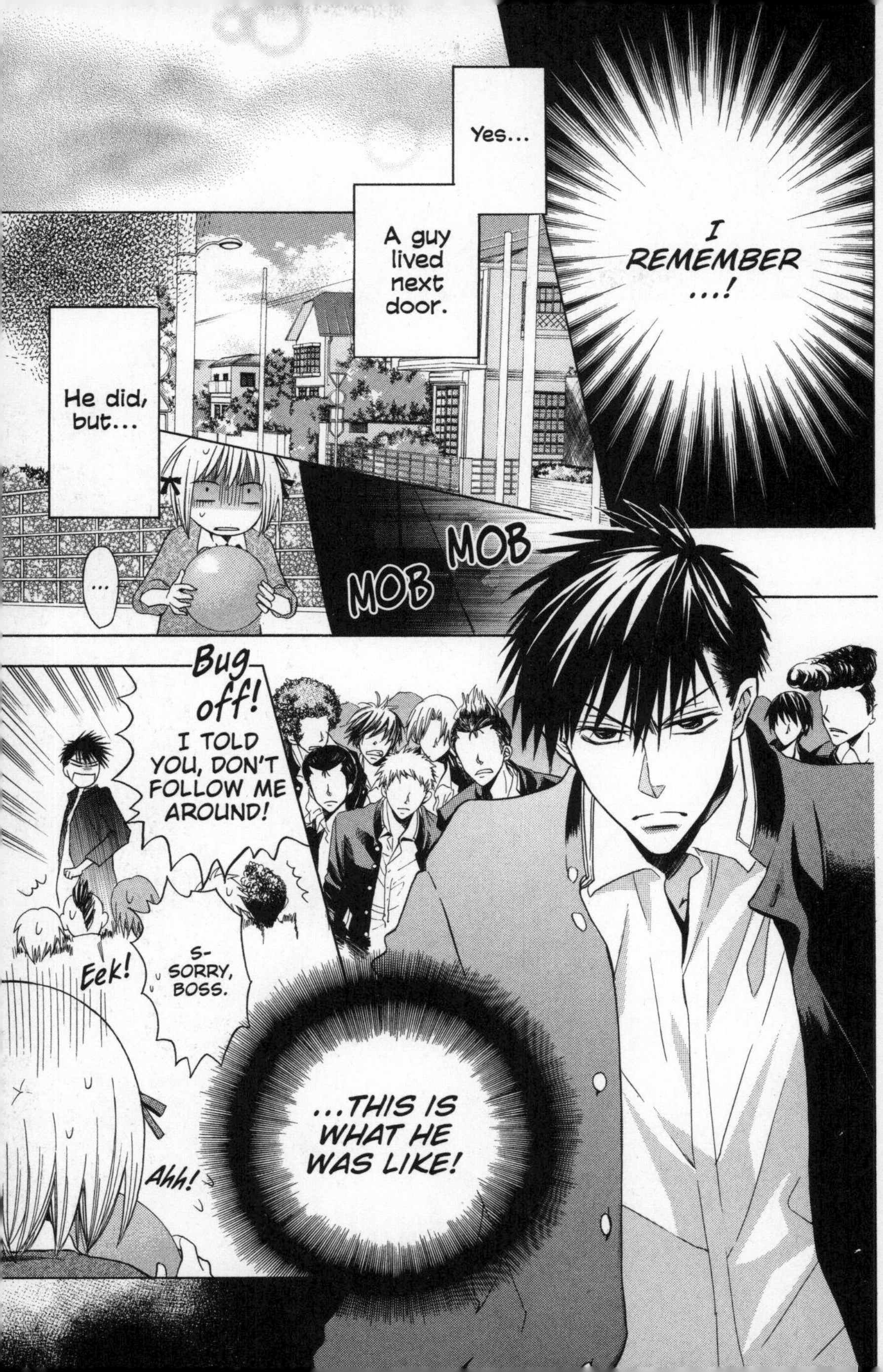
I REMEMBER...!
Yes...
A guy lived next door.
He did, but...
...
MOB MOB
MOB
Bug-off! I TOLD YOU, DON'T FOLLOW ME AROUND!
Eek!
S-SORRY, BOSS.
Ahh!
...THIS IS WHAT HE WAS LIKE!

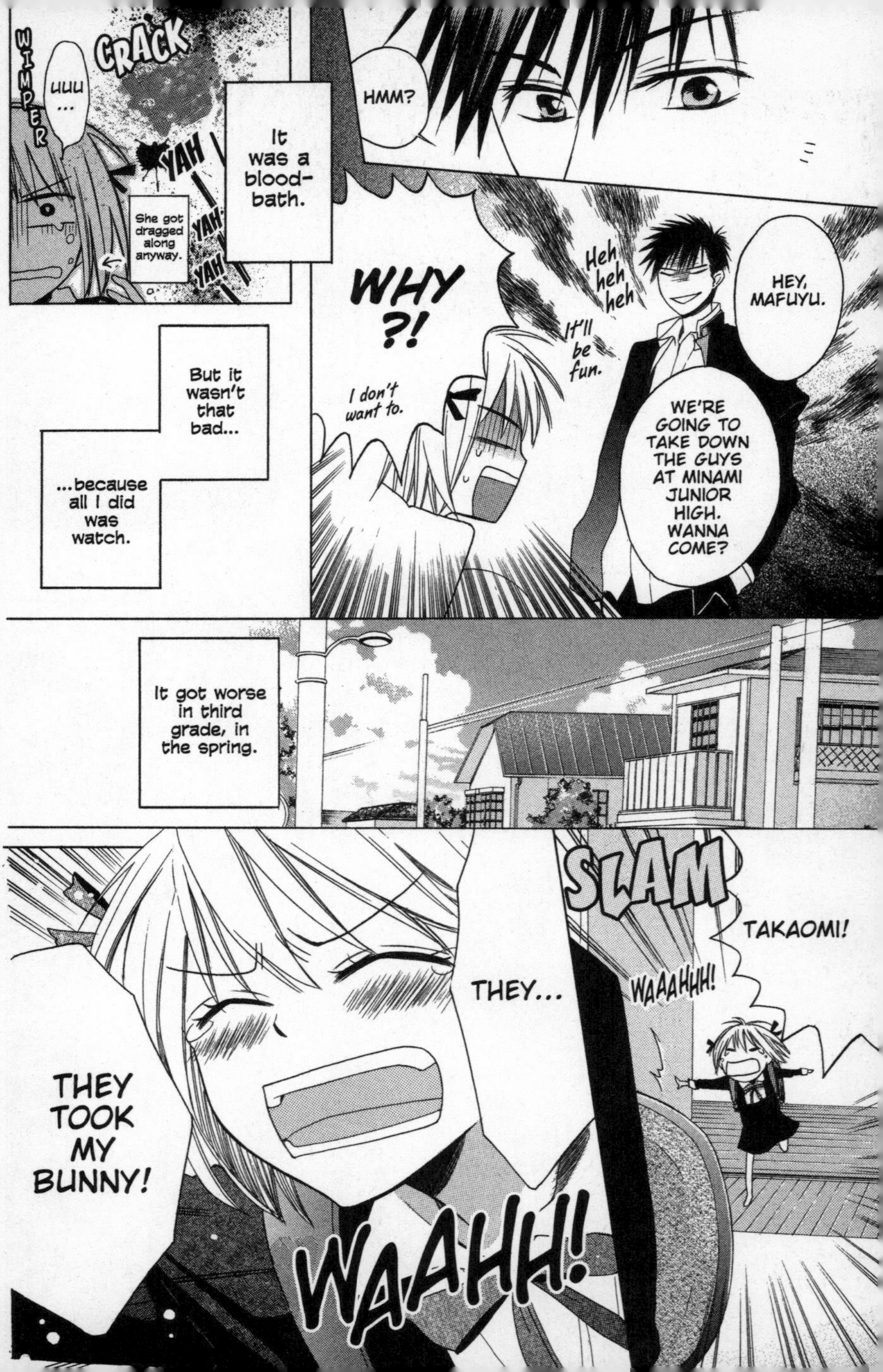

HMM?
HEY, MAFUYU.
WE'RE GOING TO TAKE DOWN THE GUYS AT MINAMI JUNIOR HIGH. WANNA COME?
Heh heh heh
It'll be fun.
WHY ?!
I don't want to.
CRACK
It was a blood-bath.
UUU ...
WIMPER
YAH
YAH
YAH
She got dragged along anyway.
But it wasn't that bad...
...because all I did was watch.
It got worse in third grade, in the spring.
SLAM
TAKAOMI!
WAAAHHH!
THEY...
THEY TOOK MY BUNNY!
WAAHH!

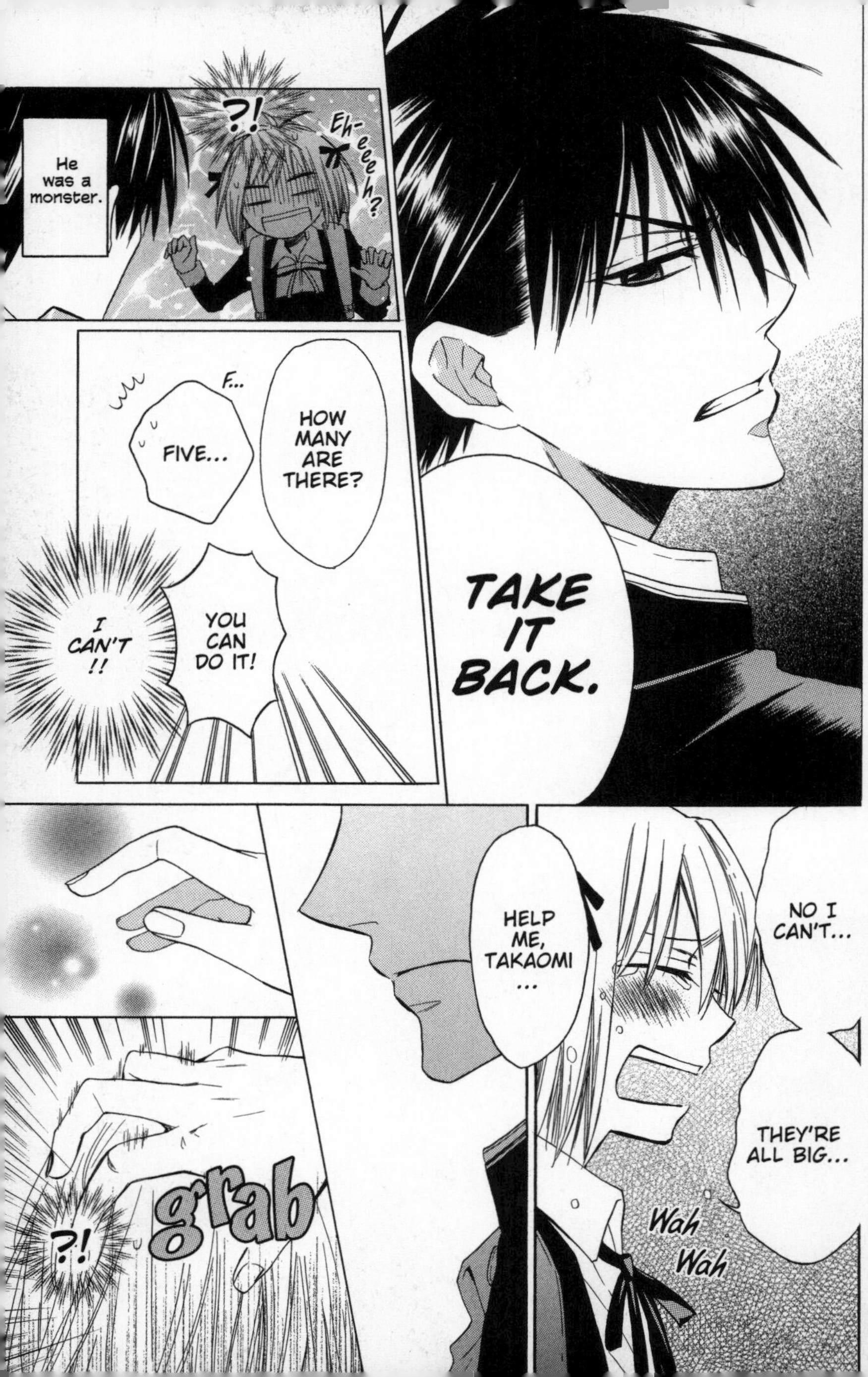
TAKE IT BACK.
Eh-eeeh?
?!
He was a monster.
HOW MANY ARE THERE?
F...
FIVE...
YOU CAN DO IT!
I CAN'T!!
NO I CAN'T...
THEY'RE ALL BIG...
HELP ME, TAKAOMI...
Wah Wah
grab
?!

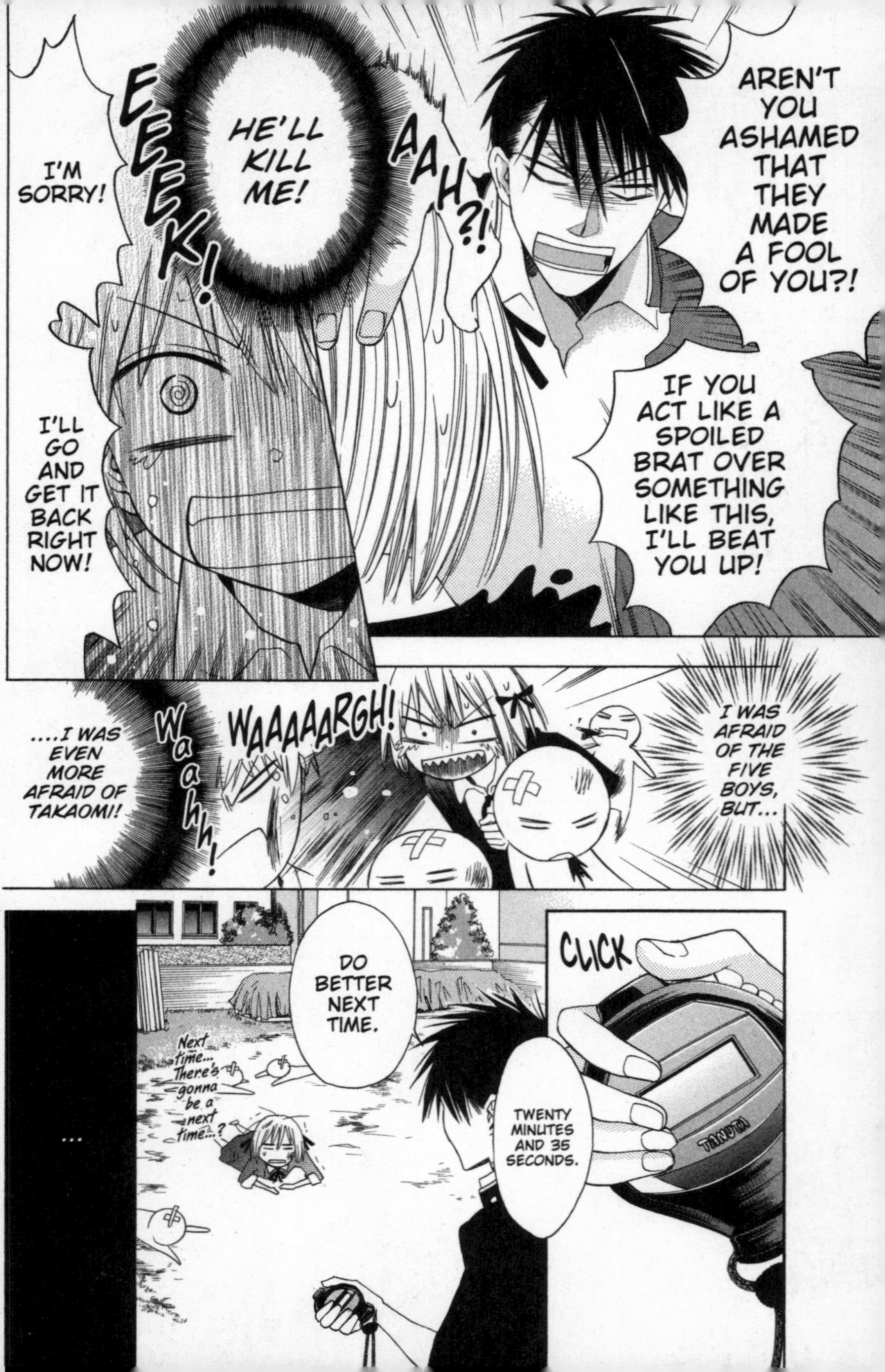

AREN'T YOU ASHAMED THAT THEY MADE A FOOL OF YOU?!
AAH?!
HE'LL KILL ME!
EEEEK!
I'M SORRY!
IF YOU ACT LIKE A SPOILED BRAT OVER SOMETHING LIKE THIS, I'LL BEAT YOU UP!
I'LL GO AND GET IT BACK RIGHT NOW!
I WAS AFRAID OF THE FIVE BOYS, BUT...
WAAAAARGH!
Waahhh!
....I WAS EVEN MORE AFRAID OF TAKAOMI!!
CLICK
TWENTY MINUTES AND 35 SECONDS.
DO BETTER NEXT TIME.
Next time... There's gonna be a next time...?
...

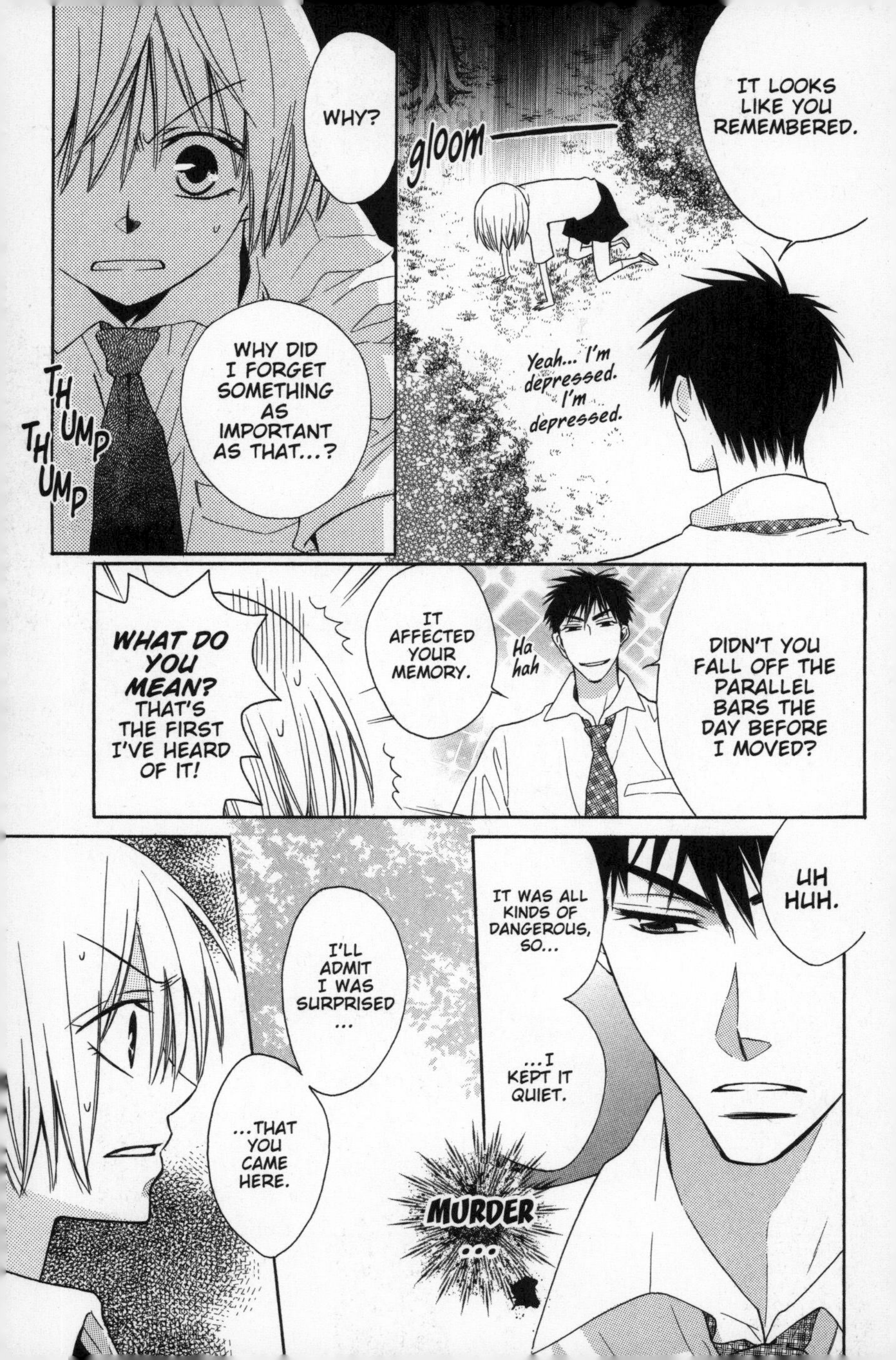
IT LOOKS LIKE YOU REMEMBERED.
gloom
Yeah... I'm depressed. I'm depressed.
WHY?
WHY DID I FORGET SOMETHING AS IMPORTANT AS THAT...?
THUMP THUMP
DIDN'T YOU FALL OFF THE PARALLEL BARS THE DAY BEFORE I MOVED?
Ha hah
IT AFFECTED YOUR MEMORY.
WHAT DO YOU MEAN? THAT'S THE FIRST I'VE HEARD OF IT!
UH HUH.
IT WAS ALL KINDS OF DANGEROUS, SO...
...I KEPT IT QUIET.
MURDER...
I'LL ADMIT I WAS SURPRISED...
...THAT YOU CAME HERE.

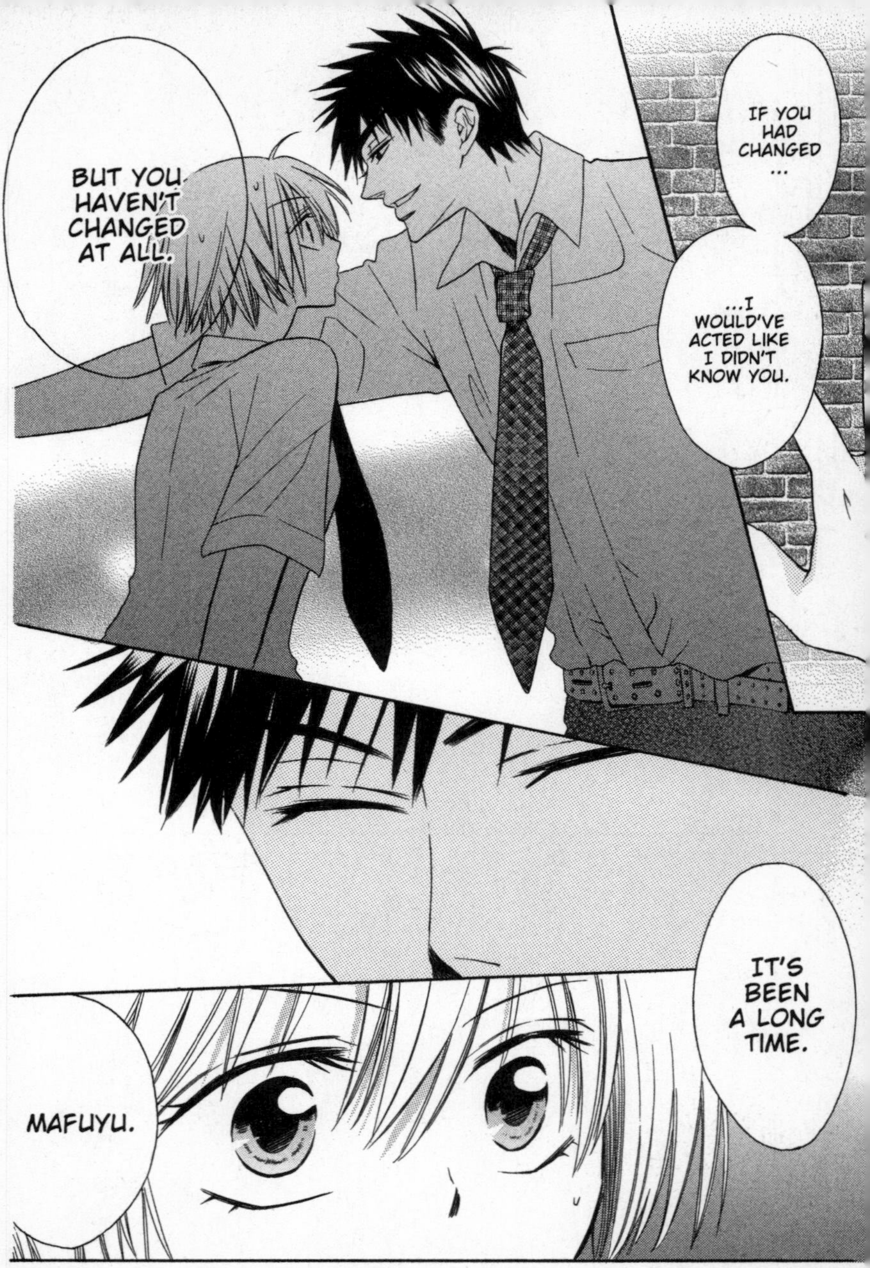
IF YOU HAD CHANGED ...
...I WOULD'VE ACTED LIKE I DIDN'T KNOW YOU.
BUT YOU HAVEN'T CHANGED AT ALL.
IT'S BEEN A LONG TIME.
MAFUYU.

Chapter 4

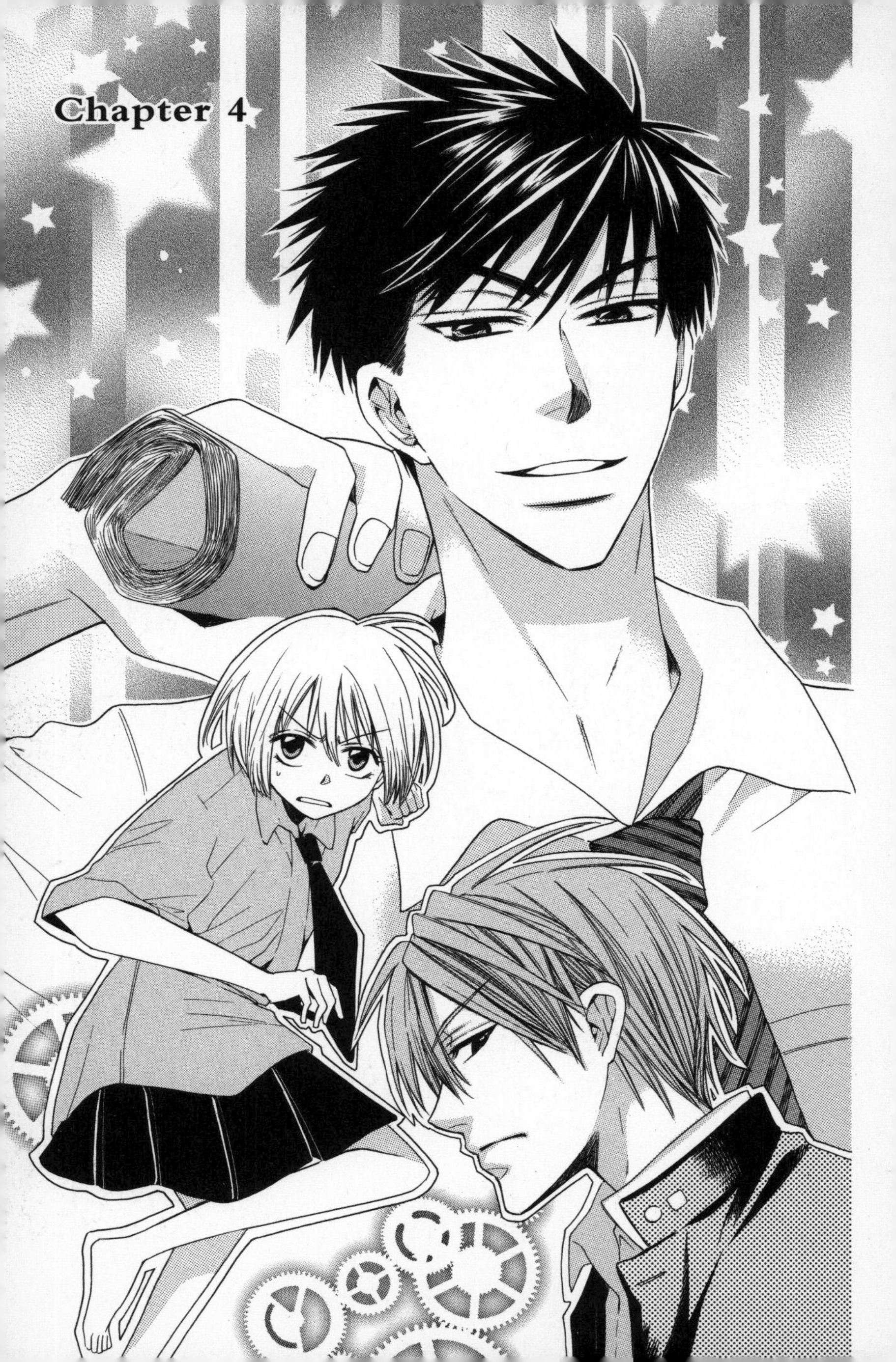

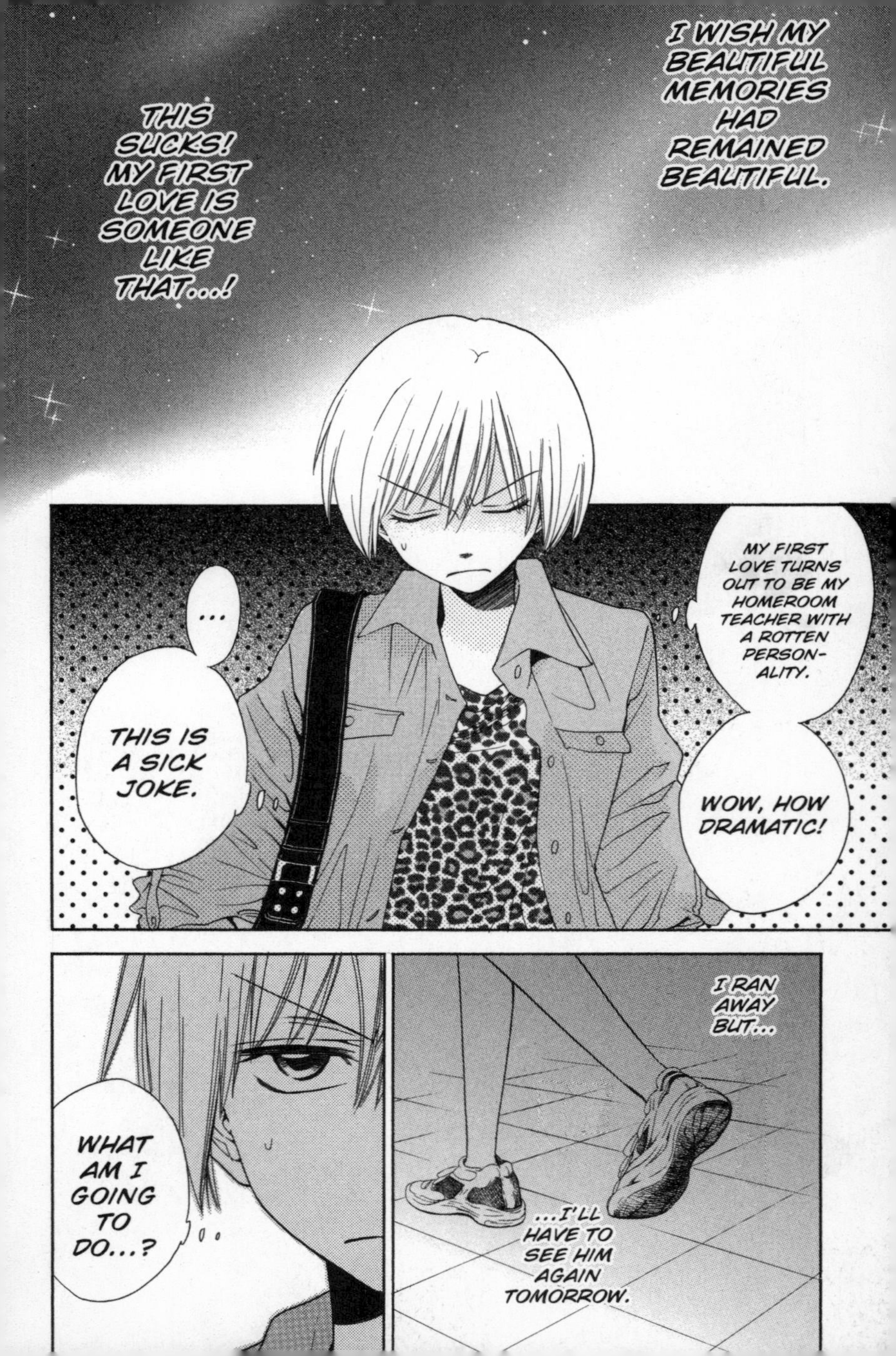
I WISH MY BEAUTIFUL MEMORIES HAD REMAINED BEAUTIFUL.
THIS SUCKS! MY FIRST LOVE IS SOMEONE LIKE THAT...!
MY FIRST LOVE TURNS OUT TO BE MY HOMEROOM TEACHER WITH A ROTTEN PERSON-ALITY.
WOW, HOW DRAMATIC!
...
THIS IS A SICK JOKE.
I RAN AWAY BUT...
...I'LL HAVE TO SEE HIM AGAIN TOMORROW.
WHAT AM I GOING TO DO...?

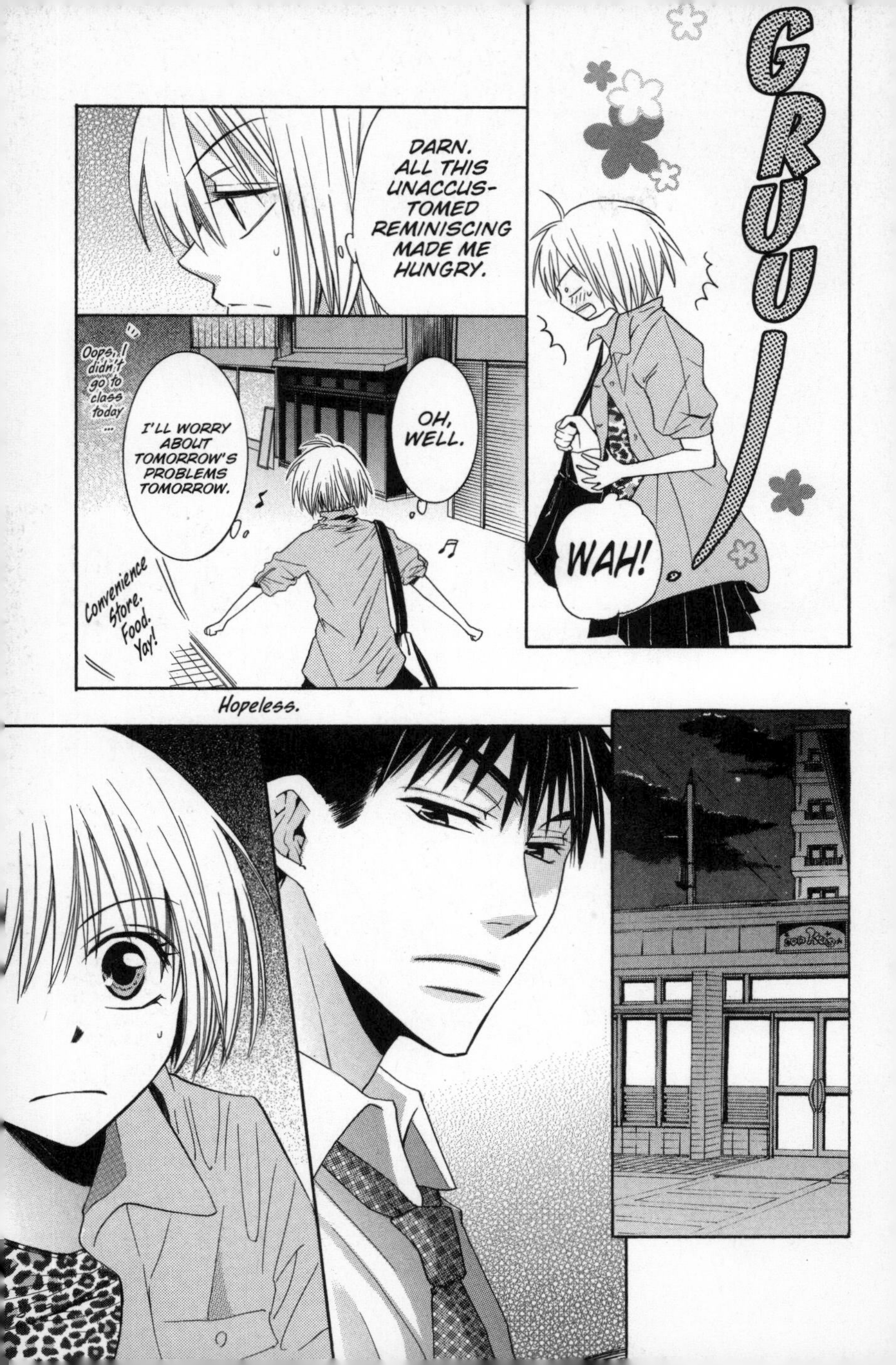
GRUU
WAH!
DARN. ALL THIS UNACCUS-TOMED REMINISCING MADE ME HUNGRY.
OH, WELL.
I'LL WORRY ABOUT TOMORROW'S PROBLEMS TOMORROW.
Oops, I didn't go to class today...
Convenience Store. Food. Yay!
Hopeless.

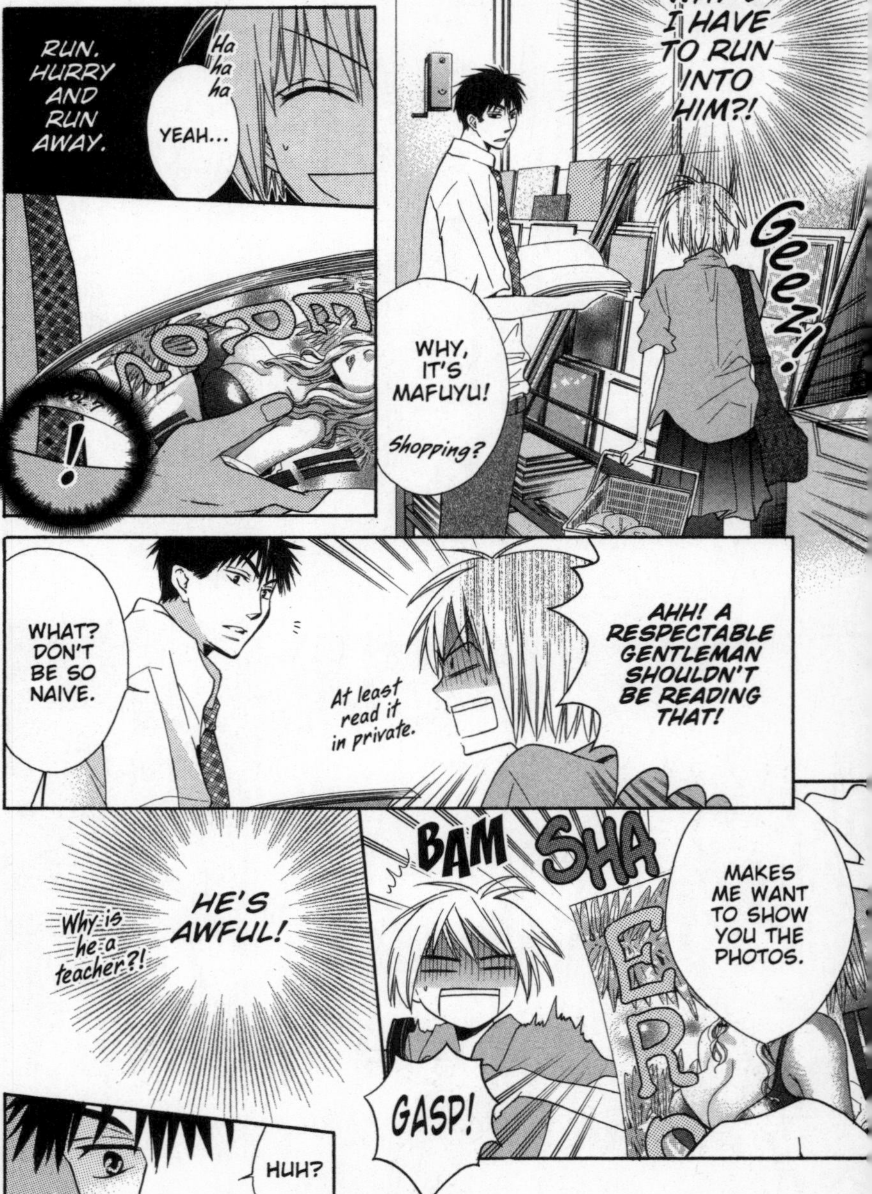
WHY'D I HAVE TO RUN INTO HIM?!
GEEZ!
WHY, IT'S MAFUYU!
Shopping?
Ha ha ha
YEAH...
RUN. HURRY AND RUN AWAY.
!
AHH! A RESPECTABLE GENTLEMAN SHOULDN'T BE READING THAT!
At least read it in private.
WHAT? DON'T BE SO NAIVE.
MAKES ME WANT TO SHOW YOU THE PHOTOS.
SHA
BAM
GASP!
HE'S AWFUL!
Why is he a teacher?!
HUH?

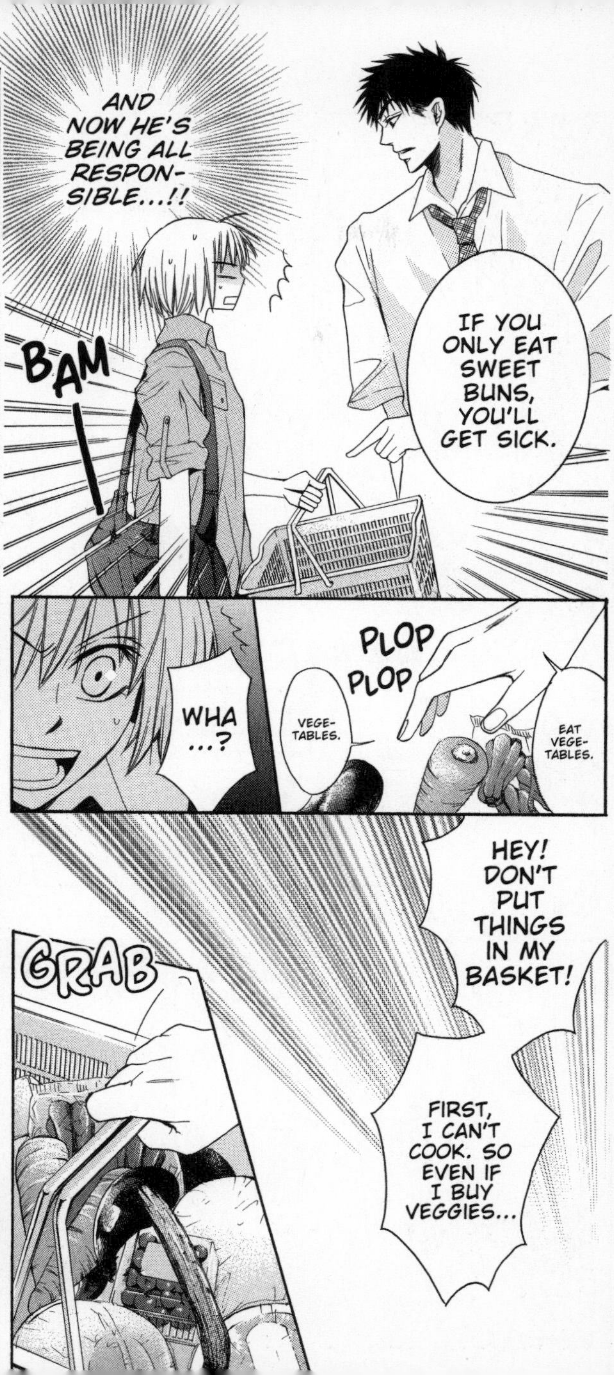

IF YOU ONLY EAT SWEET BUNS, YOU'LL GET SICK.
AND NOW HE'S BEING ALL RESPON-SIBLE...!!
BAM
PLOP PLOP
EAT VEGE-TABLES.
VEGE-TABLES.
WHA ...?
HEY! DON'T PUT THINGS IN MY BASKET!
GRAB
FIRST, I CAN'T COOK. SO EVEN IF I BUY VEGGIES...

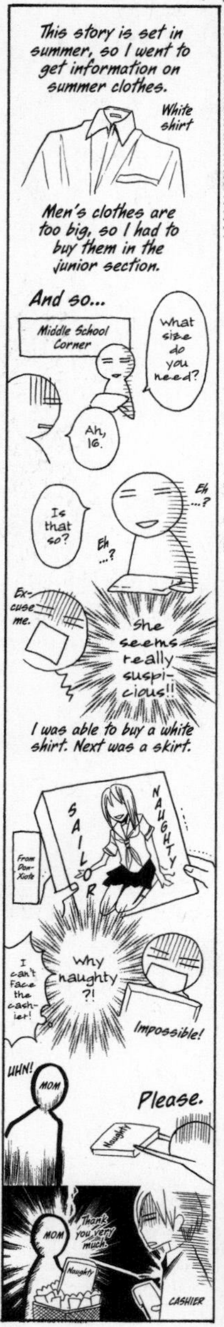

This story is set in summer, so I went to get information on summer clothes.
White shirt
Men's clothes are too big, so I had to buy them in the junior section.
And so...
Middle School Corner
What size do you need?
Ah, 16.
Is that so?
Eh ...?
Eh ...?
Ex-cuse me.
She seems really suspi-cious!!
I was able to buy a white shirt. Next was a skirt.
SAILOR
NAUGHTY
From Don-Xiote
Why naughty ?!
I can't face the cash-ier!
Impossible!
UHN!
MOM
Please.
Naughty
MOM
Thank you very much.
Naughty
CASHIER

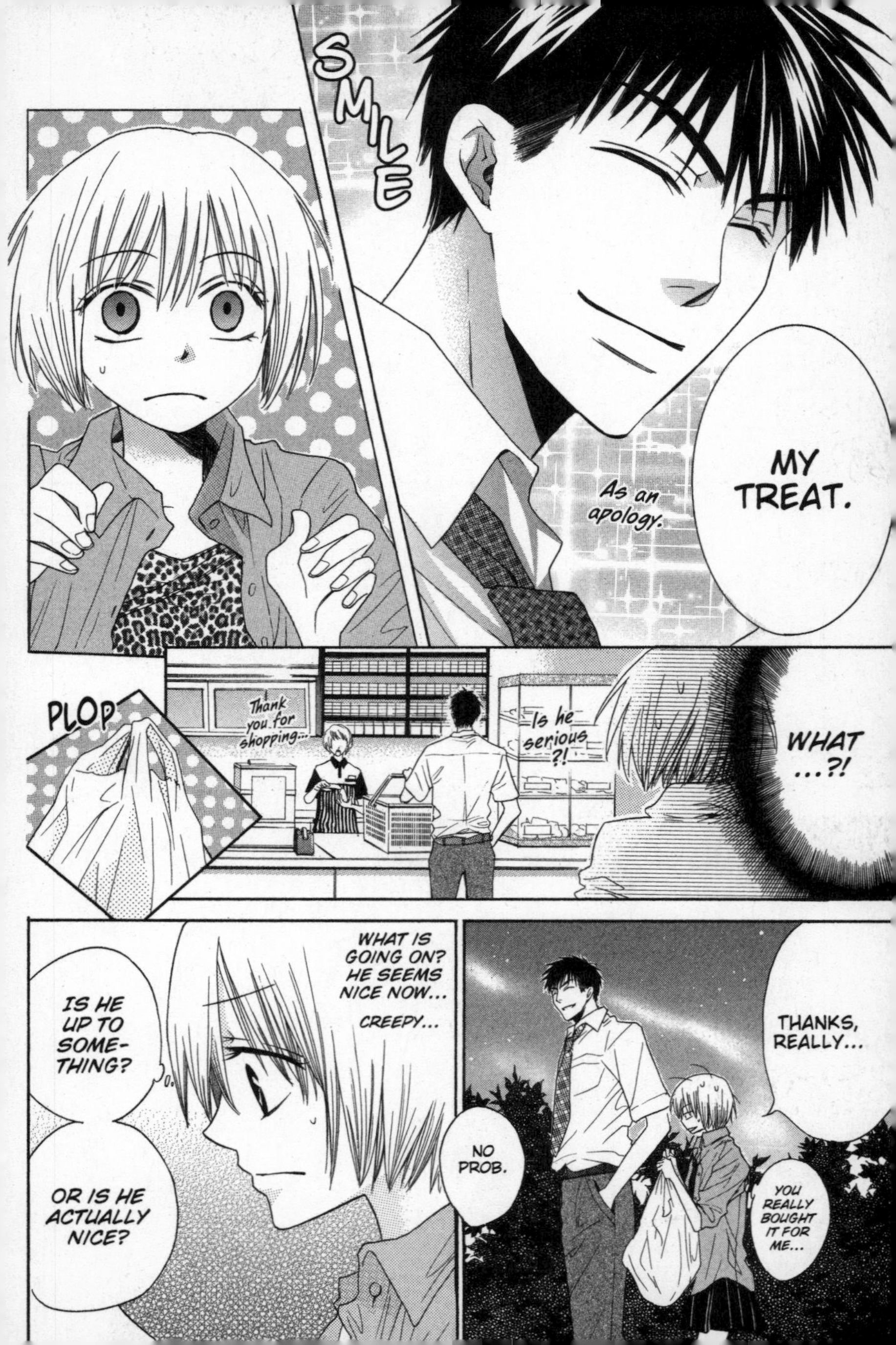
SMILE
MY TREAT.
As an apology.
WHAT ...?!
Is he serious ?!
Thank you for shopping...
PLOP
THANKS, REALLY...
YOU REALLY BOUGHT IT FOR ME...
NO PROB.
WHAT IS GOING ON? HE SEEMS NICE NOW...
CREEPY...
IS HE UP TO SOME-THING?
OR IS HE ACTUALLY NICE?

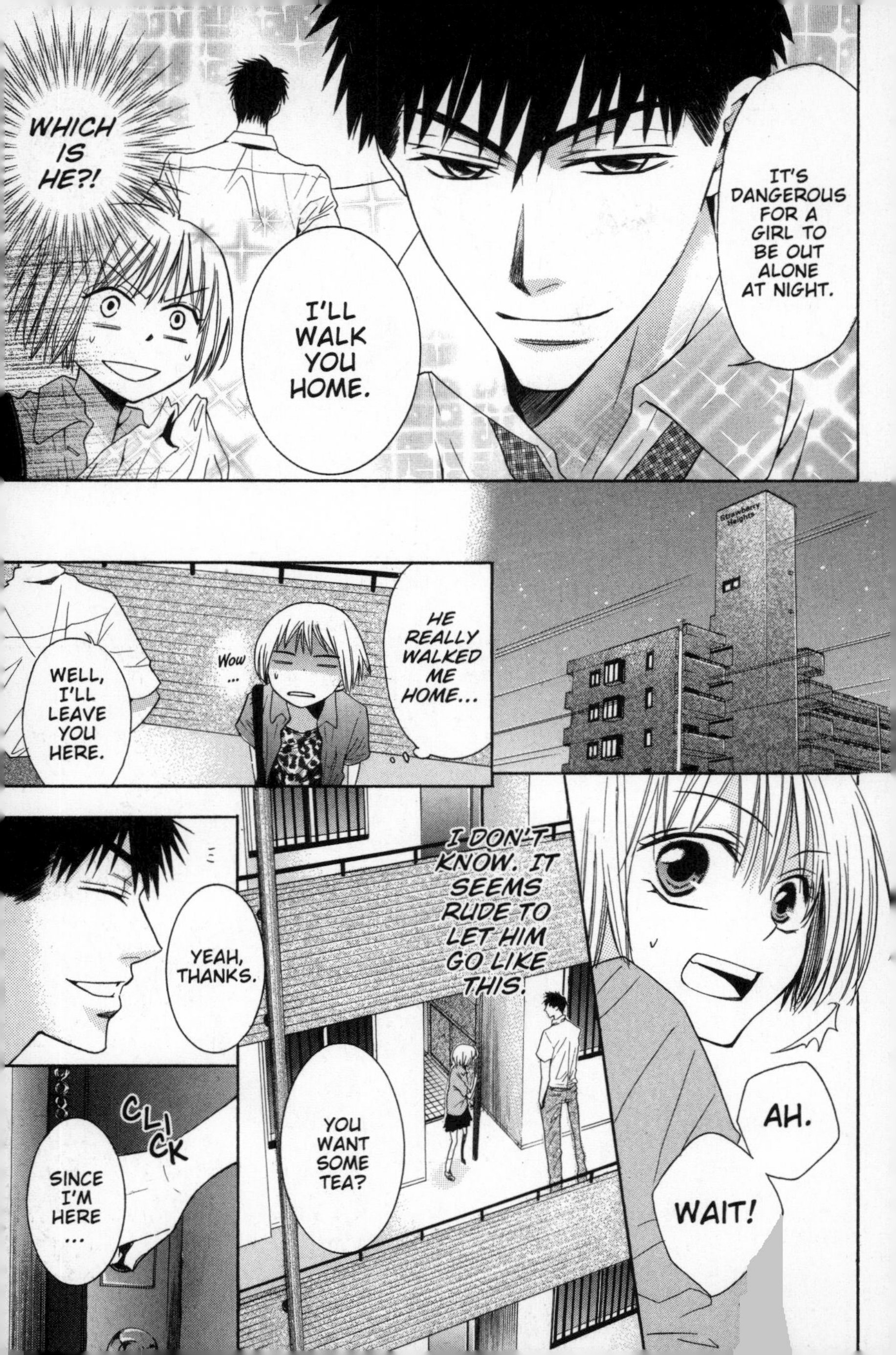
IT'S DANGEROUS FOR A GIRL TO BE OUT ALONE AT NIGHT.
I'LL WALK YOU HOME.
WHICH IS HE?!
Strawberry Heights
HE REALLY WALKED ME HOME...
Wow ...
WELL, I'LL LEAVE YOU HERE.
AH.
WAIT!
I DON'T KNOW. IT SEEMS RUDE TO LET HIM GO LIKE THIS.
YOU WANT SOME TEA?
YEAH, THANKS.
CLICK
SINCE I'M HERE ...

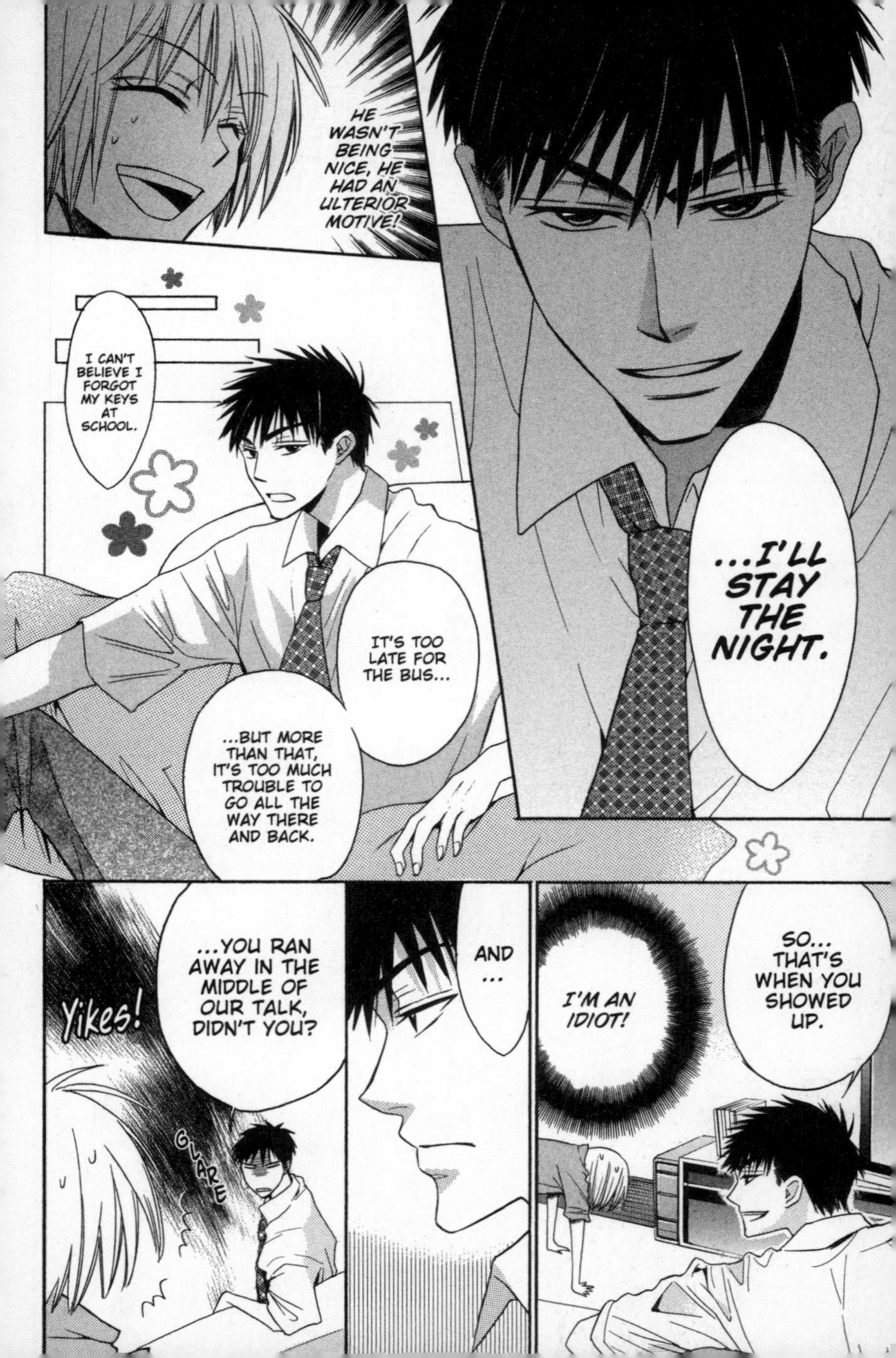
...I'LL STAY THE NIGHT.
HE WASN'T BEING NICE, HE HAD AN ULTERIOR MOTIVE!
I CAN'T BELIEVE I FORGOT MY KEYS AT SCHOOL.
IT'S TOO LATE FOR THE BUS...
...BUT MORE THAN THAT, IT'S TOO MUCH TROUBLE TO GO ALL THE WAY THERE AND BACK.
SO... THAT'S WHEN YOU SHOWED UP.
I'M AN IDIOT!
AND ...
...YOU RAN AWAY IN THE MIDDLE OF OUR TALK, DIDN'T YOU?
Yikes!
GLARE

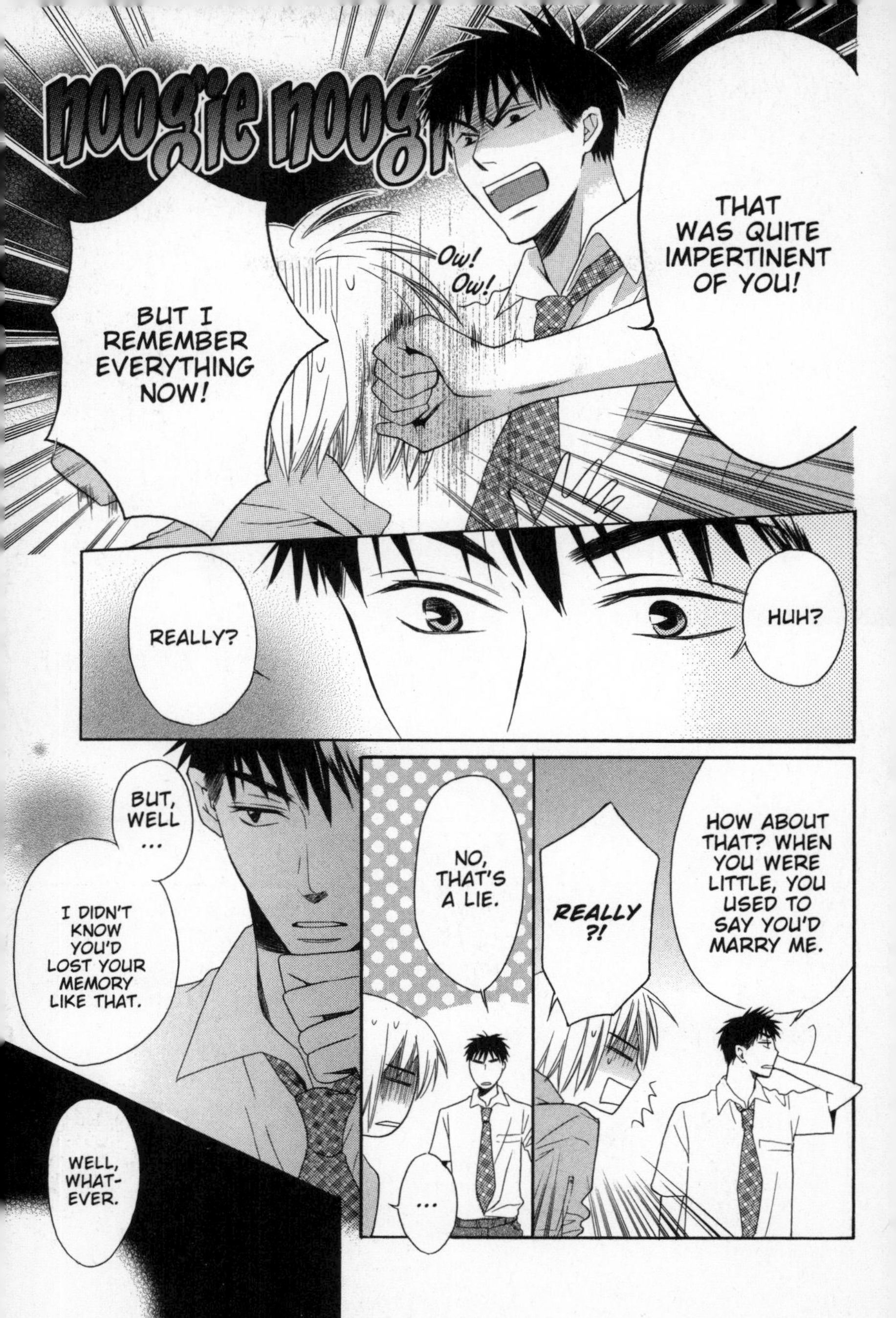
THAT WAS QUITE IMPERTINENT OF YOU!
noogie noog
Ow! Ow!
BUT I REMEMBER EVERYTHING NOW!
HUH?
REALLY?
HOW ABOUT THAT? WHEN YOU WERE LITTLE, YOU USED TO SAY YOU'D MARRY ME.
REALLY?!
NO, THAT'S A LIE.
...
BUT, WELL ...
I DIDN'T KNOW YOU'D LOST YOUR MEMORY LIKE THAT.
WELL, WHATEVER.

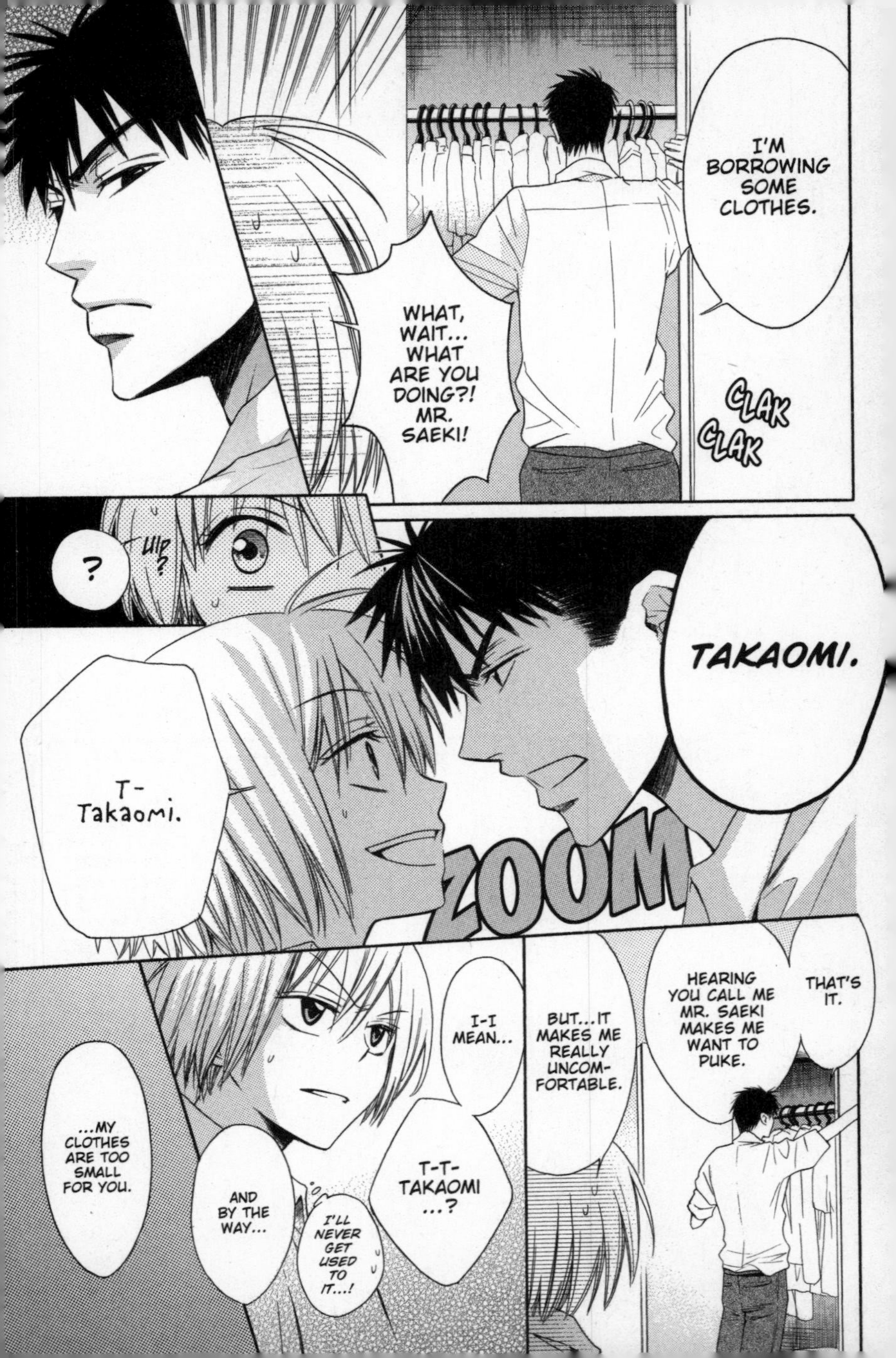
I'M BORROWING SOME CLOTHES.
CLAK CLAK
WHAT, WAIT... WHAT ARE YOU DOING?! MR. SAEKI!
TAKAOMI.
ZOOM
T- Takaomi.
?
Ulp?
THAT'S IT.
HEARING YOU CALL ME MR. SAEKI MAKES ME WANT TO PUKE.
BUT...IT MAKES ME REALLY UNCOM- FORTABLE.
I-I MEAN...
T-T- TAKAOMI ...?
I'LL NEVER GET USED TO IT...!
AND BY THE WAY...
...MY CLOTHES ARE TOO SMALL FOR YOU.

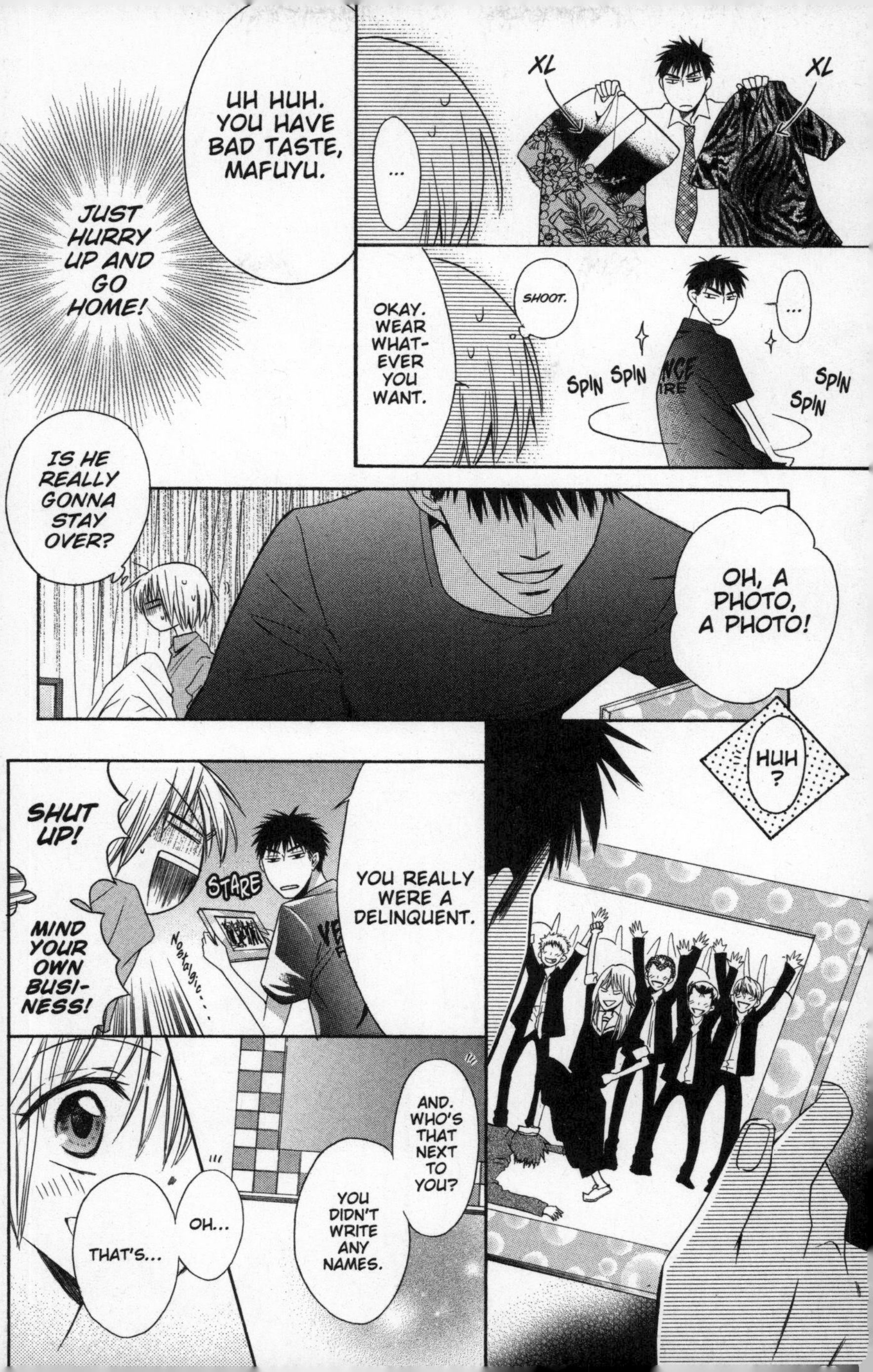
XL
XL
...
UH HUH. YOU HAVE BAD TASTE, MAFUYU.
...
SHOOT.
SPIN SPIN SPIN SPIN
OKAY. WEAR WHATEVER YOU WANT.
JUST HURRY UP AND GO HOME!
OH, A PHOTO, A PHOTO!
IS HE REALLY GONNA STAY OVER?
HUH?
YOU REALLY WERE A DELINQUENT.
STARE
Nostalgic...
SHUT UP!
MIND YOUR OWN BUSINESS!
AND. WHO'S THAT NEXT TO YOU?
YOU DIDN'T WRITE ANY NAMES.
OH...
THAT'S...

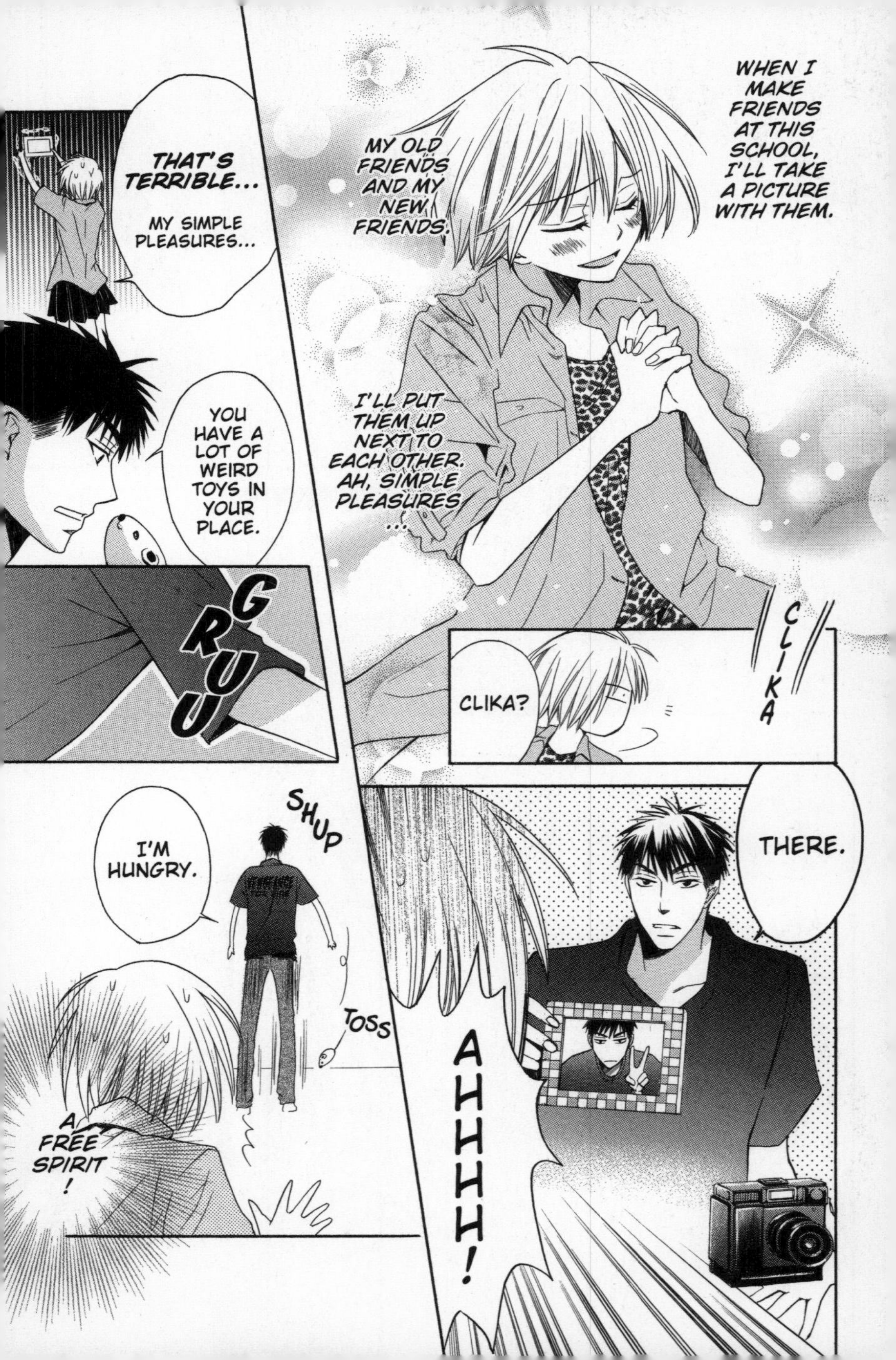

WHEN I MAKE FRIENDS AT THIS SCHOOL, I'LL TAKE A PICTURE WITH THEM.
MY OLD FRIENDS AND MY NEW FRIENDS.
I'LL PUT THEM UP NEXT TO EACH OTHER. AH, SIMPLE PLEASURES...
CLIKA
CLIKA?
THERE.
AHHHH!
THAT'S TERRIBLE... MY SIMPLE PLEASURES...
YOU HAVE A LOT OF WEIRD TOYS IN YOUR PLACE.
GRUUU
I'M HUNGRY.
SHUP
TOSS
A FREE SPIRIT!

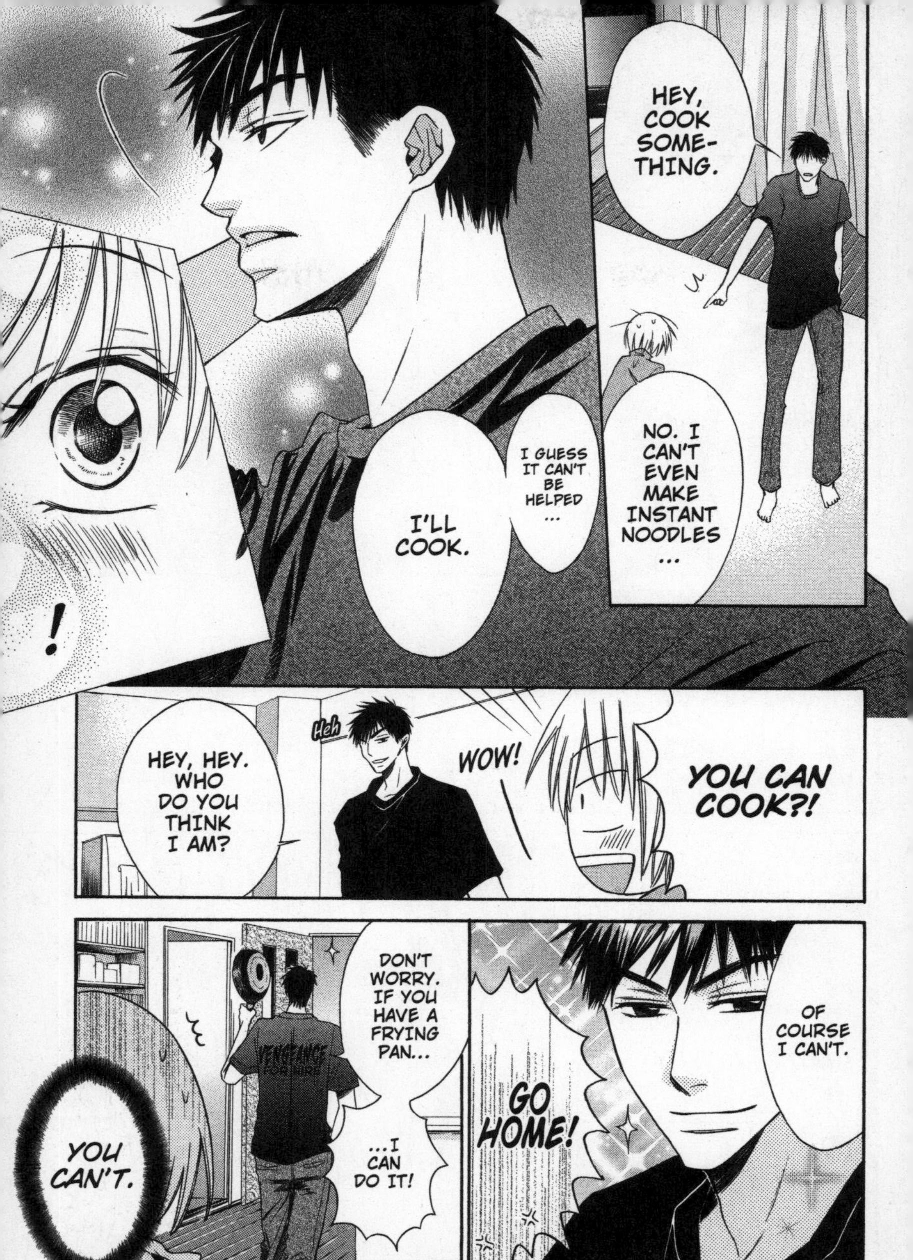
HEY, COOK SOME-THING.
NO. I CAN'T EVEN MAKE INSTANT NOODLES...
I GUESS IT CAN'T BE HELPED...
I'LL COOK.
!
YOU CAN COOK?!
WOW!
Heh
HEY, HEY. WHO DO YOU THINK I AM?
OF COURSE I CAN'T.
GO HOME!
DON'T WORRY. IF YOU HAVE A FRYING PAN...
VENGEANCE
...I CAN DO IT!
YOU CAN'T.

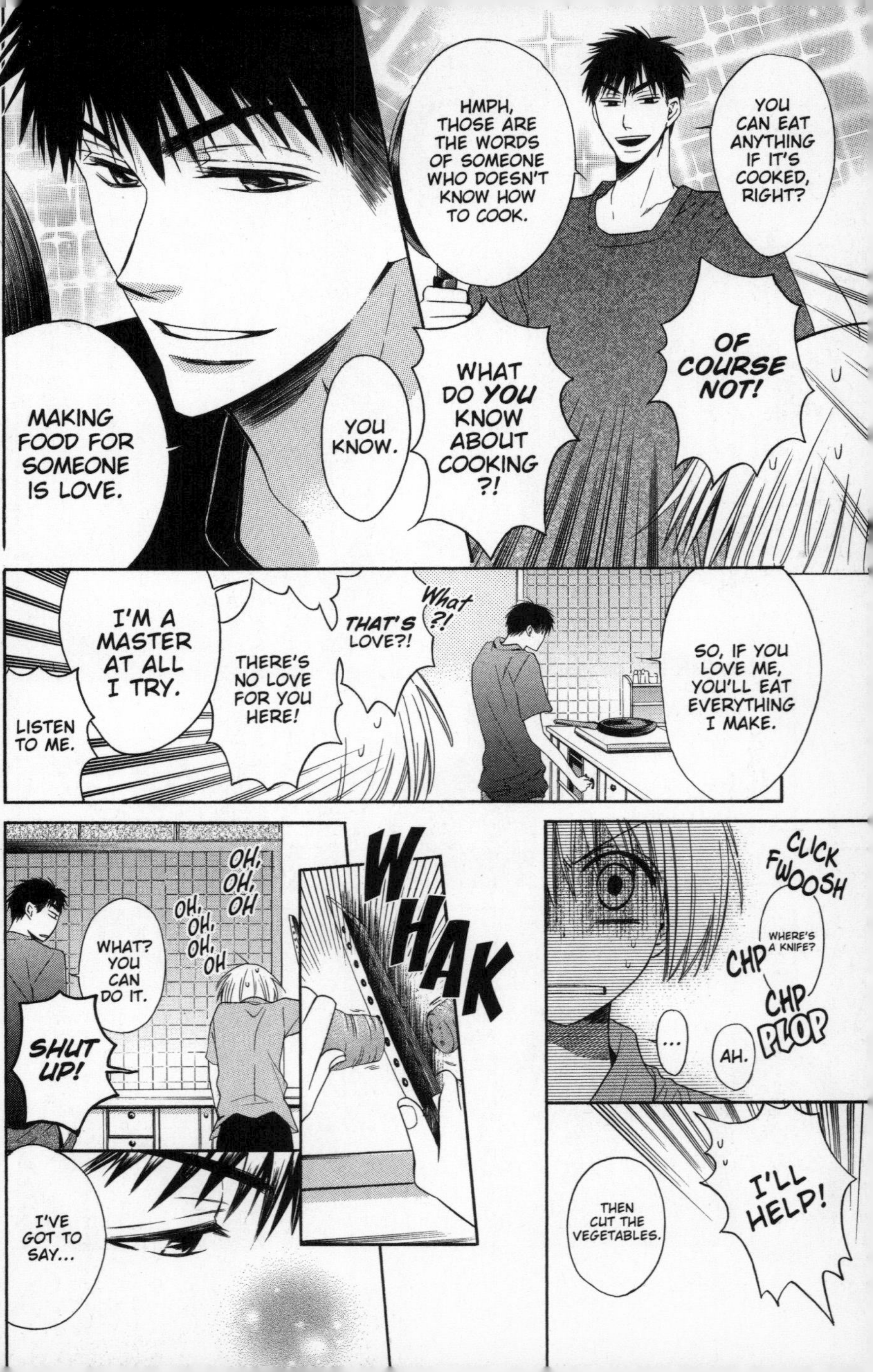
YOU CAN EAT ANYTHING IF IT'S COOKED, RIGHT?
HMPH, THOSE ARE THE WORDS OF SOMEONE WHO DOESN'T KNOW HOW TO COOK.
OF COURSE NOT!
WHAT DO YOU KNOW ABOUT COOKING?!
YOU KNOW.
MAKING FOOD FOR SOMEONE IS LOVE.
SO, IF YOU LOVE ME, YOU'LL EAT EVERYTHING I MAKE.
What?!
THAT'S LOVE?!
THERE'S NO LOVE FOR YOU HERE!
I'M A MASTER AT ALL I TRY.
LISTEN TO ME.
CLICK
FWOOSH
WHERE'S A KNIFE?
CHP
CHP
PLOP
AH.
...
I'LL HELP!
THEN CUT THE VEGETABLES.
WHAK
OH, OH, OH
OH, OH, OH, OH
WHAT? YOU CAN DO IT.
SHUT UP!
I'VE GOT TO SAY...

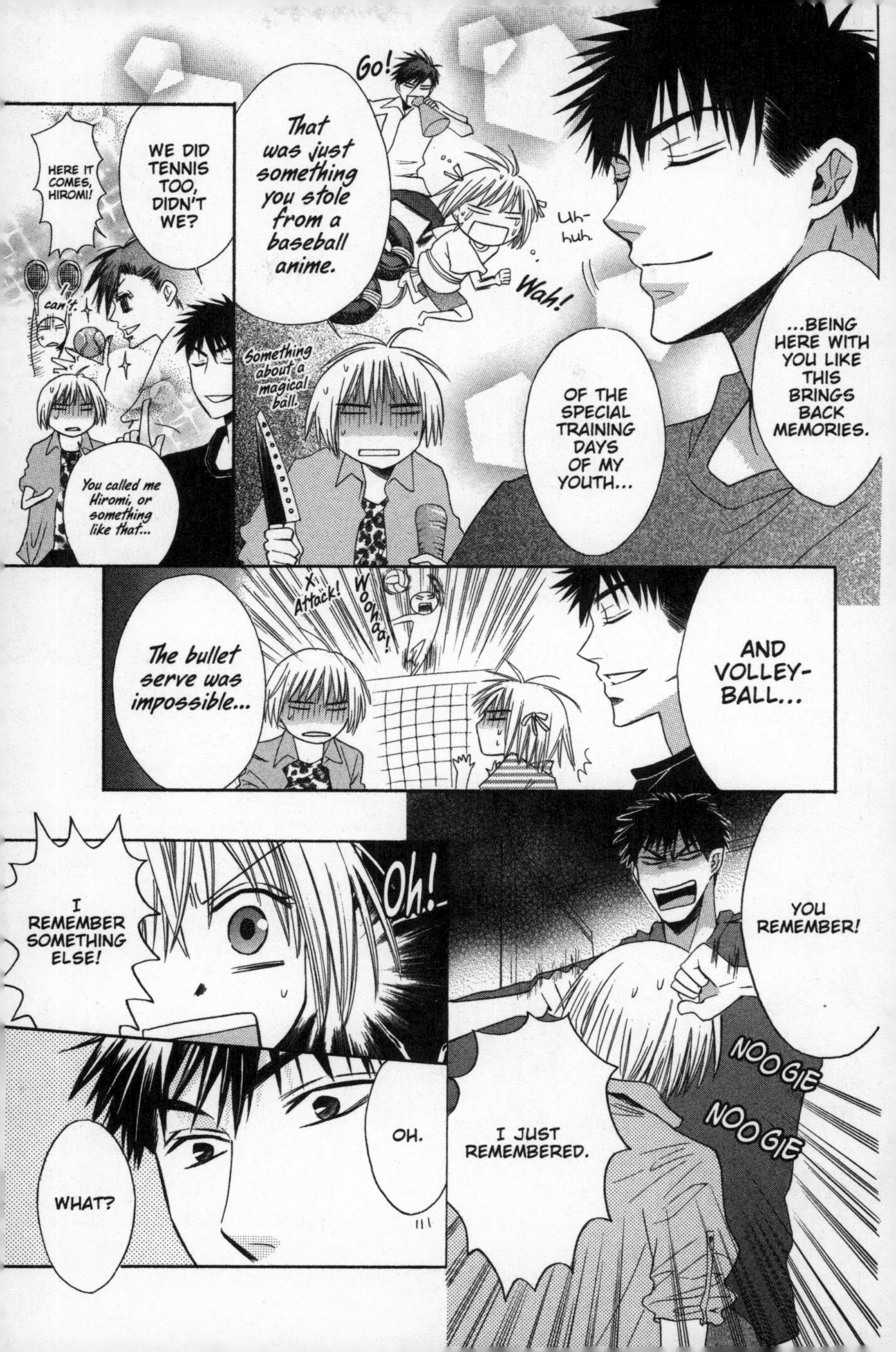
...BEING HERE WITH YOU LIKE THIS BRINGS BACK MEMORIES.
OF THE SPECIAL TRAINING DAYS OF MY YOUTH...
Go!
That was just something you stole from a baseball anime.
Uh-huh.
Wah!
Something about a magical ball.
WE DID TENNIS TOO, DIDN'T WE?
HERE IT COMES, HIROMI!
can't.
You called me Hiromi, or something like that...
AND VOLLEY-BALL...
X Attack!
Woohaa!
The bullet serve was impossible...
YOU REMEMBER!
NOOGIE
NOOGIE
I JUST REMEMBERED.
OH.
Oh!
I REMEMBER SOMETHING ELSE!
WHAT?

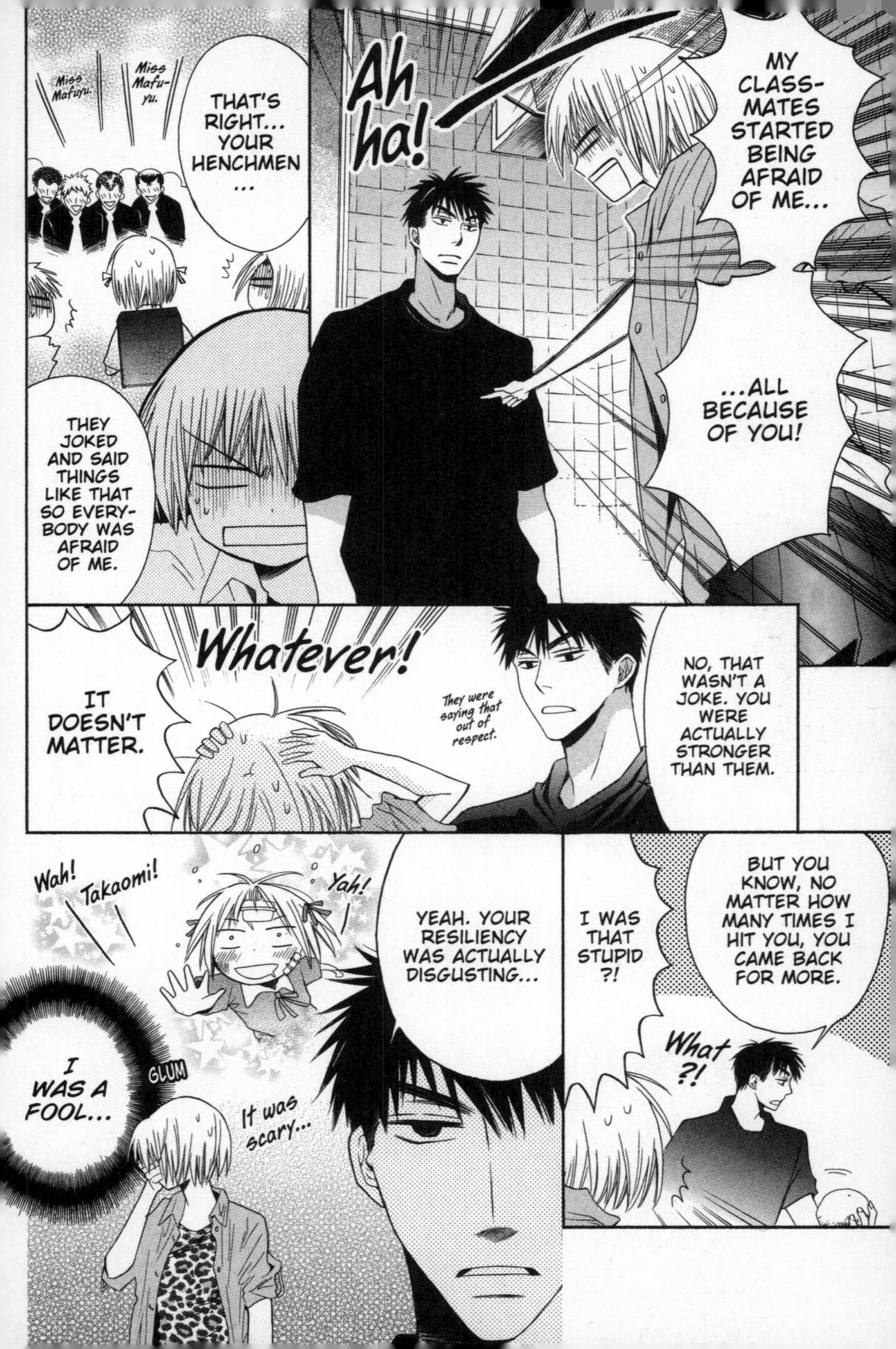
MY CLASS-MATES STARTED BEING AFRAID OF ME...
...ALL BECAUSE OF YOU!
Ah ha!
THAT'S RIGHT... YOUR HENCHMEN...
Miss Mafu-yu.
Miss Mafuyu.
THEY JOKED AND SAID THINGS LIKE THAT SO EVERY-BODY WAS AFRAID OF ME.
NO, THAT WASN'T A JOKE. YOU WERE ACTUALLY STRONGER THAN THEM.
They were saying that out of respect.
Whatever!
IT DOESN'T MATTER.
BUT YOU KNOW, NO MATTER HOW MANY TIMES I HIT YOU, YOU CAME BACK FOR MORE.
What?!
I WAS THAT STUPID?!
YEAH. YOUR RESILIENCY WAS ACTUALLY DISGUSTING...
Yah!
Takaomi!
Wah!
I WAS A FOOL...
GLUM
It was scary...

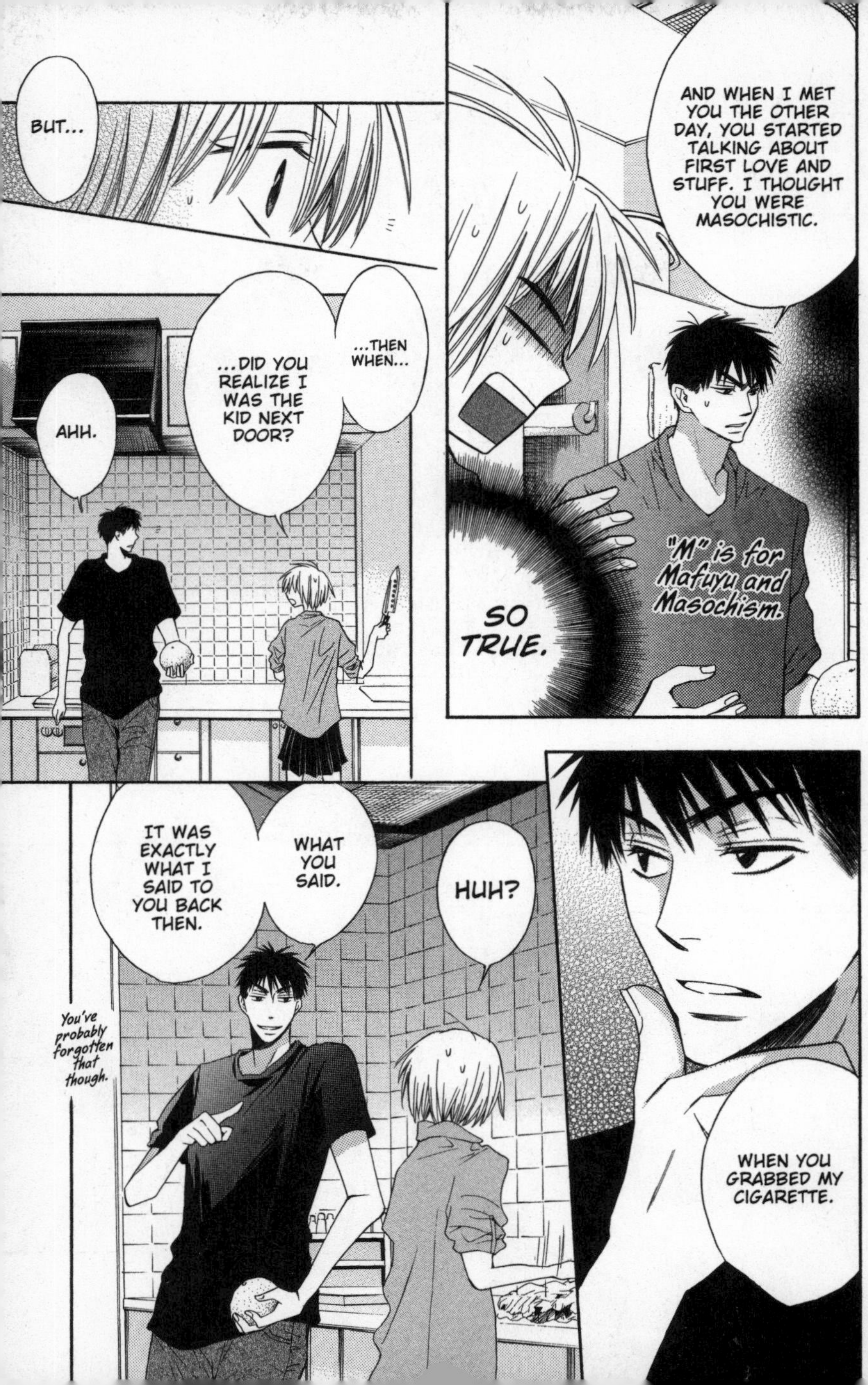
AND WHEN I MET YOU THE OTHER DAY, YOU STARTED TALKING ABOUT FIRST LOVE AND STUFF. I THOUGHT YOU WERE MASOCHISTIC.
"M" is for Mafuyu and Masochism.
SO TRUE.
BUT...
...THEN WHEN...
...DID YOU REALIZE I WAS THE KID NEXT DOOR?
AHH.
WHEN YOU GRABBED MY CIGARETTE.
HUH?
WHAT YOU SAID.
IT WAS EXACTLY WHAT I SAID TO YOU BACK THEN.
You've probably forgotten that though.

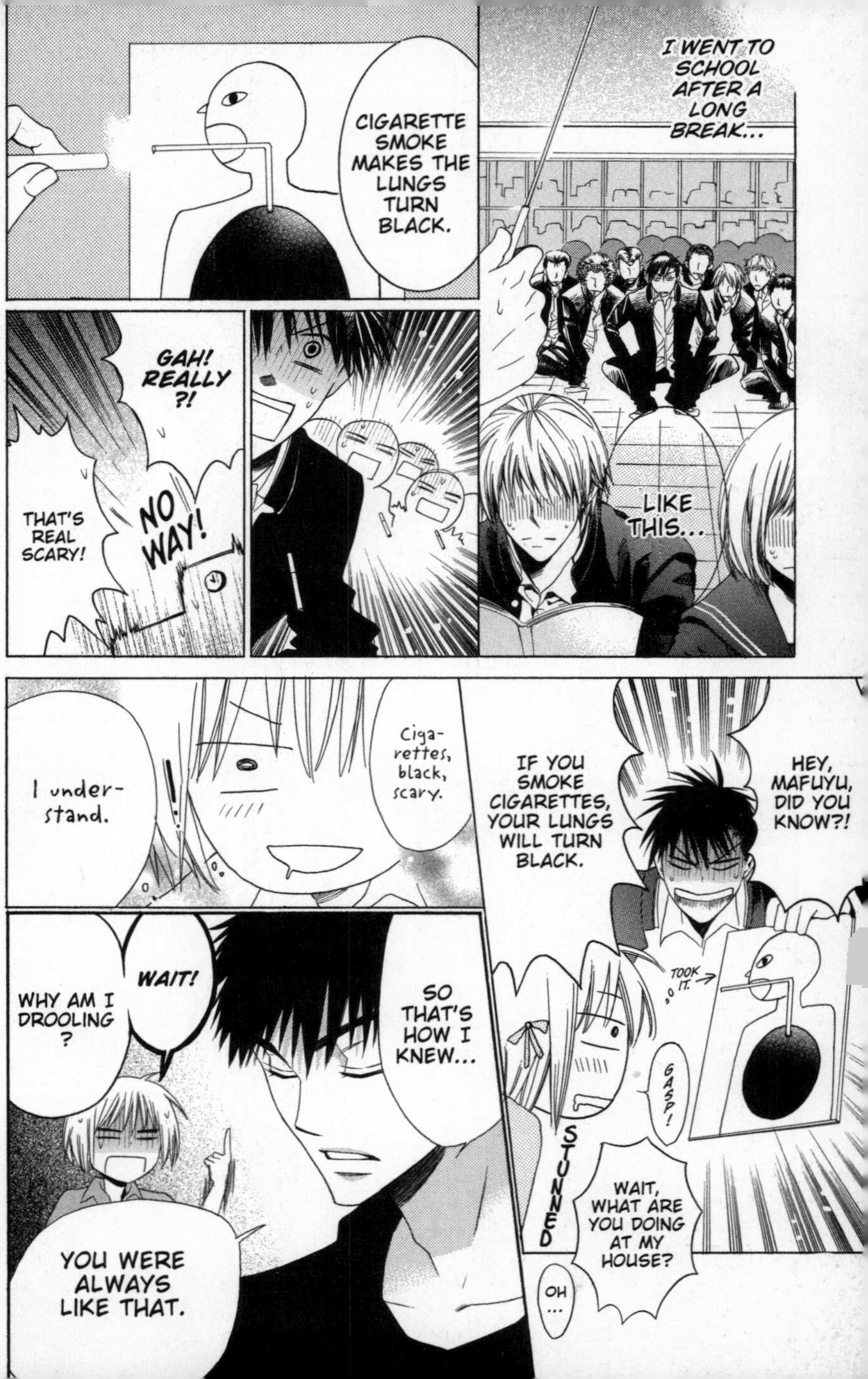
I WENT TO SCHOOL AFTER A LONG BREAK...
LIKE THIS...
CIGARETTE SMOKE MAKES THE LUNGS TURN BLACK.
GAH! REALLY?!
NO WAY!
THAT'S REAL SCARY!
HEY, MAFUYU, DID YOU KNOW?!
IF YOU SMOKE CIGARETTES, YOUR LUNGS WILL TURN BLACK.
TOOK IT.
GASP!
STUNNED
WAIT, WHAT ARE YOU DOING AT MY HOUSE?
OH...
Cigarettes, black, scary.
I understand.
SO THAT'S HOW I KNEW...
WAIT!
WHY AM I DROOLING?
YOU WERE ALWAYS LIKE THAT.

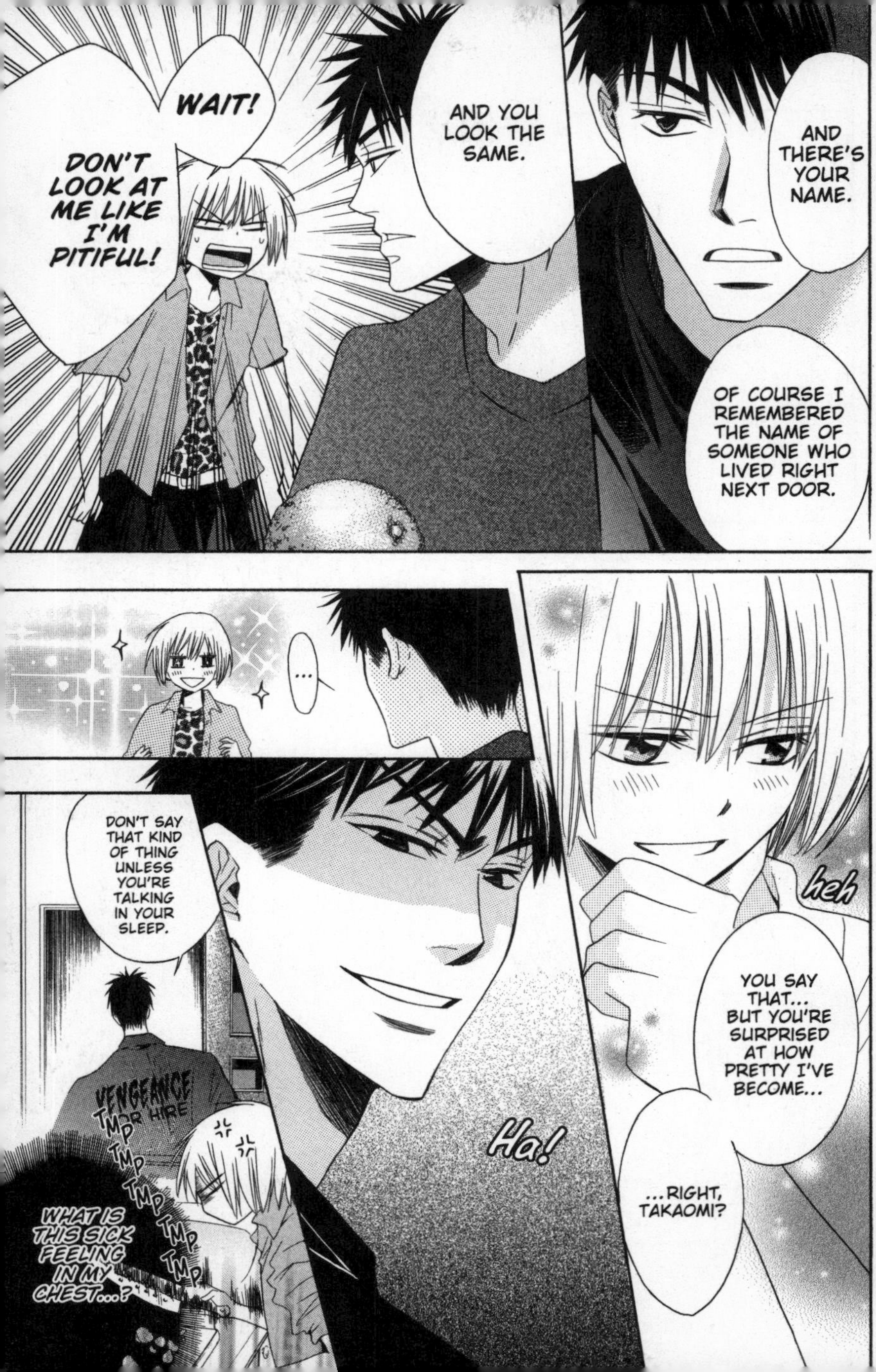
AND THERE'S YOUR NAME.
OF COURSE I REMEMBERED THE NAME OF SOMEONE WHO LIVED RIGHT NEXT DOOR.
AND YOU LOOK THE SAME.
WAIT!
DON'T LOOK AT ME LIKE I'M PITIFUL!
heh
YOU SAY THAT... BUT YOU'RE SURPRISED AT HOW PRETTY I'VE BECOME...
...RIGHT, TAKAOMI?
...
Ha!
DON'T SAY THAT KIND OF THING UNLESS YOU'RE TALKING IN YOUR SLEEP.
VENGEANCE
TMP TMP TMP TMP TMP TMP
WHAT IS THIS SICK FEELING IN MY CHEST...?

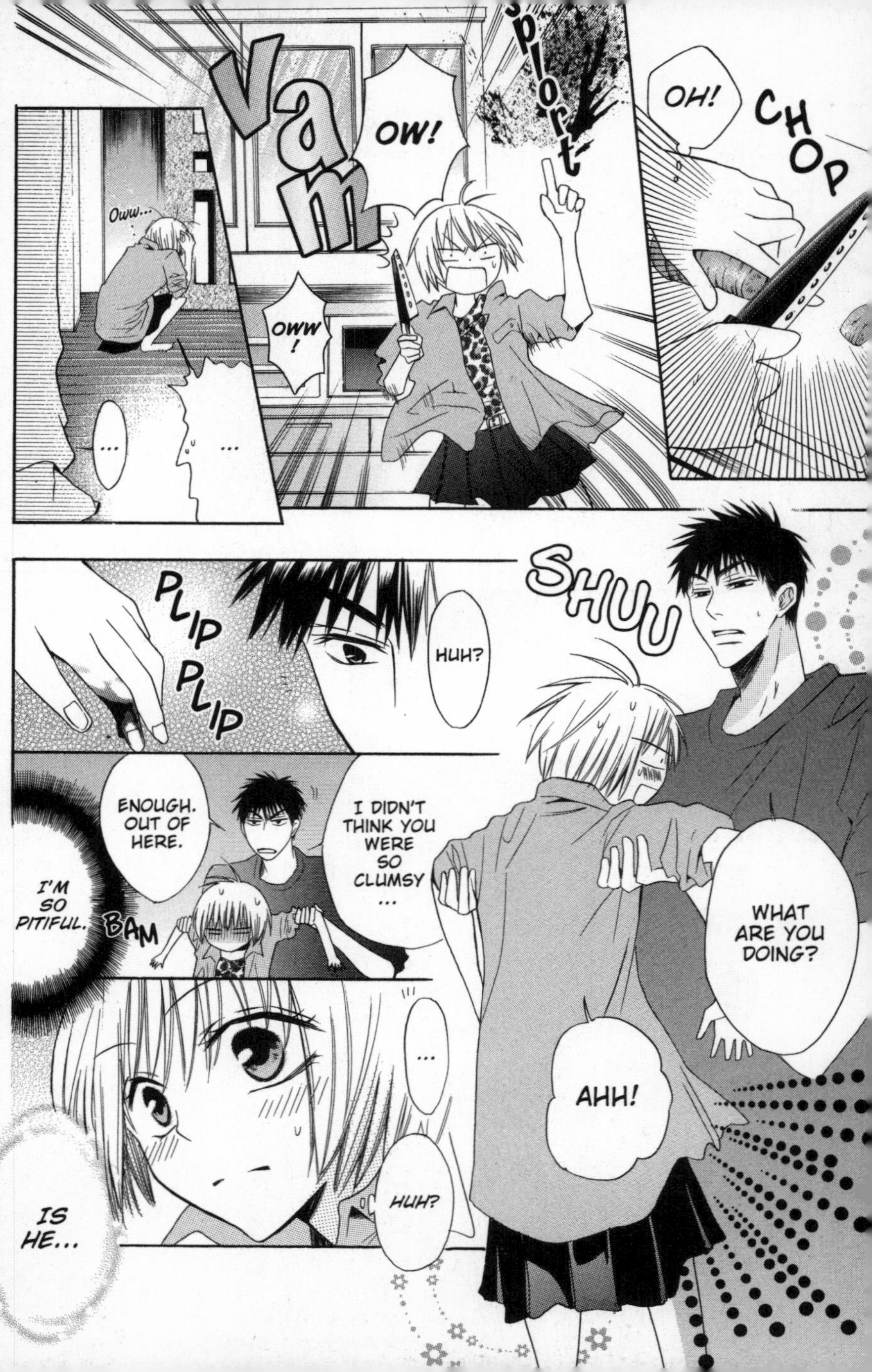
OH!
CHOP
splort
vam
OW!
OWW!
Oww...
...
...
SHUU
WHAT ARE YOU DOING?
AHH!
HUH?
PLIP PLIP
I DIDN'T THINK YOU WERE SO CLUMSY ...
ENOUGH. OUT OF HERE.
BAM
I'M SO PITIFUL.
...
HUH?
IS HE...

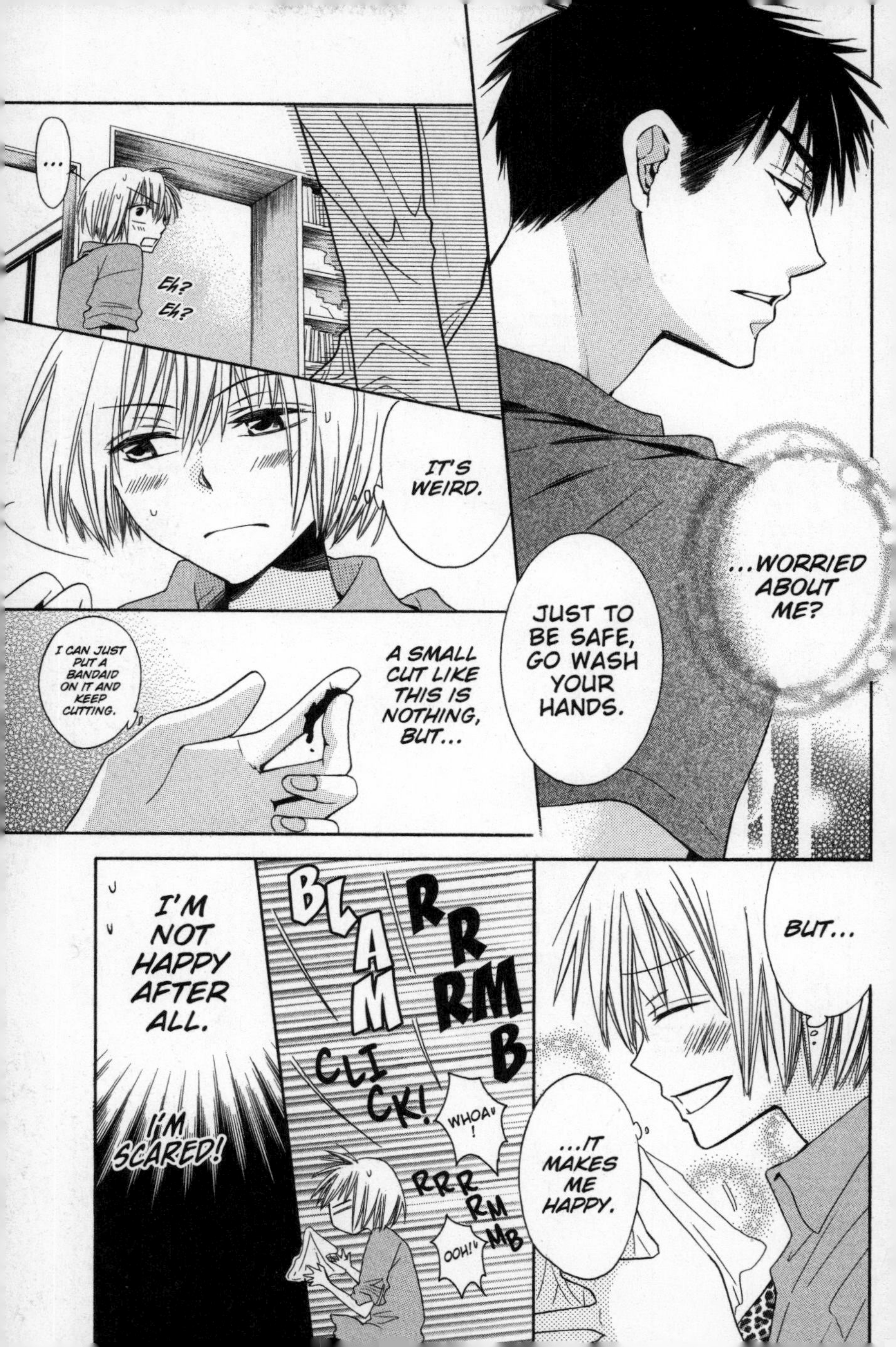
JUST TO BE SAFE, GO WASH YOUR HANDS.
...WORRIED ABOUT ME?
...
Eh? Eh?
IT'S WEIRD.
A SMALL CUT LIKE THIS IS NOTHING, BUT...
I CAN JUST PUT A BANDAID ON IT AND KEEP CUTTING.
BUT...
...IT MAKES ME HAPPY.
BLAM
RRRRMB
CLICK!
WHOA!
RRRRMMB
OOH!
I'M NOT HAPPY AFTER ALL.
I'M SCARED!

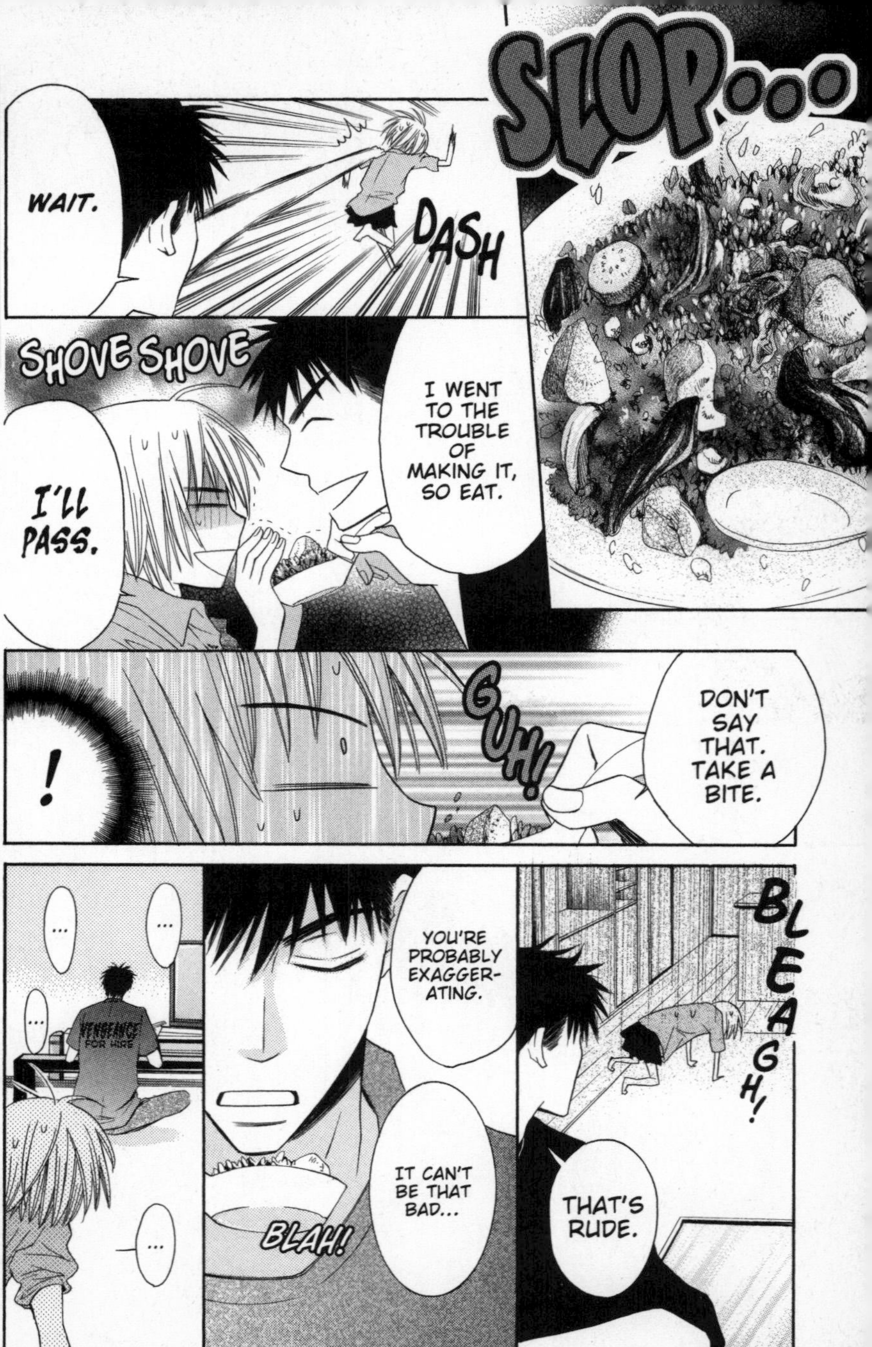
SLOP...
WAIT.
DASH
I WENT TO THE TROUBLE OF MAKING IT, SO EAT.
SHOVE SHOVE
I'LL PASS.
DON'T SAY THAT. TAKE A BITE.
GUH!
!
BLEAGH!
THAT'S RUDE.
YOU'RE PROBABLY EXAGGER-ATING.
IT CAN'T BE THAT BAD...
BLAH!
...
...
...
VENGEANCE FOR HIRE
...

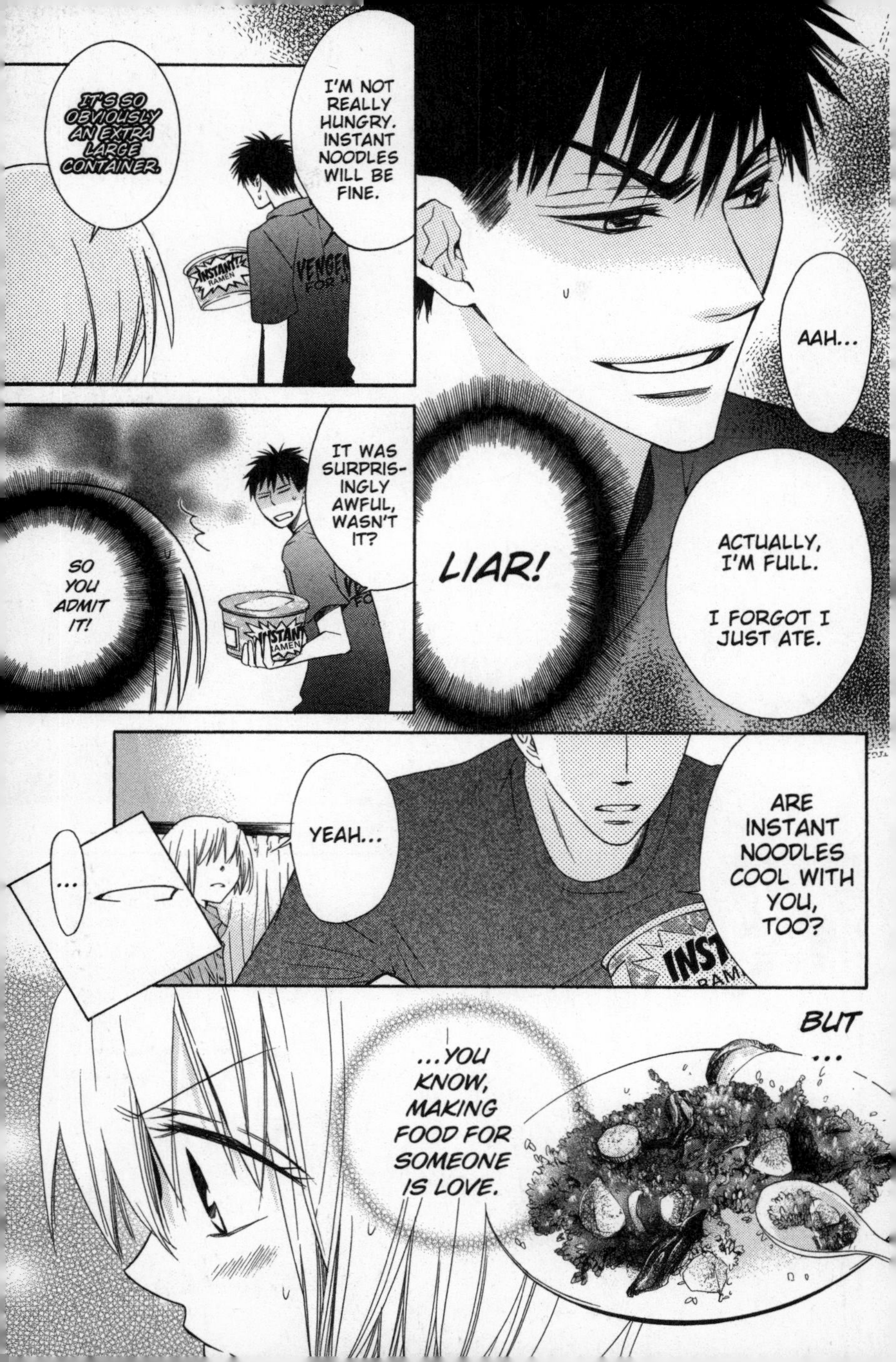
AAH...
ACTUALLY, I'M FULL.
I FORGOT I JUST ATE.
LIAR!
I'M NOT REALLY HUNGRY. INSTANT NOODLES WILL BE FINE.
IT'S SO OBVIOUSLY AN EXTRA LARGE CONTAINER.
INSTANT! RAMEN
VENGE
FOR
IT WAS SURPRISINGLY AWFUL, WASN'T IT?
SO YOU ADMIT IT!
INSTANT RAMEN
ARE INSTANT NOODLES COOL WITH YOU, TOO?
YEAH...
...
BUT...
...YOU KNOW, MAKING FOOD FOR SOMEONE IS LOVE.

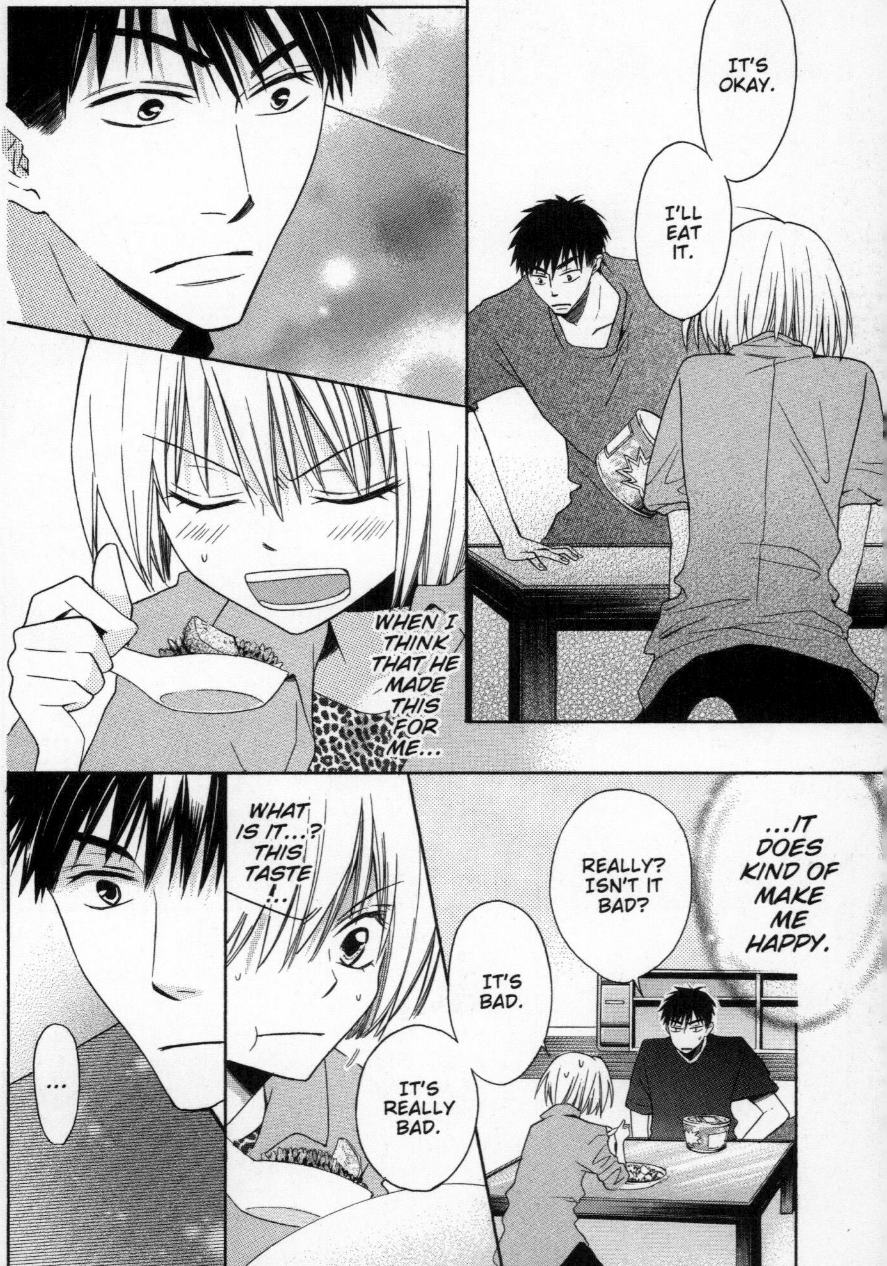
IT'S OKAY.
I'LL EAT IT.
WHEN I THINK THAT HE MADE THIS FOR ME...
...IT DOES KIND OF MAKE ME HAPPY.
REALLY? ISN'T IT BAD?
IT'S BAD.
IT'S REALLY BAD.
WHAT IS IT...? THIS TASTE...!
...

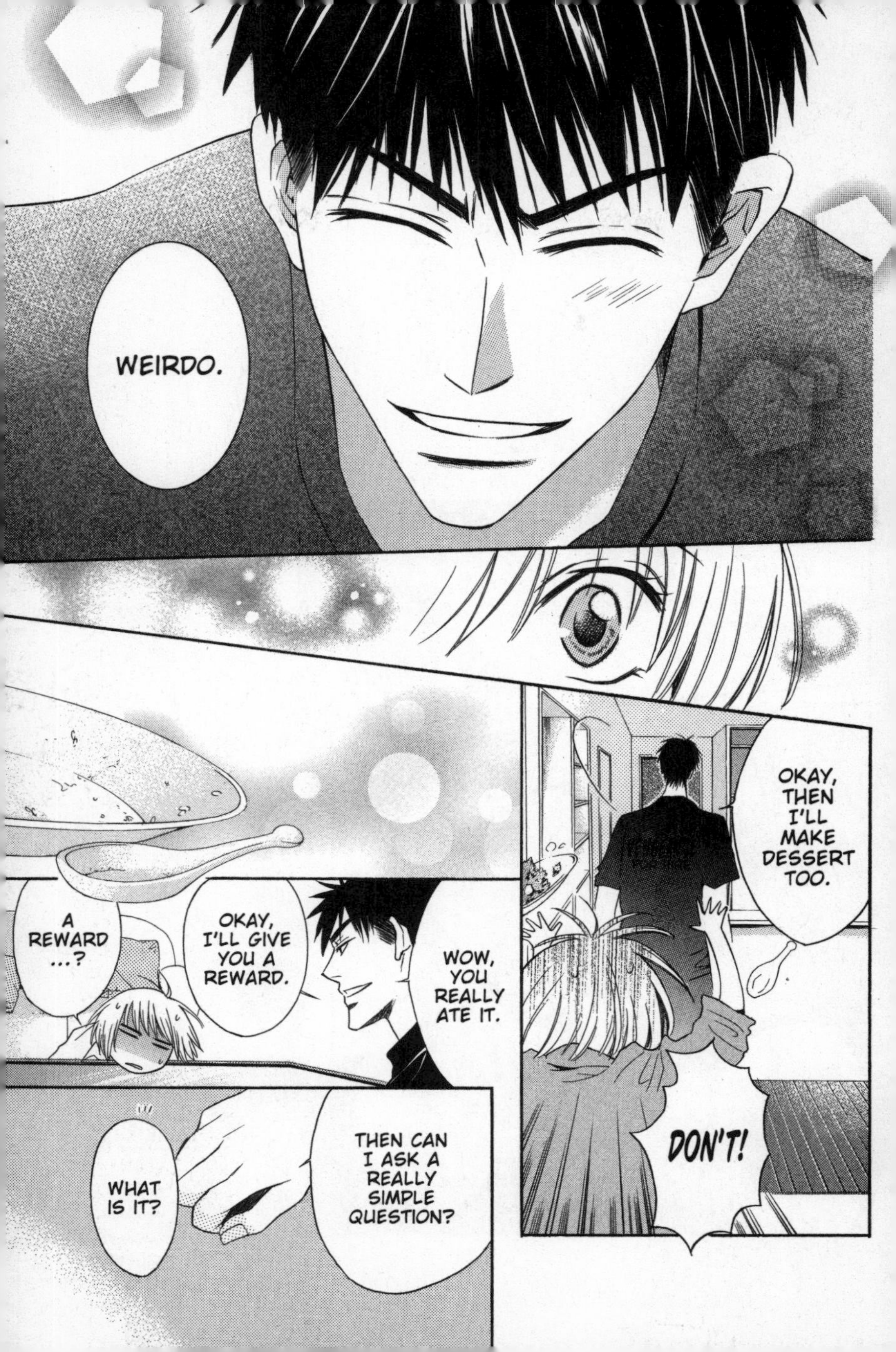
WEIRDO.
OKAY, THEN I'LL MAKE DESSERT TOO.
DON'T!
WOW, YOU REALLY ATE IT.
OKAY, I'LL GIVE YOU A REWARD.
A REWARD ...?
THEN CAN I ASK A REALLY SIMPLE QUESTION?
WHAT IS IT?

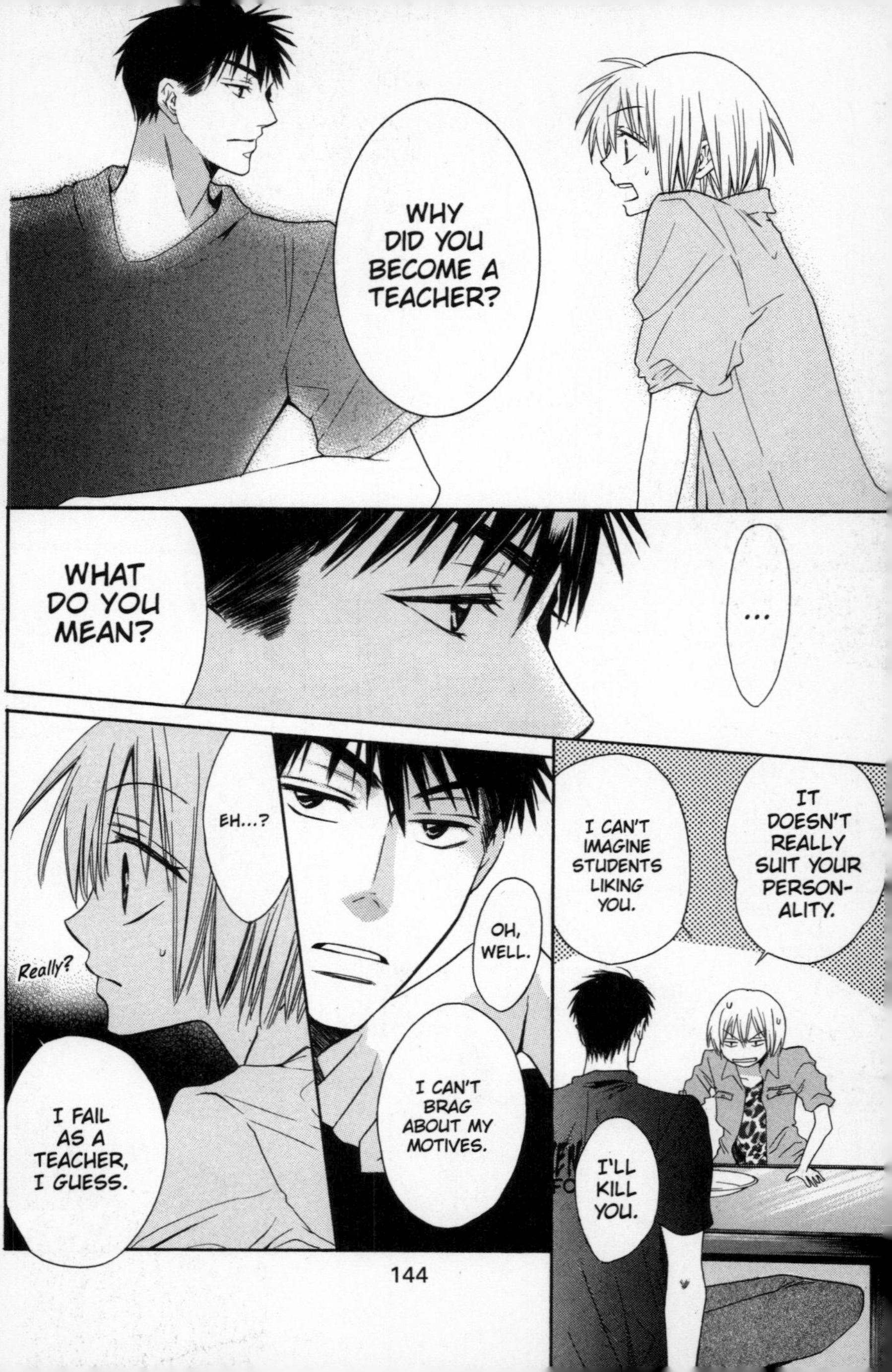
WHY DID YOU BECOME A TEACHER?
...
WHAT DO YOU MEAN?
IT DOESN'T REALLY SUIT YOUR PERSON-ALITY.
I CAN'T IMAGINE STUDENTS LIKING YOU.
I'LL KILL YOU.
OH, WELL.
I CAN'T BRAG ABOUT MY MOTIVES.
EH...?
Really?
I FAIL AS A TEACHER, I GUESS.

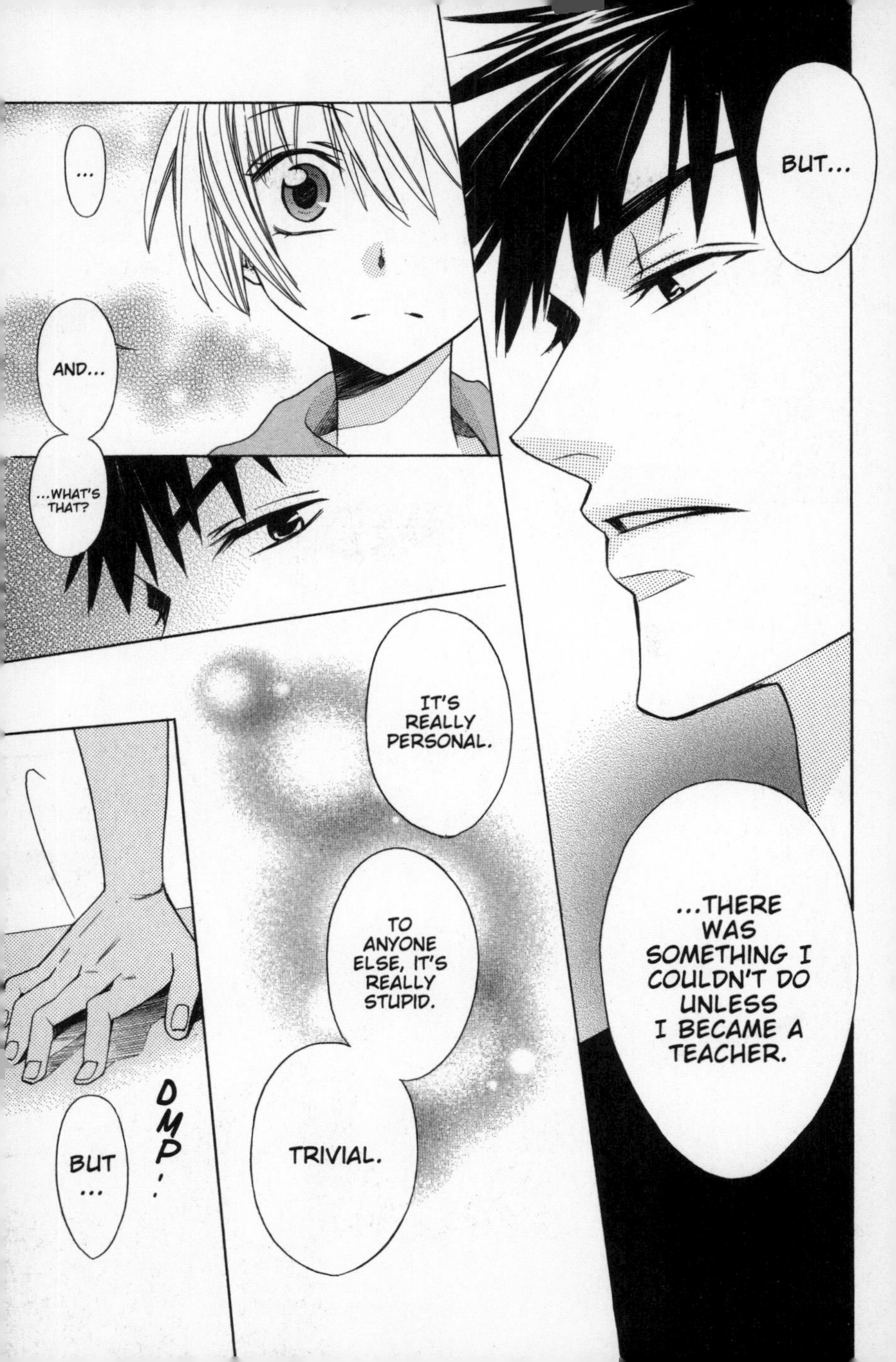
BUT...
...THERE WAS SOMETHING I COULDN'T DO UNLESS I BECAME A TEACHER.
...
AND...
...WHAT'S THAT?
IT'S REALLY PERSONAL.
TO ANYONE ELSE, IT'S REALLY STUPID.
TRIVIAL.
DMP!
BUT ...

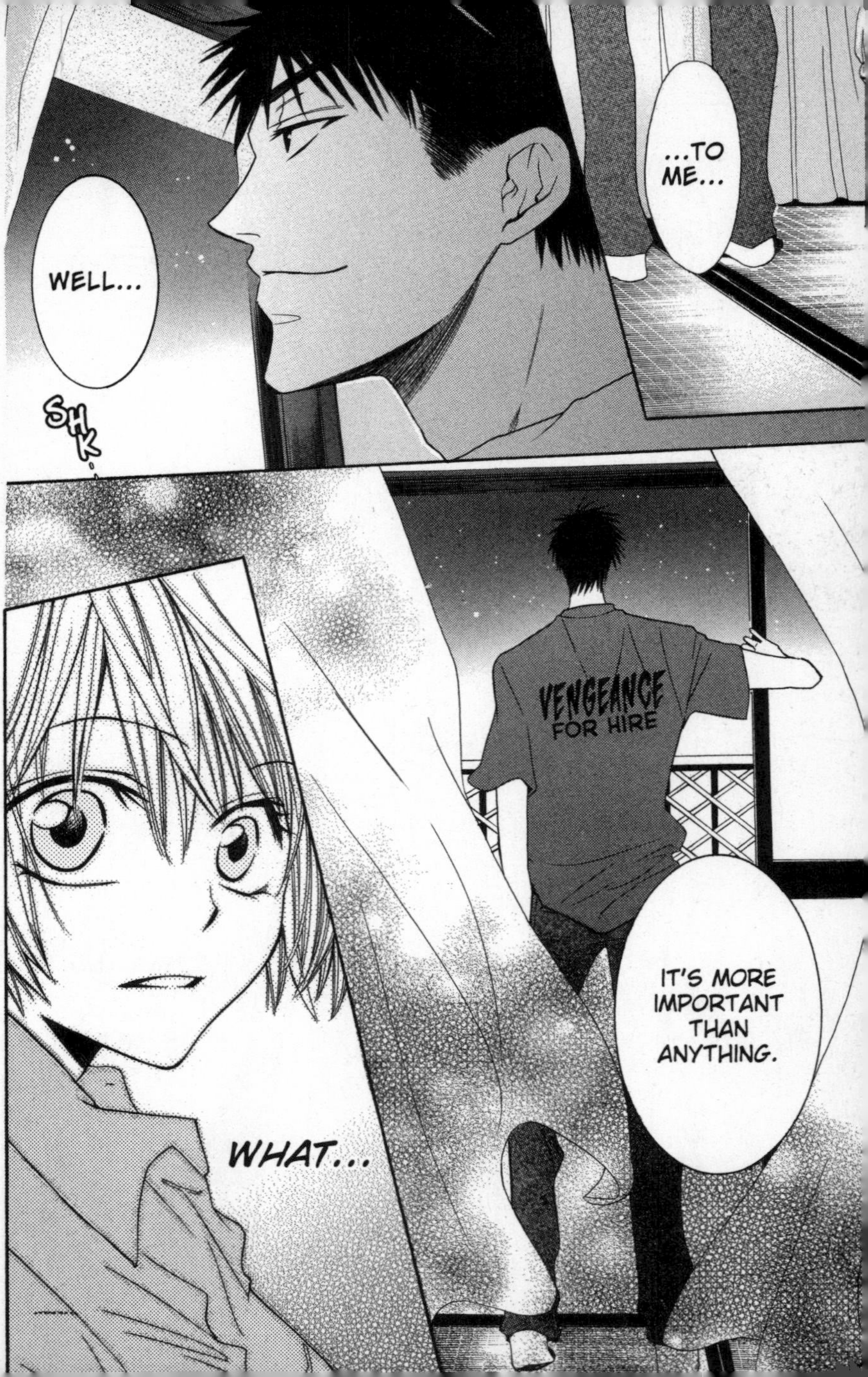
...TO ME...
WELL...
SHK
VENGEANCE FOR HIRE
IT'S MORE IMPORTANT THAN ANYTHING.
WHAT...

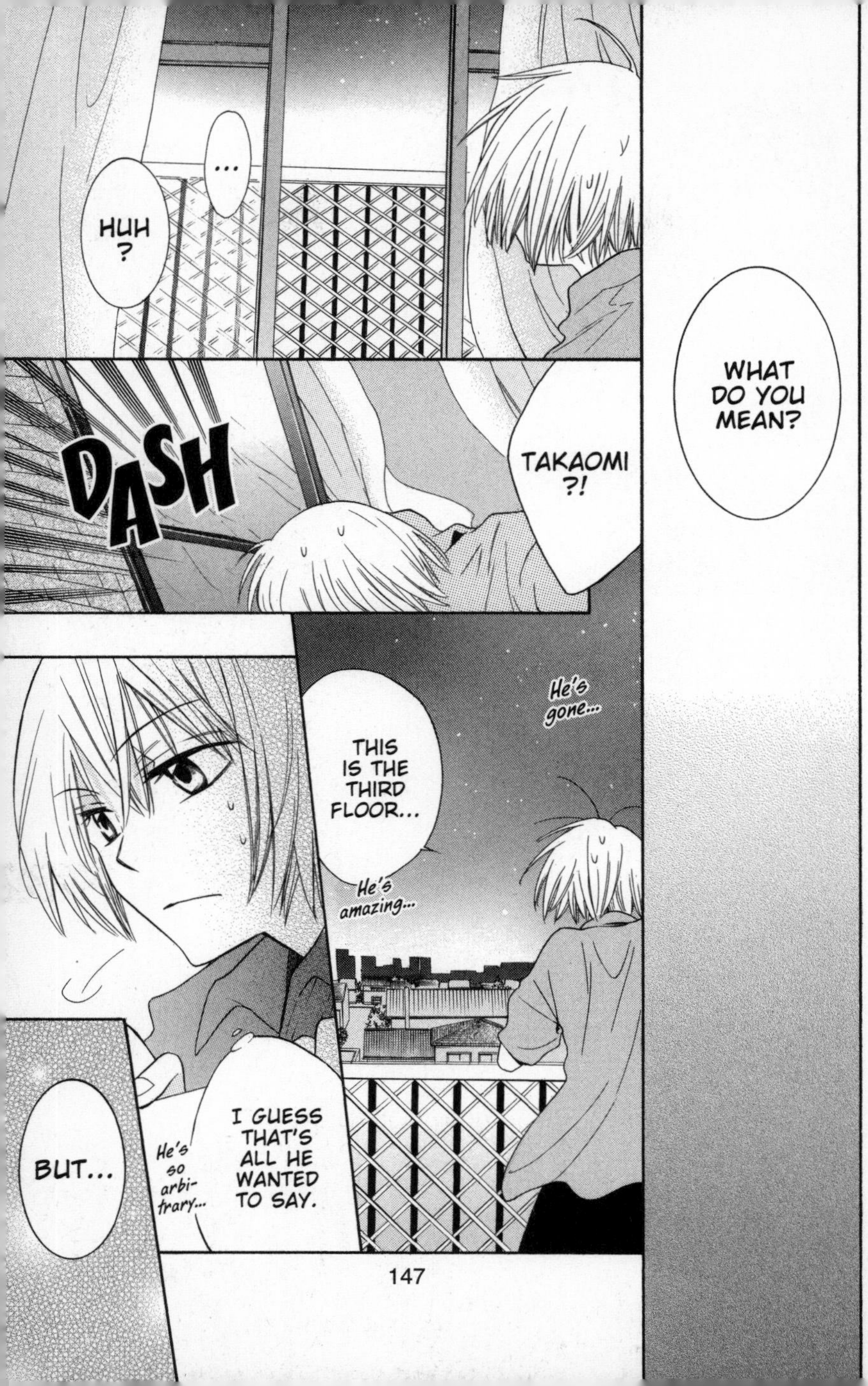
WHAT DO YOU MEAN?
...
HUH ?
TAKAOMI ?!
DASH
He's gone...
THIS IS THE THIRD FLOOR...
He's amazing...
I GUESS THAT'S ALL HE WANTED TO SAY.
He's so arbi-trary...
BUT...

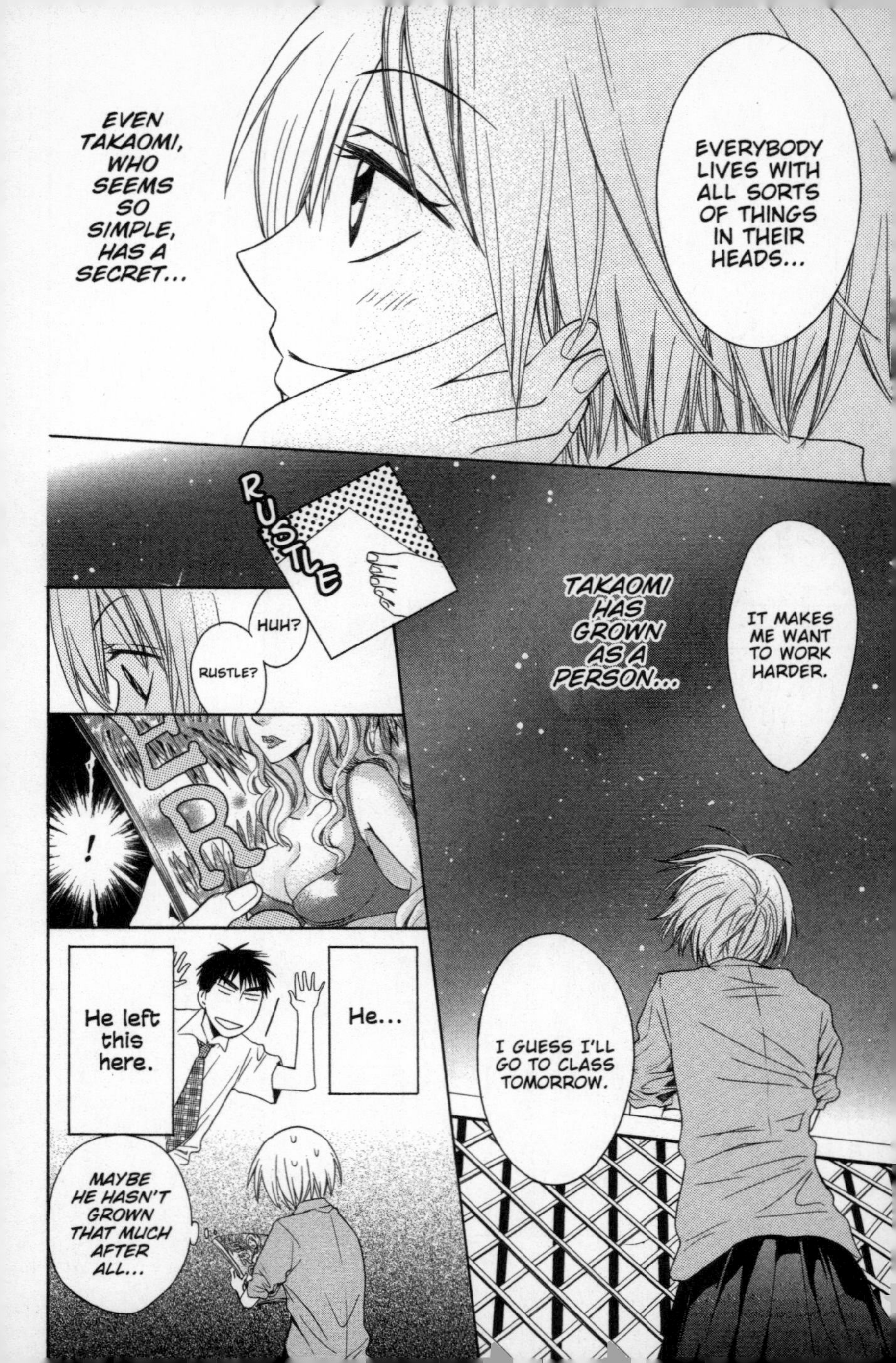
EVERYBODY LIVES WITH ALL SORTS OF THINGS IN THEIR HEADS...
EVEN TAKAOMI, WHO SEEMS SO SIMPLE, HAS A SECRET...
IT MAKES ME WANT TO WORK HARDER.
TAKAOMI HAS GROWN AS A PERSON...
I GUESS I'LL GO TO CLASS TOMORROW.
RUSTLE
HUH?
RUSTLE?
!
He...
He left this here.
MAYBE HE HASN'T GROWN THAT MUCH AFTER ALL...

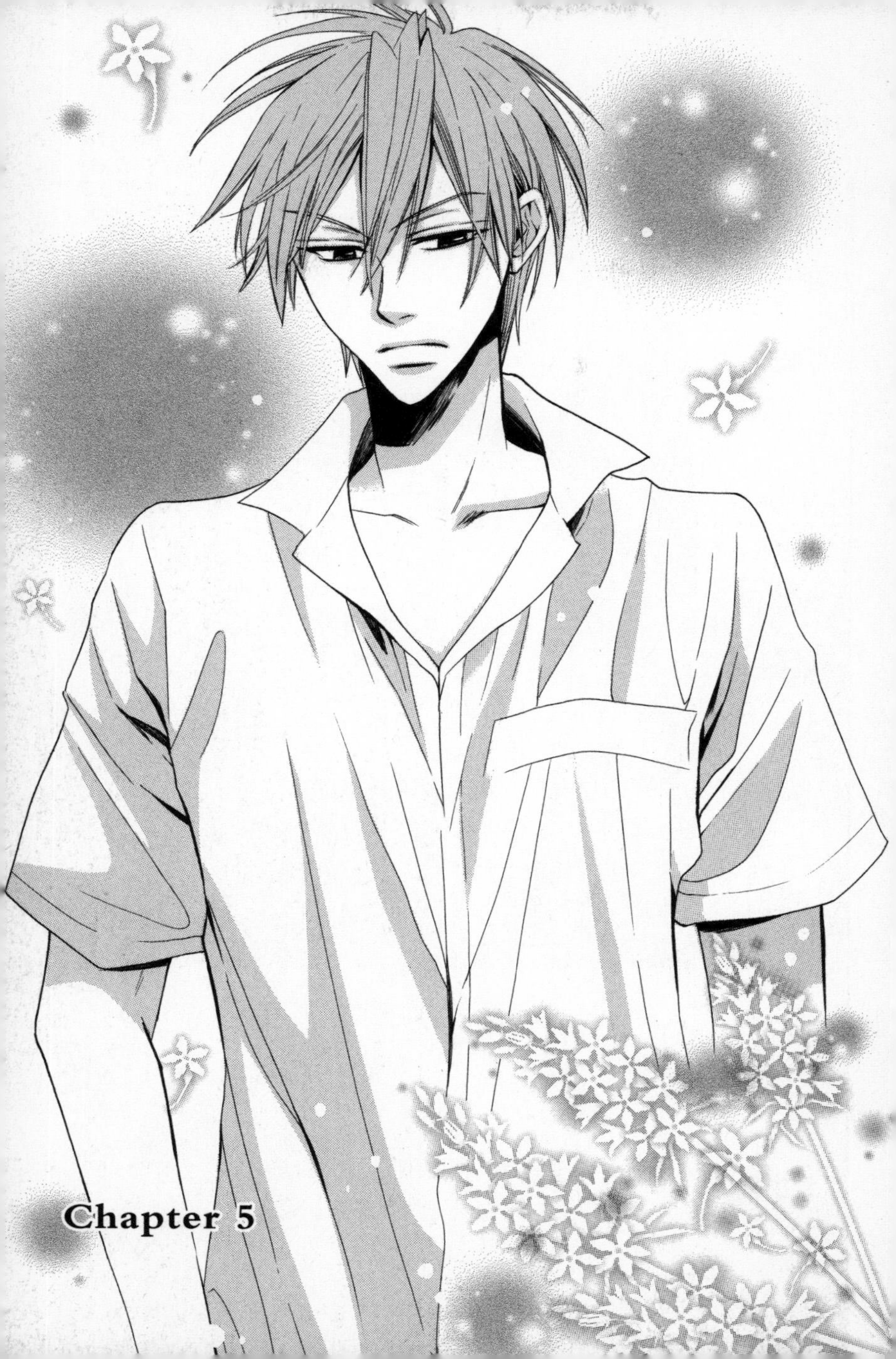

Chapter 5

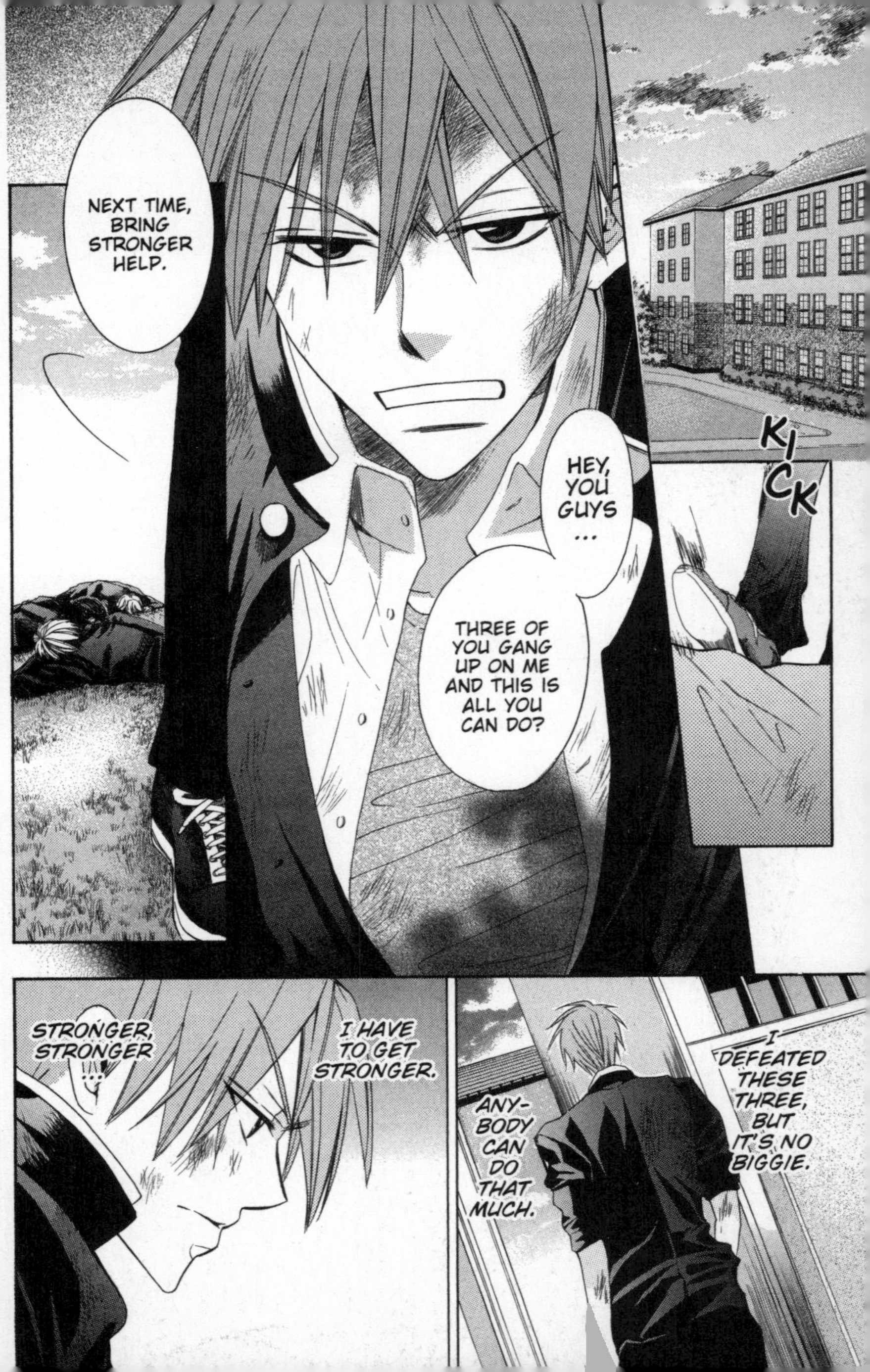
KICK
HEY, YOU GUYS...
THREE OF YOU GANG UP ON ME AND THIS IS ALL YOU CAN DO?
NEXT TIME, BRING STRONGER HELP.
I DEFEATED THESE THREE, BUT IT'S NO BIGGIE.
ANY-BODY CAN DO THAT MUCH.
I HAVE TO GET STRONGER.
STRONGER, STRONGER...

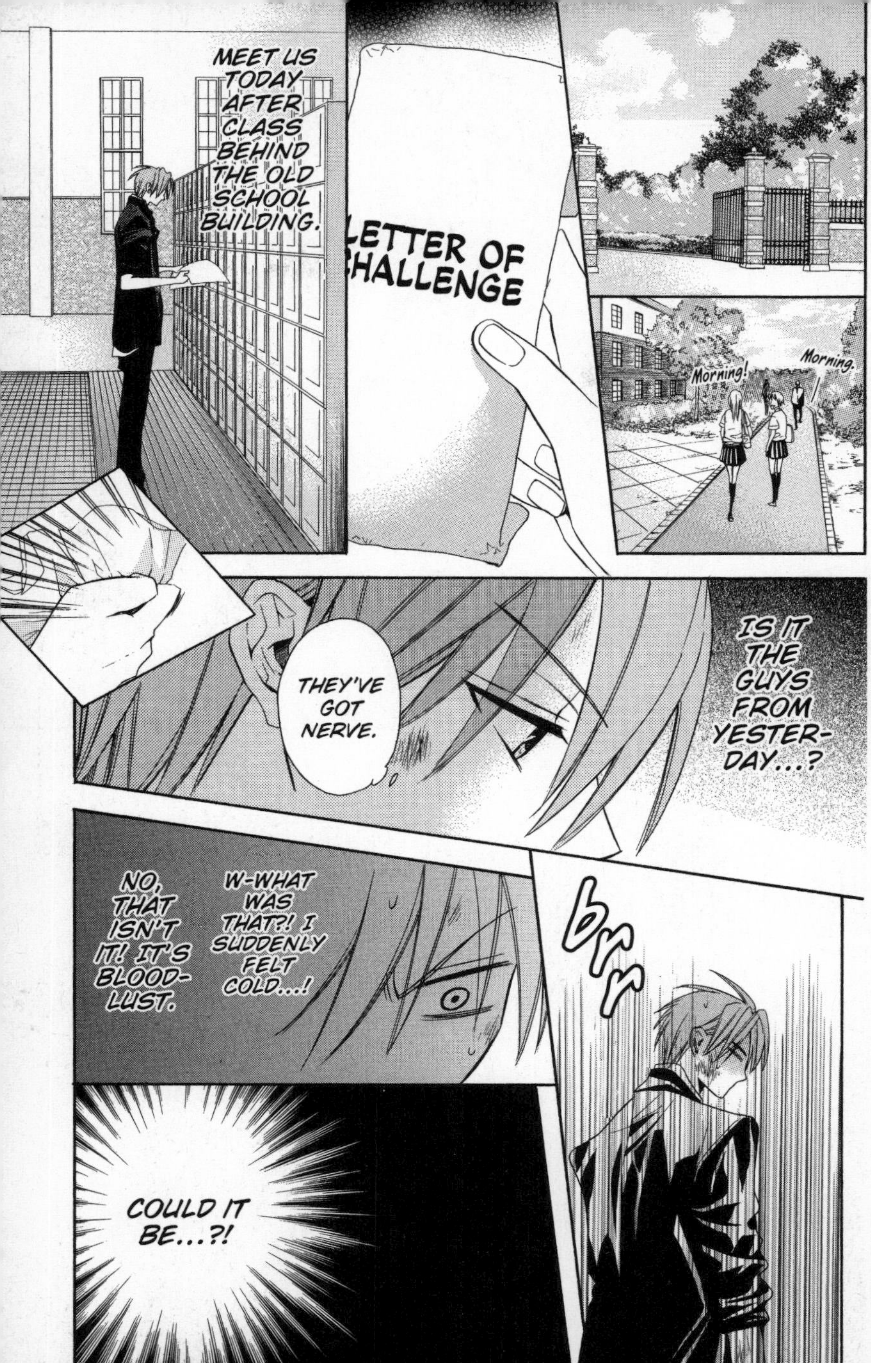
Morning.
Morning!
LETTER OF CHALLENGE
MEET US TODAY AFTER CLASS BEHIND THE OLD SCHOOL BUILDING.
IS IT THE GUYS FROM YESTER-DAY...?
THEY'VE GOT NERVE.
brr
W-WHAT WAS THAT?! I SUDDENLY FELT COLD...!
NO, THAT ISN'T IT! IT'S BLOOD-LUST.
COULD IT BE...?!

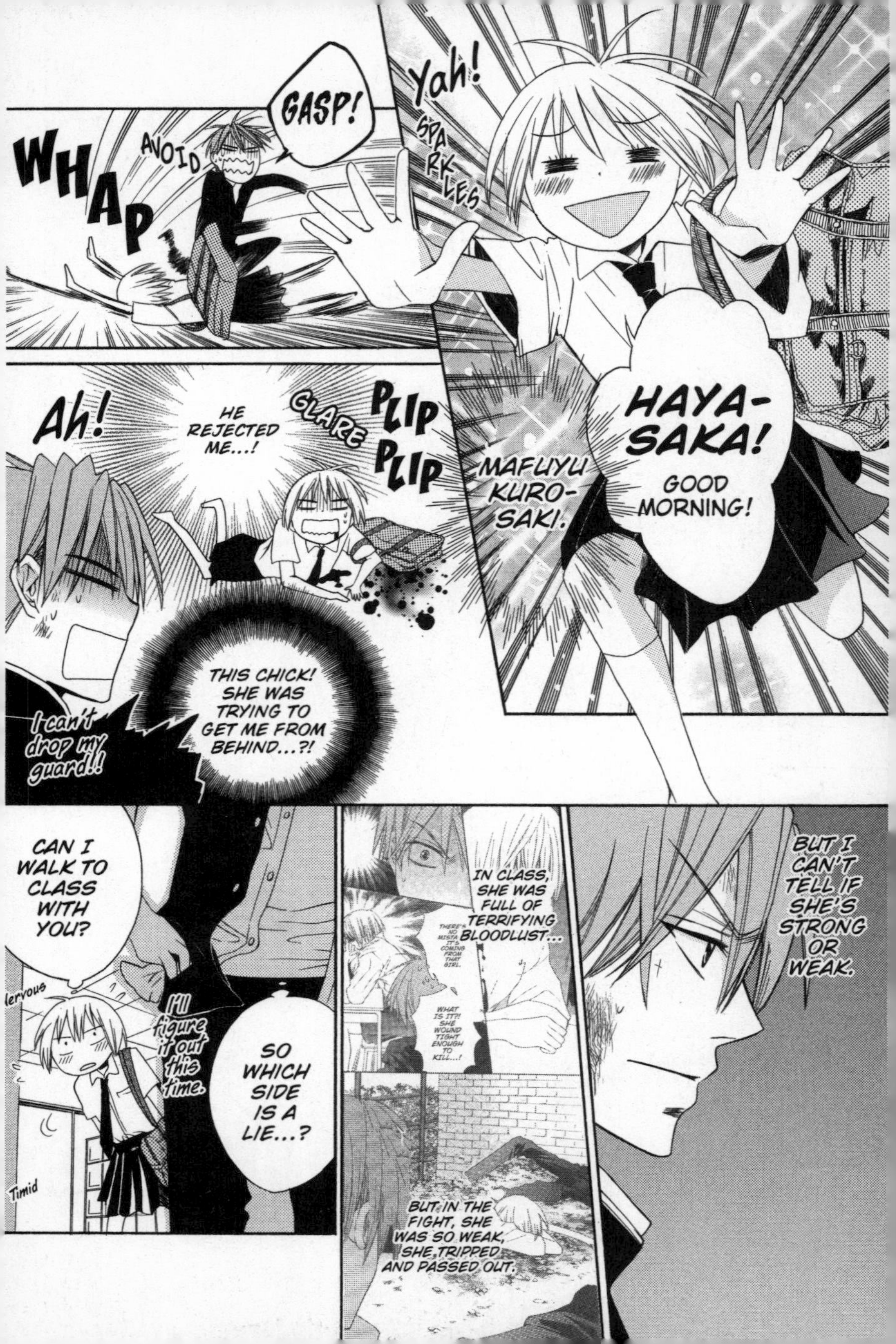
Yah!
SPARKLES
HAYA-SAKA! GOOD MORNING!
MAFUYU KUROSAKI.
GASP!
AVOID
WHAP
Ah!
HE REJECTED ME...!
GLARE
PLIP PLIP
THIS CHICK! SHE WAS TRYING TO GET ME FROM BEHIND...?!
I can't drop my guard!!
BUT I CAN'T TELL IF SHE'S STRONG OR WEAK.
IN CLASS, SHE WAS FULL OF TERRIFYING BLOODLUST...
THERE'S NO MISTA... IT'S COMING FROM THAT GIRL.
WHAT IS IT?! SHE WOUND TIGHT ENOUGH TO KILL...!
BUT IN THE FIGHT, SHE WAS SO WEAK, SHE TRIPPED AND PASSED OUT.
CAN I WALK TO CLASS WITH YOU?
Nervous
Timid
I'll figure it out this time.
SO WHICH SIDE IS A LIE...?

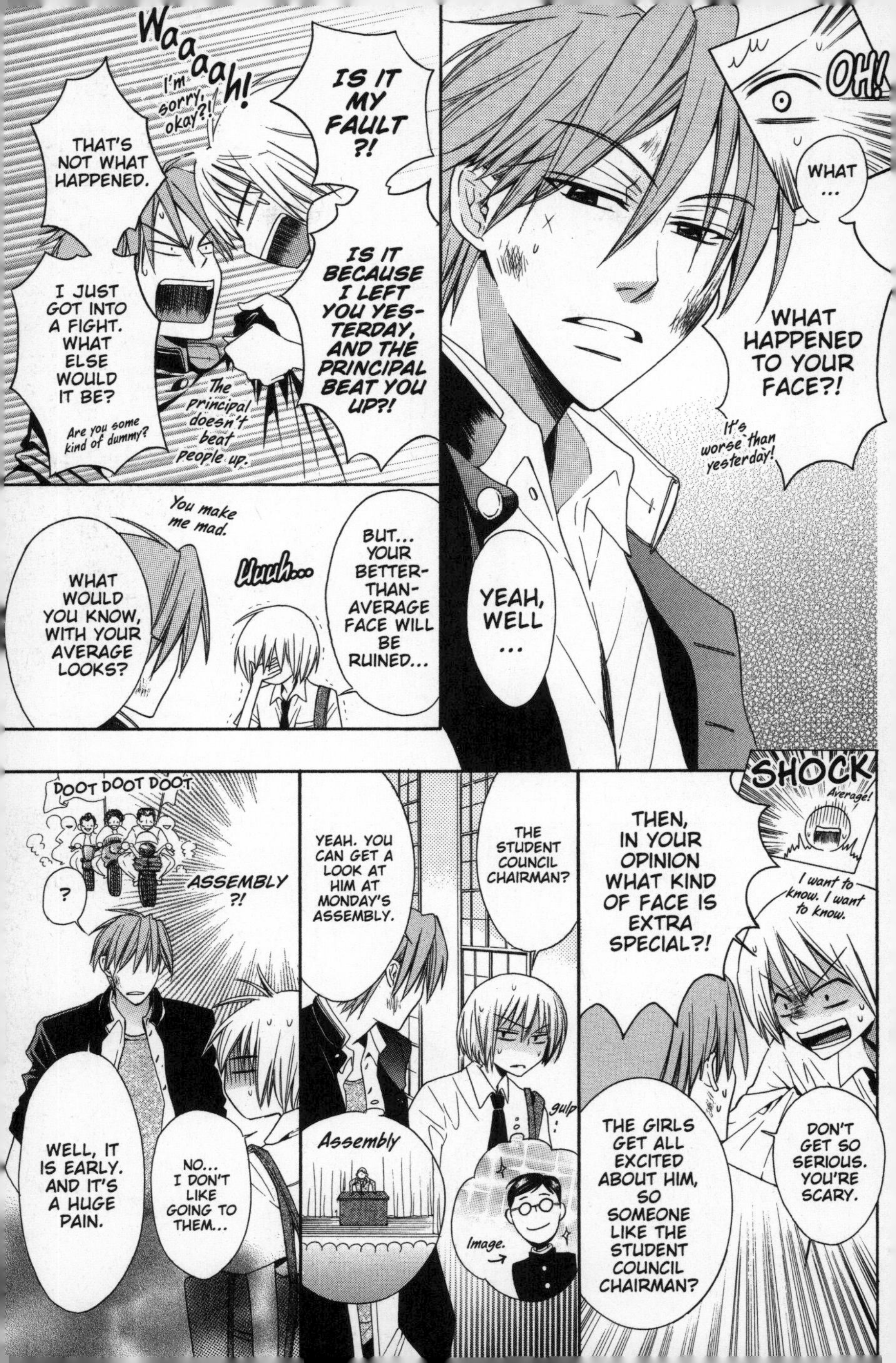
OH!
WHAT...
WHAT HAPPENED TO YOUR FACE?!
It's worse than yesterday!
YEAH, WELL...
IS IT MY FAULT?!
IS IT BECAUSE I LEFT YOU YES-TERDAY, AND THE PRINCIPAL BEAT YOU UP?!
Waaaaah!
I'm sorry, okay?!
THAT'S NOT WHAT HAPPENED.
I JUST GOT INTO A FIGHT. WHAT ELSE WOULD IT BE?
The Principal doesn't beat people up.
Are you some kind of dummy?
BUT... YOUR BETTER-THAN-AVERAGE FACE WILL BE RUINED...
Uuuh...
You make me mad.
WHAT WOULD YOU KNOW, WITH YOUR AVERAGE LOOKS?
SHOCK
Average!
THEN, IN YOUR OPINION WHAT KIND OF FACE IS EXTRA SPECIAL?!
I want to know. I want to know.
DON'T GET SO SERIOUS. YOU'RE SCARY.
THE GIRLS GET ALL EXCITED ABOUT HIM, SO SOMEONE LIKE THE STUDENT COUNCIL CHAIRMAN?
Image.
THE STUDENT COUNCIL CHAIRMAN?
YEAH. YOU CAN GET A LOOK AT HIM AT MONDAY'S ASSEMBLY.
gulp
Assembly
DOOT DOOT DOOT
ASSEMBLY?!
?
NO... I DON'T LIKE GOING TO THEM...
WELL, IT IS EARLY. AND IT'S A HUGE PAIN.

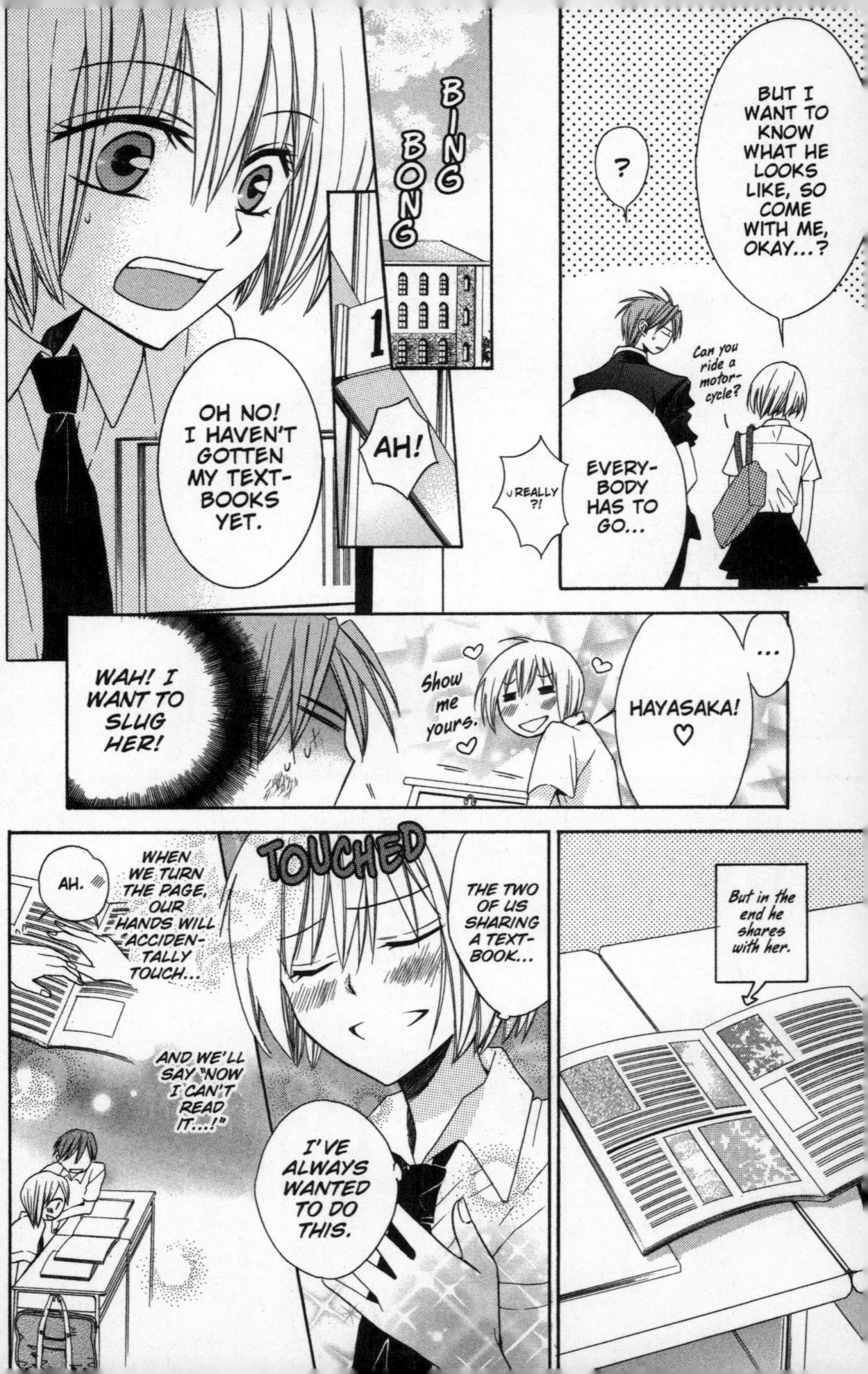
BUT I WANT TO KNOW WHAT HE LOOKS LIKE, SO COME WITH ME, OKAY...?
?
Can you ride a motorcycle?
EVERY-BODY HAS TO GO...
REALLY ?!
BING BONG
AH!
OH NO! I HAVEN'T GOTTEN MY TEXT-BOOKS YET.
...
HAYASAKA! ♡
Show me yours.
WAH! I WANT TO SLUG HER!
But in the end he shares with her.
THE TWO OF US SHARING A TEXT-BOOK...
TOUCHED
WHEN WE TURN THE PAGE, OUR HANDS WILL ACCIDEN-TALLY TOUCH...
AH.
AND WE'LL SAY "NOW I CAN'T READ IT...!"
I'VE ALWAYS WANTED TO DO THIS.

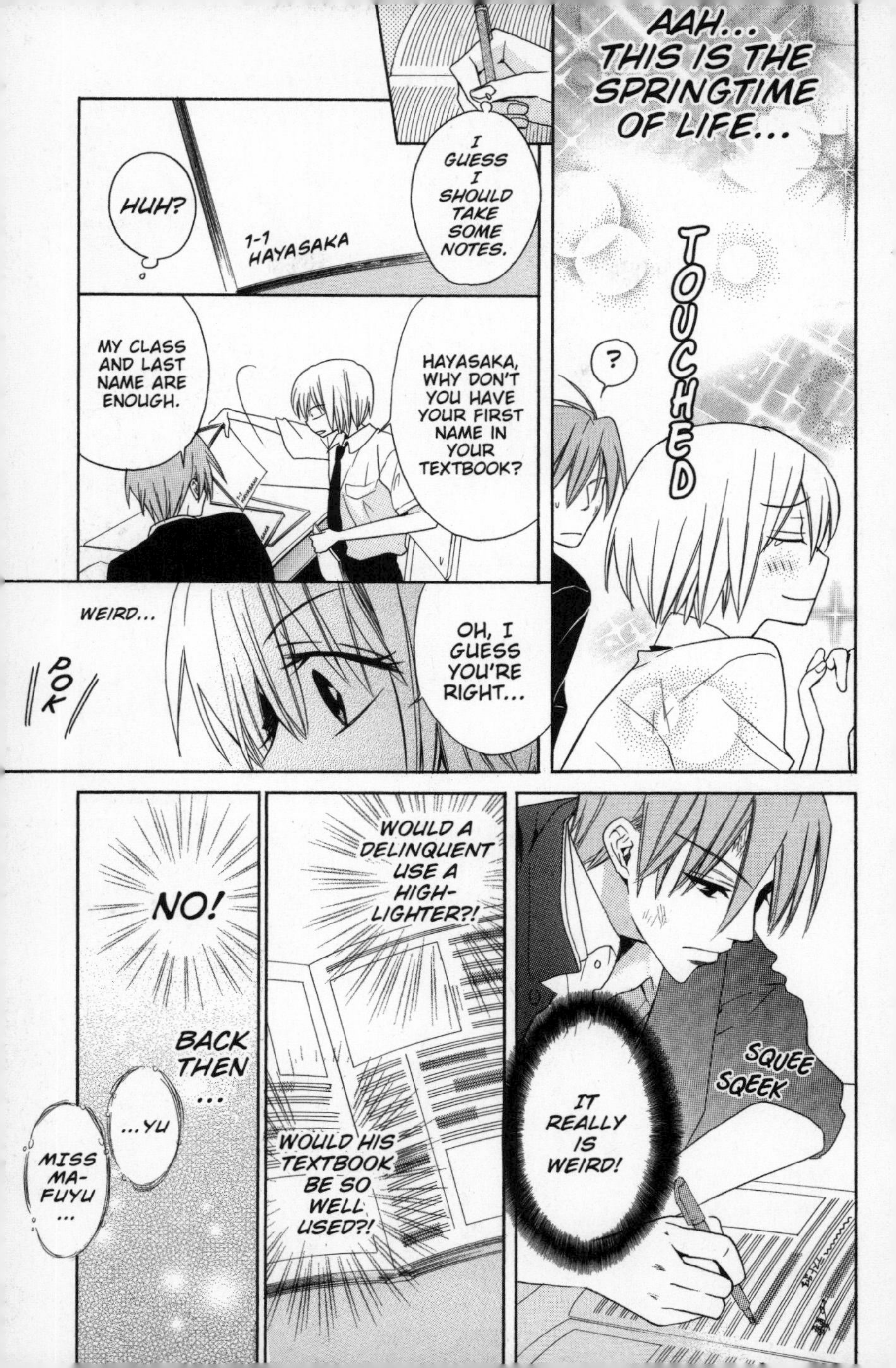
AAH... THIS IS THE SPRINGTIME OF LIFE...
TOUCHED
?
I GUESS I SHOULD TAKE SOME NOTES.
1-1 HAYASAKA
HUH?
HAYASAKA, WHY DON'T YOU HAVE YOUR FIRST NAME IN YOUR TEXTBOOK?
MY CLASS AND LAST NAME ARE ENOUGH.
OH, I GUESS YOU'RE RIGHT...
WEIRD...
POK
SQUEE SQEEK
IT REALLY IS WEIRD!
WOULD A DELINQUENT USE A HIGH-LIGHTER?!
WOULD HIS TEXTBOOK BE SO WELL USED?!
NO!
BACK THEN ...
...YU
MISS MA-FUYU ...

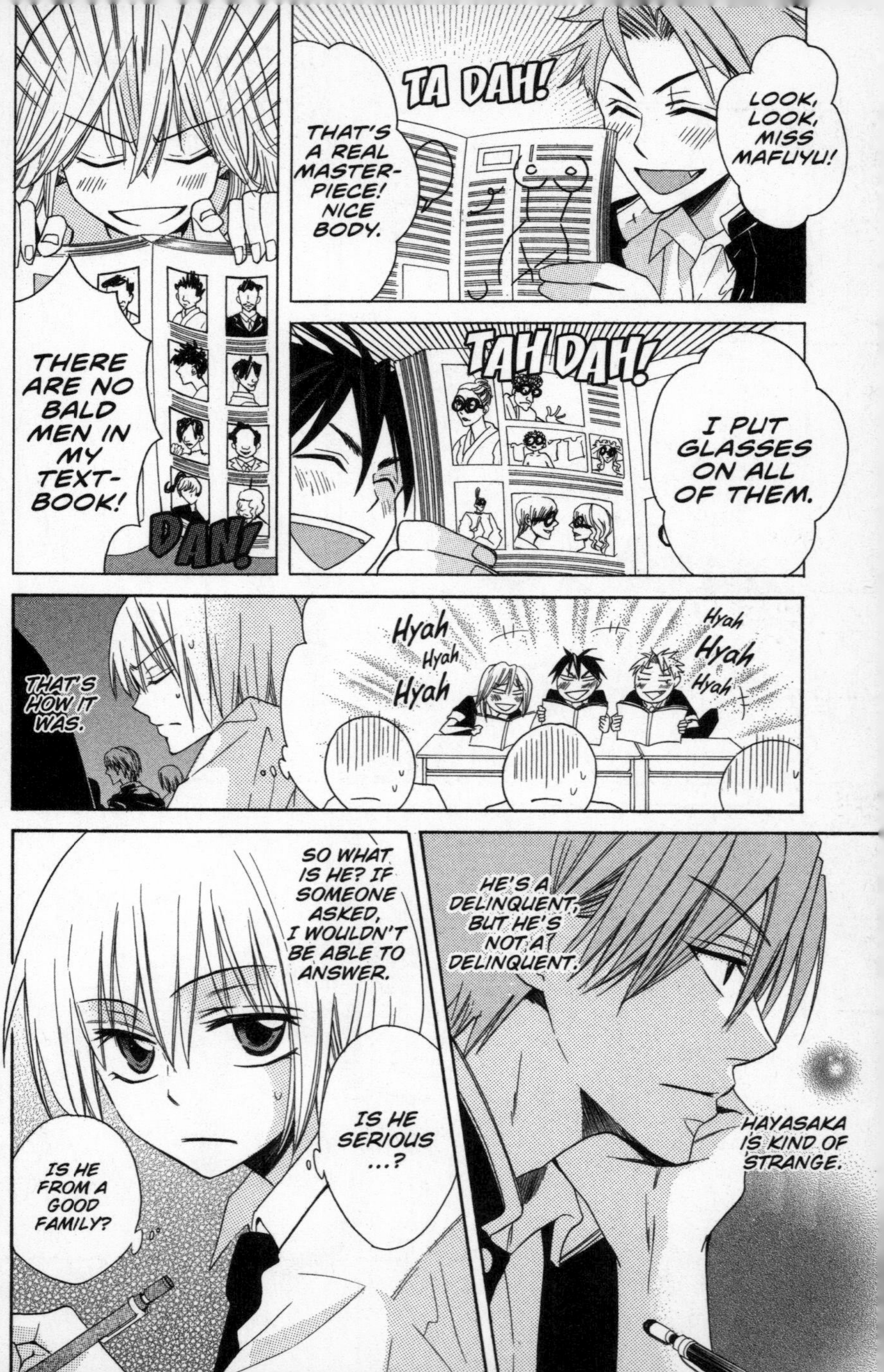
LOOK, LOOK, MISS MAFUYU!
TA DAH!
THAT'S A REAL MASTER-PIECE! NICE BODY.
TAH DAH!
I PUT GLASSES ON ALL OF THEM.
THERE ARE NO BALD MEN IN MY TEXT-BOOK!
DAN!
Hyah Hyah Hyah Hyah
Hyah Hyah Hyah
THAT'S HOW IT WAS.
HAYASAKA IS KIND OF STRANGE.
HE'S A DELINQUENT, BUT HE'S NOT A DELINQUENT.
SO WHAT IS HE? IF SOMEONE ASKED, I WOULDN'T BE ABLE TO ANSWER.
IS HE SERIOUS ...?
IS HE FROM A GOOD FAMILY?

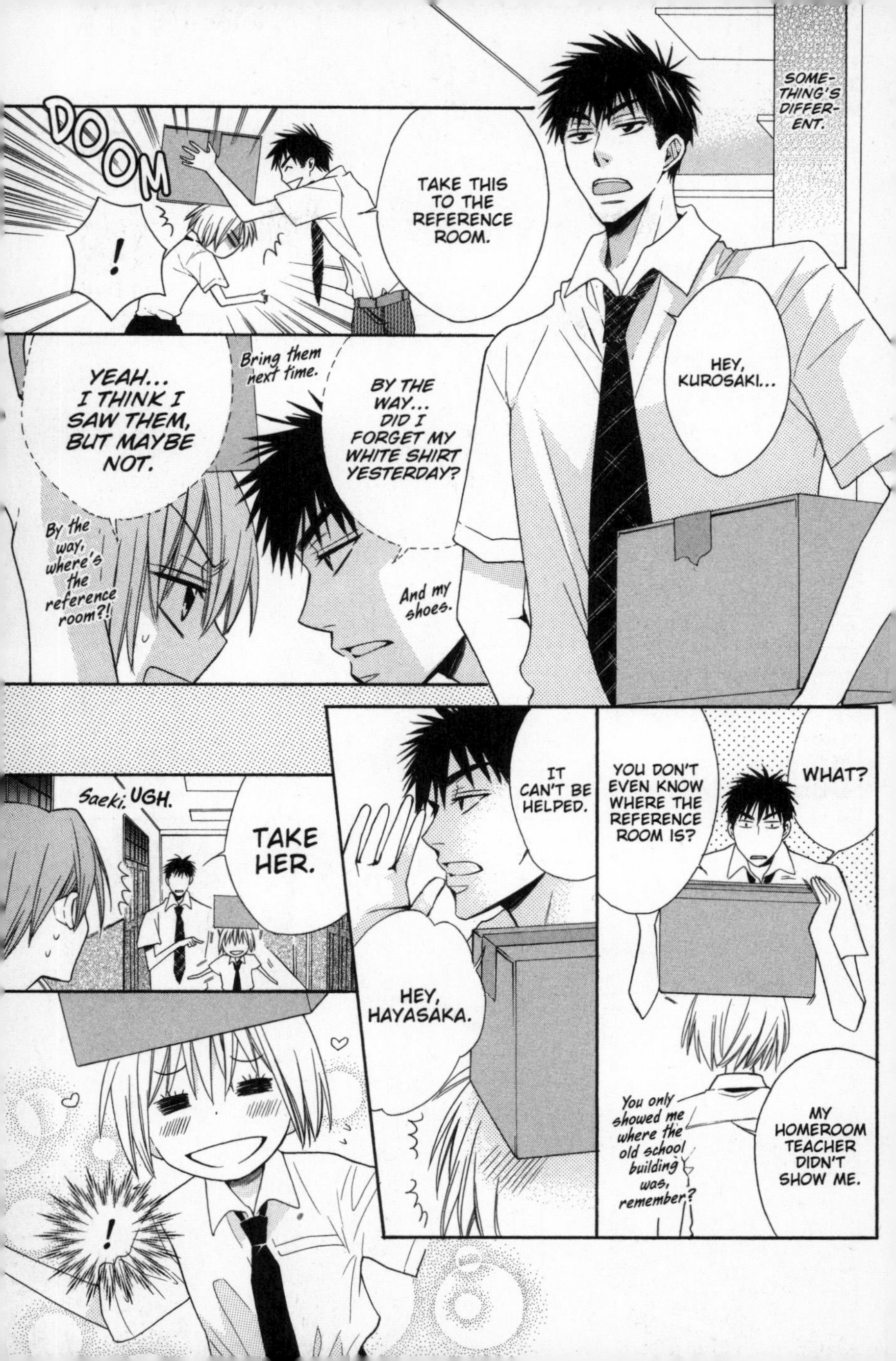
SOMETHING'S DIFFERENT.
HEY, KUROSAKI...
TAKE THIS TO THE REFERENCE ROOM.
DOOM
!
BY THE WAY... DID I FORGET MY WHITE SHIRT YESTERDAY?
YEAH... I THINK I SAW THEM, BUT MAYBE NOT.
Bring them next time.
And my shoes.
By the way, where's the reference room?!
WHAT?
YOU DON'T EVEN KNOW WHERE THE REFERENCE ROOM IS?
MY HOMEROOM TEACHER DIDN'T SHOW ME.
You only showed me where the old school building was, remember?
IT CAN'T BE HELPED.
HEY, HAYASAKA.
TAKE HER.
UGH.
Saeki.
!

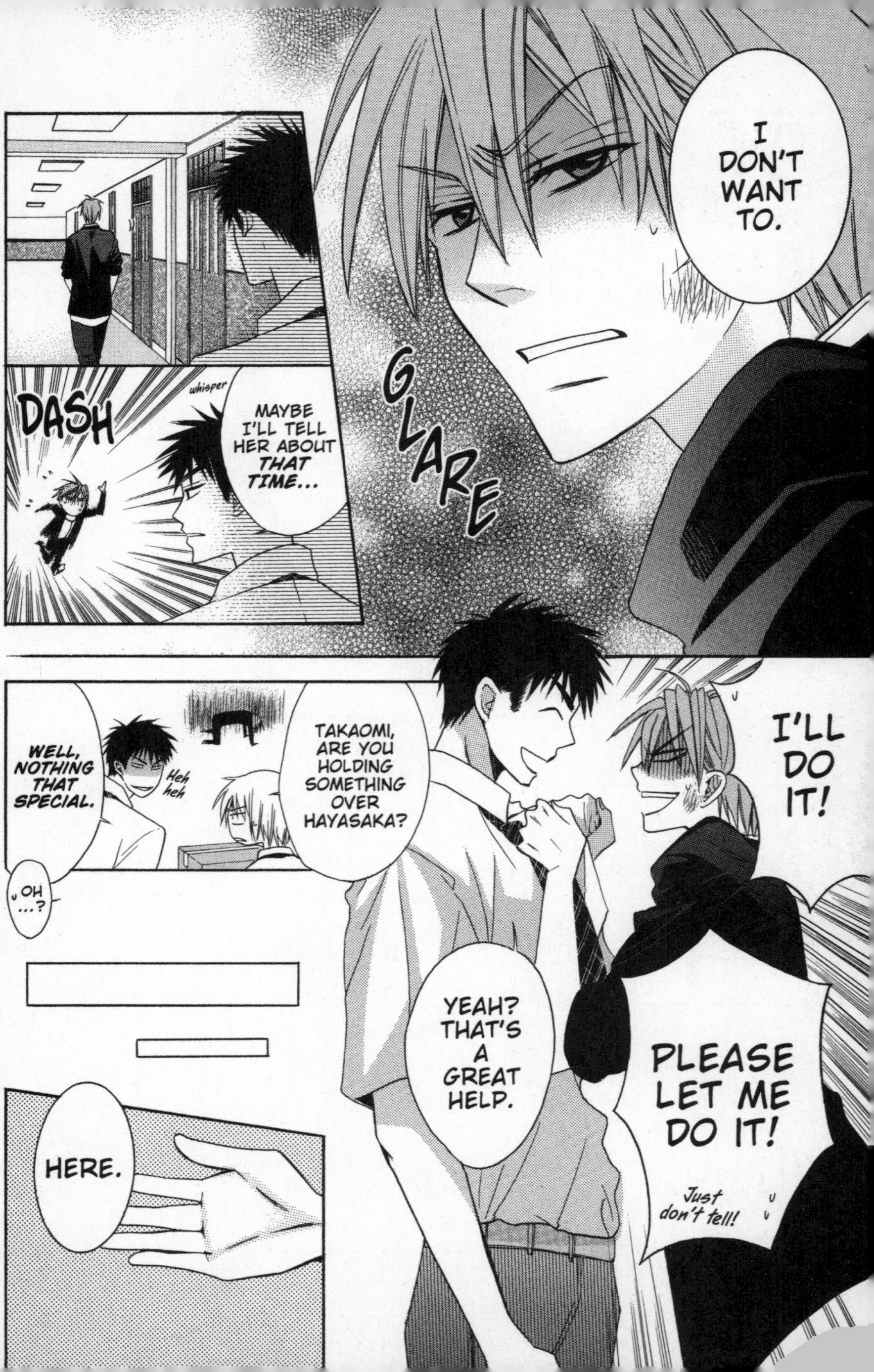
I DON'T WANT TO.
GLARE
whisper
MAYBE I'LL TELL HER ABOUT *THAT TIME*...
DASH
I'LL DO IT!
PLEASE LET ME DO IT!
Just don't tell!
YEAH? THAT'S A GREAT HELP.
TAKAOMI, ARE YOU HOLDING SOMETHING OVER HAYASAKA?
WELL, NOTHING THAT SPECIAL.
Heh heh
OH ...?
HERE.

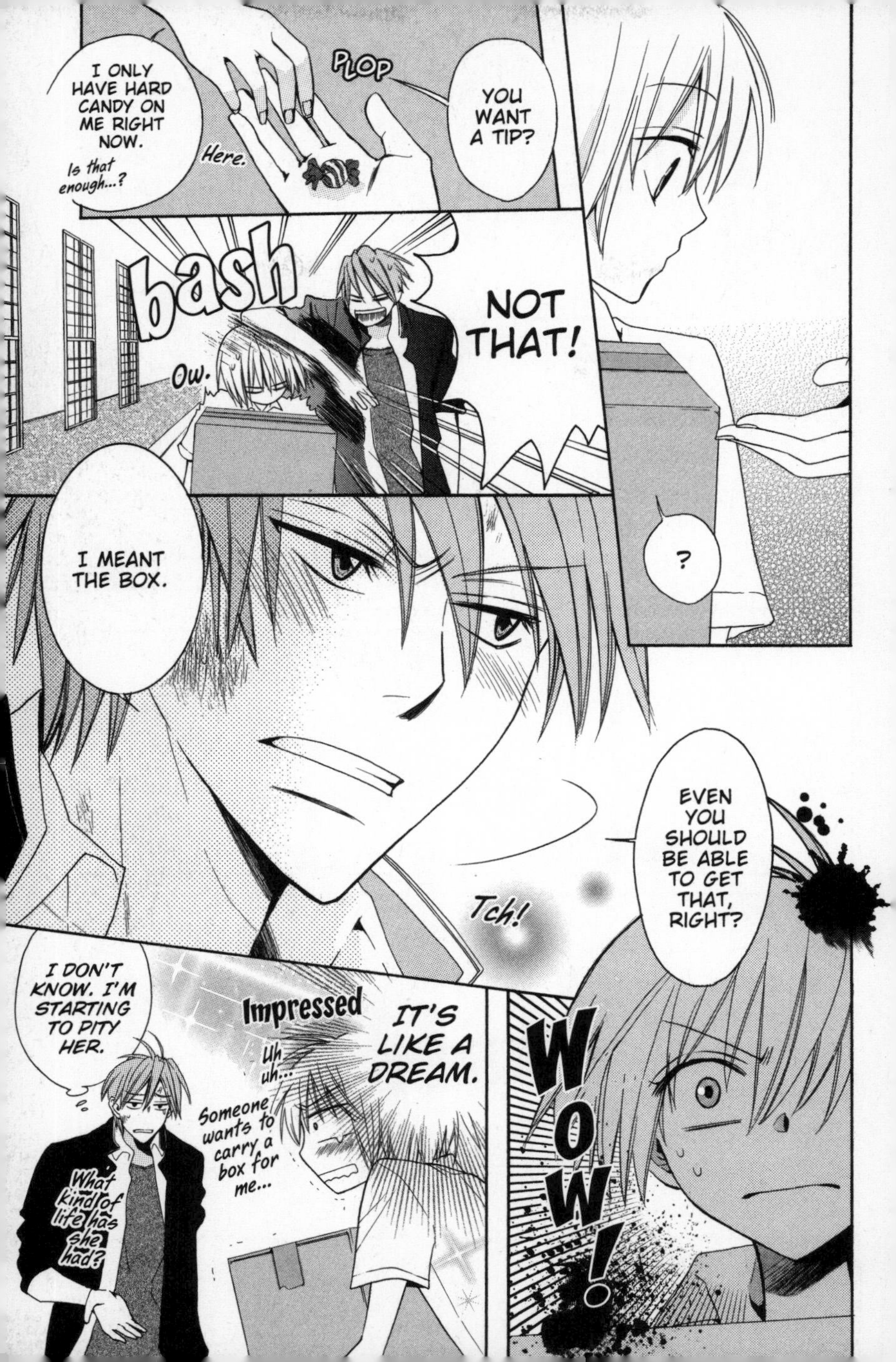

PLOP
YOU WANT A TIP?
I ONLY HAVE HARD CANDY ON ME RIGHT NOW.
Here.
Is that enough...?
?
bash
NOT THAT!
Ow.
I MEANT THE BOX.
EVEN YOU SHOULD BE ABLE TO GET THAT, RIGHT?
Tch!
WOW!
IT'S LIKE A DREAM.
Impressed
Uh uh...
Someone wants to carry a box for me...
I DON'T KNOW. I'M STARTING TO PITY HER.
What kind of life has she had?

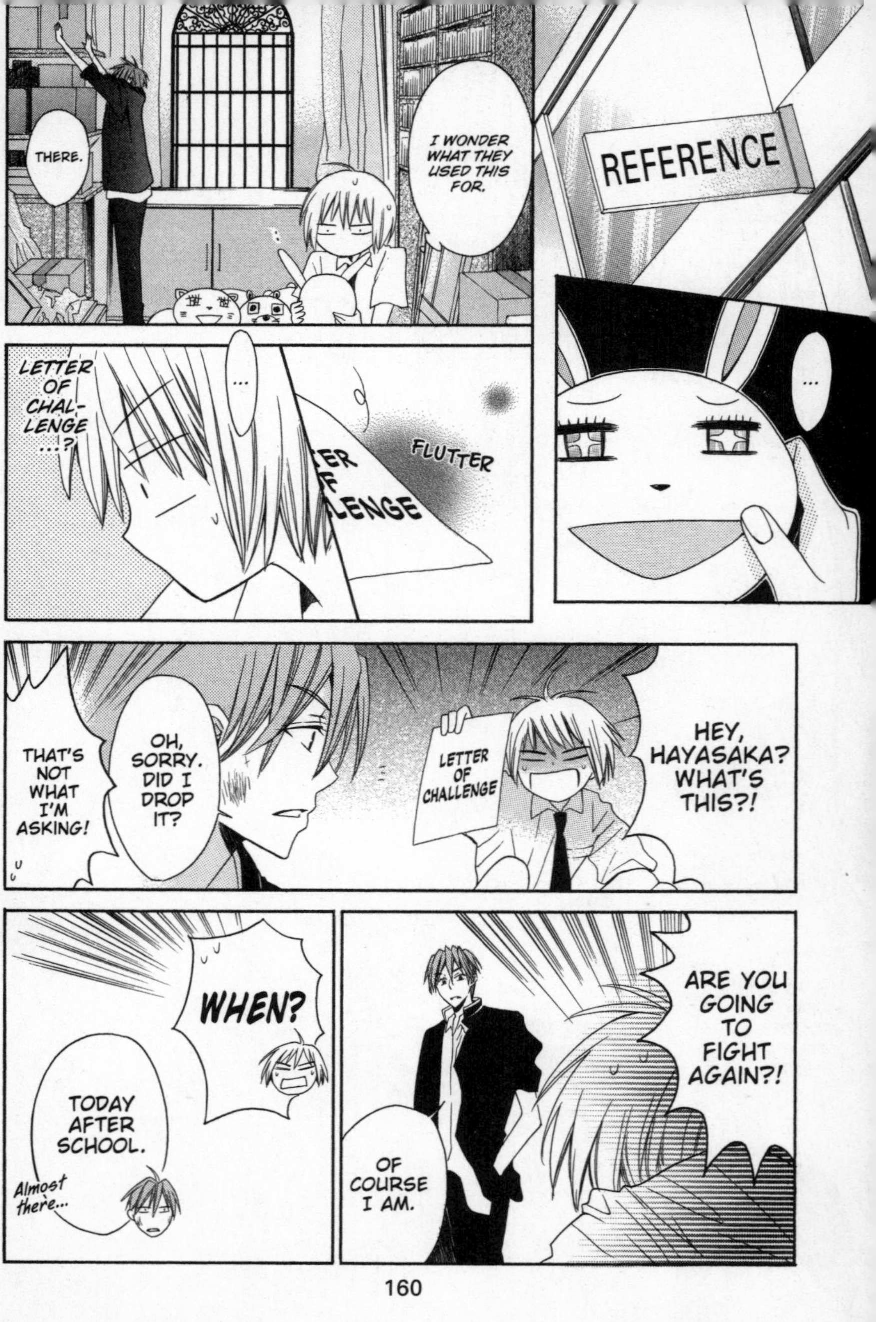
REFERENCE
I WONDER WHAT THEY USED THIS FOR.
THERE.
...
FLUTTER
...
LETTER OF CHAL-LENGE ...?
HEY, HAYASAKA? WHAT'S THIS?!
LETTER OF CHALLENGE
OH, SORRY. DID I DROP IT?
THAT'S NOT WHAT I'M ASKING!
ARE YOU GOING TO FIGHT AGAIN?!
OF COURSE I AM.
WHEN?
TODAY AFTER SCHOOL.
Almost there...

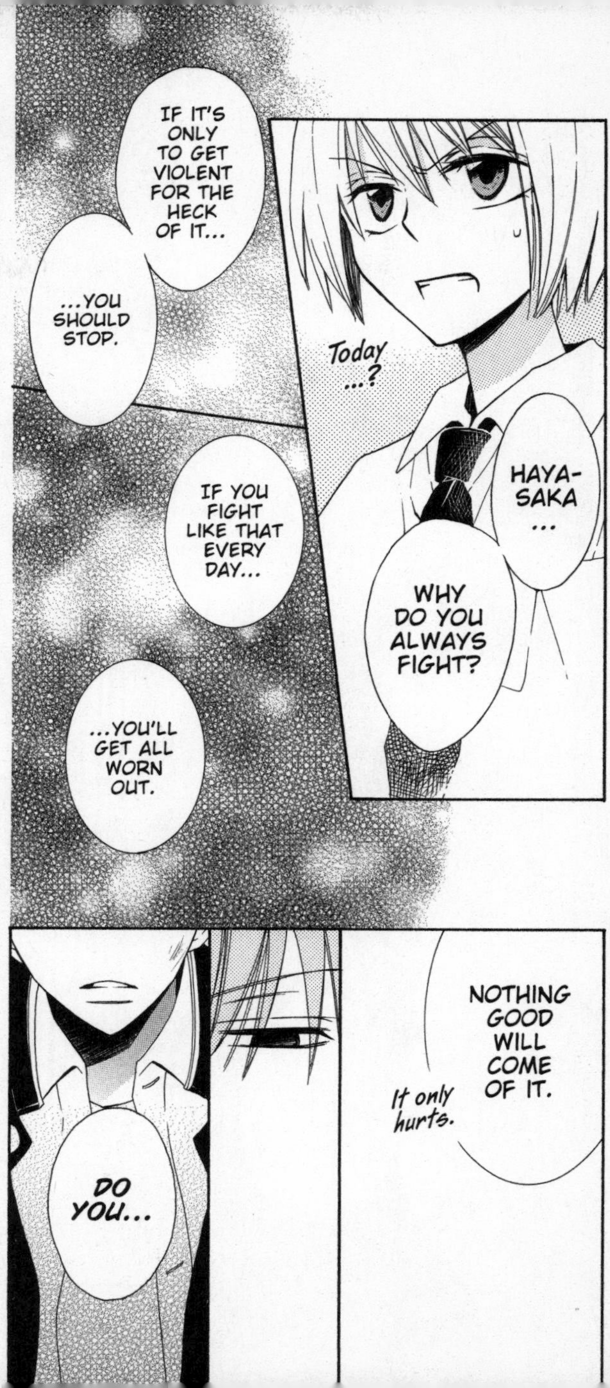
Today ...?
HAYA-SAKA...
WHY DO YOU ALWAYS FIGHT?
IF IT'S ONLY TO GET VIOLENT FOR THE HECK OF IT...
...YOU SHOULD STOP.
IF YOU FIGHT LIKE THAT EVERY DAY...
...YOU'LL GET ALL WORN OUT.
NOTHING GOOD WILL COME OF IT.
It only hurts.
DO YOU...

NEW YEAR'S WISHES

Those years when New Year's and my deadlines don't overlap, I go to a nearby shrine for hatsumode, the first visit of the year. There are many wish tablets. Just reading them is satisfying.

A student writes

Let me be accepted at XX High School!!

A couple writes

Let me be with XX always and forever! ♡

The springtime of life... It comforts me.

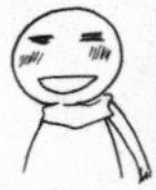

But sometimes there are strange ones.

I want to become a princess.

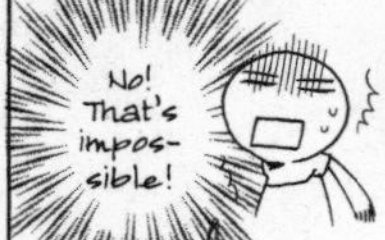
No! That's impos-sible!

Eat a bit of gold. Fermented beans that don't smell. It's delicious!

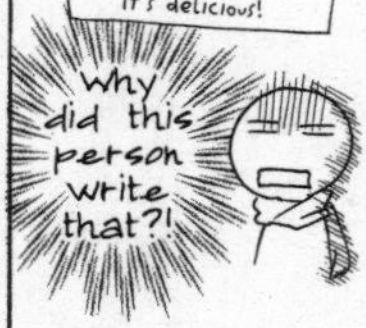
Why did this person write that?!

It's a lot of fun.

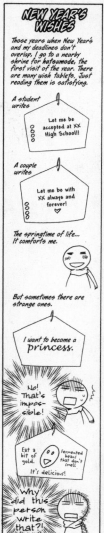

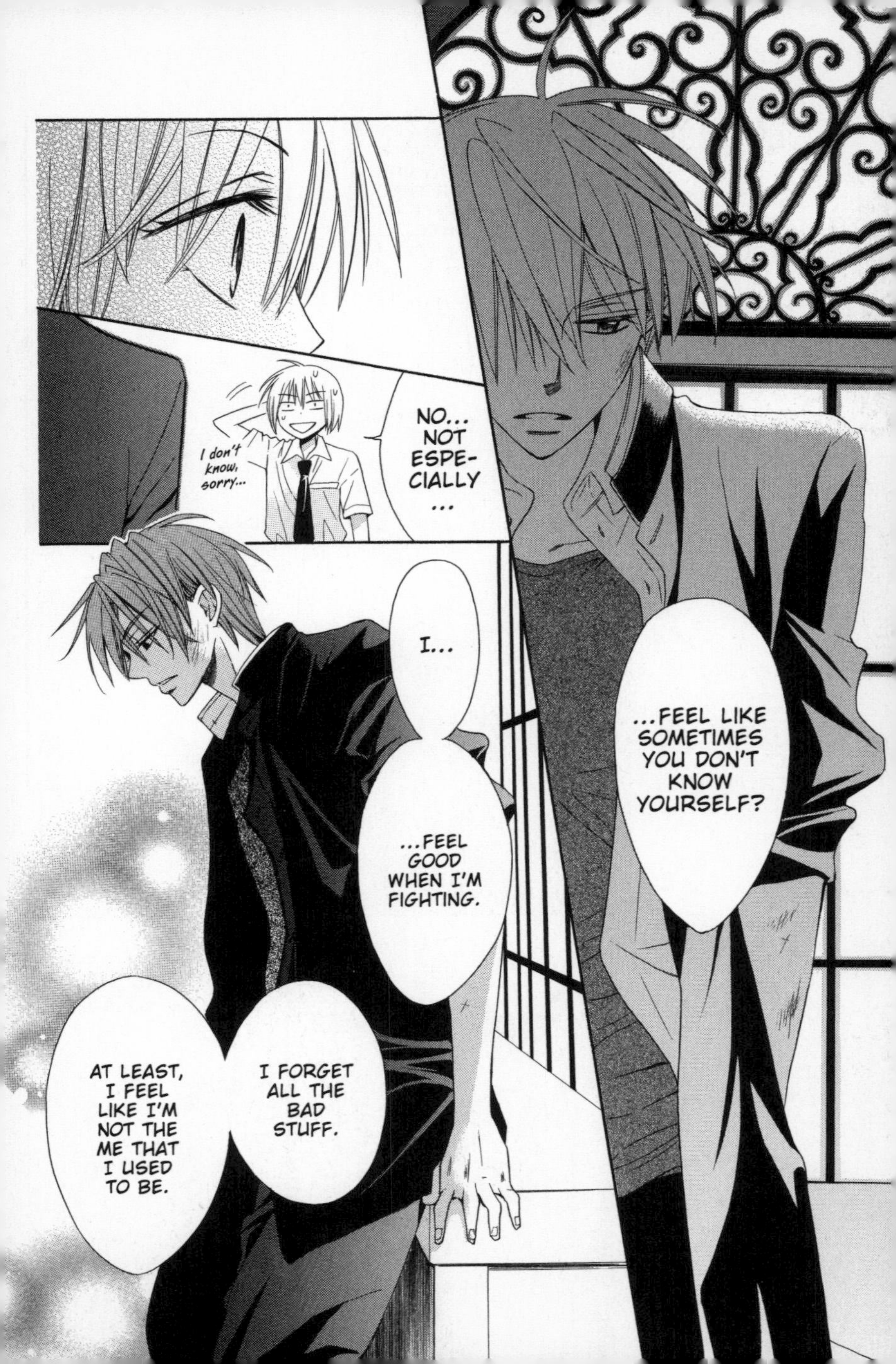
...FEEL LIKE SOMETIMES YOU DON'T KNOW YOURSELF?
NO... NOT ESPE-CIALLY...
I don't know, sorry...
I...
...FEEL GOOD WHEN I'M FIGHTING.
I FORGET ALL THE BAD STUFF.
AT LEAST, I FEEL LIKE I'M NOT THE ME THAT I USED TO BE.

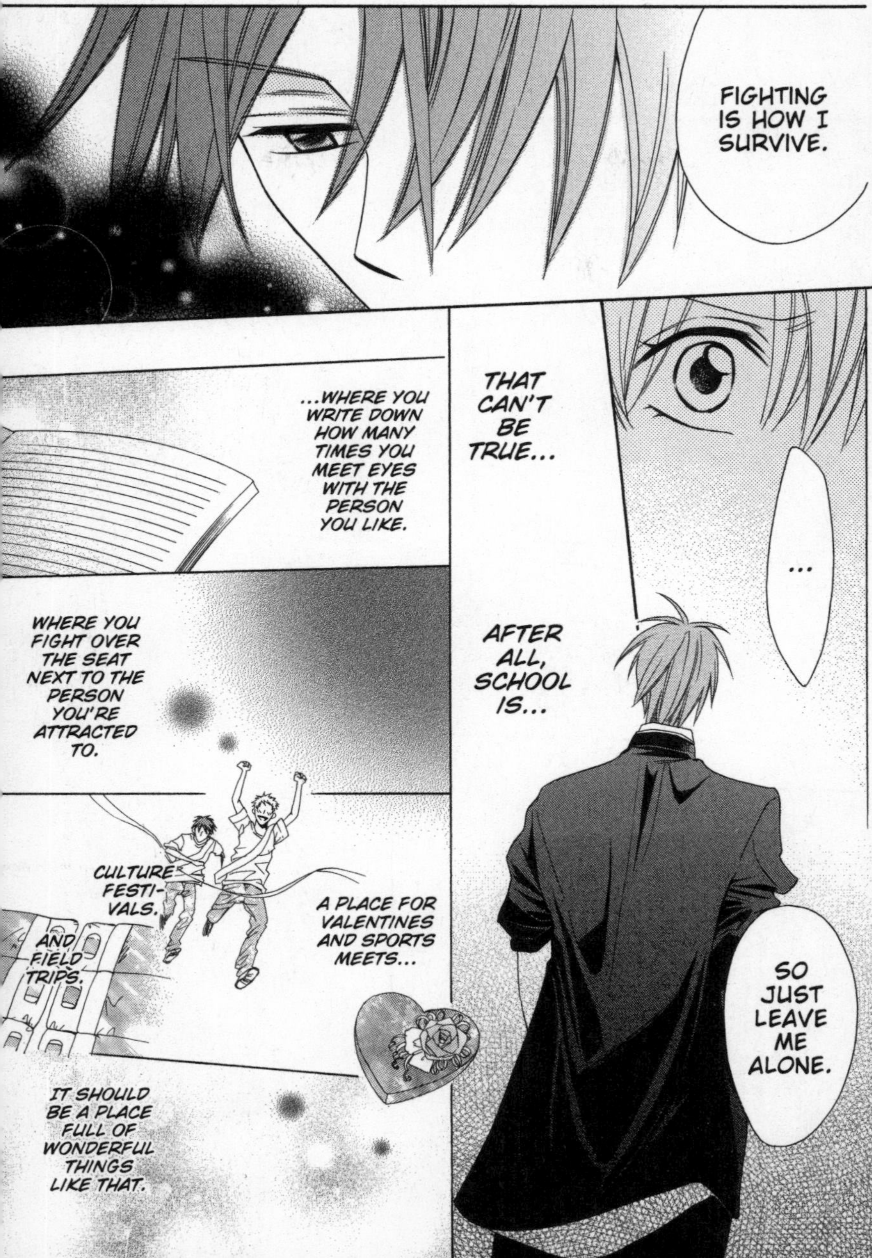
FIGHTING IS HOW I SURVIVE.
...
THAT CAN'T BE TRUE...
AFTER ALL, SCHOOL IS...
SO JUST LEAVE ME ALONE.
...WHERE YOU WRITE DOWN HOW MANY TIMES YOU MEET EYES WITH THE PERSON YOU LIKE.
WHERE YOU FIGHT OVER THE SEAT NEXT TO THE PERSON YOU'RE ATTRACTED TO.
A PLACE FOR VALENTINES AND SPORTS MEETS...
CULTURE FESTI-VALS.
AND FIELD TRIPS.
IT SHOULD BE A PLACE FULL OF WONDERFUL THINGS LIKE THAT.

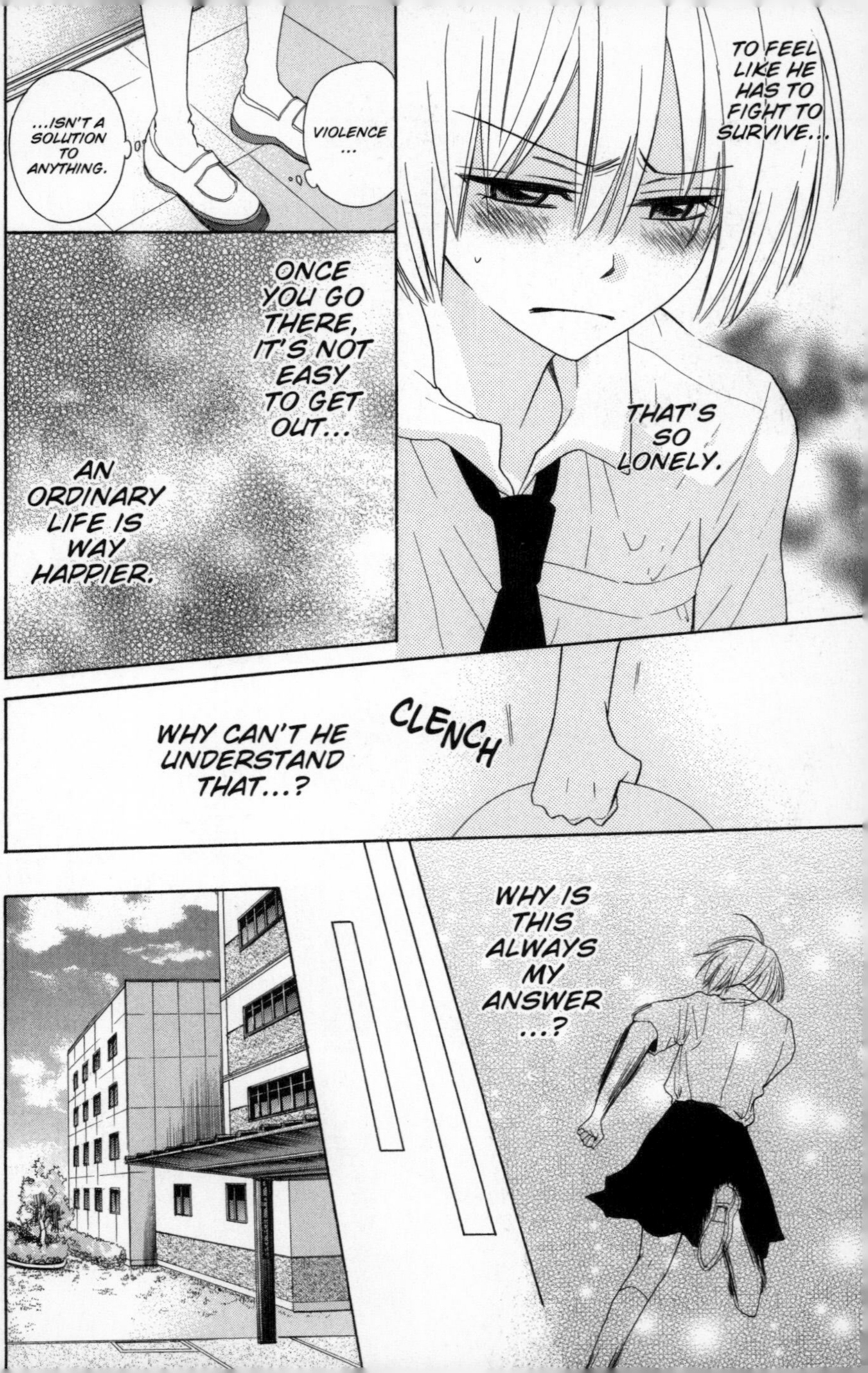
TO FEEL LIKE HE HAS TO FIGHT TO SURVIVE...
THAT'S SO LONELY.
VIOLENCE...
...ISN'T A SOLUTION TO ANYTHING.
ONCE YOU GO THERE, IT'S NOT EASY TO GET OUT...
AN ORDINARY LIFE IS WAY HAPPIER.
CLENCH
WHY CAN'T HE UNDERSTAND THAT...?
WHY IS THIS ALWAYS MY ANSWER...?

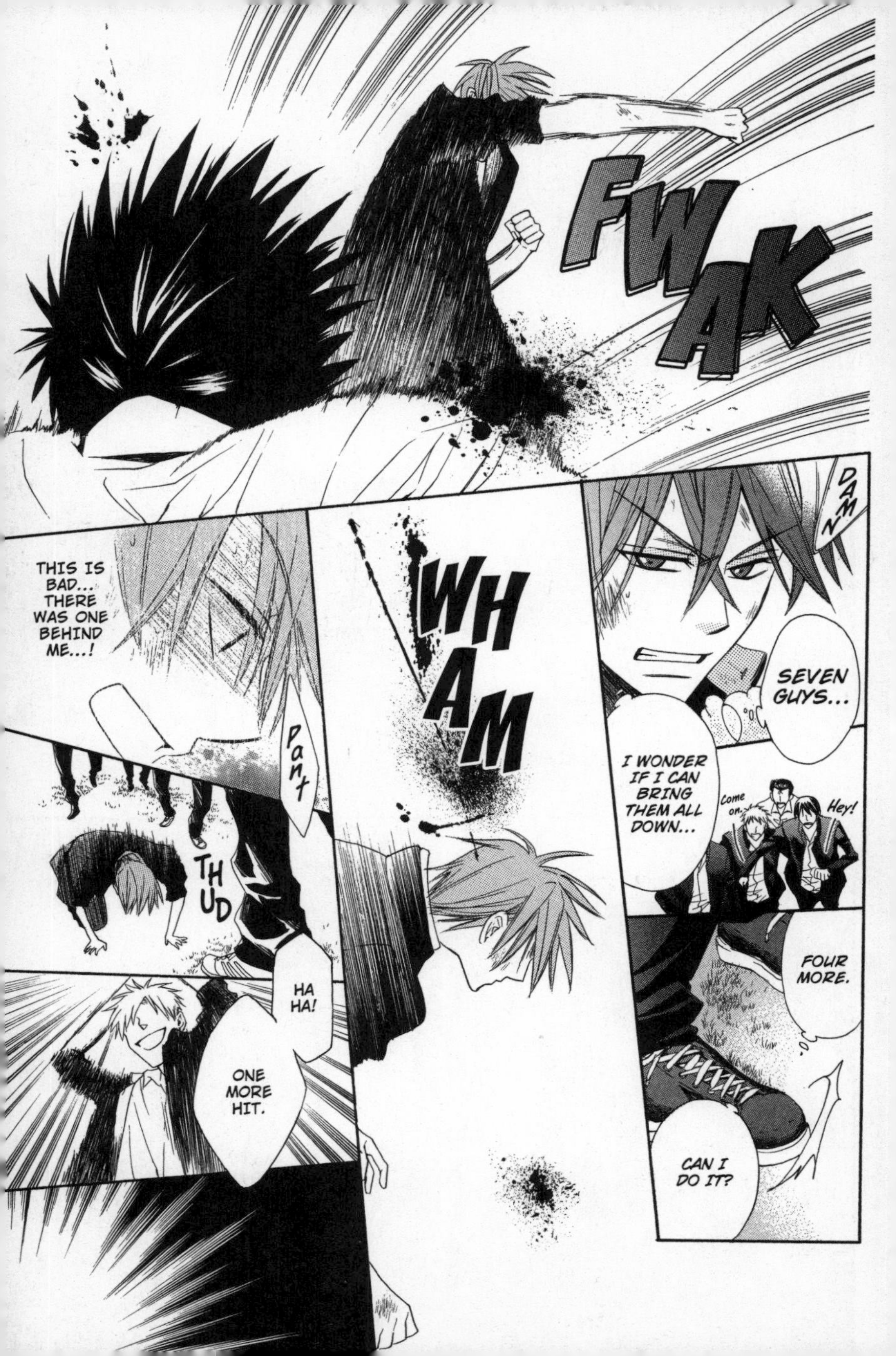
FWAK
DAMN
SEVEN GUYS...
I WONDER IF I CAN BRING THEM ALL DOWN...
Come on.
Hey!
FOUR MORE.
CAN I DO IT?
WHAM
THIS IS BAD... THERE WAS ONE BEHIND ME...!
Pant
THUD
HA HA!
ONE MORE HIT.

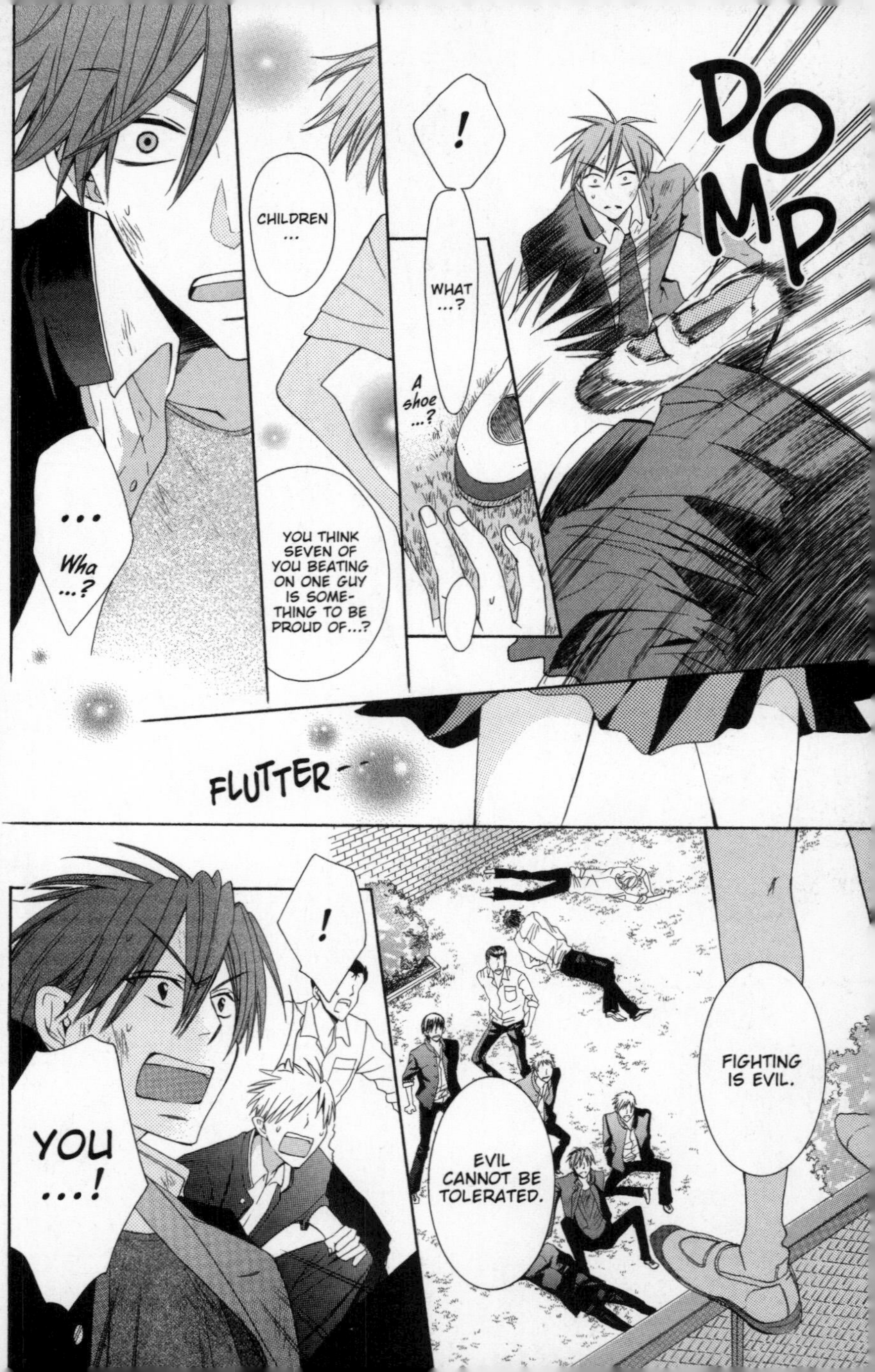
DOMP
!
WHAT ...?
A shoe ...?
CHILDREN ...
YOU THINK SEVEN OF YOU BEATING ON ONE GUY IS SOME-THING TO BE PROUD OF...?
... Wha ...?
FLUTTER
FIGHTING IS EVIL.
EVIL CANNOT BE TOLERATED.
!
YOU ...!

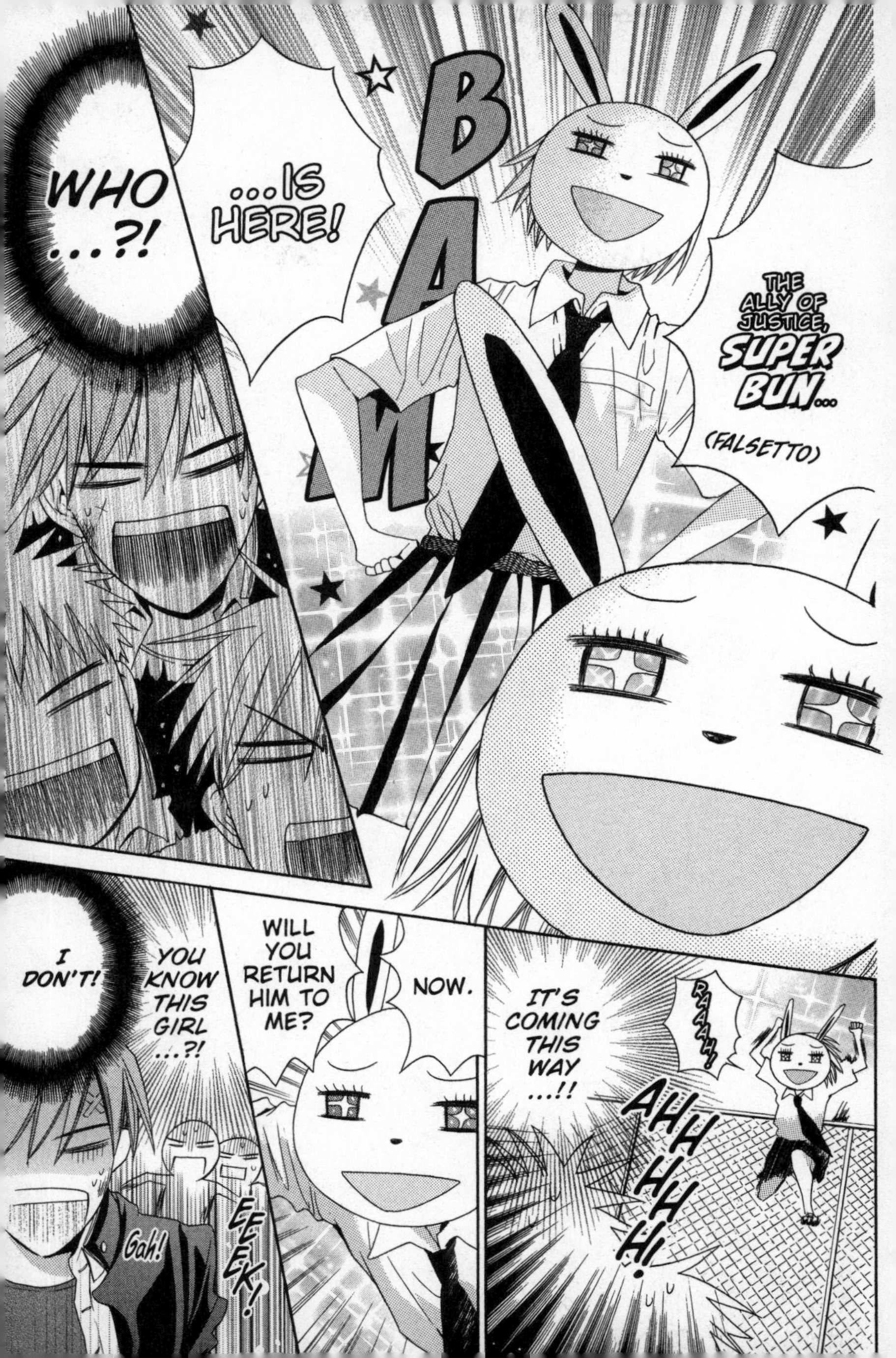
THE ALLY OF JUSTICE, SUPER BUN...
(FALSETTO)
BAM
...IS HERE!
WHO ...?!
RAAAH!
AHHHHHH!
IT'S COMING THIS WAY ...!!
NOW.
WILL YOU RETURN HIM TO ME?
YOU KNOW THIS GIRL ...?!
I DON'T!
EEEEK!
Gah!

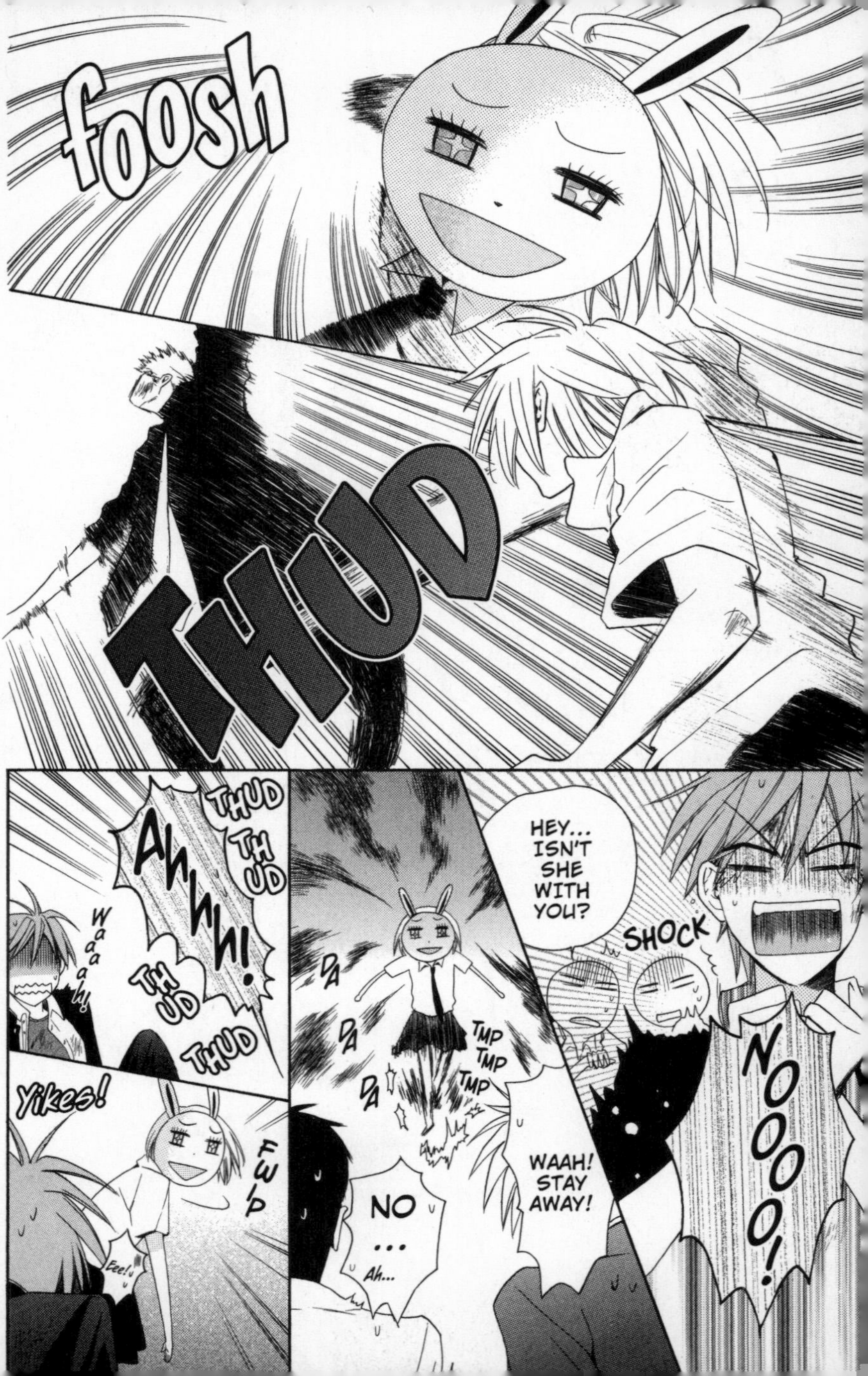
foosh
THUD
HEY... ISN'T SHE WITH YOU?
SHOCK
NOOOO!
DA
DA
DA
TMP TMP TMP
WAAH! STAY AWAY!
NO ...
Ah...
THUD
Ahhhh!
THUD
Waaaah!
THUD
THUD
Yikes!
FWIP
Eee!

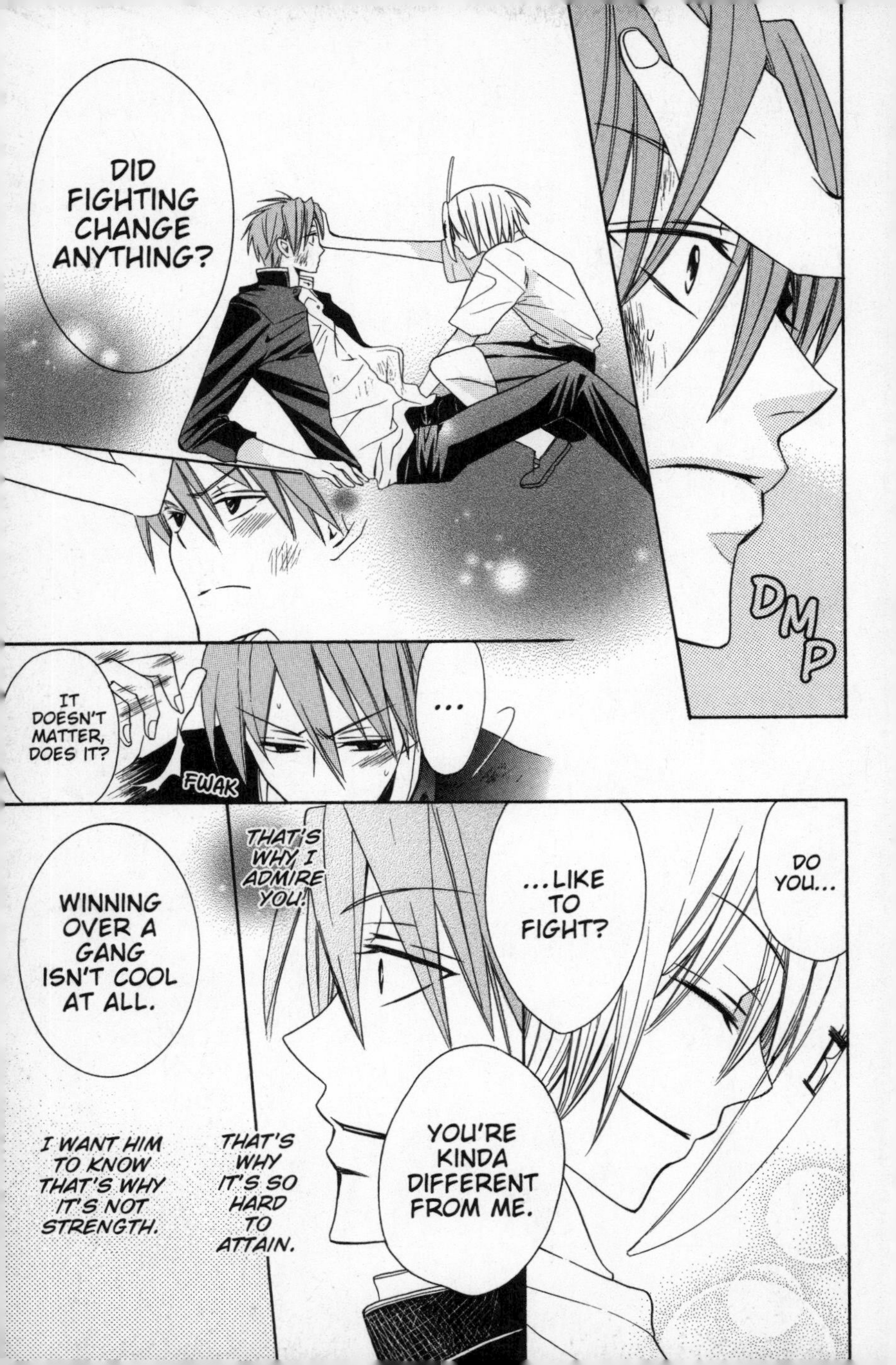
DMP
DID FIGHTING CHANGE ANYTHING?
...
FWAK
IT DOESN'T MATTER, DOES IT?
DO YOU...
...LIKE TO FIGHT?
THAT'S WHY I ADMIRE YOU.
WINNING OVER A GANG ISN'T COOL AT ALL.
YOU'RE KINDA DIFFERENT FROM ME.
THAT'S WHY IT'S SO HARD TO ATTAIN.
I WANT HIM TO KNOW THAT'S WHY IT'S NOT STRENGTH.

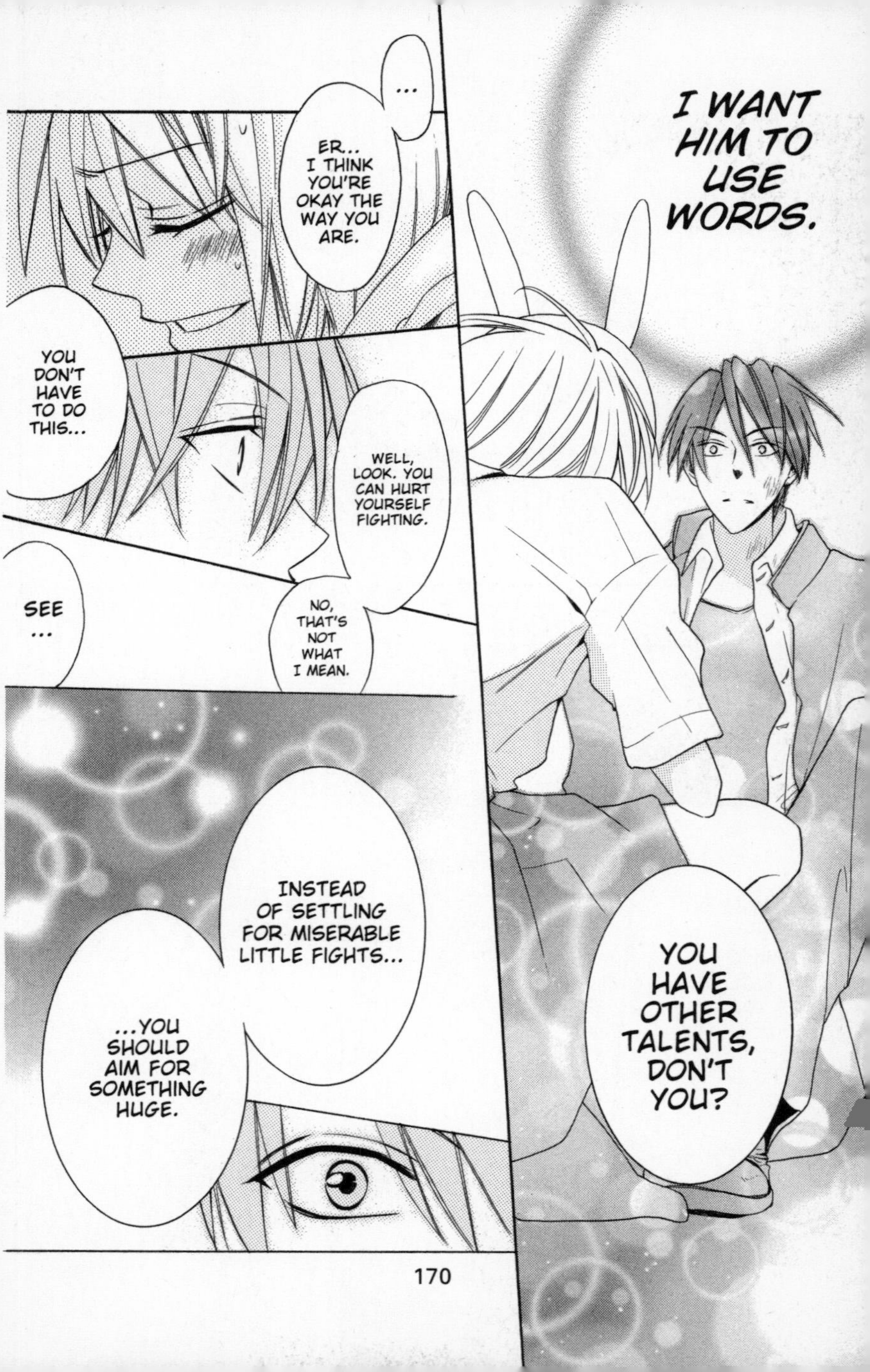
I WANT HIM TO USE WORDS.
YOU HAVE OTHER TALENTS, DON'T YOU?
...
ER... I THINK YOU'RE OKAY THE WAY YOU ARE.
YOU DON'T HAVE TO DO THIS...
WELL, LOOK. YOU CAN HURT YOURSELF FIGHTING.
NO, THAT'S NOT WHAT I MEAN.
SEE ...
INSTEAD OF SETTLING FOR MISERABLE LITTLE FIGHTS...
...YOU SHOULD AIM FOR SOMETHING HUGE.

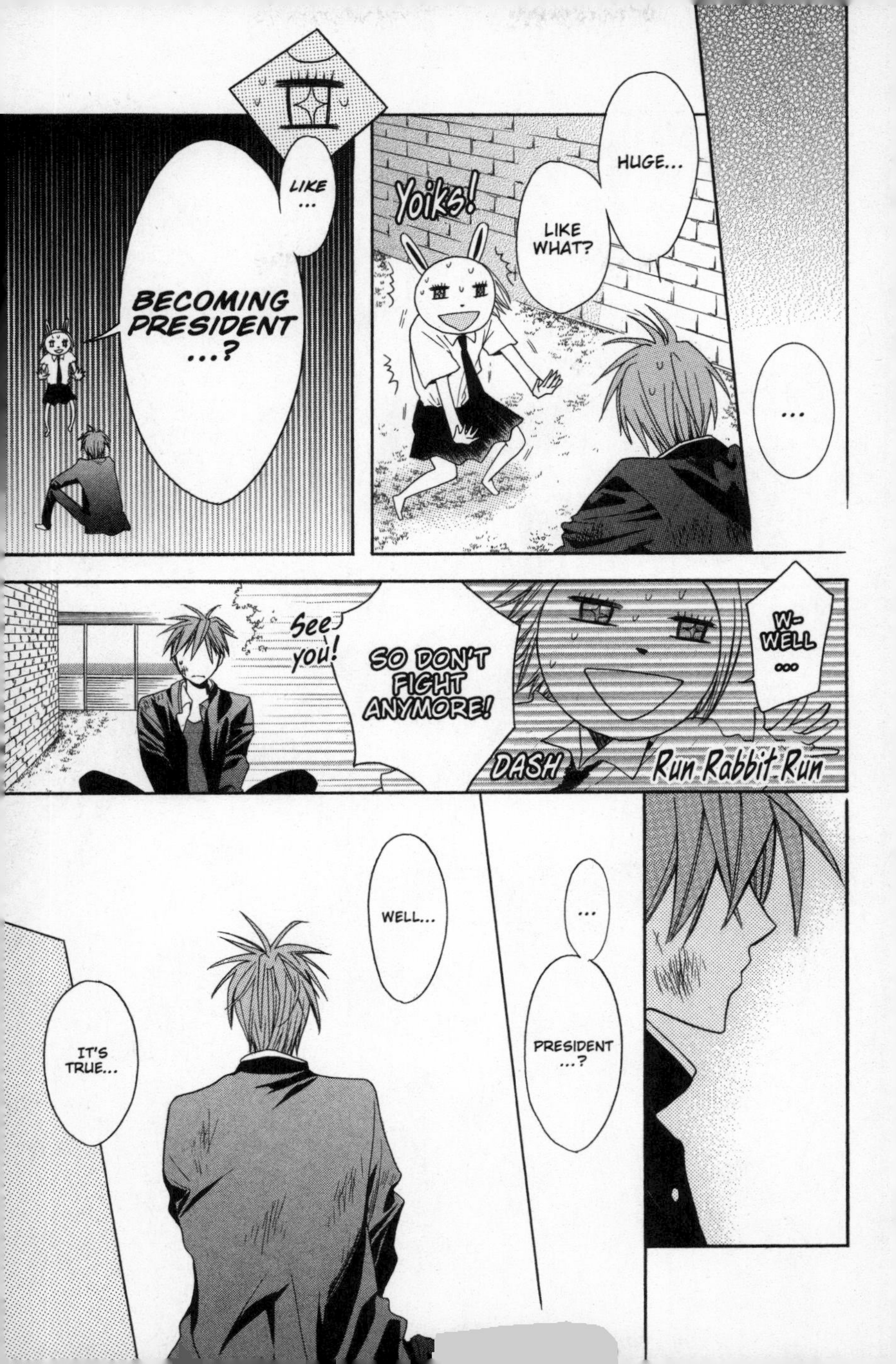
...
HUGE...
LIKE WHAT?
Yoiks!
LIKE ...
BECOMING PRESIDENT ...?
W-WELL ...
Run Rabbit Run
DASH
SO DON'T FIGHT ANYMORE!
See you!
...
PRESIDENT ...?
WELL...
IT'S TRUE...

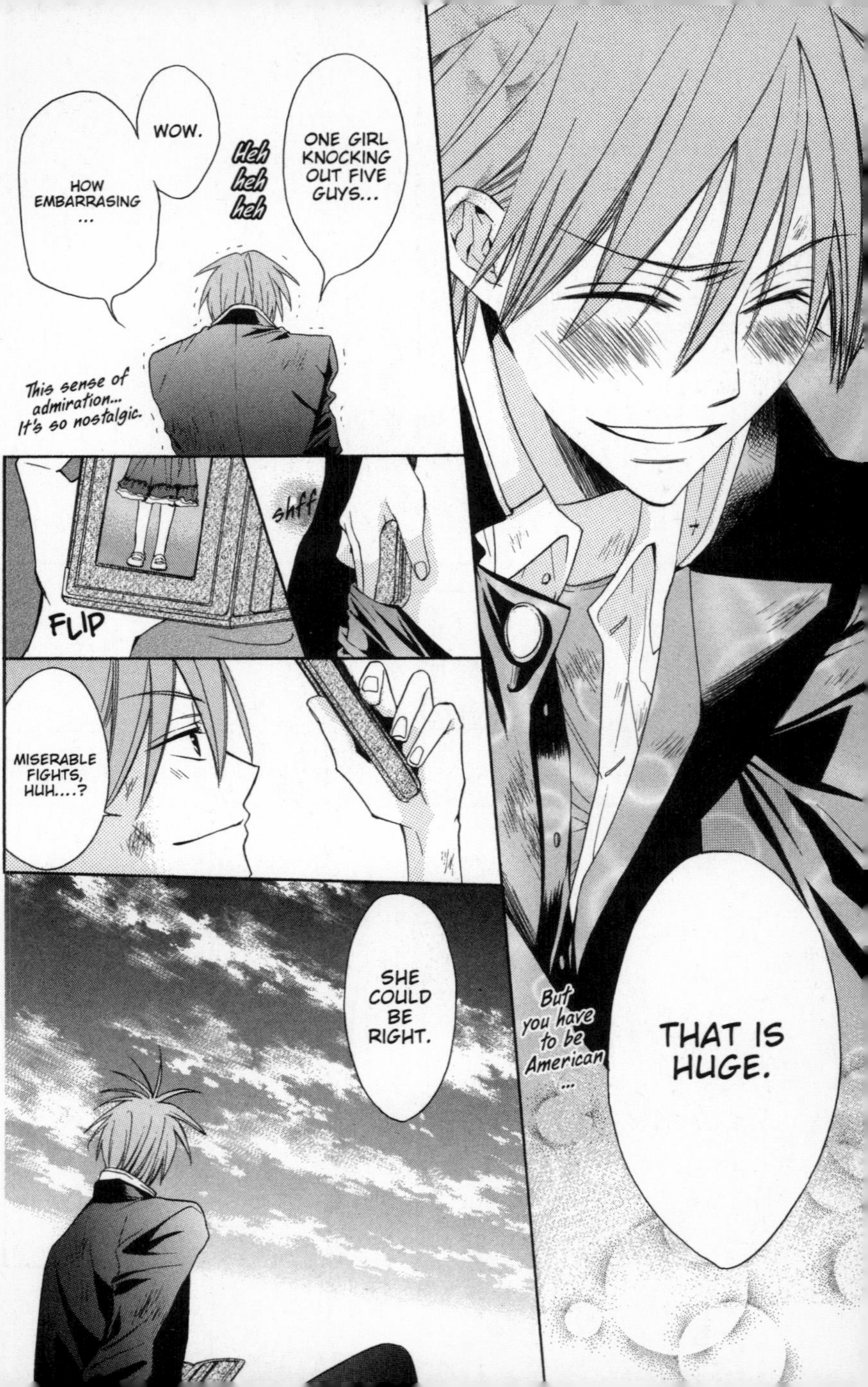
But you have to be American...
THAT IS HUGE.
ONE GIRL KNOCKING OUT FIVE GUYS...
Heh heh heh
WOW.
HOW EMBARRASING ...
This sense of admiration... It's so nostalgic.
shff
FLIP
MISERABLE FIGHTS, HUH....?
SHE COULD BE RIGHT.

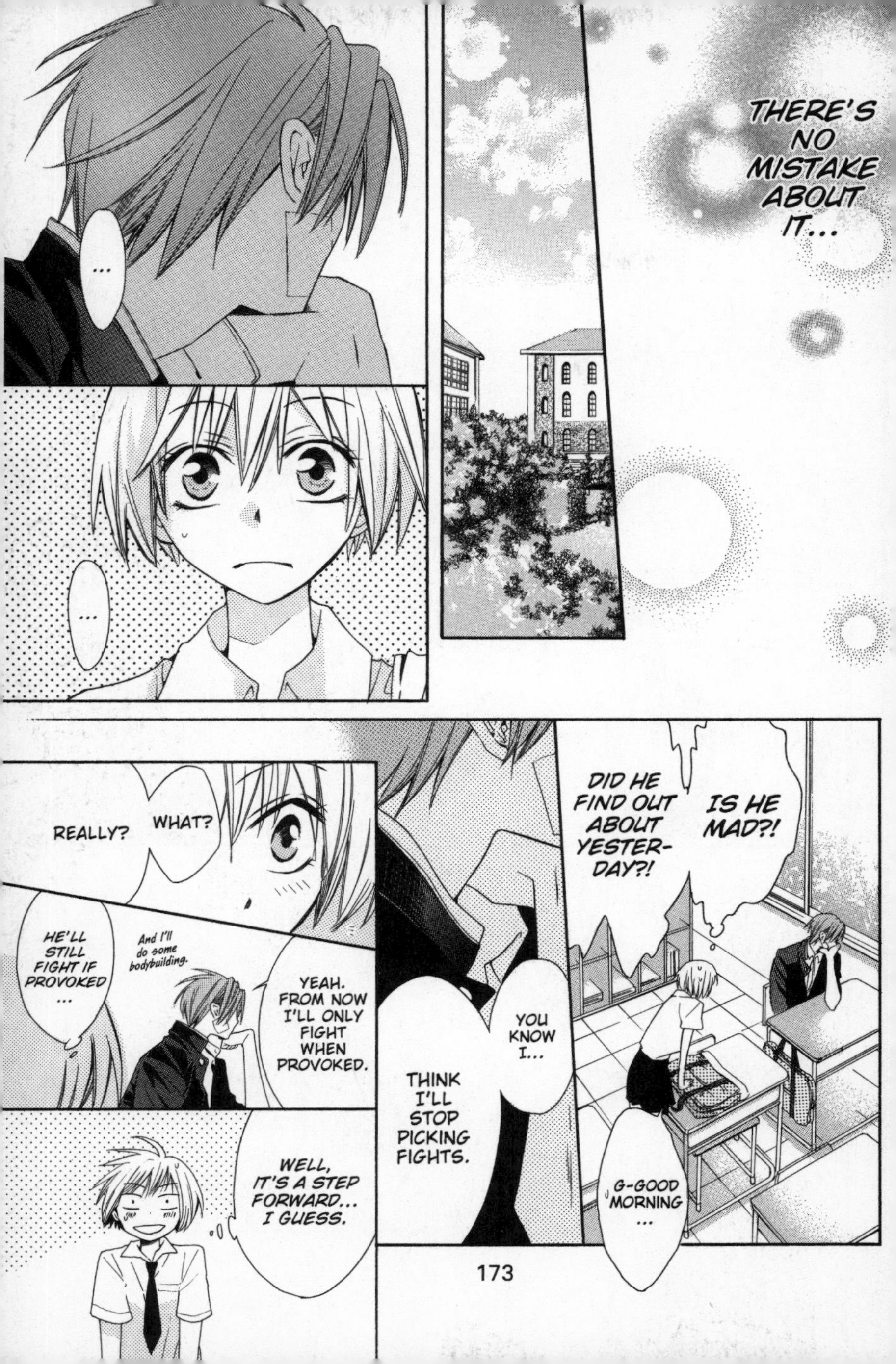
THERE'S NO MISTAKE ABOUT IT...
...
...
IS HE MAD?!
DID HE FIND OUT ABOUT YESTER-DAY?!
G-GOOD MORNING...
YOU KNOW I...
THINK I'LL STOP PICKING FIGHTS.
WHAT?
REALLY?
YEAH. FROM NOW I'LL ONLY FIGHT WHEN PROVOKED.
HE'LL STILL FIGHT IF PROVOKED...
And I'll do some bodybuilding.
WELL, IT'S A STEP FORWARD... I GUESS.

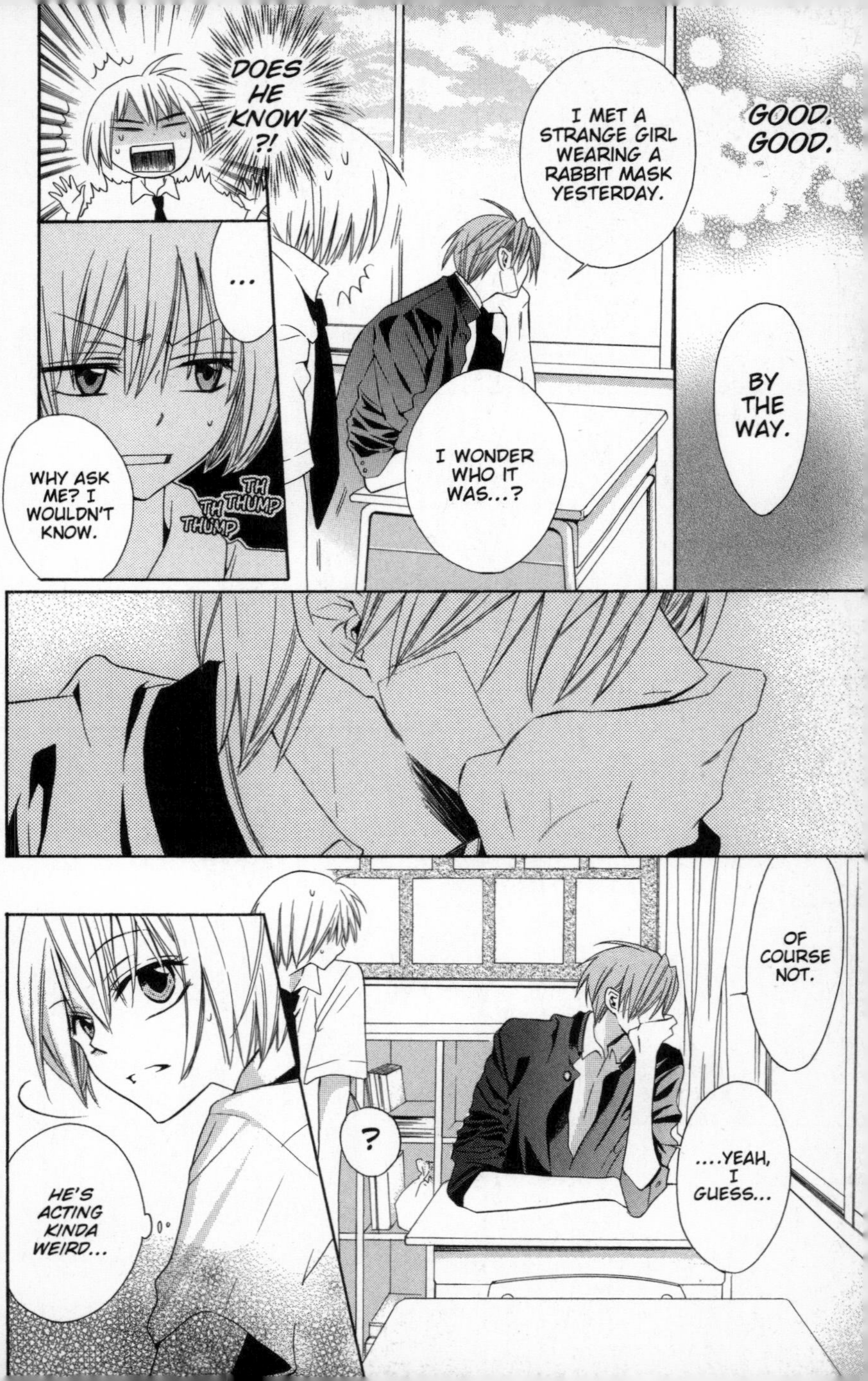
GOOD. GOOD.
BY THE WAY.
I MET A STRANGE GIRL WEARING A RABBIT MASK YESTERDAY.
I WONDER WHO IT WAS...?
DOES HE KNOW ?!
...
WHY ASK ME? I WOULDN'T KNOW.
TH THUMP
TH THUMP
OF COURSE NOT.
....YEAH, I GUESS...
?
HE'S ACTING KINDA WEIRD...

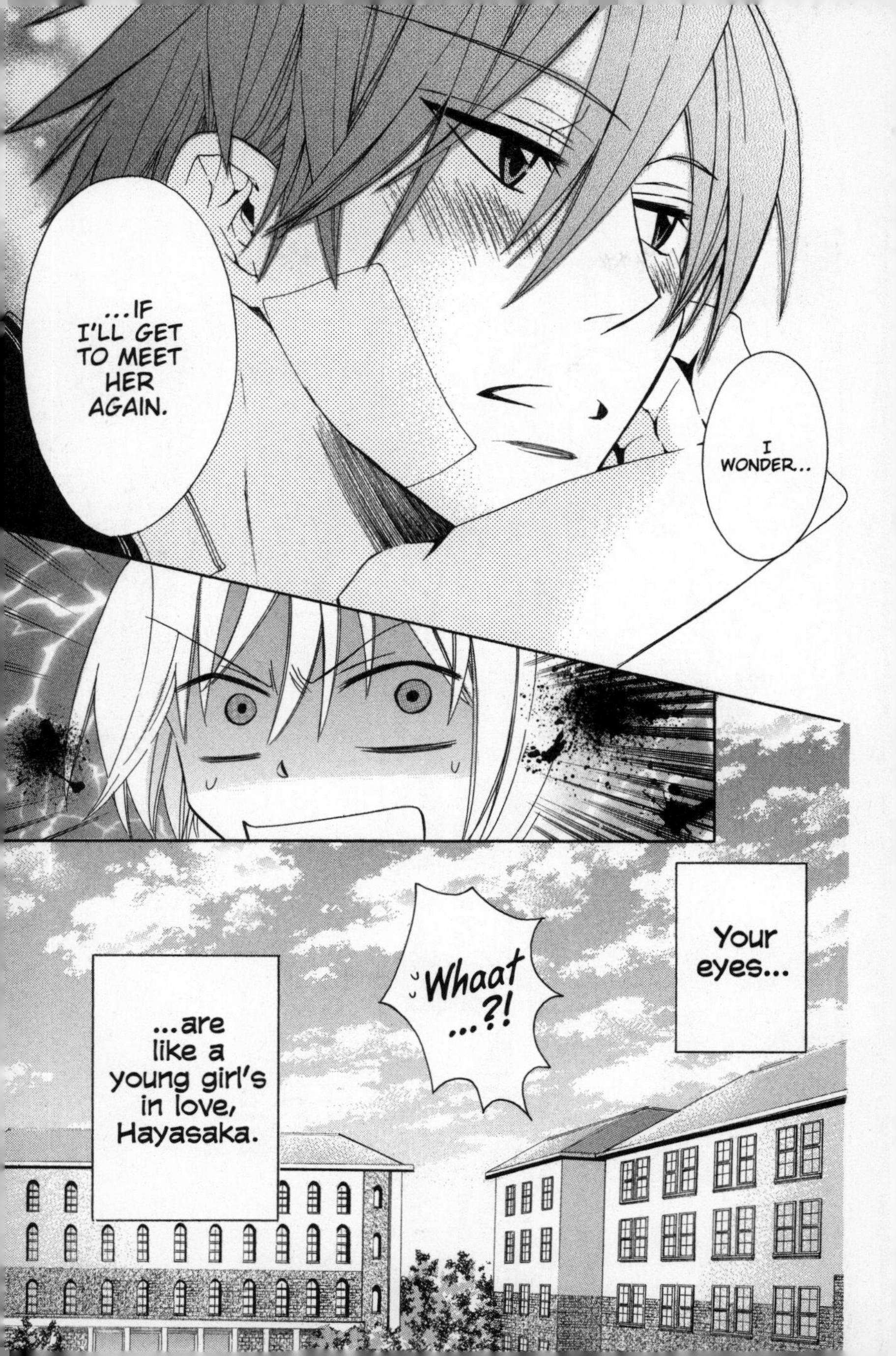
I WONDER..
...IF I'LL GET TO MEET HER AGAIN.
Your eyes...
Whaat ...?!
...are like a young girl's in love, Hayasaka.

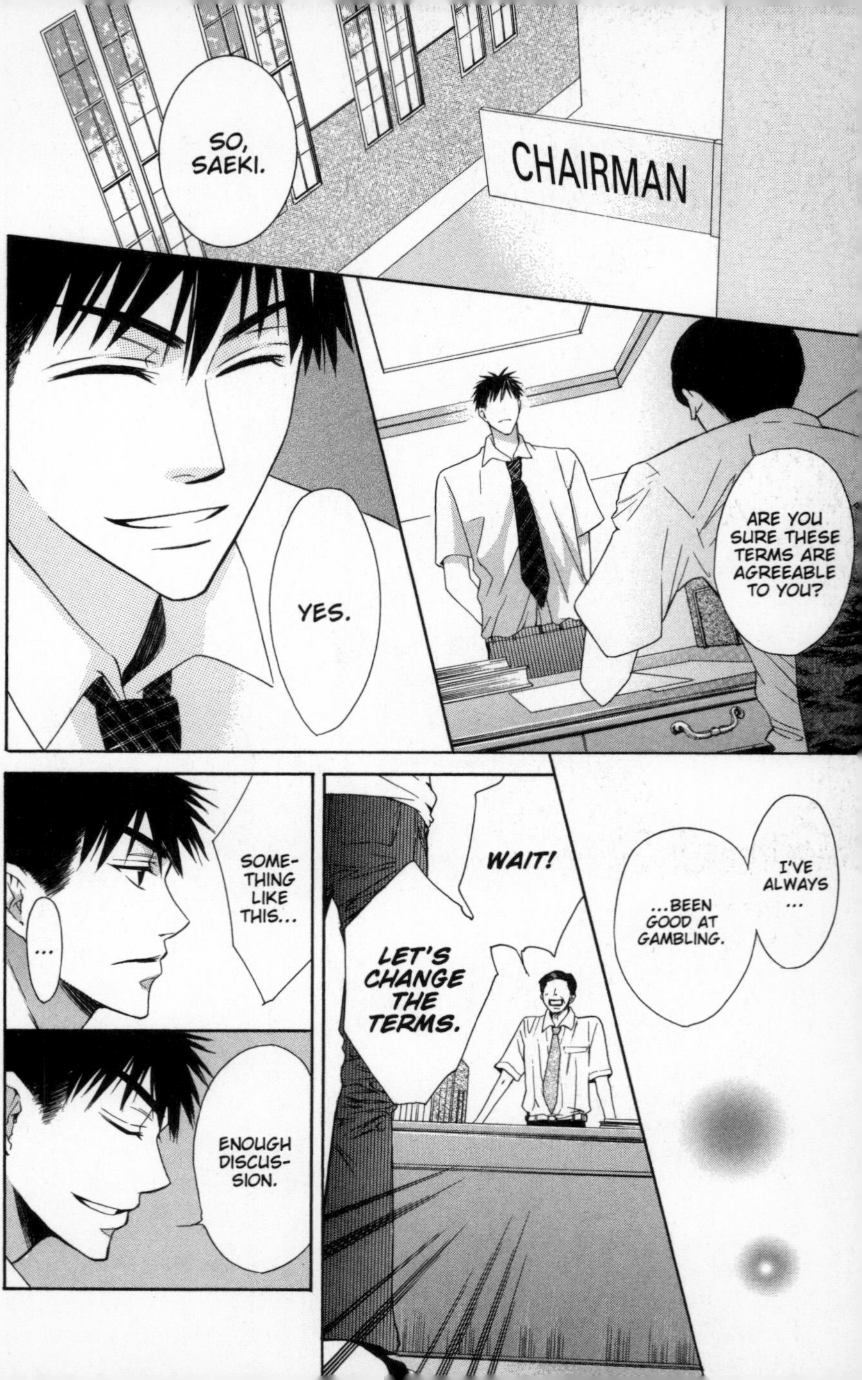
CHAIRMAN
SO, SAEKI.
ARE YOU SURE THESE TERMS ARE AGREEABLE TO YOU?
YES.
I'VE ALWAYS...
...BEEN GOOD AT GAMBLING.
WAIT!
LET'S CHANGE THE TERMS.
SOME-THING LIKE THIS...
...
ENOUGH DISCUS-SION.

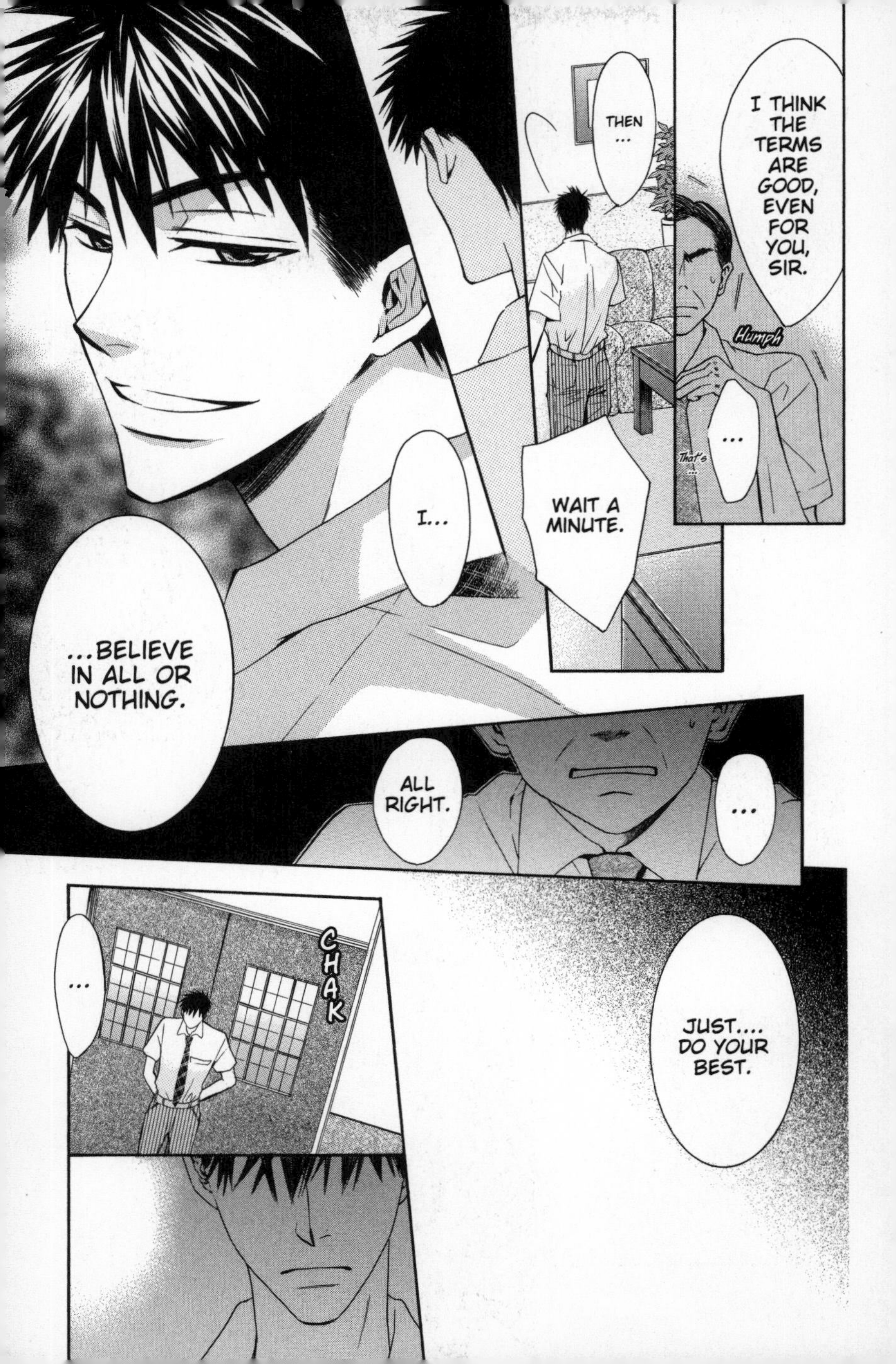
I THINK THE TERMS ARE GOOD, EVEN FOR YOU, SIR.
Humph
...
That's ...
THEN ...
WAIT A MINUTE.
I...
...BELIEVE IN ALL OR NOTHING.
...
ALL RIGHT.
JUST.... DO YOUR BEST.
CHAK
...

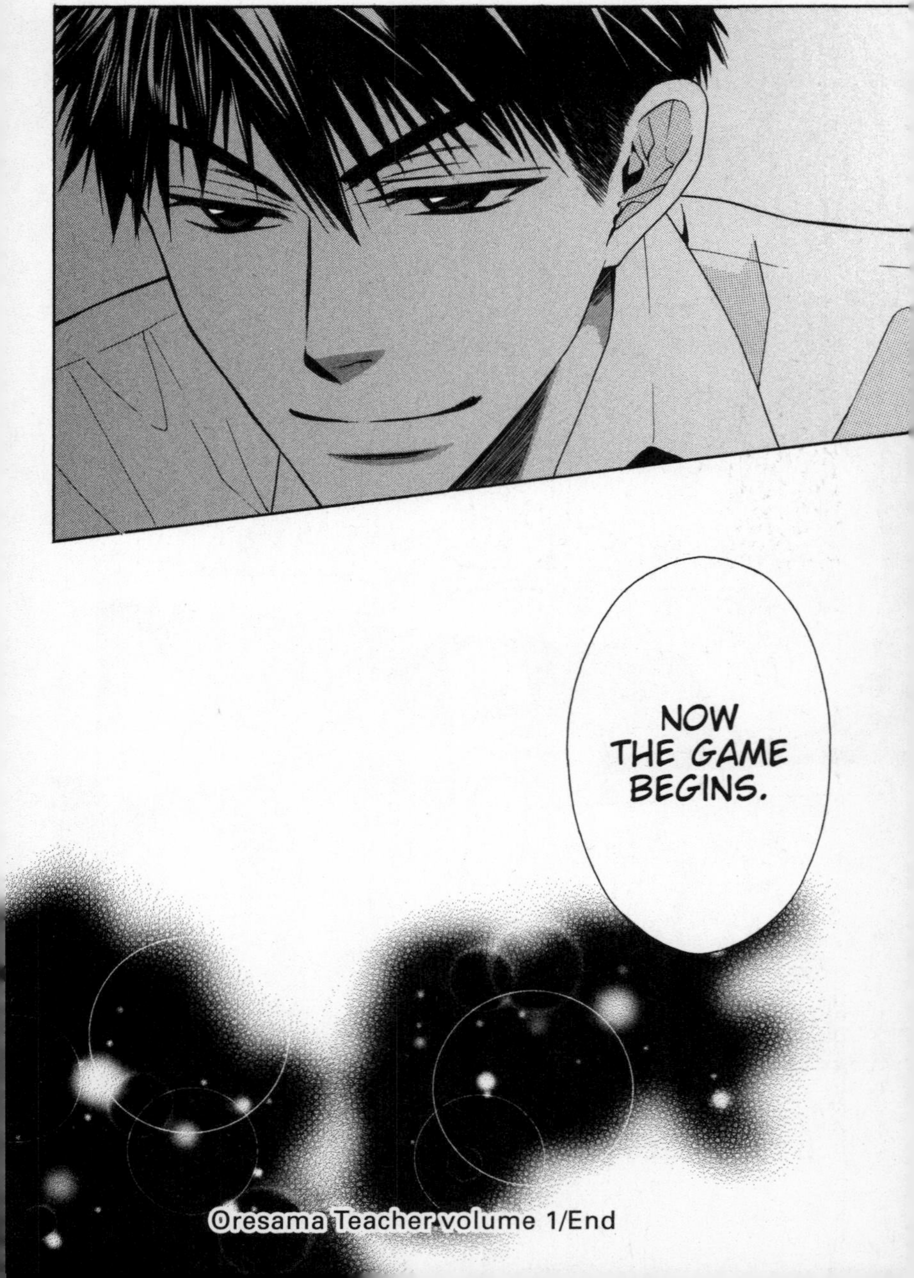
NOW THE GAME BEGINS.
Oresama Teacher volume 1/End

Visually, Takaomi looked more like a teacher, so that's how the story came out. This is a project showing what would happen if Hayasaka were the teacher.

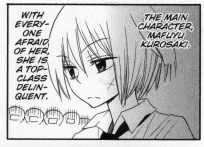

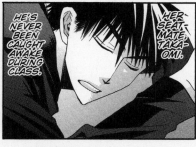

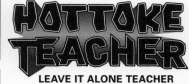

HOTTOKE TEACHER

LEAVE IT ALONE TEACHER

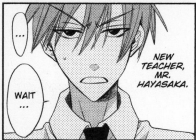

Characters

THE MAIN CHARACTER, MAFUYU KUROSAKI.
WITH EVERYONE AFRAID OF HER, SHE IS A TOP-CLASS DELINQUENT.
HER SEATMATE, TAKAOMI.
HE'S NEVER BEEN CAUGHT AWAKE DURING CLASS.
NEW TEACHER, MR. HAYASAKA.
...
WAIT ...
WHY IS KUROSAKI AN ORDINARY DELINQUENT?!
WELL, I THOUGHT I'D GO ORTHODOX ...
Zzz
Zzz

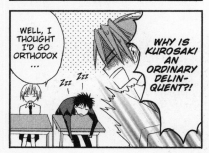

HERE IT BEGINS!

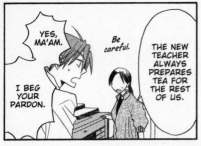

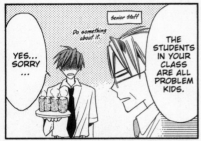

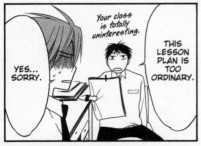

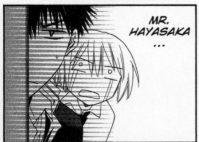

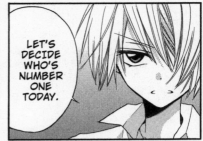

LET'S DECIDE WHO'S NUMBER ONE TODAY.
HA!
DO YOU THINK YOU CAN BEAT ME?
HEY, YOU!
WE ARE...
...HAVING CLASS RIGHT NOW!!

It's looking to be an ordinary school story.

MR. HAYASAKA

THE NEW TEACHER ALWAYS PREPARES TEA FOR THE REST OF US.
Be careful.
YES, MA'AM.
I BEG YOUR PARDON.
Senior Staff
THE STUDENTS IN YOUR CLASS ARE ALL PROBLEM KIDS.
Do something about it.
YES... SORRY ...
THIS LESSON PLAN IS TOO ORDINARY.
Your class is totally uninteresting.
YES... SORRY.
MR. HAYASAKA ...

Very ordinary...

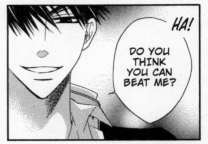

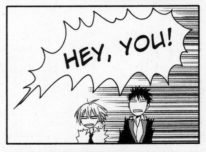

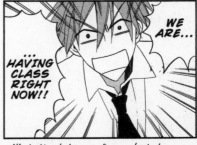

CALLED OUT #1

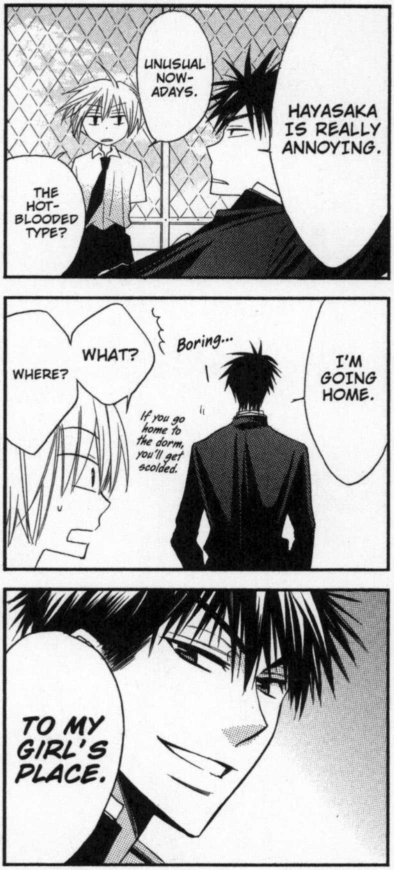
HAYASAKA IS REALLY ANNOYING.
UNUSUAL NOW-ADAYS.
THE HOT-BLOODED TYPE?
I'M GOING HOME.
Boring...
If you go home to the dorm, you'll get scolded.
WHAT?
WHERE?
TO MY GIRL'S PLACE.
THIS ONE'S A COLLEGE COED WITH BIG BOOBS.
I don't expect it to last a week though.
So what...?
heh heh heh
YOU SUCK!

I think the student Takaomi is very bad.

CALLED OUT #2

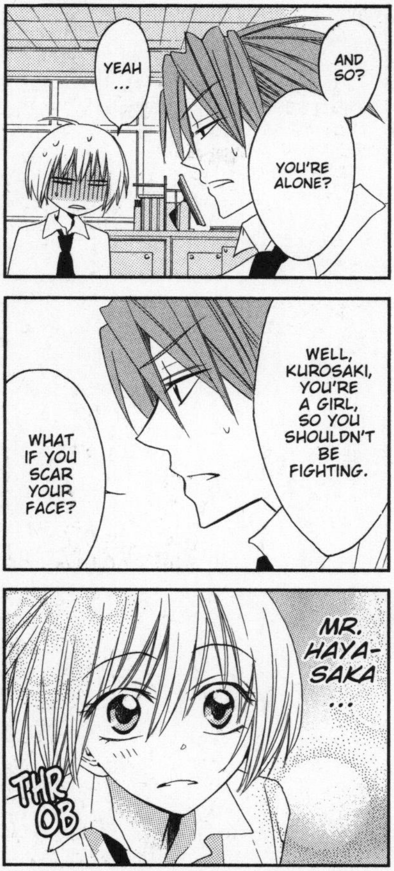
AND SO?
YOU'RE ALONE?
YEAH ...
WELL, KUROSAKI, YOU'RE A GIRL, SO YOU SHOULDN'T BE FIGHTING.
WHAT IF YOU SCAR YOUR FACE?
MR. HAYA-SAKA ...
THROB
They didn't realize this single sentence would be the start of a forbidden love...
MR. HAYA-SAKA... YOU MUSTN'T ...
STOP THAT!
Mr. Hayasaka...
NO! I DIDN'T MEAN THAT!
SHUT UP!

He's kind of pitiful.

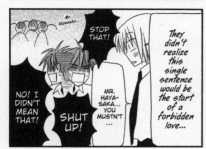

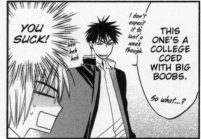

CONFESSION #1

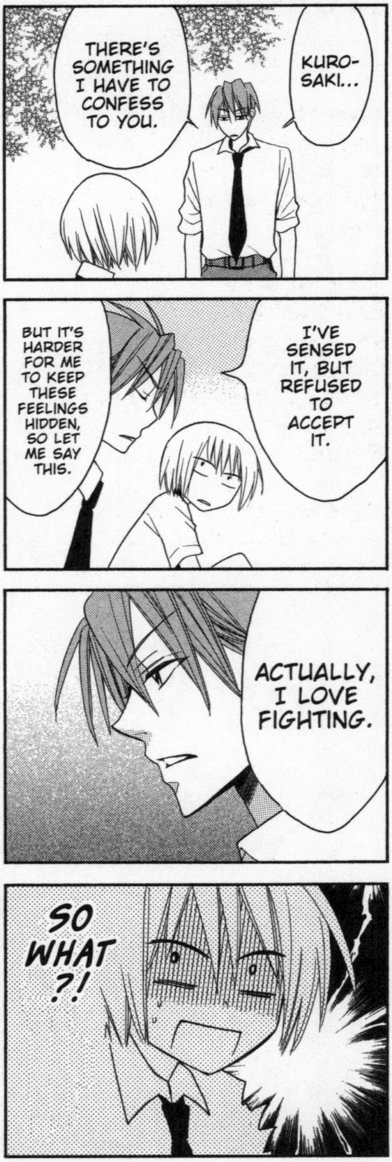
KURO-SAKI...
THERE'S SOMETHING I HAVE TO CONFESS TO YOU.
I'VE SENSED IT, BUT REFUSED TO ACCEPT IT.
BUT IT'S HARDER FOR ME TO KEEP THESE FEELINGS HIDDEN, SO LET ME SAY THIS.
ACTUALLY, I LOVE FIGHTING.
SO WHAT?!

CONFESSION #2

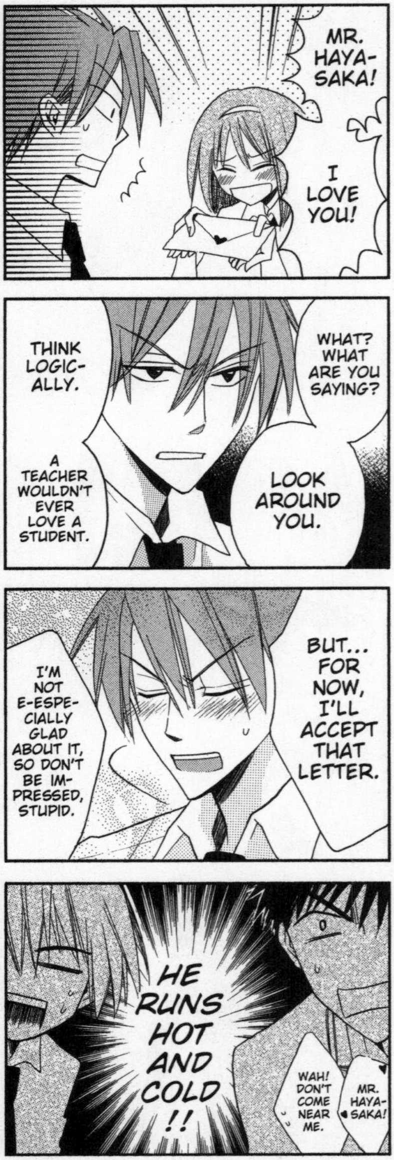
MR. HAYA-SAKA!
I LOVE YOU!
WHAT? WHAT ARE YOU SAYING?
THINK LOGIC-ALLY.
LOOK AROUND YOU.
A TEACHER WOULDN'T EVER LOVE A STUDENT.
BUT... FOR NOW, I'LL ACCEPT THAT LETTER.
I'M NOT E-ESPECIALLY GLAD ABOUT IT, SO DON'T BE IM-PRESSED, STUPID.
MR. HAYA-SAKA!
WAH! DON'T COME NEAR ME.
HE RUNS HOT AND COLD!!

THE END

HOTTOKE TEACHER/END

End Notes

Page 16, panel 5: First Meal
The stereotypical first meal
in police custody in Japan is
katsudon, or breaded fried pork
cutlet over rice.

Page 59, panel 2:
Bleaches his hair
In Japan, bleaching your hair
has a negative connotation,
similar to the way tattoos are
sometimes viewed in the United
States.

Page 98, panel 2: Akihabara
The electronics district in Tokyo.

Izumi Tsubaki began drawing manga in her first year of high school. She was soon selected to be in the top ten of *Hana to Yume's* HMC (*Hana to Yume* Mangaka Course), and subsequently won *Hana to Yume's* Big Challenge contest. Her debut title, *Chijimete Distance* (Shrink the Distance), ran in 2002 in *Hana to Yume* magazine, issue 17. Her other titles include *The Magic Touch* (*Oyayubi kara Romance*) and *Oresama Teacher*, which she is currently working on.

ORESAMA TEACHER
Vol. 1
Shojo Beat Edition

STORY AND ART BY
Izumi Tsubaki

English Translation & Adaptation/JN Productions
Touch-up Art & Lettering/Jose Macasocol
Design/Yukiko Whitley
Editor/Pancha Diaz

ORESAMA TEACHER by Izumi Tsubaki © Izumi Tsubaki 2008
All rights reserved. First published in Japan in 2008 by HAKUSENSHA, Inc., Tokyo.
English language translation rights arranged with HAKUSENSHA, Inc., Tokyo.

Printed in the U.S.A.

Published by VIZ Media, LLC
P.O. Box 77010
San Francisco, CA 94107

10 9 8 7 6 5 4 3 2 1
First printing, March 2011

www.viz.com   www.shojobeat.com

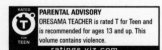

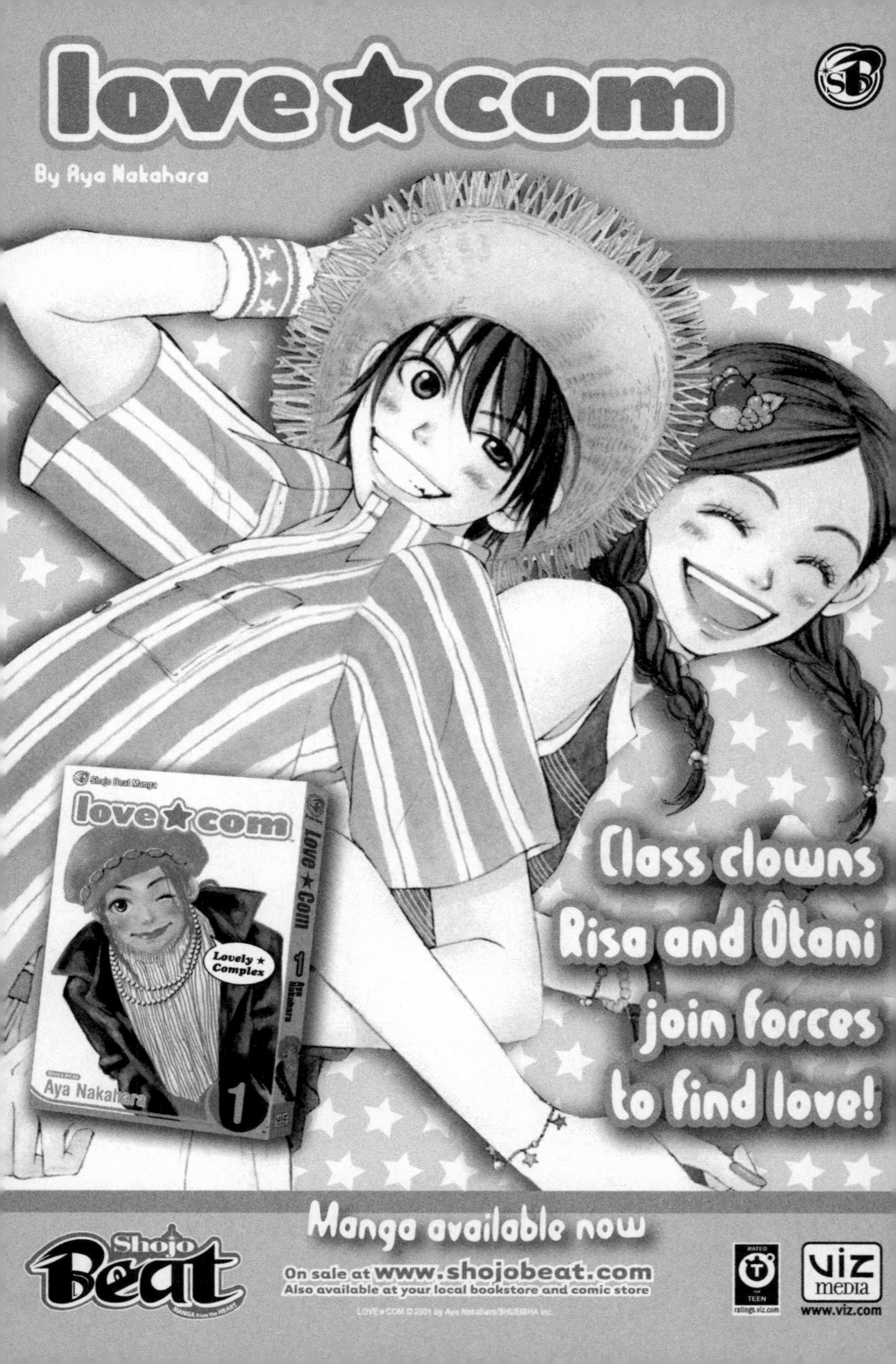
love★com
By Aya Nakahara
Shojo Beat Manga
love★com
Lovely ★ Complex
Aya Nakahara
1
Class clowns Risa and Ôtani join forces to find love!
Manga available now
Shojo Beat
On sale at www.shojobeat.com
Also available at your local bookstore and comic store
LOVE★COM © 2001 by Aya Nakahara/SHUEISHA Inc.
RATED T TEEN
ratings.viz.com
viz media
www.viz.com

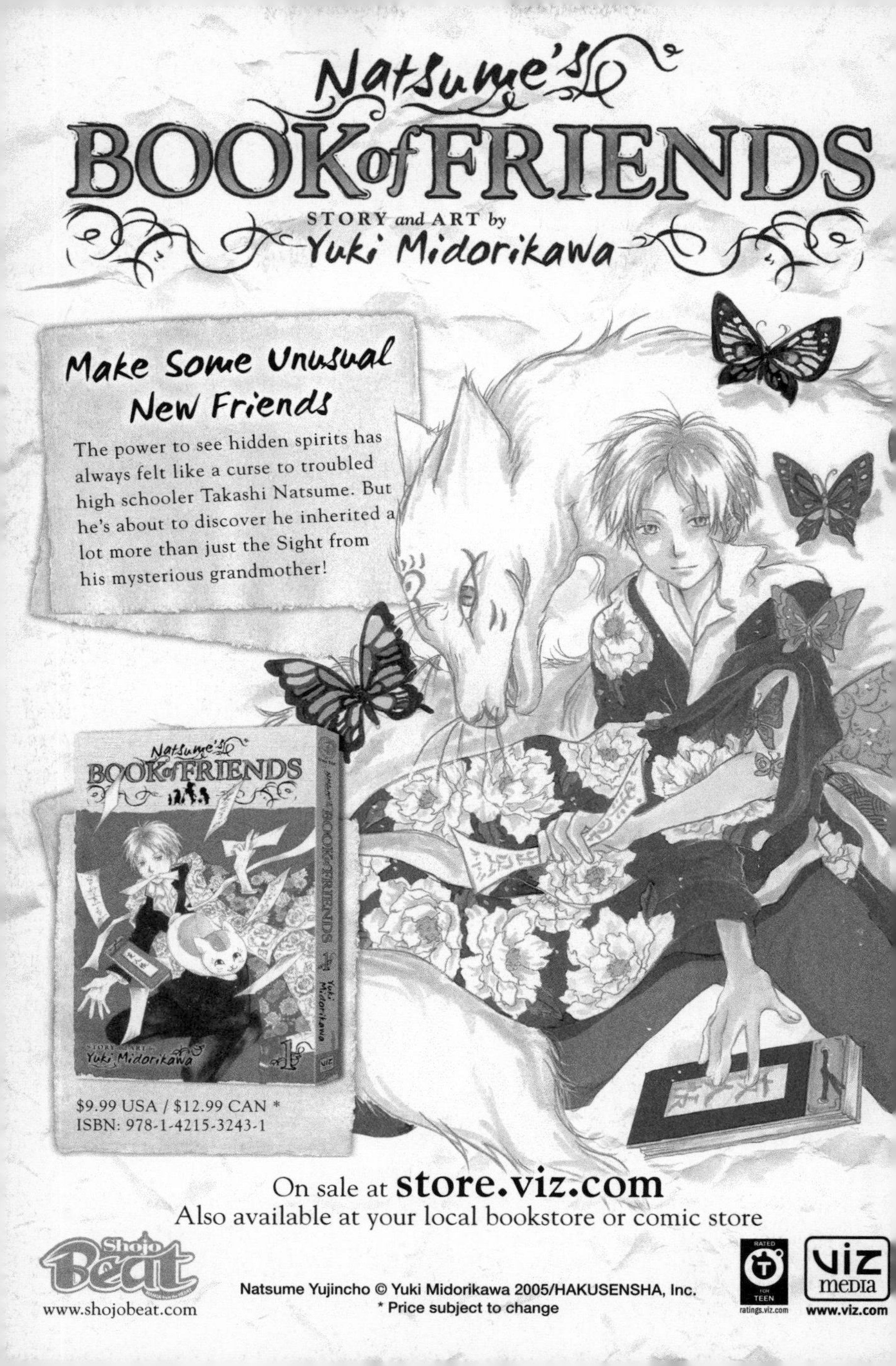
Natsume's BOOK of FRIENDS
STORY and ART by
Yuki Midorikawa
Make Some Unusual New Friends
The power to see hidden spirits has always felt like a curse to troubled high schooler Takashi Natsume. But he's about to discover he inherited a lot more than just the Sight from his mysterious grandmother!
Natsume's BOOK of FRIENDS
STORY and ART by Yuki Midorikawa
$9.99 USA / $12.99 CAN *
ISBN: 978-1-4215-3243-1
On sale at store.viz.com
Also available at your local bookstore or comic store
Shojo Beat
www.shojobeat.com
Natsume Yujincho © Yuki Midorikawa 2005/HAKUSENSHA, Inc.
* Price subject to change
RATED T FOR TEEN
ratings.viz.com
VIZ media
www.viz.com

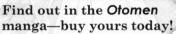